THE BASES OF ECONOMIC GEOGRAPHY

The Bases of Economic Geography:

An Essay on the Spatial Characteristics of Man's Economic Activities

Ronald Reed Boyce
University of Washington

Holt, Rinehart and Winston, Inc.
New York   Chicago   San Francisco   Atlanta
Dallas   Montreal   Toronto   London   Sydney

To
Norma Rae, Renée, Susan, and Christy

Preface

When I told an illustrious colleague that I was planning to write a college text-book in economic geography, his response was swift and sure: "Anyone would be a fool to undertake such a work." First, as he so correctly pointed out, there are about fifteen textbooks on economic geography available right now, more than there are on any other aspect of geography. Second, he was dismayed at the prospect of having to recapitulate and rewrite all the seemingly endless chapters on commodities and products commonly covered in economic geography texts — a task both monotonous and pointless. He further maintained that textbooks, by their very nature, are boring; that he avoids reading them, even those he uses in his own classes; and that he has taken a sacred vow never to write one himself. His final and somewhat flattering observation was to the effect that it would be particularly wasteful for a scholar to write a textbook since it would take valuable time and energy from "research."

This conversation reminded me of Samuel Johnson's *Preface to the English Dictionary* (1755), in which he wrote: "It is the fate of those who toil at the lower employments of life, to be rather driven by the fear of evil, than attracted by the prospect of good; to be exposed to censure, without hope of praise; to be disgraced by miscarriage, or punished for neglect, where success would have been without applause, and diligence without reward. . . . Among these unhappy mortals is the writer of dictionaries." To this I might add, ". . . and the writer of textbooks."

Obviously, given these clear difficulties, one must indeed have a good and strong reason for writing yet another textbook. I have undertaken this work precisely because my illustrious colleague was so right. It occurred to me that if such books are unappreciated by professionals, as seems to be the case, how then could one expect them to inspire novices? Perhaps a new approach to "texts" and the nature of texts was needed. Thus, this work might be considered as an experiment in finding a better approach. Moreover, I have

vii

written this text because I too am dissatisfied with many of our existing economic geography texts and feel that I have something positive to offer.

Possibly the most boring single element of economic geography texts is, paradoxically, the great amount of encyclopedia material they contain — a characteristic long considered the hallmark of a "true text." A true text in economic geography by this standard would require many volumes — a task clearly beyond the capabilities and requirements of any single course. Nonetheless, in following this tradition, the authors of most economic geography texts make some attempt at complete coverage. For example, a scanning of the contents of several leading economic geography texts shows chapterlike sections devoted to the following agricultural crops: wheat, rice, corn, sugar beets, sugar cane, coffee, tea, grains, bananas, pineapples, oranges, grapefruits, lemons, limes, grapes, prunes, figs, apples, peaches, pears, apricots, potatoes, nuts, yams, tomatoes, lettuce, cacao, soybeans, olives, peanuts, rye, and copra. By the time the author discusses the characteristics of the plant, the conditions under which it is grown and harvested, its marketing features, and various other factors that might affect the distribution of each of these crops, to say nothing of their consumption patterns, it is no wonder that most students succumb to frustration and loss of interest.

By contrast, the present work makes no pretense of covering, even superficially, all the commodities, products, goods, services, or whatever that might be relevant to economic geography. Rather than trying to explain the locational character of all things relevant to economic geography, this book simply uses selected phenomena as examples in order to convey a better appreciation of the locational characteristics of various kinds of things relevant to economic geography. By proceeding in a graduated way through a series of selected activities, in order to avoid duplication of locational problems, a framework is set for geographic analysis. It is hoped that the student will thus become acutely aware of the characteristics and changing nature of the spatial world about him.

Pedagogically, this book explores the spatial characteristics of man and his economic activities within a framework that progresses from the simple to the more complex. With each new topic treated, greater depth is achieved. The topics treated earlier in the work, however, are not necessarily easier to understand spatially than those treated later. For purposes of progression, the earlier topics are treated in a simpler way than those discussed later. For example, to truly understand the locational characteristics of an agricultural crop such as, for example, peaches, it is necessary to know an awful lot about peaches. In truth, it is a complex rather than a simple locational problem. Therefore, it is largely the way in which the topics are treated here that makes them simple or complex in the locational context rather than the inherent features of the topics themselves.

The book is divided into six sections, plus an introduction. Part A lays the bases for geographical understanding. This includes the general distributional effects of the following on various types of other activities: transportation, physical features, economic systems, human and institutional systems, and population and cities. The topics in Parts B through E are calculated to illustrate differing spatial arrays in a progression from the most simple to the most complex locational patterns. In general, the order of spatial complexity as treated here are noncommercial economies, extractive activities, agriculture, manufacturing, and intraurban land use. Part F, the final section, is regional and problem-oriented in an attempt to place certain spatial problems in a meaningful, public-policy perspective.

It is hoped that the book will not be boring. It is written largely in a "nontextbook style" in order to maintain smoothness of word flow. The reader will not be interrupted with detailed maps, tables, and other materials more complicated than the verbal discussion. No distracting "filler-type" material is included. Therefore, this book does not attempt to be a substitute for atlases, the U.S. Census, the United Nations' Yearbooks, various picture magazines, dictionaries, research articles, or indeed for certain other "true texts."

Finally, the book is written for adults rather than for children. Dictionary-defined and common terms are not italicized, nor does the book digress to define them. Proper definitions are found in any good dictionary. I believe that the student will have other reference materials at hand or will know where to get them. In this regard, this text assumes a high level of student maturity, competence, knowledge, and curiosity.

R. R. B.

Woodway, Washington
November 1973

Contents

Part f
PROBLEMS OF ACTIVITY PLACEMENTS:
MICRO AND MACRO REGIONALIZATIONS   309

THE BASES OF ECONOMIC GEOGRAPHY

1

What is Economic Geography?

If man and his activities were distributed evenly over the earth, there would perhaps be little interest in economic geography. Any economic atlas, however, will attest to the uneven distribution of man and his activities. Thus the purpose of this book is to provide some explanation for this uneven distribution.

Geography is the discipline that attempts to explain the *uneven* placements, distributions, extents, and uses of selected things over the surface of the earth. Economic geography is concerned with explaining the locational characteristics of things of utilitarian value to man—particularly the things he considers valuable enough to move from one part of the earth to another. By focusing on the spatial dimensions of items of economic value to man, partial explanation is provided for the distribution of man himself.

The major premise in economic geography, as in all geography, is that despite an uneven placement, man and his activities are distributed in an orderly and therefore understandable manner. However, such underlying orderliness is usually neither so simple that it can be explained by a single factor such as environment, nor so complicated that it defies explanation except through approximation, probability, and randomization procedures. Those who argue that single factors, such as environment or a few physical factors, offer satisfactory explanation, claim far too much spatial orderliness and give man too little response choice. Those who argue that the distribution of things can be approached only through randomization and probability assume far too little spatial orderliness. The truth lies somewhere in between and, as such, involves an interplay among a number of variables.

If we accept the premise that man and his activities are distributed in a logical and orderly manner, then such distributions can be understood through the use of concepts, theories, and general spatial principles. It is not necessary, therefore, to spend a great amount of time learning the distributions and placements of thousands of different items. Instead, through various conceptual principles and insights, the causes for a particular pattern can be readily understood.

Even so, a blend of factual and conceptual (that is, theoretical) information is necessary for sound geographical understanding. By observing reality through a conceptual framework, imperfections, peculiarities, and deviations from a general concept can be identified. Conversely, examination of factual reality is necessary, if for no other reason than to suggest needed improvements in theory. Moreover, theory is rarely good enough, nor is it designed, to explain fully any given distribution.

Thus a careful blend of facts and theory is a prerequisite to sound geographical understanding. Theory without facts, or with only a few facts calculated to verify the theory, often leads to blind acceptance of presumed spatial arrangements—arrangements that may exist only in the mind of the theoretician. A person who relies solely on theory for geographical understanding commonly thinks he knows all; in reality, however, such a person is shallow in that he knows nothing for certain about the real earth. On the other hand, a person who relies solely on facts for geographical understanding may be superficially impressive; he may be a walking gazetteer and a marvel at quiz shows and cocktail parties, but he knows little of meaningful or lasting value. His tendency is to look for the peculiar and the unique because the common or general are not appreciated by him—they are beyond his interpretive powers. Without a conceptual base, this fact-laden person will not be able to differentiate the forest from the trees; he will not be able to differentiate the general from the unique. Finally, the "facts only" advocate has taken on an impossible task and, unless constantly renewed with new facts, will soon find himself hopelessly out-of-date and irrelevant. Thus it is evident that an exclusive emphasis on either theory or facts contains great dangers.

Yet there are also certain inherent dangers in attempting to achieve a proper blend of theory and facts, which is one of the goals of this book. Two dangers are evident: one is factually based; the other, theoretically based. These two approaches are more formally labeled the *inductive* and the *deductive*. In the inductive approach one takes facts and then tries to "make sense" of them. In the second approach one tries to deduce, based on certain logical premises or theories, what the spatial effect will be. Both methods are sound when properly used and properly tested—one against theory, the other against facts.

A common pitfall of the factually-based inductive approach involves the correlation of one spatial distribution with another. For example, wheat yield might be correlated spatially with the degree of field slope in a particular area. Such spatial covariation is often valuable in providing meaningful insights and in removing incorrect assumptions. Nonetheless, such spatial correlation does not necessarily provide explanation in any causative way.

Yet such a procedure often gives the deceptive appearance of having explained something when it has merely showed that it relates to other similar patterns—patterns that may have no direct casual relationships.

An equally serious fallacy in the pursuit of a proper blend of fact and theory is to use only selected facts to "verify" a particular theory. In geography a misapplication often results when a particular area, in which things operate much as the theory predicts, is purposely selected. The tendency here is to seek out only those facts and those areas that coincide with the theory in question. By so doing, one fails to see how well, or how poorly, the theory works to provide any general explanation. As a fair test of the theory, data from a number of areas should be examined.

Aside from a judicious selection of facts and theories, this work will attempt to build spatial knowledge through the use of the *ceteris paribus,* or "other things being equal," approach. Often it will be stated that given certain postulates and premises, such and such should follow, other things held constant. Such use of *ceteris paribus* is extremely common in economics, and its use here will follow much in that tradition. In fact, most statements implicitly contain other-things-being-equal arguments. For example, one might say that a structure should have a physical life of, say, fifty years—if fire, earthquake, or other forces do not destroy it. This makes the problem of verifying or denying theoretical statements by facts extremely complex and difficult. In fact, the tests required for valid verification are often quite complex, so that only a few will be demonstrated here. Therefore, some faith, based on logical (deductive) proof, will be required.

Nonetheless, the most important principle utilized here is simply common sense—an uncommon commodity—applied in a spatial context. It is hoped that, once explained, the reasons behind any particular spatial response will become fairly clear, and in some cases, even seemingly obvious. At any rate, most of the material here, although unfamiliar to the average person, is not complicated and does seem rather simple and obvious once it is discussed. This is truly the nature of most discovery and surely an attribute of common sense.

Geography is sometimes defined in a tongue-in-cheek manner as consisting of what geographers do. By the same token, economic geography might be defined as consisting of what is included in the economic geography texts. This may not provide a very satisfactory definition, but it will surely reveal a great deal of the philosophy of what economic geography has been and ought to be. If anything is abundantly clear, it is that the content of economic geography texts has changed drastically in the past several decades.

The first college-level economic geography text in the United States was written by J. Russell Smith in 1913 for Henry Holt & Co., the forerunner of the publisher of this work. It was a best seller. (In fact, it had no competition. Today, there are more texts available on economic geography than on any other aspect of geography.) In organization and approach, Smith's book was largely limited to those activities directly associated with the physical features of the earth. Discussion was largely on farming, fishing, foresting, mining, and general trade patterns.

During the 1930s and 1940s manufacturing was gradually added to economic geography texts. The inclusion of these *secondary* activities greatly strengthened the coverage of, and gave greater coherence to, a body of knowledge. Still the general focus was on particular food crops, materials for industry, and the manufacturing of basic industrial materials such as iron and steel. Transportation was also included, particularly international movements of commodities and minerals. Thus these economic geography texts emphasized the locational characteristics of critical components of production, particularly those types which are highly correlated with certain physical characteristics (for example, climates, soils, natural vegetation, geology) of the earth. Consequently, by today's standards, these texts gave only passing attention to economic principles affecting location of things.

It was also during the pre-World War II period that a general theory of economic geography was developed. Clarence Jones summed up this "new" viewpoint of economic geography as follows:

> Not all types of work are included in the field of economic geography. Many people — doctors, teachers, ministers, politicians, bankers, writers, musicians, etc. — obtain their living through other types of work. Economic geography deals with the productive occupations. . . . The statement that the classes of goods—food, clothes, shelter, fuel, tools, and materials of industry, and luxuries—have physical bases, called the factors of the natural environment, is axiomatic.[1]

By this he meant that only economic activities with direct physical bases have a legitimate place in economic geography. Thus not even all types of manufacturing were included. Cities and the placement of people and activities within them simply did not qualify for inclusion.

For the past decade or so, these and many other activities have usually been included in standard textbooks on economic geography. Foremost among the new topics treated are cities and the distribution of things within them. Nonetheless, some writers still hold that urban geography concerns "unproductive uses" of the land and should not be part of economic geography. Your author takes the predominant current stance: Whether a given activity is or is not directly tied to the physical bases of the earth is irrelevant in determining if that activity should be included as part of economic geography. The distribution of anything that has utilitarian value is considered a legitimate candidate for economic-geographic inquiry. This would include

[1]Clarence Fielden Jones, *Economic Geography* (New York: The Macmillan Company, 1950), p. 7.

anything that men judge to be worth buying, begging, borrowing, selling, bartering, stealing, or moving. Such a stance also means that there are more topics than can possibly be treated in any one economic geography text.

The Activity Components of Economic Geography

Six major sectors, or activity components, can be recognized in any study of economic geography. These components include the (1) *procurement*, or primary sector, (2) *production*, or secondary sector, (3) *marketing*, or tertiary sector, (4) *servicing*, or quaternary sector, (5) *consumption*, or quinquenary sector, and (6) *transportation*, a connecting link among them (Figure 1.1).

The primary sector — procurement

In the primary production sector, commodities are obtained in natural form from the earth's land, seas, mines, forests, and farms. Such resources are taken directly as found, or as grown on the earth in collaboration with man. Therefore, most commodities might be considered as being in a "wild" state. They are taken pretty much as provided by nature.

The major activities in this category include: (1) primitive hunting and gathering of wild plants, animals, and fish, and gathering of certain minerals; (2) commercial exploitation of such products; (3) augmentation of nature's bounty through farming methods; (4) "private" sports use of such items. In commercial economies the first three include fishing, forestry, mining, and agriculture. The recreation activity of hunting and fishing, however, is another major activity which utilizes such extractive procedures.

Primary production often provides the first link in a vast chain of production before these commodities are consumed as goods in the marketplace. Usually it is only in very primitive societies that such goods are consumed without going through some of the other major activity sectors.

In the United States, only a small percentage of the total labor force is employed in the primary activities (actually less than 10 percent today). Nevertheless, the primary sector might be thought of as a basic catalyst for the addition of employment in other sectors. Paradoxically, the smaller the proportion of workers in the primary sector, the more advanced the economy.

The secondary sector — manufacturing

In the secondary production sector, materials produced in the primary

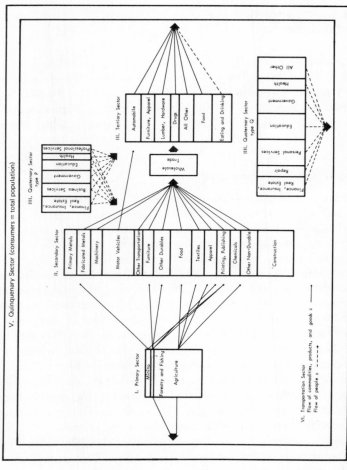

FIGURE 1.1 The Activity Components of Economic Geography. The height of the various columns represents the proportionate numbers of workers in each sector for the United States. Note how commodities produced in the primary sector are moved through the secondary and tertiary sectors to the consumer. The quaternary sector is divided to differentiate schematically those services which aid the flow of material items from those services which are primarily consumer-oriented.

sector are changed in form through the process of manufacturing. Whereas *commodities* are produced in the primary sector, *products* are produced in the secondary sector. Thus, manufacturing is the intermediate step between initial acquisition of materials from nature and their consumption by man in the retailing or tertiary sector. These are more appropriately called consumer products as contrasted with producer products—that is, products used in the production process.

The manufacturing sector is a very complex one. Only rarely does material move in a one-stop process from the primary to the tertiary sector. In most cases, a series of steps within the secondary sector are involved (see Figure 1.1). One firm's "finished product" often becomes another's raw materials. These are commonly labeled secondary transfer products.

The major locational forces for secondary activities are of three types: (1) the need to be near the source of raw material—that is, near the primary sector; (2) the need to be near the market—that is, near the tertiary sector; (3) the need to be near other things that are critical in the production process, such as labor, power, transportation, and so forth. Thus it is evident that the choices available for the location of manufacturing are more numerous than for activities in the primary sector.

The tertiary sector — retailing and wholesaling of goods

There is much confusion among economic geographers as to what constitutes the tertiary sector. Historically, it was simply added as a third sector to complement the primary and secondary sectors; it included all other activities, but particularly those associated with cities. Over time, the tertiary sector has been referred to as the "service" sector. Consequently some present-day authors take this literally and exclude from the tertiary sector retailers, wholesalers, and handlers of goods. Others, however, have made a distinction among kinds of services and have labeled most of the office, governmental, educational, and health services as the quaternary sector and have left business services such as barber shops and lawyers in the tertiary sector. Still others have limited retailing and wholesaling to an *exchange* category—yet exchange is more a facet of transportation than anything else. Thus there is a wide difference of opinion and a wide variance in the use of the term tertiary.

It therefore seems appropriate at this point to define the term in a way that is most meaningful in light of the flow of material from the primary sector to the consumption sector. Clearly, if manufacturing is the secondary sector and produces products to be shipped to wholesaling and retailing establishments, then these latter establishments should be properly labeled the third stage, or tertiary sector. Business establishments dealing not in products but in services should not be labeled as tertiary. Thus, tertiary activities are simply the third step in a triad of sectors ranging from the first stage (primary), where commodities are taken pretty much as mother nature provided them, to the third stage (tertiary), where products are displayed for purchase by the final customer.

The quaternary sector — business and consumer services

As here defined, the quaternary sector includes the provision of all types of services to the productive sectors (primary, secondary, and tertiary) and to the consumer sector. These services are logically divided between those concerned with the extraction, movement, manufacturing, and selling of material items (type P) and those provided to the consumer (type Q) (see Figure 1.1). The former are labeled *producer services* and the latter, *consumer* or *personal services.*

It is difficult to break them into these two categories, logical though they may be, for the reason that most such quaternary activities have dual purposes within the same establishment. For example, a legal firm rarely serves only corporations, particular types of businesses, or consumers. It is even more difficult to make a hard-and-fast separation between such services as communications, education, public administration, finance, and insurance.

Quaternary activities often have locational variables similar to those of tertiary activities, and are often found in conjunction with tertiary activities. For example, in a typical "retail business district" there might be a post office, a telephone exchange, a lawyer, a doctor, a real estate office, a barber and beauty shop, an insurance company office, several financial institutions, plus various "business repair" services—all quaternary activities. None of these deal directly in products or goods. All perform services, either for businesses or for consumers.

From the standpoint of total space use of the earth, the tertiary and quaternary sectors are of little consequence. All together, tertiary and quaternary uses cover no more than one-hundredth of one percent of the land surface of the earth. On the other hand, the territory used for primary activities alone covers more than one-tenth of the earth's land surface.

Tertiary and quaternary activities are highly market-oriented, but they are not therefore necessarily simple to understand. Paradoxically, their locational choice is so restricted that there is considerable competition for sites among the various commercial activities. Within this limited territory, various firms bid for sites, and presumably those best able to pay the highest rents receive the best sites. But this is an oversimplication of the problem and understanding must await detailed treatment later.

The quinquenary sector — consumer demands

The consumer or quinquenary sector includes the total population: workers in all sectors, their wives and dependents, unemployed persons. Basically, this is a sector to which goods and services are supplied. As such, the *quinquenary* sector is the initiating demand sector for the many activities distributed over the earth. By contrast, the primary sector is the initial response, or supply, sector. Of course, the nature of the response will be influenced by transportation conditions, by the various governmental features that differentiate one economic system from another, as well as many other factors.

This residential land-use base, while utilizing less than one percent of the land surface, is the home of the consumer, the ultimate utilizer of material and service products, who is clearly a key to the spatial understanding of the other activities.

One might quickly argue that man lives near his work and hence merely follows his work. This may be true, but he only lives *near* his work in most cases. Moreover, his choice of residence has direct impact on the placement of the tertiary and quaternary employment sectors—sectors that account for the majority of the employed population in postindustrialized countries such as the United States.

The transportation sector

The transportation component consists of several major linkage types (Figure 1.1). First it supplies a series of material flow links among the primary, secondary, tertiary, and consumer sectors. In order to distinguish among the types of materials moved among these sectors, different terminology is usually employed, namely, *commodities, products,* and *goods.* The material items physically transferred from the primary to the secondary sector will be called *commodities;* those transferred from the secondary to the tertiary sector, *products;* and those transferred from the tertiary sector to the consumer, *goods.*

These increase in value as they proceed through each sector. Their value increases not only because of the cost inputs like transportation, storage, and labor, but because things are worth more in some areas than in others. Items also generally increase in value as they change ownership and as they change in form. Thus, transportation is the vehicle whereby value is increased along the path from point of initial production to final consumption. As things are conveyed along the road to the consumer, they often change in form (manufacturing) and in ownership (exchange).

There is also the flow of people who travel from their residences or places of work to purchase goods in the tertiary sector. The broken lines in Figure 1.1 depict the flow between the consumer and eating and drinking establishments where the good is consumed on site. Thus the broken lines represent *people.* The solid lines, however, represent *material items* — goods — transported by the consumer himself from the tertiary sector. Connections from the quaternary sector to other sectors are also mostly people flows. The services of the quaternary sector, of course, also include the flows of communication and information (not distinguished on the diagram).

Finally, there is the flow of ideas, energy, money, credit, and know-how. These flows, unlike all those mentioned above, are not considered as transportation. The term *transportation* pertains only to the physical flows of commodities, products, goods, and people. The flow of nonmaterial items is discussed under the broader topics of communication and circulation.

It is informative to rank the sectors of economic activity according to their proximity to the sector of final consumption (quinquenary sector). In the case of primitive economies and sports-recreation, production and consumption are direct and often immediate. For most other activities, however, there is a decreasing series of steps between initial production and final consumption. In the case of fishing, there are three intermediate steps before the fish reaches the final consumer: processing, wholesaling, and retailing. In mining, too, many processing and manufacturing activities take place between the initial point of production and final consumption.

Within this connectivity system, the question might be raised as to which is the critical, or catalytic, sector in the flow. Although this is difficult to determine, it is clear that the final consumption sector, which triggers the demand through which all other activities directly or indirectly respond, is the prime sector. Man is clearly the key to locational understanding. All goods and services are ultimately aimed at him, albeit in a complex web. In terms of the consumer, residential land use is the only sector connected locationally with all other sectors.

In the analysis of any particular location problem, however, a complex feedback situation occurs. One approach used in this work will be from the vantage point of these linkages. Such linkages among the procurement, production, service, exchange, and consumption sectors provide a key element of spatial understanding.

Varying Complexity of the Locational Problem, by Sector

The degree of complexity in the locational problem varies greatly among the various sectors of economic activity. In general, the degree of locational freedom (and hence the difficulty of spatial understanding) increases as one proceeds from the primary through the quinquenary sectors. Thus it will be noted that there is only one freedom of locational choice for extractive activities (at the resource site), two degrees of choice in agriculture (because of slippage between land-based production costs and accessibility to market), three degrees of choice in the secondary sector (raw material, market, or some intermediate location), and a great number of locational choices among the other sectors (Table 1.1).

TABLE 1.1
GENERAL DEGREE OF COMPLEXITY IN THE LOCATION PROBLEM

Type of Activity	One Location Fixed or Given	Major Locational Component Variables*							Rank of Locational Complexity	Degrees of Locational Choice
		(a)	(b)	(c)	(d)	(e)	(f)	(g)		
Primitive Economies	X	X	X					—	A	1
Primary: Extractive	X	X	X					—	A	1
Primary: Agriculture		X	X	X				—	B	2
Secondary		X	X	X	X			—	C	3
Tertiary		X	X	X	X	X	X	—	D	Many
Quaternary		X	X	X	—	X	X	X	D	Many
Quinquenary		X	X	X	—	X	X	X	D	Many

*Locational component variables are: (a) accessibility, (b) site quality, (c) regulation and control, (d) on-site procurement costs, (e) site competition for strategic sites on a microscale, (f) site affinities and disaffinities among activity types, and (g) a host of additional variables not otherwise identified. The symbol "X" indicates a locational component of major importance. The hyphen indicates other variables not otherwise specified.

The number of major components that provide general explanation for the location of each activity also generally increases as choices in location become more numerous. Note that for primitive, noncommercial economies and the extractive activities, the location of the site of production is given—for production to occur at all, it must be at the location of the resource in question. There are choices among resource sites, however, based on quality of the resource and accessibility to points of consumption. Moreover, the primary activities often have a regulatory variable imposed. The secondary activities are even more complicated in locational understanding because of additional variables pertaining to raw material procurement costs. Finally, the tertiary and quaternary sectors are most complicated of all inasmuch as they are affected in location not only by most of the variables of the other sectors, but also by intensive competition for particular sites within cities.

Conclusions

The realm of economic geography consists of five activity sectors, plus transportation. Our purpose here will be to attempt to understand the spatial dimensions of each. In one sense, of course, understanding them fully involves tracing present patterns back to the dawn of time and space. But this approach would take us out of the arena of economic geography and into the wide expanse of general philosophy. Thus we shall be content to start and to finish on a closer and firmer standing base — a base that will be accepted as given (Figure 1.2).

To be more specific, four major outside influences will be taken as they are found, with no attempt on our part at explanation — unless such a pursuit provides some direct and necessary light, otherwise unavailable, on the activity under investigation. These four givens are: (1) the physical features of the earth; (2) the natural resources of the earth; (3) the human and cultural-trait features and patterns as they vary over space; and (4) the respective socioeconomic and institutional systems among different peoples over the earth. Explanation of these outside influences belongs more properly to disciplines other than economic geography — to physical geography, geology, anthropology, psychology, sociology, economics, and many others. Thus our purpose will be simply to employ such features as ontological agents for the locational explanation and understanding of still other features, specifically those features comprising the various sectors of economic geography. And from this analytical thrust we shall examine other factors that will provide even greater understanding of the placement of man and his activities on earth.

As a cautionary note to the above, it cannot be overemphasized that economic geography is not simply a fusion of economics and geography. To regard it as such would be no more true than to view political geography as a combination of political science and geography, or social geography as a combination of sociology and geography. While it may well be true that economic geography needs more economics, economic geography is geography pure and simple. As such, it has a strong core bias and focus. That bias is spatial: What concerns the geographer is the locational elements of things. Anything that does not contribute to his improved spatial understanding of the object being studied is of no interest to him as a geographer. However, the explanations for the spatial positioning of things must necessarily come from a wide assortment of inputs not always obvious or clearly defined; for economic geography, however, these most often include physical, cultural, historical, institutional, and certainly not least, economic factors. These critical inputs will henceforth be called *The Bases of Economic Geography.*

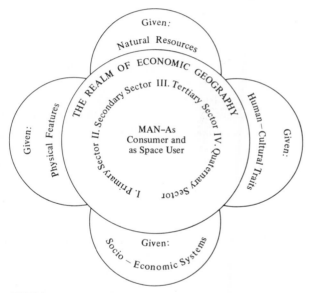

FIGURE 1.2 The Realm of Economic Geography. Economic geography is arbitrarily differentiated from connected influences — influences which must, for pedagogic purposes, be taken as given.

Because the content of economic geography is so extremely comprehensive, no one book can possibly cover all topics. This work will focus on the general types of locational patterns and problems that are encountered as one progresses from the primary through the quinquenary activity sectors. Part A lays the groundwork by which the subjects next discussed can be understood. These bases include transportation, physical features, economic principles, and social and institutional conditions. The distribution of cities is also presented in Part

A, inasmuch as their placement strongly affects the location of most all other activities to be studied. In many of the following chapters, the location of cities is taken as fixed and is one of the factors used in locational explanation. Part B then proceeds in a graduated way to discuss the more simple types of location problems, namely the primitive or noncommercial economies and the extractive activities. Part C deals with agriculture, slightly more difficult an activity to understand spatially. Parts D and E (manufacturing and internal spatial structure of cities) deal with problems treated in a more complex manner. Finally, in Part F the ultimate in spatial understanding and application is attempted: regional synthesis within a public policy framework.

BIBLIOGRAPHY

Selected texts in economic geography

(Most of the following contain materials that will be of use throughout this book.)

Alexander, John. *Economic Geography*. Englewood Cliffs N.J.: Prentice-Hall, 1963.

Dohrs, Fred E., and Sommers, Lawrence M., eds. *Economic Geography: Selected Readings*. New York: Thomas Y. Crowell Co., 1970.

Fryer, D. W. *World Economic Development*. New York: McGraw-Hill, 1965.

Griffin, Paul F.; Chatham, Ronald L.; Singh, Ajmer; and White, Wayne R. *Culture, Resources, and Economic Activity: An Introduction to Economic Geography*. Boston: Allyn and Bacon, 1971.

Highsmith, Richard M., Jr., ed. *Case Studies in World Geography: Occupance and Economy Types*. Englewood Cliffs N. J.: Prentice-Hall, 1961.

Highsmith, Richard M., Jr., and Northam, Ray M. *World Economic Activities: A Geographic Analysis*. New York: Harcourt, Brace & World, 1968.

Hoffman, Lawrence A. *Economic Geography*. New York: The Ronald Press, 1965.

Jones, Clarence Fielden, and Darkenwald, Gordon Gerald. *Economic Geography*. New York: The Macmillan Co., 1965.

Klimm, Lester E.; Starkey, Otis P.; and Russell, Joseph A. *Introductory Economic Geography*. New York: Harcourt, Brace & World, 1956.

McCarty, H.H., and Lindberg, James. *Preface to Economic Geography*. Englewood Cliffs N. J.: Prentice-Hall, 1966.

Roepke, Howard G., ed. *Readings in Economic Geography*. New York: John Wiley & Sons, 1967.

Smith, Robert H. T.; Taaffe, Edward J.; and King, Leslie J., eds. *Readings in Economic Geography*. Chicago: Rand McNally & Co., 1968.

Thoman, Richard S.; Conkling, Edgar C.; and Yeates, Maurice H. *The Geography of Economic Activity*. New York: McGraw-Hill, 1968.

Van Royen, William, and Bengston, Nels A. *Fundamentals of Economic Geography*. Englewood Cliffs N.J.: Prentice-Hall, 1964.

White, C. Langdon; Griffin, Paul F.; and McKnight, Tom L. *World Economic Geography*. Belmont Calif.: Wadsworth Publishing Co., 1964.

Zimmermann, Erich W. *World Resources and Industries.* New York: Harper and Brothers, 1951.

Other sources

Berry, Brian J. L. "Further Comments Concerning 'Geographic' and 'Economic' Economic Geography." *The Professional Geographer*, January 1959, pp. 9–12.

Commission on College Geography. *A Systems Analytic Approach to Economic Geography.* Washington: Association of American Geographers, 1968.

Ginsburg, Norton. *Atlas of Economic Development.* Chicago: The University of Chicago Press, 1961.

Ginsburg, Norton, ed. *Essays on Geography and Economic Development.* Chicago: University of Chicago Press, 1960.

Lukermann, Fred. "Toward A More Geographic Economic Geography." *The Professional Geographer*, July 1958, pp. 2–11.

McCarty, H. H. "Toward a More General Economic Geography." *Economic Geography*, October 1959, pp. 283–289.

McNee, Robert B. "The Changing Relationships of Economics and Economic Geography." *Economic Geography*, July 1959, pp. 189–198.

Webb, Martyn J. "Economic Geography: A Framework for a Disciplinary Definition." *Economic Geography*, July 1961, pp. 254–257.

part a

The Bases of
Geographic Understanding

"What concerns the geographer is the locational elements of things. Anything that does not contribute to his improved spatial understanding of the object being studied is of no interest to him as a geographer. However, the explanations for the spatial positioning of things must necessarily come from a wide assortment of inputs not always obvious or clearly defined; for economic geography, however, these must often include physical, cultural, historical, institutional, and certainly not least, economic factors. These critical inputs will henceforth be called *The Bases of Economic Geography.*"

Chapter 1, "What Is Economic Geography?" p. 13

II

Transportation: A Determinant of Locational Choice and A Mirror of Spatial Interactions

The effects of transportation on the location of economic activities will be a recurrent theme throughout this book. Nevertheless, it is important that the general principles affecting movement be presented before analysis of any specific activity pattern is attempted. The principles of spatial interaction and of transportation costs supply the framework for assessing any given area or activity. Transportation is thus a strong determinant of the amount of locational choice afforded any given activity. The effects of these transportation characteristics and preconditions for interaction are reflected in the actual patterns of economic activity over the earth. Finally, the interaction patterns among such economic activities are further mirrored by the physical transportation routes themselves.

Thus transportation provides the initial key for the spatial understanding of economic activity and also reflects the territorial differentiation of man's activities. Paradoxically, transportation represents both the beginning and the summation of spatial understanding. Anyone who fully understands the reasons underlying the earth's network of routes and their flow patterns surely understands the economic geography of the world.

Transportation and Locational Choice — A Paradox

The general effect of transportation improvement is to allow more locational choice for any given economic activity. In a primitive economy, for example, with very limited transportation, people can only choose from resources close at hand — poor though those resources may be — to meet their major life requirements. Often such people will select the *one* best resource near them, whether it be fishing, hunting, herding, gathering, or "slash-and-burn agriculture." In this way they often become highly dependent on one activity. Thus, in a primitive economy, the choice and actual use of materials is highly restricted.

As transportation improves, these people can fan out and begin to select from resources scattered over a much wider area. It is probable that they will find more and even better resources than they had before. If so, they may use several of these new-found materials to satisfy their needs. And because the new-found resources may be much richer in quality, these people will be more efficient than formerly.

As transportation improves still further, expanding their range of selection, there is an even greater likelihood that such people will find several different high-quality resources. Their economy thus becomes more diversified in terms of material used, but more specialized in terms of the division of labor and in terms of selection of areas for use. Finally, with improved access to extended areas, they may come into contact with other people and be able to interchange some of their high-quality resources and products. In this way trade is established and the economy advances from the subsistence level to the commercial level. With trade, the area may once again become highly specialized. It will also become greatly dependent on outside areas for its existence.

But transportation is also quite paradoxical in other ways. As the world becomes more accessible, because of improvements in transportation, materials can be brought in from longer distances. Thus, paradoxically, improvements in transportation lead to greater consumption of transportation. Although transportation is a cost in the acquisition process, it is usually true that the greater the use of transportation in a given area, the more advanced are the people in that area.

Advanced economies, which today select resources almost on a world scale, have become highly reliant on nonlocal materials. The United States, for example, though rich in natural resources, is such a great consumer that it cannot supply its full needs from domestic sources. In other cases, it is a heavy importer because nondomestic resources are higher in quality or more accessible (for example, near water) than local resources.

When such materials decline in availability as a result of wars, trade controls, or the like, technological skill is used to manufacture substitutes. For example, synthetics and artificial products of all types have been developed to remove dependency on resources no longer readily available. These substitutes, in turn, cut down the necessity of transporting the original materials. Yet synthetics may also result in trade. The United States, for example, is now a major exporter of synthetic rubber. Thus there is a constant play-off between activities — creating substitutes, for example — designed to minimize the use of transportation, and man's incessant desire to improve transportation and hence use more of it.

Three Principles of Spatial Interaction

Materials will not be transferred from one part of the earth to another unless their increased worth at their destination justifies the costs of transporting them. The basic reason for most things having different values in different places is that the distribution of the earth's resources is unequal; consequently a surplus of a particular item is found in some areas while elsewhere that item exists in short supply or not at all. By connecting areas, transportation helps to remove the inequity of resource distribution. Because materials usually vary in value from one part of the earth to another, transportation is said to "add value" to them. They are, therefore, always moved toward the place where they are worth more. Of course, whenever materials are moved, value is always added simply because transportation is costly.

In more specific terms, materials will not move over the surface of the earth unless (1) there is a supply, or surplus, of an item in one place and a demand for that specific item in another — a condition hereinafter labeled *complementarity;* and (2) the item can "reasonably" be moved from supply area "S" to demand area "D." This latter prerequisite will hereinafter be labeled *transferability*. In addition to these two primary requirements, supply area "S" must represent the closest, or best, opportunity for which demand area "D" can receive such an item; in other words, there must be no *intervening area* which offers a better opportunity for trade of this item with area "D" than does area "S." Thus it can be assumed that from the vantage point of area "D," area "S" has a *comparative advantage* over other areas. (This principle will be further discussed in Chapter 4.) Implicit in these interactions, or flows, is also the assumption that appropriate methods of payment, or exchange, are available so that area "D" is able to pay for the item from area "S."

Complementarity as a necessary prerequisite for interchange and physical flow of commodities, products, and goods merely means that the demand area and the supply area must complement each other specifically with regard to the material to be transported. Just to have a surplus of "food" in one area and a demand for "food" in another tells us very little about the possibilities of interaction because nothing has been said about *specific* types of food. People do not demand just food, manufactured products, or stores, but rather such specific things as soft wheat, dried beef, Volkswagens, and bib overalls. Man is particular about his demands. An understanding of spatial interaction from the vantage point of complementarity involves a consideration of specific items of demand and supply.

Transferability, like complementarity, means exactly what the word suggests — how transferable are things over the earth? First, some items cannot be moved physically. You may want a particular climate or view, but such things are immobile. Second, some items are not moved because the high cost of moving them cancels out the initial demand for them. For example, if you wanted a bushel of apples and were willing to pay $2.00 for it, and if this were available in another area for $1.80, specific complementarity would exist. But if transportation costs amounted to $0.30, your demand would no longer operate because the price to you would be $2.10 — $0.10 more than you would be willing to pay. Your demand is not operable at $2.10 and cannot be met at $2.00. In this way the cost of transportation prevents many items from being moved over the earth. You either must go without apples or substitute something else in their place.

Such cancellations of demand create a large number of substitutions. As a general rule, when transferability problems prevent fulfillment of the specific complementarity, a substitution of another item for that initially demanded usually occurs. Moreover, substituting an item also often involves substituting one area for another — one area intervenes for another.

This is another factor which discourages movement. Often the demand is short-lived and immediate. If the demand time is limited, a mode of transportation may be used that is faster and thus more expensive than the one usually employed. There may also be time restraints as to when an item can be supplied. Seasonality plays a very strong role in the movement of agricultural commodities.

These principles can be formally presented by a Gravity Model as follows: $I = P/dn$ where P represents the size, or importance of a place, d represents distance, time, or cost, and where the exponent n represents the expected deterioration of interaction with distance. Generally this exponent is 2, thereby squaring the time-distance measure. Thus P substitutes for the above notions of complementarity, d for transferability, and the exponent n represents intervening opportunity. As an example, assume that area A is ten miles from a place, P, of 10,000 population. If so, A would have an interaction index of one hundred with P, as compared with another area, B, only five miles distant, which would have an index value of four hundred. Thus area B's interaction potential with regard to place P would be four times greater than area A's. The general interaction between two places, say $P1$ and $P2$, can be determined according to the derived formula $P1\ P2/dn$.

Factors Affecting Transportation Costs

The major factor affecting the transferability of materials over the earth is the cost of shipping a particular item a given distance. Although factors like time and perishability may in some cases be present, they can often also be treated as transportation cost factors. For example, perishable items may require special transport facilities such as refrigerated ships, trucks, and railroad cars, or speedy shipment that can be supplied only by airplane. Thus the main requisite for understanding interaction, given complementarity, is the cost of transportation. The following are the major factors affecting the costs of transportation:

1. Length of haul
2. Area characteristics between complementary places
3. Mode of transportation
4. Nature of item shipped
5. Volume of interaction
6. Back-haul possibilities
7. Extent of competition
8. Government regulation and control

Length of haul

In general, the greater the distance between any two places, the greater will be the total cost of transportation for any given item. Thus it costs more to ship Washington timber to Iowa than to Wyoming. This cost relationship is an indirect measure of proximity, or accessibility, of various places on the earth relative to each other.

Perhaps the most interesting aspect of length of haul and transportation cost is that the *cost per unit* decreases with increasing distance. For most transportation modes, the greater the distance shipped, the lower the *rate* per unit. Actually the cost of transportation increases, but at a decreasing rate, with distance from point of origin. This occurs primarily because loading and unloading costs (terminal costs) are constant regardless of length of haul. Thus short trips are relatively more costly per unit mile as compared to longer trips. However, as will be demonstrated, this varies greatly among modes. The practical result of this exponential cost-distance relationship is often a series of steplike rates, with each horizontal plateau becoming greater in distance and each vertical rise becoming less with increasing distance (Figure 2.1).

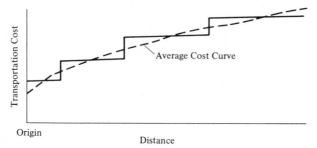

FIGURE 2.1 The Cost of Transportation as Affected by Distance Shipped. Transportation costs increase with distance shipped but at a decreasing rate. Thus longer distance shipments cost less per unit-mile than do shorter distance shipments. The general increase is characterized by steplike changes in cost rather than by a smooth curve.

This pricing and distance factor causes much longer flows of material to occur than would be initially supposed. First, the more distant areas are charged much less per unit than their distances would suggest. For example, a place four times as far away as another place usually pays only about twice as much per unit mile. Second, distant areas are often generally blanketed with the same rate. As might be expected, the breaks in transportation charges often makes such places desirable as transfer points.

Another rather common method of favoring more distant areas is the "postage stamp" rate procedure — that is, charging the same price per item no matter where it is purchased or sent. A first-class letter, for example, will go anywhere in the United States for the same cost to the sender (hence the label "postage stamp rate"). In fact, it costs more for the postal authorities to send a letter across the United States than to the next state, but perhaps not so much more that it would be worth the labor costs involved in having varying rates, to say nothing of the general confusion and trouble varying rates would cause the public. The United States Congress must also feel some subsidization to more distant areas is appropriate in this case. But postage stamp rates are also used by many firms. Nevertheless, under such a policy people near the source of the product pay more and those further away pay less than the true costs of shipment.

The distinction between true actual costs, which are normally exponential, and rates charged should be noted, since the two rarely coincide in the real world. But in terms of economic location, both may prove important for complete understanding.

Area characteristics between complementary places

A first major modification of the distance-cost factor is the nature and composition of the territory between any two places. For example, areas characterized by water, land, mountains, plains, and rivers all have differing transportation costs. If it is necessary to change modes of transportation between places, costs will rise because of transfers of cargo at these *break of bulk points.* Ports are clearly places where cargo must be changed from ship to land transportation.

On the other hand, as will be demonstrated, land transportation is generally five or six times more costly than water transportation. Thus two places separated by land might be considered about five times further apart in cost-distance than are two equally distant places connected by water. For example, Northern Europe and the East Coast of the United States are closer in terms of transportation costs than are New York and Omaha, Nebraska — though not in terms of time nor, perhaps, in actual costs when tariffs and various international trade controls are taken into account.

The result of the land-water surface cost discrepancy is to cause a refractive route phenomenon between such areas. Refraction occurs when light passes through two different media having different densities — air and water, for example. The denser medium (analogous to higher transportation cost area) causes the light to bend to meet the less dense material in a shorter distance than would otherwise be the case if light traveled in a straight line (Figure 2.2). This is precisely what happens given different transportation costs over various surfaces, for example, between land and water. The land transportation route is generally much shorter than it would be by a direct line route between *A* and *B*. If water transportation costs were zero, or so small relative to land transportation as to be of no locational consideration, the land route would take the shortest route to the sea *(BXA)* rather than a direct route between *A* and *B (BYA)*. In Figure 2.2 it is assumed that there are two ports on the mainland: *W* and *Z*. Therefore neither route *BYA* nor *BXA*, nor any combination between them, is possible. Instead, shipment must go either by way of *BWA* or *BZA*. Clearly, the *BWA* route is less costly than *BZA* inasmuch as it uses the least land transportation. Yet it is by far the longest route in terms of total distance.

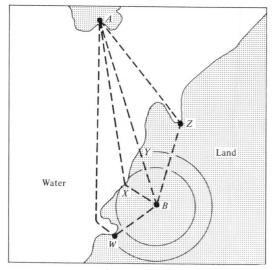

FIGURE 2.2 Variation in Transportation Costs over Land and Water Surfaces.   Water transportation per unit mile is much cheaper than land transportation. Thus the cheapest route is the one that maximizes the use of water mileage and minimizes the land mileage. The location of ports, perhaps related to shoreline features, may dictate a more costly route than the one that is theoretically the cheapest.

In fact, in most water-land breaks, the port is generally found in a place that lengthens distance by the direct route (that is, the water route) and shortens the direct land route. Of course, ports cannot be put just anywhere along a coast, so that this primary goal of minimizing transportation costs between any two points is rarely achieved perfectly in practice. And, of course, the port may preexist because of other flows. This may be but a minor flow and will simply have to ship through the port as it is found.

The cost over land also varies greatly because land has many different surface characteristics. Where different territorial cost surfaces are traversed, a "bending" and shortening of costs — but a lengthening of distance — generally occurs, much the same as with water and land surfaces. Undoubtedly, the cheapest territory for land transportation is a flat area. Crossing plains is therefore less costly than traversing hilly or mountainous areas. This is easily demonstrated in the United States where "slightly higher rates" are charged for shipments west of the Rocky Mountains. (Terrain here, however, is not the only factor involved. Volume of traffic and back-haul problems are other factors.)

In order to be operationally understood, land surface characteristics must be very carefully examined. For example, even a rather rolling terrain may require considerable cut-and-fill for railroad routes. There may also be numerous small bridges required to cross small streams. On the other hand, low-lying and very flat land may require that roadbeds be raised. In cold climates, where permafrost exists, still another problem in roadbed construction is presented. In many areas, vegetation presents clearance and control problems. Thus, while important, terrain alone is inadequate as any full physical guide to variable transportation costs with distance.

The effect of terrain also varies greatly in importance among transportation modes. Air traffic is least affected, although terrain surely plays a cost role in the restriction of opportunity for airport placements, the flight patterns as the result of mountain peaks and ranges, and by various weather conditions associated with terrain in certain climatic types. Nonetheless most surface transportation involves greater costs in hilly areas because of differential costs of route construction and over-the-road operating costs. Yet pipelines can operate, albeit with more pumping, at grades of forty degrees and above; trucks, too, can handle relatively steep grades, but at high cost. On the other hand, any grade over five degrees is considered excessive for rail transportation. This explains in large part the circuity of rail routes in hilly areas as they seek out low grade passes and river grades.

Thus it is evident that some parts of the earth have much greater cost advantages with regard to interaction than have others. Because of complementarity among areas, however, many routes are constructed in high-cost territory. In fact, most of the transportation movement in the United States and the world is "cross-grain," that is, transportation routes run counter to the easiest directions of movement. Thus territorial character, while affecting costs and causing variations in routes, does not determine the nature and extent of transportation routes. It is rather the *flows*, the reflection of the principles of spatial interaction, that determine such route location.

Mode of transportation

It does little good to discuss the costs of transportation with regard to distance and territorial characteristics without specifying the mode involved. Some modes have an advantage for short distances (for example, truck), whereas others have the advantage for longer distance (for example, rail). Nevertheless, some ranking of the costs of these modes can be made in terms of *ton-mile costs* — the cost of transporting one ton of material one mile. In general, ton-mile costs of various modes increase in the following order: (1) ships and barges, (2) pipelines, (3) trains, (4) trucks, (5) airplanes, and (6) human-powered carriers. Ships generally cost less than one cent, trains one to three cents, trucks six or more cents, and airplanes about twenty-five cents per ton-mile. Transportation by human porter, even in underdeveloped, cheap labor areas, amounts to one dollar or more per ton-mile.

Such cost data, however, does not settle the question of which mode is best. In terms of speed, a typical shipment from New York to San Francisco takes only half as long (seven days versus fifteen days) by train as by ship because of the slower speed of ships (about twenty miles per hour versus sixty miles per hour for trains) and the longer route required of ships — in this case, through the Panama Canal. But truck transportation is even faster than train for this trip, not because trucks are so much faster in traveling speed, but because no single railroad connects New York and San Francisco. To make this trip by train, several freight-car changes must be made in various classification yards as the cars are moved from one railroad line to another. Yet the two days saved by truck costs about $65 per ton ($90 by truck versus $35 by train). It becomes a question of how much two days' time is worth. In fact, if time is of the essence, the trip can be made by air in four and a half hours — but at a cost of about $400 per ton.

Another determinant of mode advantages is the amount of material that needs to be moved. Each mode has differing carrying capacities. A supertanker can carry some 200,000 tons of petroleum. A typical general-freight cargo ship can carry 20,000 tons. (Incidentally, the supertanker has speeds of only about sixteen to seventeen knots per hour whereas the general cargo ship has speeds of over 20 knots. But the 20,000 tons carried by the general cargo ship requires a 72,000 horsepower engine as compared with a 32,000 horsepower engine in the supertanker — factors that clearly affect costs.) A train on fairly flat terrain can carry almost 10,000 tons (two diesel engines). By comparison, the typical semitruck carries only about twenty-five tons. Thus, for large shipments, ship and train are clearly superior to truck and air.

Another key to differential mode costs is the ratio of the horsepower to freight hauled. A single train locomotive, using a 6000 horsepower diesel engine and crew of only four men, can pull some 200 freight cars or 5600 tons of freight. It would take 200 trucks, in all using some 40,000 horsepower and at least 200 drivers, to carry the same freight. Thus the horsepower tonnage ratio for a train is about 1.0 (6000 horsepower and 5600 tons) compared to 4.0 for trucks (100 horsepower and 25 tons). The hypothetical cost advantage is therefore at least four to one. However, the railroad must build and maintain its own track — an additional cost — whereas routes are only partially paid for by trucks. The supertanker's horsepower-to-tonnage ratio is 0.16, and the fastest general-container ships have a horsepower-to-tonnage ratio of about 3.0. But the private automobile is by far the most inefficient mode inasmuch as over 200 horsepower is often used to move less than one-tenth of a ton — a ratio of 2000 to 1.

Nevertheless, it is not difficult to understand why, despite their greatly differing costs, all these modes are used and needed. Each has special advantages relative to the other. Some have a special advantage with regard to carrying particular commodities. It is also obvious that in specific areas, some modes are out of the question, for example, rail transportation over extremely rugged terrain.

Sometimes the specialties of each are used by combining several modes in one shipment. Combination most commonly takes place at break-of-bulk areas, where materials are transferred from one mode to another. Of course, such loading, unloading, and reloading also involve considerable costs, and it is only on fairly long trips, or where there is little alternative but to transfer, that such breaks occur. However, containerization has made transfers much cheaper and easier.

Another rapidly developing dual mode practice is to use a combination of modes through such practices as *fishy-back* and *piggy-back*. In the first case, railroad cars are carried on ships and in the second, trucks, or more recently truck bed containers, are carried on railroad cars. Thus, the loading and unloading problem is fairly easy.

The question of which mode is best, or even cheapest, can be answered only with regard to a particular territory and shipment. For example, barges and tankers are less costly per ton-mile for shipping petroleum than are pipelines. But pipelines are little affected by grade and often avoid circuitous routes and port location restrictions imposed on ocean and river shipping. Thus the shorter distance needed by pipelines may override the slight ton-mile cost advantage of ocean shipping. On the other hand, constant pumping and full flow are necessary for pipeline operation. Only the large fields and demand areas can support such a system. In fact, until recently the United States was the only country with major "large inch" pipelines, and these were built primarily because German submarines posed a threat to tanker shipments from the Gulf Coast to the East Coast during World War II. (Now Western Europe, the Middle East, and the U.S.S.R. also have major oil pipelines.)

In terms of flow, a twenty-four-inch pipeline (about the average size) will deliver about 45,000 tons per day. Yet one supertanker will deliver more than five times as much. In most areas of the world, the supertanker is the most efficient carrier of petroleum, even where pipelines run quite directly between demand and supply areas.

Nature of items being shipped

The general principle with regard to types of items shipped is to "charge what the traffic will bear." Therefore, the higher the value of the material being shipped, the higher the transportation charge. In this regard, the rate charged for products is generally higher than for commodities. This principle, like several of the others, tends to favor long distance flows of raw material; thus items like coal, wheat, iron ore, and petroleum are shipped over much larger distances than might initially be supposed. On the other hand, many high-value items can "stand the cost of transportation" better than can low-value items. Thus products of high value are also moved over vast areas of the earth.

Another major principle relating to type of material carried is the difficulty involved in its shipment, particularly with regard to loading and unloading problems. Commodities that can be moved in large bulk by mechanized handling and special carriers and facilities can be transported at relatively low cost. In fact, the use of such facilities on the Great Lakes for the movement of wheat, iron ore, and coal has resulted in some of the lowest per ton-mile costs in the world.

By the same token, highly perishable and breakable items, which require special care in shipment and handling (refrigeration, for example), are properly charged higher rates than otherwise. These perishable items include fruits, especially bananas, and vegetables. Some items are so perishable and bulky (milk, for example) that they must often be produced close to their points of consumption. In other cases, however, when the perishable products are of high value (flowers, for example), they can stand the cost of high speed transportation.

Special refrigerator railroad cars and trucks were also developed to increase the distance range of perishable products, but only at added cost. (In fact, this improvement in transportation was primarily responsible for the growth of Southern California's fruit and vegetable industry.) Most often, however, perishability difficulties are overcome near production areas by changing the form of the product through packing, canning, and processing. In other cases, the produce is picked green and calculated to arrive at the market ready for immediate consumption. This is done, for example, with bananas and apples.

Highly breakable items must also be carefully packed and shipped. This special care will raise shipping costs, but innovations like containerization have been a great boon to the shipment of such materials.

In fact, most materials move by special types of vehicles — oil tankers, ore barges and boats, moving vans, and automobiles. There are over forty different types of customized railroad cars alone. Such cars include piggy-back, automobile rack, coal, coke, plasterboard, lumber, refrigerator, stock, container, automotive parts, pulpwood, cushioned underframe (for fragile shipments), log, insulated, and various other types of gondola, hopper, tank, and flat cars.

Volume of traffic

The lower the volume of traffic between any two places, the higher the rate charged and generally the higher the actual shipment cost. This occurs because, for all modes except air (pipelines *must* carry full loads), it is not much more expensive to carry a full load than part of a load. In fact, less than carload (LTC) shipments are commonly higher per unit cost than the general commodity rate. Full carloads are made up from LTC shipments by freight-forwarding companies. These companies charge the customer at the LTC rate, but ship at carload rates. In turn, they provide the customer with other services, such as door-to-door pickup and delivery.

Higher volumes for many carriers also allow efficiencies in transportation. Trains can be longer and "unitized," that is, all cars carry the same item and go to the same destination. In addition, special railroad cars, trucks and ships can be used to handle single items. Where volume is high, great efficiencies can often be obtained in loading and unloading. In fact, on major routes with high traffic volume, the rule is the use of special carrier types such as oil tankers, grain ships, ore ships, and many truck types particularly suited to a particular commodity or product.

Extent of competition

Generally, the greater the amount of competition among modes, the lower will be the rate charged between any two places. The tendency to "meet or beat competition" is so strong that cutthroat competition sometimes occurs among carriers. So severe was this practice among railroads in the United States during their early development that many were forced into bankruptcy. Railroads are particularly vulnerable to such competitive responses because they can cut costs down to actual operating costs by temporarily neglecting roadbed and rolling stock maintenance. Labor costs often have to be met whether freight is hauled or not, so that it is actually beneficial to use the truck and car rather than to leave them idle.

Regulatory agencies such as the Interstate Commerce Commission no longer allow carriers to engage in wars of competition. Even so, rates are usually lower on routes that have several alternative modes available, for example, along the Mississippi River valley, where barge, truck, and railroad compete. Of course, carried to extreme, such a protectionist policy (setting rates to protect the high-cost producer) has the effect of subsidizing inefficient transportation modes. Thus it is conceivable that where transportation rates should be the lowest because of competition, they might actually be kept higher by artificial means. Fortunately, the advantages of various modes with regard to factors other than cost create fewer competitive cost responses than would otherwise be the case.

Without regulation, on the other hand, a route having monopolistic freight rights to an area might gouge that area by charging the maximum costs it could bear. Even with regulations, places served by single modes or single carriers usually have higher rates than other more comprehensively served places. However, low volume as well as other factors are also usually involved in most such high-rate decisions.

Back-haul possibilities

Generally, the smaller the possibility for a return shipment, or backhaul, the higher will be the rate charged. This is a reasonable practice inasmuch as returning cars or trucks empty costs about as much as returning them with a full load. In fact, ships are especially handicapped since they must load rocks or other items merely for ballast before proceeding to the next port.

The result of back-haul demands are such that if *A* and *B* are 50 miles apart and the flow is only to *B*, then the shipping cost will perhaps be the equivalent of 75 or 100 miles rather than 50. The rate per ton-mile might be based on about a 30-mile shipment. What normally occurs is that the rate is set considerably lower from *B* to *A* and considerably higher than could otherwise be justified from *A* to *B*. The general attitude toward reducing the *B* to *A* rate is presumably a reflection of the standard dictum that any freight is better than no freight.

Yet almost all trade routes have unbalanced flows. Raw materials move to factories and finished products move in return. Inasmuch as there is almost always some weight-loss in the manufacturing process, the flow is invariably greater toward manufacturing areas than away from them. (The product shipments may be more bulky or perishable, however, thus compensating for the weight-loss factor.) In the United States, major flows are toward the industrial belt — that area roughly circumscribed by lines connecting Boston-Milwaukee-St. Louis-Baltimore-Boston. Thus there is commonly a boxcar shortage in the West and South. This is made even more apparent because of the seasonal nature of agricultural production in these areas.

It should be noted that the principle of backhaul runs counter to the principle of volume. In the case of volume, the heaviest flows receive the cheaper rates. In the case of one-way flows, these high volumes may nonetheless have high rates because of the paucity of back-haul possibilities. Indeed, the low-volume backhaul may have extremely low rates.

Regulation and control

The effect of regulation and control on the transfer costs of commodities and products is enormous. First, regulatory agencies often set rates among carriers within countries for the reasons described above. Second, various restrictions are often placed on various modes with regard to routes and general network configuration. This is especially true with regard to the interstate highway system, where the federal government, which has borne 90 percent of the costs, has made almost all the decisions regarding the extent of the network and what places the routes will or will not serve. Route pattern in this case is largely dictated by the needs of national defense, the existence of large cities, and, of course, by politics. Thus, compared to the railroad network, the highway system appears to be overbuilt in the South and underbuilt in the industrial belt.[1]

Nowhere is regulation and control more evident in affecting costs than in international trade. Such controls are of two types: those that restrict trade by raising the costs of transportation, and those that facilitate trade by offering special advantage to certain areas through "trade blocs" of various kinds. The effect of most regulation, however, is to raise the costs of transportaion by tariffs and other import duties. Tariffs set for revenue-raising purposes, although numerous, are calculated to have little effect on flows.

However, the general effects of tariffs on transportation costs can be considerable, as shown in Figure 2.3. Note that international trade tariffs add costs to what already often amounts to a break-of-bulk condition, inasmuch as most international trade moves through ports from which transfers to land transportation have to be made. Thus tariffs are an additional charge at break-of-bulk points and therefore a restraint on world trade.

Regulation and control also have a transportation effect on land transportation between countries (Figure 2.4). Only certain border crossings (X) are permitted. (Physically, too, there are often no places to cross these borders other than the designated ones.) Thus the length of haul must often be much increased to meet these border-crossing requirements. Given a tariff charge in addition to the route distortion, a major increase in transportation costs can result.

Tariffs are generally imposed to protect local economic activities and sometimes to favor one area of the world over another. For example, England has no import duties on tea but heavy import duties on coffee. This, of course, is a favor to Britain's former colonies. By contrast, the United States has no tariff on coffee but heavy quotas on sugarcane imports. This latter quota system favors local sugar beet production, which is noncompetitive with sugarcane production in other areas of the world. Similarly, the United States has almost prohibitive policies with regard to Argentine beef — another commodity in

[1]William L. Garrison, "Connectivity of the Interstate Highway System," *Papers and Proceedings of the Regional Science Association* (1960), pp. 121–37.

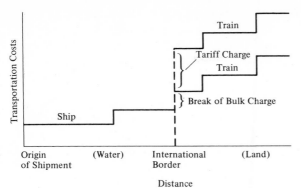

FIGURE 2.3   Effect of Tariff on Transportation Costs. A tariff charge has the effect of increasing transportation costs. Such charges commonly occur at international borders. If a transportation mode change is involved, this further increases the "shipping costs" at this point. Even if no tariff is charged at a break-of-bulk point, a new step-system of transportation cost is developed.

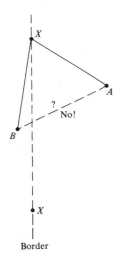

X● = Border Crossing

FIGURE 2.4   Effect of Border Crossings on Direct Shipments. Assuming a shipment from place *A* to *B* and an international border with crossings only at places *X*, the direct shipment route between *A* and *B* is negated by the necessity to cross at a specific border crossing. This has the effect, therefore, of lengthening the distance shipped and thereby increasing the cost of shipment over what otherwise would occur.

competition with similar activities within the United States. Although most countries talk in favor of "free trade" and do lower some import duties, heavy import duties are the rule — and outright embargoes are not uncommon. (Nontariff distortions of trade through trade agreements, quotas, and the like, which also strongly affect movements among countries, will be discussed in Chapter 5.)

In cases where competition is injurious to a country, embargoes, quotas, and especially high tariffs are imposed. (For example, great concern has been expressed over U.S. importation of European motor vehicles, textiles, and a wide range of manufactured products that sell better than domestic products in the United States.) These restrictions represent increased costs of transportation and general impediments to movement. As such, they diminish or curtail many potentially heavy flows among areas.

Trade Routes and Spatial Interaction

Examination of the physical routes of various transportation modes over the earth provides a first approximation of the manner in which the regions of the earth are interrelated and tied together. These routes are a direct mirror of the extent of interaction over the earth as affected by costs of transportation (and hence the possibilities for movement) and by organizational and institutional arrangements between countries. The pattern of routes is also a direct confirmation of actual complementarities among areas.

Trade routes thus reflect interactions over the earth. Anyone who understands all the flows and the reasons for them has a fairly comprehensive understanding of economic geography. The purpose here, therefore, is not to explain all the various flows but to impart some understanding of the nature and spatial configuration of such routes, as they are affected by the general principles of spatial interaction discussed earlier.

First of all, trade routes and their flows reflect the uneven distribution of population over the earth, and differing habits and customs. This is particularly significant in the large, overpopulated areas of Southeast Asia. Foodstuffs must be imported to many of these areas, to bolster the local agricultural economy. Rice and wheat from the United States and Canada have been major commodities shipped to these places.

The routes, their placements, volumes, and specific flows are also indicative of the inequalities of resources distributed over the earth. Some areas are endowed with rich deposits of materials for industry, such as petroleum, iron ore, coal, and bauxite, whereas other areas have few of the resources so critical to attaining an advanced industrial economy. Consequently, such materials are moved from the "haves" to the "have-nots." Paradoxically, the have-nots in this case are often the most industrially advanced nations. Conversely, some of the nations quite richly endowed with materials of industry are also the least advanced industrially. Thus the flows of these materials are preponderantly from the underdeveloped nations in Southeast Asia, Africa, and South and Central America to the industrially advanced nations of Western Europe, the United States, and, increasingly, Japan. It should not be inferred, however, that the industrially advanced nations have no such resources; they just do not have enough. Undoubtedly, some of the richest mineral resources in the world are found within the United States, but still more are needed.

Such flows also reflect the climatic inequities over the earth; the most striking of which is the inequity between the tropical and semitropical climatic areas, on the one hand, and the midlatitude areas of the industrially advanced countries, on the other. Inasmuch as many agricultural commodities can be produced efficiently only in certain latitudes, climatic areas favorable for producing particular crops have a distinct advantage. Thus products like sugar cane, bananas, rubber, coffee, and tea are important exports from tropical countries. On the other hand, some agricultural products, for example, corn, rice, wheat, potatoes, tobacco, and cotton, grow better in midlatitude climates. Thus surpluses in two different areas set up good possibilities for interchange.

Other areas have good potential with regard to industry but have poor food resources. England, a case in point, follows a long-standing procedure of importing raw materials for industry, as well as foodstuffs, and exporting its manufactured products in return. In fact, this is a typical pattern for most of the economically advanced nations. They import selected foodstuffs and various raw materials, but export manufactured items. This cycle increases transportation to a much greater extent than might be expected, because of long-distance flows of both raw materials and finished products.

Another feature mirrored by trade routes and flows is the degree of economic development. The more economically developed nations constitute the nucleus of world trade. Of particular importance are Western Europe and the United States. Except for the Communist-Bloc countries, most countries of the world are heavily hinged to this dual industrial complex on either side of the North Atlantic Ocean.

People in the more industrially advanced countries have much higher per capita incomes than do those in less developed countries. They also have rather diversified tastes in food and material. Thus they demand food from around the world. By contrast, people in the less developed countries of the world carry on a much more limited trade. Most of their trade consists of raw-material and commodity exports to the richer nations, in return for which they receive small flows of high-value products as well as food for their burgeoning populations. The United States, for example, is the world's foremost rice exporter. Canada is the world leader in wheat exports.

In this regard, the greater the degree of economic development in a country, the greater the trade. This is confirmed by the fact that the greatest trade route in the world, in terms of value of items shipped, is the North Atlantic route between Western Europe and the United States. The route between highly industrialized Japan and Western countries, particularly the United States, is also heavily used. In this latter case, however, Japan appears to be more advanced for it imports many of its raw materials from the United States (for example, timber, scrap iron) and exports finished products such as automobiles, photographic equipment, and other high-priced and high-quality items in return. However, other important indicators of economic advancement clearly demonstrate that the economy of the United States is superior to Japan.

Even many items of the same kind are interchanged among the industrially advanced countries. For example, there is a heavy flow of automobiles both to and from Western Europe, the United States, and Japan. Similarly, there are reciprocal flows of textiles, foodstuffs, and many manufactured items. This further demonstrates the importance of specific complementarity in predicting or understanding spatial interaction. Nonetheless, there are general patterns. Exports to Europe from the United States mainly include aircraft, automobiles, agricultural machinery, wheat, tobacco, cotton, and soybeans. Significant flows from Europe to the United States and Canada include alcoholic beverages, textiles, watches, and automobiles.

Conclusions

Transportation both sets the conditions for potential interaction and mirrors actual spatial movements. Before movement can occur between any two areas, there must be specific complementarity, the possibility of effecting transfers, and various institutional arrangements. If these conditions are fulfilled, then a flow may occur — provided no better area can be substituted. Thus the physical flows and route patterns over the earth summarize and ossify such theoretical possibilities.

Many factors effect the transferability of things over the earth. Among them are degrees of perishability, fragility, and bulkiness. These and other factors are most easily seen in terms of general costs of transportation, which reflect considerations such as mode, distance to be shipped, mode-change needs, volume of movement, back-haul possibilities, the extent of competition among modes, the nature of the item shipped, and various controls and regulations. In combination, these considerations favor some areas and disadvantage others. Thus, transportation-cost parameters are largely responsible for a great multitude of spatial inequalities.

In another sense, transportation trade routes simply mirror the earth's differences in resources. Some areas have great iron ore deposits but no coal; some have great forests but no farmland; some have one climate and some another. The physical connection of these diverse areas and potential interchange among them is summed up in transportation. Thus transportation, by enabling resources to be moved to more profitable areas, makes possible the use of otherwise useless resources. Paradoxically, by so doing, it also allows an area to specialize in its greatest surplus — a surplus which otherwise would be of little use.

By shifting things among areas, transportation is largely the cause of territorial specialization. With poor transportation, areas are often unable to use some of their resources because of the need for a critical complement, such as coal for iron ore. When an area must obtain everything locally, a relatively inefficient system generally results. Thus, isolated areas often have subsistence-type economies and must depend largely on themselves simply to survive. In contrast, an area highly connected to other areas can often enjoy a great diversity in life style by concentrating on the export of one or a few items in which it has a comparative advantage over other areas. This principle of territorial specialization is the fundamental essence of trade and, by definition, of transportation — truly a two-edged sword.

BIBLIOGRAPHY

Alexander, John W.; Brown, S. Earl; and Dahlberg, Richard E. "Freight Rates: Selected Aspects of Uniform and Nodal Regions." *Economic Geography*, January 1958, pp. 1–18.

Clark, Colin. "Transport: The Maker and Breaker of Cities." *Town Planning Review*, 1958, p. 239.

Hoover, Edgar M. *The Location of Economic Activity.* New York: McGraw-Hill, 1948.

Locklin, D. Philip. *Economics of Transportation.* Homewood, Ill.: Richard D. Irwin, 1954.

McDowell, Carl E., and Gibbs, Helen M. *Ocean Transportation.* New York: McGraw-Hill, 1954.

Olsson, Gunnar. *Distance and Human Interaction: A Review and Bibliography.* Bibliography Series no. 2. Philadelphia: Regional Science Research Institute, 1965.

Sealy, Kenneth R. *The Geography of Air Transport.* Chicago: Aldine Publishing Co., 1968.

Taaffe, Robert N. "Transportation and Regional Specialization: The Example of Soviet Central Asia." *Annals of the Association of American Geographers*, March 1962, pp. 80–98.

Ullman, Edward L. *American Commodity Flow.* Seattle: University of Washington Press, 1957.

Wallace, William H. "Railroad Traffic Densities and Patterns." *Annals of the Association of American Geographers*, December 1958, pp. 352–74.

Warntz, William. "Transatlantic Flights and Pressure Patterns." *Geographical Review*, April 1961, pp. 187–212.

Wolfe, Roy I. "Transportation and Politics: the Example of Canada." *Annals of the Association of American Geographers*, June 1962, pp. 176–90.

III

The Physical Bases of Economic Geography

In economic geography some things must be taken as given — that is, we will not try to explain their causes but only their consequences with regard to the location of economic activities. This is especially true with regard to the physical features of the earth. Although understandable and good reasons exist for the placement of such features as climates, soils, land forms, and rivers, it is not our purpose here to explain them. Our purpose is rather to discuss and explain the general influences of such physical bases on economic geography.

The importance of certain physical features in modifying transportation routes and costs was discussed in Chapter 2. Even though these physical features are important, they rarely play a deterministic role; they are only some of the many factors that modify transportation and thereby affect spatial interaction. Understanding the proper role of the physical features with regard to transportation is relatively easy. However, with regard to agriculture and other activities, it is often difficult to avoid an exaggerated view of the importance of these physical features.

Given the obvious fact that many of the relatively unoccupied parts of the earth have foreboding environments — for example, the polar ice caps and tundra, the high plateaus and mountains, the major deserts, and various jungle and tropical areas — economic geographers soon postulated the "too" concept. According to the developers of this concept, man has avoided the extreme environments but has sought out the "good lands." The avoided areas are thereby considered too hot, too dry, too cold, too steep, or too something else for major settlement and land use.

The positive version of the "too" concept is that man has sought out the good lands, the areas most suitable for agriculture and, subsequently, for cities and industry. In short, he has settled in the midlatitude areas having good soil and good access to the sea — he has chosen the best of all possible worlds. This Goldilocks type of reasoning is quite obviously too deterministic and surely too simple.

Nonetheless, an examination of the general distribution of population and major economic activities over the earth strikingly demonstrates the tremendous concentration of these in only a few areas. Some 90 percent of the earth's population live and work on less than 10 percent of the land surface. Moreover, certain broad physical features are strongly associated with the distribution of mankind. These selected places are in midlatitude areas and climatically temperate zones; they are accessible to the seas, and are characterized by relatively level terrain or rolling plains. Such physical correlations have not only led to the formation of the "too" concept, but to other highly restrictive and physically based concepts in economic geography. In extreme cases, these concepts presume that the physical bases of the earth provide *the* primary explanation for man's distribution.

The undeniable importance of certain physical features was carried to the extreme about a half-century ago. At that time it was asserted that what man does is determined primarily by his environmental conditions. This concept was called *environmental determinism*. Although geographers have long since formally rejected it, some still persist in placing too heavy an emphasis on environmental factors. Several of these latter practitioners have coined a neodeterministic phrase called *environmental possibilism*. They hypothesize that the environment sets the stage for a range of possibilities for economic activity, and that man selects, through his culture, from among these limited choices. This concept, while generally correct, also commonly overstates the role of the physical bases in man's placement of activities. (Other equally, if not more, important factors will be discussed in Chapters 4 and 5.) Many new books still contain rather strong assumptions of the influence of physical features on man and his activities.

Although the man-land connection is often very close, man has exhibited considerable latitude of choice in his response. Close observation of economic activity patterns reveals that man has more choices open to him than such deterministic or possibilistic concepts suggest. Other variables in land use, such as location and culture, may also play a restrictive role, causing otherwise good land to be left unused or very poor land to be heavily used.

Even if physical factors were determining elements, there would still be different optimum environments for different activities. For example, optimum environmental conditions for bananas are not the same as for cotton, and those for cotton are not ideal for wheat. In fact, an impossible environment for one crop may actually be an optimum environment for another. Thus, even in agriculture, it makes little sense to apply a general label of "good" to some lands and "bad" to others.

This is further the case because man has substitution capabilities whereby he may play off costs of production and yields. Even where an optimum physical

condition can be found — for example, just the right combinations of temperature and precipitation (Figure 3.1) — yield and cost substitution factors enter
the picture. Even so, there is a limit beyond which a crop cannot be produced
because of zero yield at infinite costs. To find an optimum, as illustrated in
Figure 3.1, it must be tailor-made to a specific crop. And the limits of profitability
are wide, indeed, for most crops. In other words, it is still difficult to judge
on the basis of physical features the best place for a crop to be grown.

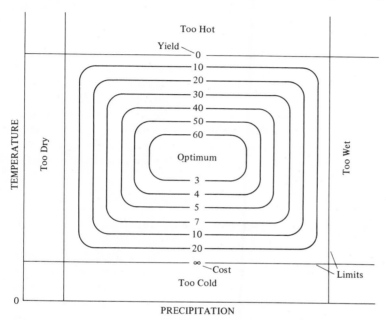

FIGURE 3.1 A Simple Physical-Restraint Model.   This model demonstrates the effects of varying combinations of temperature and precipitation on crop yields and production costs. For any given crop an optimum
combination and a limit of production is hypothesized. Note that yields
naturally fall off with more adverse physical conditions, but can be
increased by more dollar inputs. Source: Harold H. McCarty and James
B. Lindberg, *A Preface to Economic Geography*, (C) 1966. By permission
of Prentice-Hall, Inc., Englewood Cliffs, New Jersey.

Therefore, it should be evident that physical features do not limit production of a particular crop only to that location which is physically optimum.
Instead, production often occurs in "marginal" areas. Here the yields may
be lower, but if the marginal area is closer to the final market, savings in
distribution costs may more than offset lower yields or higher production costs.
On the other hand, it is also possible to obtain yields even higher than those
at the physically optimum location if higher input costs (purchasing fertilizer,
for example) are made. Finally, the optimum physical space may be usurped

by some other, more profitable crop. For these reasons, any given crop is rarely produced at its most optimum physical location. The true optimum location is where greatest profitability exists, not necessarily where physical features are most advantageous.

Finally, man often modifies physical features to suit his needs. Agricultural crops are surely much affected by climate and soil variables, yet man has many ways of overcoming such natural obstacles: He can fertilize poor soil, drain wet soil, irrigate arid areas, and through the application of chemicals, overcome such problems as soil acidity and alkalinity. Given steep slopes, which in their natural conditions normally prevent agriculture because of soil erosion, he may terrace land to make it usable. In rolling topography, the land may be leveled to make it suitable for irrigation. For example, in the Palouse grain-growing area of Washington, special machinery with balancing devices has been developed, so that very steep slopes can be traversed without the machinery tipping over. (In this latter case, the soil is a windblown *loess* and erosion is rare.) Of course, such modifications of nature may be precluded because they are so costly. Nevertheless, the demand for the use of areas near markets often makes modification more feasible than using better-endowed areas farther from the markets.

Climate, Soils, Vegetation, and Economic Activity

Possibly the most important physical features to be considered in their relationship with economic activities are climate, soils, and vegetation. On a world scale, these are interconnected. Climate sets the stage for general vegetation, and vegetation strongly affects the soil types. For quick analysis, the nature of an area's wild vegetation provides the first strong clues to crop potential in that area. Tropical areas, for example, with their large, evergreen broadleaf trees, indicate a suitable physical environment for plants that require much precipitation and high, even temperatures throughout the year, and for those that can survive on heavily leached soils. On the other hand, grassland areas may have potential for growing grains like wheat and flax. In dry areas, only plants with special, deep-root systems and leaves that allow little evapotranspiration can survive. The date, palm, olive, and certain nut trees, for example, do well in the drought-stricken summers characteristic of Mediterranean climates. The temperate area of mixed forest and grasslands provides a wide array of crop possibilities. Indeed it is in this area that the greatest variety of commercial crops is found.

On a detailed area basis, however, the correlation between climate, vegetation, and soils quickly breaks down. Wild vegetation varies considerably among similar climatic areas, not only because of the succession and diffusion of plants over time but also because of differing physical conditions. For example, soil is a product of vegetation, parent material, slope, drainage, and local factors, all operating over time. Moreover, actual vegetation, often the crops raised by man, further alters the original soil conditions.

Drastic soil differences within climatic regions are caused by two of earth's major features: mountains and river valleys. Volcanic soils and alluvial river-valley soils are extremely rich. In these cases, the parent material often outweighs other factors in producing a particular soil. For example, civilization first developed along the banks of the Tigris-Euphrates, the Nile, and Indus, and the Hwang Ho rivers, which flooded each year and replenished the soil. Thus, unlike the inhabitants of most other areas of the earth, the people of these river regions did not deplete the soil. They could thus remain in one place rather than migrate to new soil areas.

Volcanic soils are possibly the only other soils on earth that are so intrinsically rich that they are almost impossible to deplete. For example, perhaps the most densely populated rural area on earth is found in Java, where the soil is volcanic. Hawaii, Japan, Southern Brazil, and river valleys in much of Oregon, Idaho, and Washington also have similar soils. Careful examination of these volcanic-based soil areas with nearby areas reveals tremendous variation in intensity of land use and density of population. For example, note that Sumatra has the same climate and physical location features as Java. Yet, by comparison, Sumatra has a low density of population. The major difference between them is a volcanic soil on Java and a basaltic soil on Sumatra. In Oregon, Washington, and Idaho a fortuitous combination occurs: volcanic soils and rivers for irrigation.

Yet, if one temporarily ignores these two distorting features, mountains and river valleys, it is safe to generalize further on the spatial variation of climates, vegetation, and soils. In this regard, geographers generally recognize five broad types of climate and associated soil and vegetation types (Figure 3.2). The climatic types, for lack of a more detailed name, might be labeled as follows, from equatorial areas to the poles: (1) tropical, (2) dry, (3) temperate, (4) snow, and (5) ice. Trees can grow in all but the very dry and the ice types. The ice climates have little soil in the traditional sense and only limited, tundralike vegetation. Grasses grow primarily in semidry and temperate areas. The soil types, in the same sequence as above, are (1) *latosols*, (2) *sierozems*, (3) a wide variety of red, brown, and yellow soils, (4) *podzols* and *tundra*, and (5) none.

As is evident from Figure 3.2, the dividing lines between the five major climatic types and their associated soil and natural vegetation zones are arbitrary. In fact, there is a general transition in all of these from the equator to the poles. The transition zone outward from the tropical zone is the *savanna* — a zone of seasonal dryness characterized by a more open pattern of vegetation and a less leached soil. The transition zone around deserts is usually called the *steppe* — a zone of grasslands and more productive soils. A transition

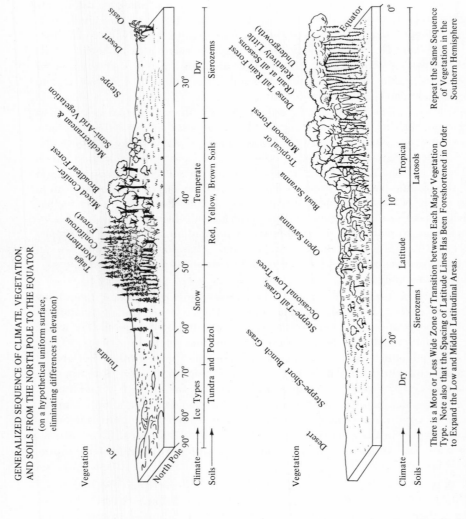

GENERALIZED SEQUENCE OF CLIMATE, VEGETATION, AND SOILS FROM THE NORTH POLE TO THE EQUATOR

(on a hypothetical uniform surface, eliminating differences in elevation)

There is a More or Less Wide Zone of Transition between Each Major Vegetation Type. Thus there is a crude relationship among these three measures which varies regularly from equator to the poles. Note also that the Spacing of Latitude Lines Has Been Foreshortened in Order to Expand the Low and Middle Latitudinal Areas.

Repeat the Same Sequence of Vegetation in the Southern Hemisphere

FIGURE 3.2 Relationships among Climate, Vegetation, and Soils for Any Latitude. Vegetation and soils are highly interrelated with climate. Thus there is a crude relationship among these three measures which varies regularly from equator to the poles. Source: Adapted from Rhoads Murphey. *An Introduction to Geography*, (C) 1961, 1963. By permission of Rand McNally & Co., Chicago.

zone on the littoral west coasts of continents is a *marine type* climate affected by ocean currents. The *tundra* is a transition zone between the northern coniferous forest (called the *taiga* in Eurasia and the Boreal forest in North America) and the ice caps. Yet even the transition zones are arbitrary. The point to remember is that there is a demonstrable change in climate, soils, and natural vegetation from the equator to polar areas.

Wet tropical lands and economic activity

The tropical areas are generally found about ten to fifteen degrees on either side of the equator. In this area, monthly mean temperatures are above 64.4 degrees. Precipitation is exceedingly high, well distributed throughout the year, and generally over sixty inches annually — more than enough for almost any kind of crop. On the outer edges of the climatic type are two areas that are alternately wet and dry, depending on the season of the year. These are the savanna climates, which have a wet season during high-sun times of the year and a relative dry period during low-sun periods, and the monsoon climate, which is related to littoral areas but especially to places where mountains bring about orographic precipitation part of the year.

The lateritic or latosolic soil in the tropics are very deep, but most of the soluble parts have been leached out. They are, however, heavy in iron hydroxides and various hydroxides of manganese and aluminum. This gives the surface soil a reddish or yellowish appearance. Organic material decomposes very rapidly under the high temperatures and heavy rainfall, so that this soil type is not very fertile. Nevertheless, it can support very heavy tree growth.

The predominant economic activities in this area are based on trees. The broadleaf trees include rubber, teak, ebony, and mahogany. Coffee, cocoa, cassava, abaca and kapok are also important products, providing employment in areas accessible to world trade. Important also are forest products such as rubber, nuts, and various other parts of the tree (see Chapter 3).

Because trees do not generally grow in stands as they do in midlatitude and northern areas, gathering activities require considerable labor. In some parts of the tropics, the development of plantations has remedied this problem. Yet few people are employed in the tropical areas. Much of the area is occupied only by subsistence-economy peoples, who eke out a living by gathering tropical products or by a primitive, slash-and-burn agricultural system (see Chapter 7).

Thus the tropical areas are generally among the most sparsely settled on earth. Nonetheless, people in the industrialized areas have long been concerned with the possibilities of greater use and development of the tropics. It is thought that with better health and sanitation methods, better transportation facilities, and the ability to "farm" many of the areas, the tropical areas will increase in importance. To date, very little has happened in this regard. Instead, population and jobs appear to continue to grow most rapidly in midlatitude areas.

Dry lands and economic activity

The dry areas of the earth (that is, those where evaporation exceeds precipitation) represent another major paucity in world population distribution (Figure 3.3). There is little doubt that this lack of population is directly related to physical factors.

One of the foremost requirements for intensive use of the area is, of course, the provision of water for irrigation and other uses. This has been possible in those dry areas traversed by rivers (*exotic streams*, that is, streams that flow through a desert or any area where there is insufficient rainfall to support them) like the Nile, the Colorado, and the Columbia, or where oasis-type conditions occur.

Desert soils are usually of the *sierozem* type and are gray in appearance. Like the soils in the tropics, they contain little humus, in this case, however, because there is little vegetation to decay. There is no leaching of the soil, as is characteristic of tropical climatic areas, because of lack of precipitation. In fact, the opposite effect occurs, so that a lime crust — that is, a calcium carbonate deposit — is often found within a foot or so of the surface. Such soil is suitable for cultivation only when finely textured and, of course, where water is available.

With the exception of exotic stream areas and oasis settlements, such as Salt Lake City where adjacent mountains are adequate in precipitation, most of the dry parts of the world are practically uninhabited. These include about one-fifth of the earth's surface. The few inhabitants in these areas are often migratory, moving seasonally with their animals to places with better vegetation.

Again, man has had great hopes for deserts, but the results to date have been disappointing. In some desert areas he has found rich mineral resources, particularly petroleum in the Middle East, and in others he has been able to develop an intensive agriculture based on irrigation. There have been great hopes, too, that desert areas near the seas could be utilized through desalinization of sea water. Desalinization has indeed been developed to serve urban settlements, but converted sea water is still too costly to be used on a large scale for irrigation. Consequently, the vast amount of dry land is still little used by man.

Cold lands and economic activity

At about fifty degrees north and south latitude and continuing to the poles are the severe winter climates. Some geographers have labeled them the snow and ice climates. Yet these cold lands should generally be divided into three types:

1. A continental, warm-summer, cold-winter type, where the growing season is about three months long and sufficient for many crops. In terms of natural vegetation, coniferous trees like fir and spruce are the rule.

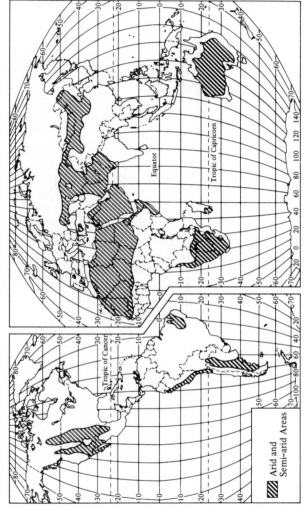

FIGURE 3.3 Arid and Semiarid Areas of the World. The dry areas of the world are primarily the result of descending air masses in subtropical, high-pressure zones. Other causes include the rain-shadow effects of mountains, offshore cool ocean currents, and extreme continentality.

2. The tundra area, where the growing season is so short and insolation so little that only mosses, lichens, and very limited grasses grow. This area often has a permanent layer of frozen soil (permafrost) beneath the thawed-out summer surface and is thereby often boggy and waterlogged. Clearly, agriculture in this area is almost nonexistent.
3. The ice caps, where no vegetation exists — nor, for that matter, do soils in the true sense.

The continental climate, which has a podzol soil and, generally, a coniferous-tree natural vegetation, thus has the greatest (though limited) potential for economic activities in the cold lands. These activities, however, are of an extensive nature, thus making population in these areas limited. Lumbering is by far the most important activity here. Inasmuch as the summers are too short for broadleaf hardwood trees, softwood conifers like spruce are predominant. The main use of such wood is for the pulp and paper industry.

Podzol soils, in contrast to the alkaline desert soils, are characteristically acid. Another distinctive feature of podzol soils is a strongly leached horizon that is whitish gray or ash gray in color, inasmuch as the coloring agents have been leached out. The leached colloids are removed only to the layer below, however, where they often form a clay layer that becomes an impervious hardpan. These soils are low in fertility also because of the coniferous tree vegetation. In fact, a podzol is characteristic of other climates in the midlatitudes that have a conifer natural vegetation. Inasmuch as conifers need little colloid material such as phosphorus, potassium, calcium, and magnesium, they do not bring these to the surface of the ground. Instead, they remain as a "hardpan" layer in a lower soil horizon. Of course, this acidic condition and the problem of leached bases can be corrected by soil treatment. However, only limited areas in this zone are usable in any case, since glaciation has left it with a highly rock-infested soil and many morainal swamps and lakes. For agriculture, then, this area also is highly limited. Because of peculiar geological conditions, however, minerals are often widespread and rich here, and mining has become a major activity.

The warm temperate lands and economic activity

It is difficult to discuss the temperate areas and economic activity because of their great physical and economic diversity. Some temperate areas, such as the southeastern portions of the United States and China, are "humid subtropical"; some, such as the "Mediterranean" climates, are characterized by summer drought. Some are moist, mild "marine" climates located in littoral areas on the west coasts of continents; and others, such as the Midwest in the United States, are "continental." Yet, all are temperate (lowest monthly mean temperature over 26.6 degrees F.) and are suitable for the growing of many crops (Figure 3.4).

It is in these areas where the most productive agriculture and the most

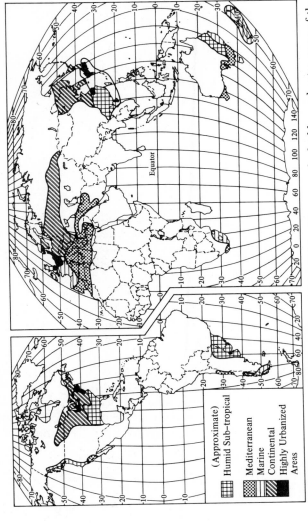

FIGURE 3.4 Warm Temperate Areas of the World. These are the highly productive areas of the world. Note their relationship to urban areas and to industrialization.

industrialized and urbanized parts of the world are found. It is in these temperate midlatitude areas where the majority of the world's population resides. In fact, most of the world population lives in the midlatitude forest area — a natural vegetation type characterized by deciduous trees intermixed with pines and other coniferous trees. Much of the northwestern part of the United States, Western Europe, Northern India, and Japan are characterized by such a vegetation type.

People are not evenly spread over these "choice" lands, however. Instead, they are clustered only in selected areas within it. The most attractive features physically for urbanization and industrialization appear to be (1) coastal and river valleys, and (2) the flatter plainlike areas at the lower elevations. Nonetheless, the primary reasons for the particular sitings of urban-industrial development in this area appear to be not physical but economic. These will be discussed in Chapter 4.

Mountains and Economic Activity

Mountains do not fit well into either a foreboding land concept or a good land concept. Certainly, they are sparsely inhabited and in this regard might be considered as foreboding for settlement. Inasmuch as there is an altitude counterpart in climate, vegetation, and soils that corresponds to the latitude-related patterns discussed above, mountains must therefore be considered a mixture of possibilities — some foreboding, others ideal.

The positive aspects of mountains are numerous and important. First, mountains change the climate because of their changes in altitude. Thus, they provide a diversity of vegetation types over a small distance. Affording the opportunity to move animals from lower to higher elevations in the summer (transhumance) is one way in which mountains might benefit a rural activity. In dry areas such a climatic change is a life-giving feature. Here, mountains often act as humid islands, or oases, inasmuch as they receive much more rain than does the surrounding arid country. Thus streams from such mountains often provide water for nearby settlements and for agricultural use. This is the case along the Wasatch Mountains in Utah, which supply water to cities like Salt Lake and Ogden.

These climatic and vegetation changes allow forests to occur in areas that would otherwise be devoid of timber. The Sierra Nevadas in California provide a growth of timber in an otherwise dry and grassladen area. In fact, mountains are a major source of timber in the United States. In forestry, steep slopes are often an asset rather than a deficit in getting the material to market.

Conversely, mountains also make deserts out of much of the earth that would otherwise be humid and potentially highly productive. Most of the deserts in midlatitude areas are the result of a rain-shadow effect produced by mountains on their leeward or eastern sides. Thus the deserts in Nevada, Utah, Idaho, Arizona, and California are largely the result of mountains.

Paradoxically, the climatic differences created by mountains also create possibilities for spatial interaction. Inasmuch as the environment is often different on either side of the mountain, such areas have differing agricultural and industrial potential. In those instances where irrigation can be applied on the leeward side of the mountains, as in Eastern Washington, tremendous interaction may occur. Thus mountains often set up the physical bases of area differentiation, and hence the potential for trade. They then act somewhat as barriers to such interaction because of the difficulty of transportation over them.

The diversity in climate and vegetation of mountains, as distinct from the homogeneity of the surrounding countryside, also makes them attractive as recreational areas for the nearby population. Because they are cooler in summer and, of course, often picturesque, they are attractive as summer resort areas. Where the nearby lower-elevation lands have mild winters — for example, along the littoral of Western United States and Western Europe — the coldness of mountains makes them excellent for skiing, which is possibly the world's fastest-growing outdoor sport. In California, Washington, and Oregon, a tremendous recreational potential is found in mountains because the lower-lying and urbanized areas nearby are usually snowless in winter.

The recreational value of mountains is clearly evident if the location of national parks and outdoor resort areas is examined. These recreational areas are located in mountains not only for the reasons cited above, but because mountains often provide highly unusual and picturesque landscapes. Yellowstone National Park, with its geysers and hot springs; Zion National Park, with its unusual rock formations; and various volcanic peaks like Mount Rainier are cases in point. However, the recreational value of mountains can be assessed only in terms of the accessibility of the mountains to those demanding the resource. Thus, most mountains of the earth, especially those not found near major concentrations of urban population, are little used for recreation and hence, as yet, of little recreational value.

Undoubtedly the most valuable asset of mountains is their mineral wealth. Even a casual examination of an economic atlas reveals the strong spatial correlation between mountains and various mineral resources. The folding, faulting, and other tectonic forces are particularly favorable to the formation of rich mineral deposits. Some resources strongly correlated with mountains include coal, iron ore, copper, many alloys, and precious metals. This in no way implies that such mineral resources are found only in mountains, but most minerals are more closely associated with mountains than with any other single physical feature.

Mountains are also often valuable for the generation of water power. The steep gradients of many rivers and streams ofttimes make for considerable water potential, even on relatively small streams. Here again, the degree to which this potential is actually used will depend largely upon the proximity of such potential to demand sites and the alternatives available for the generation of power.

It will be noted from the above that the use of mountains is often highly seasonal. Thus they have little permanent population. Activities that may operate on a year-round basis, such as mining and forestry, employ few people, are short-lived, and consequently lead to few permanent settlements. Probably no other physical feature of the earth has so many assets and generates so little permanent settlement.

Thus, mountains are places of contrast. At certain times and places they are occupied by a prosperous and dense population. Lake Tahoe, Yosemite National Forest, Yellowstone National Park and the Catskill Mountains, for example, but at other times of the year they are abandoned, isolated, and desolate. Some mountain communities are isolated, backward, and have little or no economic potential; others are tourist, mining, and recreational centers, rich and with great future prospects.

Rivers and Economic Activity

Rivers, like mountains, are in some cases assets, and in others, deficits. On the one hand, rivers and their associated alluvial soils provide some of the most productive agricultural land on earth. Certainly they support the majority of the world's population. Only some volcanic soils are richer. Rivers also provide primary channels of inland transportation, not only directly in the form of navigable waterways, but indirectly through their valleys, where railroads and other routes are numerous. The attraction of man and his activities to river valleys, however, has also led to some of the world's worst flood disasters. Rivers periodically, and naturally, flood unless dams, levees, and other flood-control devices are constructed. Even then, the greater intensity of use following installation of such flood-control features often means that a smaller flood will cause even greater hardships and damage.

Thus it is truly difficult to generalize about rivers. Their valleys contain the most dense and concentrated settlements in the world, as evidenced by the valleys of the Yangtze, the Hwang Ho, and the Ganges in Asia; the Nile in Africa; the Danube in Europe; and the Mississippi in the United States. Some of the other great rivers, however, are little used, and their valleys contain almost no population. In this respect note the Congo in Africa, the Amazon in South America, and the Ob, Yensie, and Lena in Asia; all are without significant nearby population. Aside from their great value in desert areas where they operate as exotic streams, rivers appear to be of little use for agriculture and its consequent activities unless they are found in midlatitude areas.

As is the case with mountains, it is difficult to make generalizations about rivers because of their many different, and often conflicting, use potentials. Their flood plains and nearby areas often have potential for agriculture and for transportation routes. The rivers themselves can be used for a variety of activities. They can be recreational areas or the site of sewerage and industrial disposal systems. As might be expected, there are conflicts among the various uses as, for example, irrigation, navigation, recreation, hydropower, domestic consumption, and industrial waste disposal. In fact, given the many uses to which the water alone is put, and the obvious conflicts among these uses, it is small wonder that more problems have not arisen on this score than currently exist.

It is evident from the above that the standard statistics generally given about rivers, such as "longest river in the world," are of little value in assessing a river's potential use or uses. Instead, at least seven features should be examined: (1) location, which is by far the most important; (2) flow or discharge, which affects possibilities for most uses; (3 and 4) depth and width, which are clearly critical for navigation, and sometimes for recreational purposes; (5) grade, or gradient, which is important for hydroelectric potential and perhaps for recreational use; (6 and 7) direction of flow and circuitry of stream, which have particular importance with regard to transportation potential.

Other river features, such as water quality, temperature, dendritic pattern, and character of the drainage basin slope, may also prove critical for various purposes. For example, a river may have good attributes for hydropower — discharge, gradient, and proximity to market — but may not have economic possibilities because a dam site cannot be found for reservoir impoundment.

Critical deficiencies of some of the world's "great" rivers will perhaps best illustrate the nature of these various elements. Undoubtedly, the Congo River has the greatest power potential of any river in the world. The tremendous flow and steep fall from the African plateau to the coast give it great potential as a hydropower source, but distance from market makes the river unusable. (Incidentally, the waterfall character of the river also greatly decreases its transportation potential.) On the other hand, the Amazon River has the largest flow of any river in the world and has no steep gradient to interfere with navigation. But the Amazon River is likewise little used — in fact, it has much less traffic than most small river canals in Europe. Again, location is the deterrent factor. The major rivers in Northern Asia run in the "wrong" direction. They flow northward, where the estuaries become icebound in winter, instead of westward, toward the heart of the Soviet Union. In this regard, one might say that the Mississippi River in the United States also runs pretty much in the wrong direction. Nevertheless, given the cheapness of water transportation, it still has some advantages. There are many exotic rivers in the world with potential irrigation value, but it takes tremendous amounts of money to build dams and irrigation networks; it also requires that there be a market for agricultural goods. Undoubtedly, many of these rivers, like the Indus in

Pakistan and the Nile in Egypt, will be put to more use with the building of large dams. In many dry areas, however, there is a scarcity of river water. This is particularly the case in the western part of the United States, where Utah and Colorado need more water from the Colorado River and the Rio Grande but must by law release much of it to California, Arizona, and Mexico. So critical is the water problem in many highly industrial, dry areas such as Los Angeles, that water is brought in from hundreds of miles away. There is even considerable pressure to bring water from the Columbia River in Washington to Southern California.

Conclusions

The physical bases of the earth, while important, can be fully understood only in light of a particular economy and technology, a particular culture, a particular crop and crop need, and a particular place and time. Despite extensive cautionary notes about the dangers of overplaying physical features, the physical bases are extremely important, indeed fundamental, to any full appreciation and understanding of the distribution of the many activities over the earth. They are not dictating features but one of the many bases — transportation, economic, human-cultural — that result in a particular spatial response. At best, the physical bases provide a first, albeit naïve, insight into the reasons for the spatial differentiation of land-oriented economic activities. At worst, overemphasis on them leads to a myopic and simplistic view of economic geography and is an obstacle to spatial interpretation and understanding.

BIBLIOGRAPHY

Parr, John B, "The Role of Estuaries in Regional Economic Development." *The Northern Universities Geographical Journal*, March 1966.

McCarty, Harold H., and Lindberg, James B. *A Preface to Economic Geography.* Englewood Cliffs, N.J.: Prentice-Hall, 1966.

Strahler, Arthur. *Introduction to Physical Geography.* New York: John Wiley & Sons, 1970.

Ullman, Edward L. "Are Mountains Enough?" *The Professional Geographer*, July 1953, pp. 5–8.

——— "Rivers as Regional Bonds: The Columbia-Snake Example." *Geographical Review*, April 1951, pp. 210–125.

Wolfanger, Louis A. "The Great Soil Groups and Their Utilization." In *Conservation of Natural Resources*, edited by Guy-Harold Smith, pp. 37–67. New York: John Wiley & Sons, 1958.

IV

Some Economic Bases of Economic Geography

Thus far we have accomplished three things. In Chapter 1 the content and nature of economic geography were explored. In Chapter 2, transportation, one of the most important geographical bases of economic geography, was discussed, so that we might appreciate the general matrix of interaction possibilities on the surface of the earth. In Chapter 3, the physical bases, the beginning of a many-sided framework for the analysis of any given distribution or territory, were explored. Certain of the economic factors, or bases, in economic geography will be examined in this chapter.

It may appear highly peculiar to treat the economic bases as a single chapter in a book dealing with *economic* geography. And so it is, in the sense that economic principles are emphasized throughout. One chapter could in no way cover them all, even in truncated fashion. Thus the first purpose here is to provide a brief, skeletal outline of certain pervasive economic forces that mold and shape the placement of things on the earth's surface. The second purpose of this distinct treatment of economic bases is to emphasize the fact that economic considerations, although extremely important and even paramount in many cases, are nonetheless but one of a series of bases necessary for a full comprehension of spatial reality. Economic bases should thus be viewed in a shaping framework along with transportation as well as physical, cultural, and other forces.

Devoting one chapter of a text on economic geography to economic bases makes sense also when it is realized that the word *economic* is used as an adjective to describe the kinds of activities to be considered from a geographical perspective. Economic geography is not composed of a judicious blend of the disciplines of economics and geography. Economic geography is wholly geography, but the geography of a particular set of activities. Economic geography therefore deals with the spatial aspects of those things which are of utilitarian value to man. It can easily be seen from this definitional framework that more than economic principles from the field of economics is necessary to appreciate why these kinds of activities are distributed in particular places and patterns. Among these additional principles are those pertaining to the physical bases, as they were discussed in the preceding chapter, and those pertaining to the cultural and institutional bases, to be presented in a later chapter.

In reality, all of these bases operate in a highly complex, interrelated, and contaminatory fashion. For pedagogical and organizational purposes, however, these components have been separated into rather arbitrary and isolated frameworks. This separation makes it easier to see how each of these forces, or bases, operates and combines to form any particular pattern.

The procedure for focusing on a particular relationship, while holding others in abeyance, is one of the hallmark techniques of economics. This *ceteris paribus,* or other things being equal, technique has proven highly instructive in solving economic problems and has enabled economists to gain insights into otherwise hidden operational processes. The use of the *ceteris paribus* device is equally valuable in geographical understanding and analysis and will, consequently, be heavily used throughout this work.

Another technique borrowed from economics which will be heavily employed is that of simple graphics to illustrate theoretical notions. This chapter will thus introduce the reader to such devices in a manner whereby they will be more fully appreciated and utilized in the forthcoming and more advanced discussions.

Although the analytical and theoretical techniques of economics are valuable and necessary to our spatial understanding, there are also certain pitfalls in their use. Recall, for example, how the physical bases have been overplayed by geographers and others. Likewise, it is possible to overplay certain of the economic bases. Such analytical devices, if not judiciously applied, can lead to conclusions as naïve as conclusions based on strictly physical features. Nonetheless, if the reader keeps in mind that principles and forces are being discussed, not the real earth, little misinterpretation and misapplication should result.

One final cautionary note: The economic principles discussed below are in no way meant to provide a digest of what economics is all about. Only those general economic principles that bear heavily and directly on locational problems will be discussed. For this reason, the student who is competent in economics may find much of the discussion quite different from the typical economic approach. The focus is deliberately distorted to gain a view of geographical content. The point to remember is that we are trying to understand the *effect* of such forces on the arrangement, placement, and distribution of man and his activities. Our goal is not to understand the reasons for or behind the economic principles themselves; these, like mountains, are taken as given.

As with transportation, economic principles will constitute a continuing theme throughout the text. In fact the blend between these economic principles and transportation principles is involved in many of the theories later discussed. Only the more general and simple principles will now be presented. Specific applications of these principles to agriculture, industry, or land use within cities will be discussed under those subject categories. Certain tailormade, economically based principles that pertain to these activities will be discussed at the appropriate time. The only purpose here is to provide an introduction to geographic understanding within an economic framework.

The Principle of Comparative Territorial Advantage

The principle of comparative territorial advantage, in part, means that areas having the greatest advantage for a particular activity will specialize in that activity if it brings them the greatest return. Areas less favorable for producing various items — whether physically poorer, less accessible to markets, having less productive labor, and so on — must take second or third choice in the things they do. In a territorial context this means that the better areas get first choice of production, and will specialize in producing the more profitable crop or product, but that less fortunate areas will be left with residual choices.

At first, this sounds rather bleak for less-endowed areas, but it is in fact the saving grace for the many disadvantaged and remote areas of the earth. Let us take the example of Area A, which is fertile, close to market, and well endowed in all respects. Let us assume that in Area A the profit per acre on potatoes is $200; on wheat, $100; and for grazing purposes, $50. Now compare these with the profits per acre in the less endowed Area B and Area C as shown below:

| | *Profit Per Acre on* | | |
Area	Potatoes	Wheat	Grazing
A	$200	$100	$50
B	100	50	25
C	50	25	5

It is evident that Area A has an *absolute* advantage in growing all crops. Therefore, why would there be anything left for Areas B and C to do? In some cases, there is not. But the general rule is for each area to specialize in the activity that gives it the greatest advantage and to import from other areas items produced at a comparatively lower cost. Under this system, Area A would grow potatoes (first choice), Area B would grow wheat (second choice), and Area C would be used for grazing (third choice). Incidentally, if the profit from grazing in Area C were to be $0, and these were all the options open to it, then Area C would be unused. According to the principle, Area A would import wheat from Area B and cattle from Area C even though, theoretically, it could produce such things more cheaply itself. By producing such things, however, it would make less than by specializing in the activity that brings it the greatest profit.

Another saving grace for the poorly endowed areas is that they may be closer to the market than the physically well-endowed area. If transportation costs are greater than the difference in costs between the two, then the closer but poorer area will have a comparative advantage over the better endowed but more distant area. Such a phenomenon was particularly evident during the last century in the United States, where intensive and highly profitable garden-type agriculture was found near almost every major city, even though such territory was often otherwise inferior to areas more distant from the market. The general effect of improved transportation, however, is to allow the areas with the greatest advantage to do the producing. For example, Southern California, at great distance from the major market center of the United States, now grows many of the nation's garden crops. The result of this situation is to cause nearer, but intrinsically poorer, land to be put out of production or at least in a "second choice" position. Today, many farms near large cities in the Eastern United States and elsewhere are being abandoned.

On an international scale, where artificial restraints on trade — such as trade agreements, tariffs, and outright embargoes — are very much in effect, a different condition holds. (These institutional types of economic factors are considered in Chapter 5.) Nevertheless, the general principle is still applicable. This principle is succinctly stated by Towles, as follows:

> Just as a given community, or nation, may increase its real income and the incomes of its individual citizens by abandoning individual self-sufficiency for individual specialization, so may the world increase its real income and the income of the individual nations by foregoing national self-sufficiency for national specialization. Nations, like individuals, are endowed by nature with special facilities; and nations, like individuals, acquire special skills. Minerals can be produced only in those nations where nature has stored them: nickel in Canada; tin in Bolivia, the East Indies, and Malay States; manganese in Brazil and Russia; petroleum in the United States, certain Latin American countries, Russia, Iraq, and the Dutch East Indies [Indonesia]. Nations not endowed by nature with stores of these minerals can acquire them only through exchange with nations more favorably endowed. Many agricultural products require for their cultivation a special climate. Coffee, tea, rubber, and silk, for example, demand a warm or tropical climate, while most of the cereal crops do much better in the cooler lands of the temperate zones. Consequently, the United States imports its coffee, tea, rubber, and silk, while tropical countries import from countries in the temperate zone most of their cereals.[1]

[1]Lawrence W. Towle, *International Trade And Commercial Policy* (New York: Harper and Brothers, 1956), pp. 10–11.

For confirmation of this rule in operation, one only has to look at an economic atlas.

The most distinctive feature of the world distribution of economic activities is the tremendous specialization of areas. In fact, places having a mixed farming system — the Midwest, for example — or cities having a diversified industrial base are oddities of the world rather than the rule. The general rule is one of great territorial specialization. Thus within the United States, monoculture reigns: the Great Plains area stands out as specializing in wheat; Wisconsin is primarily a dairying region; and the Mississippi Valley of Arkansas shows a concentration of rice. Territorial specialization is so prominent that we label certain areas "the corn belt," "the cotton belt," and the "industrial belt." Specialization with regard to minerals is equally prominent and is not just the result of nature's bounty. For example, coal, copper, iron ore, and many other minerals are found in many areas, but they are heavily exploited in just a few. The reason is, comparative advantage. In fact, it would make an instructive study to contrast the reserves of various minerals with the pattern of those actually used; the discrepancy is truly astounding.

Unfortunately, such exchange and specialization do not benefit all areas equally. Consequently, there are the have and have-not regions and nations of the world. Moreover, the rich are getting richer and the poor are getting poorer. Thus, perhaps this general rule, when allowed to run its natural course, may not bring about the very best of all possible worlds.

Price and the Principle of Supply and Demand

In its most simple and general form, price is the result of an interplay between the forces of supply and demand. These two forces are considered contradictory and run in opposite directions (Figure 4.1). Simply stated, from the supply side, people would opt to supply great quantities of any item at a high price, but very little, if any, at an extremely low price. Running counter to these desires is the demand for any item. If those demanding the item had their way, they would prefer to purchase a great deal at a low price, but very little, if any, at an extremely high price. Thus, the price actually used represents a kind of compromise between these two forces.

The specific shapes of these supply and demand curves for any given activity, the degrees of elasticity in them, and various other conditions are the rightful subject of economics. For our purposes, we will simply take such an interplay as given and make note that price is generated at the place where these two curves cross. Also note that there is always an interrelation between price and quantity produced, or demanded. Thus, price is in large part a reflection of the abundance or scarcity of an item and is always a function of quantity.

In Figure 4.2 it is shown that the quantity of wheat demanded and consumed is based on price. If the price is B, then only X units of wheat will be consumed

(*B, O, X*). On the other hand, if the price is over, say *A*, then *Y* units of wheat will be consumed (*A, P, Y*). Thus, such a price-quantity relationship is achieved from the general shapes of the supply and demand curves as shown in Figure 4.1.

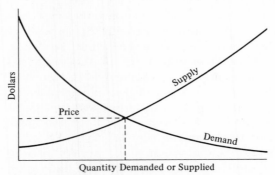

FIGURE 4.1 Price as a Compromise between Supply and Demand Curves. Price is a reflection of two contradictory relationships: (a) the supplier would prefer to supply considerable merchandise at high prices; (b) the consumer would prefer to pay lower prices and would purchase much more of the merchandise at lower prices than at higher prices. Thus there is a direct relationship between market price and the amount of merchandise that will be demanded.

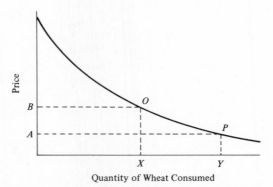

FIGURE 4.2 Market Price and Quantity of Wheat Consumed. Note that at price *B*, only *OX* amount of wheat will be demanded, but that at lower price *A*, *PY* amount of wheat will be demanded. This relationship generally holds for most items although, as is commonly the case with agricultural commodities, price will have small effect on amount of food demanded. This latter inflexibility is the result of inelasticity of demand.

It is evident that price, and hence profit, is not a simple matter of general cost plus some markup, but occurs in a complicated marketing system. For example, a change in the supply or demand of an item will affect its price, and a change in price will in turn affect its supply and demand curves. To see how this operates, note that an increase in the price of a commodity such as wheat — due perhaps to an increase in the demand or a temporary decrease in supply — will cause more wheat to be produced the coming year. With more wheat then being produced, however, the consumer will be in a better bargaining position (that is, a changed supply curve) and the price should fall. This price decline must occur if the wheat then available is to be purchased. Theoretically, assuming demand elasticity, the amount of wheat produced would not be purchased at the old price.

Any quantitative change in production of an agricultural crop, perhaps as the result of weather conditions, may have a considerable effect on price. Thus, farming is a fairly risky pursuit compared with manufacturing and retailing. In these latter cases the demand curve can be manipulated by adjustments in production. This is especially so if a firm has a monopoly on the manufacture or sale of a product through patents or if it is the only firm in a particular area. In such cases it is in a supreme bargaining position with the demand sector and can charge considerably more than would be the case under a fully competitive situation. Therefore, it is much more profitable to grow some crops than to grow others, to manufacture certain products, to sell some kinds of goods, to render certain services.

Such relationships also have spatial implications. For example, all locations do not have equal opportunities for production of various items. Given the principle of comparative advantage, that area which has the greatest advantage gets first choice. The less favorably endowed areas will have to take second best.

It is also evident that there is only so much demand for various goods, regardless of price. Thus, even if the earth were one vast, physically perfect area, not all of it would be put to use; nor would it, because of accessibility differences, be put to equal use. There still would be vast areas of good lands left vacant. For example, let us assume that tomatoes were the most profitable of all agricultural crops, and that all the earth's land was equally fertile and climatically suited for tomato production. Clearly, man would not demand solely tomatoes. Also, if only tomatoes were produced, there would be such a glut on the market, that their price would drop. Consequently, tomatoes would be an unprofitable crop in many areas. Indeed, they would no longer be a very profitable crop at all.

At this stage the reader should be somewhat perplexed. First, even if this supply and demand principle is operating to determine some proper mix of commodities produced, how is it that some crops are still more profitable than others? Why does this principle not also operate to bring about equal profit for all crops? In one way it does. The degree of profit to be made on any given crop varies from year to year and changes in rankings often occur. But this explanation is still unsatisfactory.

The real explanation is a geographic one. The earth is not homogeneous. All areas are not equally good for tomatoes. The amount of land for some crops is limited indeed — for example, olives can be grown only in a Mediterranean climate. This geographic inequity places a premium on certain lands and on the values of certain crops that must use such lands. Thus, other things being equal, it would follow that those crops with the most exacting physical demands would bring higher prices than others. Such crops also would have the first choice of suitable land.

However, there are a number of ways to "beat the system," so to speak. It is possible to make high profits in marginal locations by judiciously substituting land, labor, and capital inputs. For example, wheat is typically a frontier crop, and theoretically, since it is less profitable per acre than many other crops, it is squeezed out at some distance from the market and from better physical areas. (Storage capabilities and ability to grow in physically marginal areas are other reasons for its being a frontier crop.) But a wheat farmer can also make considerable amounts of money by increasing the land scale of operation. Instead of farming a 300-acre farm, as is typical in the corn belt, he may farm several thousand acres. Thus, while he is making only a small profit per acre as compared to the Midwest farmer, his overall accumulative profit on a farm-unit basis, may actually be higher.

Scale Economies and Locational Strategies

The general principle of profit is that the average costs per unit of output decrease as the quantity of output or volume, increases. Average costs tend to decrease with an increase in scale of operation until a critical point is reached, a point where diseconomies of scale occur. Even so, economists have become somewhat skeptical about the diseconomies of scale relationship inasmuch as a number of industries and activities appear to be unable to reach this critical point. In other words, while theoretically there should be penalties for growth beyond a certain point, many activities appear to be in little danger at the moment.

This relationship is shown graphically in Figure 4.3. Note that the average cost of producing one unit of output — for example, a bushel of wheat, a car, or a Ping-Pong table — is much higher at quantity X, where the cost is C, than at Y, where the cost per unit is B, and much higher than at quantity Z, where the average cost per unit would be only A. However, when more than quantity Z is produced, average costs per unit begin to rise rather than decrease. Obviously, a firm would have to have extremely good arguments for increasing the size of any operation beyond quantity Z. Economists argue that the optimum scale size for a firm is where the marginal cost (the cost of producing an additional unit of output) curve intersects the average costs curve.

The general reasons that average costs decrease with increasing volume of output relate to four major cost components. Such components are applicable, although in different ways, to all types of agriculture — to manufacturing and to wholesale and retail sales. These basic ingredients are (1) specialization, (2) "discount" purchases of raw materials, (3) vertical integration and bifurcation possibilities, and (4) possibilities for standardization.

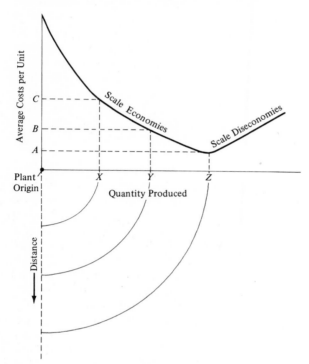

FIGURE 4.3 Scale Economies and Diseconomies in a Spatial Context. As quantity produced at the plant increases, average per-unit costs decrease until quantity Z is reached. Beyond this production amount the average costs per unit increase as the result of scale diseconomies. With increasing production, more territory is generally covered by the plant. However, increasing territorial extent, as the result of increased production, also necessitates higher transportation costs to the consumer.

Of these four, specialization, in the form of labor, machinery, or some other item, is the most universal and perhaps the most important. For example, a small operation will have to use one person to do several different jobs. Hence that person does not become a real specialist in any one of these jobs — his labor is spread about. In a large plant or on a large farm, however, each person can do a specialized job. On a large farm, there might be a manager, an equipment maintenance man, and various other persons doing specialized farm jobs. Labor efficiencies in the manufacturing of automobiles, where each person does a single job fast and well, are a well-known example of the kinds of efficiencies created from labor specialization.

Second, a large firm can get materials and services at a discount compared to prices paid by smaller concerns. A large operation often solicits bids for work to be done and then makes a choice; a small operation is often at the mercy of the sellers. A large operation also gets its needed materials cheaper than does a small operation. Again, it is the old principle of volume, or quantity, being related to cost, and hence to price. For example, a large farm operation would be able to purchase machinery, fuel, seed, and fertilizer, and get better financing and many items at less cost than a small operation. A large firm also uses things in greater volume and does not have to maintain proportionally as great an inventory as a small firm. This, of course, generally puts small operators at a disadvantage. In fact, the disappearance of many farm and manufacturing operations is the result of just such competition based on this type of scale economy.

Third, large firms often achieve notorious success by owning and thereby controlling related operations. This is called *vertical integration* and is often achieved by mergers or amalgamations. In industry, certain large firms, especially before antitrust legislation, controlled both forward and backward linked activities with regard to their operation. For example, an oil company might own not only the wells, but the pipeline and tanker companies used to transport the petroleum to the refinery and to market. At the market, such a company would also own retail and service outlets like service stations, and so on. There is still considerable vertical integration in the petroleum business, but full control of outlets is prevented through regional jurisdictional restrictions and by the maintenance of effective competition. In agriculture today, however, there are practically no safeguards in this direction. Some large farm operations, for example, not only control banks, machinery companies, fuel companies, and so on, but are also heavily involved in the marketing and processing of their products.

On the positive side, such large-scale operations do provide the possibilities for taking full advantage of formerly unused or waste products. In a large-scale potato farm operation, for example, the cull potatoes might be processed into dehydrated potatoes, and the waste juices from this process might be used to feed cattle. From the cattle, a packing plant business is opened — and so it goes. By achieving such size, a firm can capitalize on items that would be too small to bother with in a less extensive operation.

Vertical integration and "spin-off" also often allow a large firm to bifurcate its activities spatially, thereby placing the particular components of the firm's activities in the most beneficial places. For example, power and light companies have long been spatially bifurcated in that they have their accounting and administrative offices in one location, usually downtown, and their service yards elsewhere. Likewise, large manufacturing operations often have their administrative offices one place and their plants in another.

Fourth, standardization and possibilities for fuller utilization of the factors of production are also made more possible at increased scale. An industrial plant can begin to set up assembly line production with interchangeable parts; a farm operation is able to maintain specialized machinery for its operations. For example, a small farm can usually support only one general-purpose tractor. This tractor must be used to plow and prepare the soil and cultivate and harvest the crops. Usually, such a tractor, at best, is well suited to only one of these operations. A large-scale farm operation can maintain tractors for each purpose and can therefore make much more productive use of its machinery. It can keep such tractors more fully used than can a small operation, which would use a tractor only part time during the various operations. On big operations, for example, the plowing, cultivation, and harvesting tractors are run on an intensive basis.

These relationships have several important geographical implications. First, it is clear that any given quantity of output has spatial implications. For example, the larger the output (volume of sales) of a store serving a surrounding area, the greater will be the trade area for that store (Figure 4.3). We have seen that as production increases, so does the territory required for that much output; as the territory increases, the costs to the firm, and hence the price to the consumer, must increase with distance from the firm. If one follows the arguments above, in which it was assumed that price and quantity demanded are interrelated, then it follows that as scale increases, territory increases; and prices to the consumer increase with increasing distance from a plant. Note, however, that an increase in scale will have the effect of lowering the price at the plant, but of increasing the transportation cost component to the consumer. This increase simply would result from the fact that fewer plants would be serving the market with increasing scale of production (Figure 4.4).

If one compares the economies of scale relationships in Figure 4.3 with transportation cost implications as shown in Figure 4.4, it is evident that scale considerations often loom paramount in determining the location of production. Note that a firm producing at volume B would only be competitive at distances beyond X in Figure 4.4 At distance Y a firm producing at quantity B would have only a limited market (Q_1 to Z) as compared to a firm located at W but with a scale of production at A. If the two firms were located adjacent to each other, the firm producing at scale B would be unable to compete. Therefore, with respect to firm location, scale economies are often more important than transportation costs. Because of such economies, a firm, or farm, may not be in the optimum location from the standpoint of accessibility to raw materials or to markets, but will be in a position that will enable it to produce at high volume in order to achieve scale economies. Such a firm may prefer not to minimize such transportation costs, but to minimize the cost of on-site production through scale economies.

In this regard, scale economies often lead to geographical distortion in the placement of things. Thus, perhaps a manufacturer can open a new, larger plant and derive competitive advantages over an older, smaller plant more favorably situated. However, this is extremely difficult to accomplish except over the short run, inasmuch as the older plant may have the more favorable location and will also have possibilities for increasing volume and thereby achieving comparable scale economies.

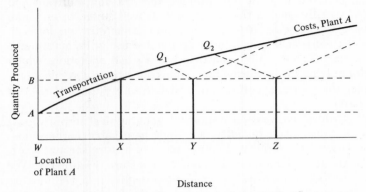

FIGURE 4.4 Relationship between Scale of Production and Costs to the Consumer at Various Distances from the Plant. The lower the costs of production at the plant, the greater the competitive range of the plant for customers (compare Figure 4.3). At production output B, plants at places Y and Z would be competitive with a plant operating at output A at location W only to the right of Q_1 and Q_2 respectively.

Another geographical implication of the scale-economies phenomenon is its relationship to the number of producers in a given market. Obviously, if economies of scale can be achieved and if the total market demand is still less than, say, quantity Z in Figure 4.3, then one firm could monopolize the entire production. Such a firm, if located so as to minimize total transportation costs as well, might make competition impossible. In fact, in a number of industries in the United States, such as steel, aluminum, and automobile production, only a few firms dominate the market. Clearly these are activities that can achieve tremendous scale economies.

On the other hand, diseconomies of scale may also occur, as demonstrated in the area of the curve to the right of quantity Z in Figure 4.3, because extension of any of the four factors discussed above with regard to economies of scale results in an increase in average costs per unit. Transportation costs may also rise to a point where the savings of such costs will outweigh further increases in quantity from any one location. Should such diseconomies occur, then the obvious spatial implications are three: (1) more firms will enter the market, (2) any given firm will wisely decentralize its operation and set up branch plants, or (3) both will occur.

This phenomenon gives outlying or marginal areas an opportunity for production as they produce for a regional or local market. This trend toward decentralization and regional plants has become particularly prominent in the United States during the past decade. New automobile assembly plants, regional offices of all kinds, and other regionally oriented manufacturing have become the rule rather than the exception. This leads to a less geographically concentrated distribution of employment, and hence population, than was formerly the case. Even so, there are many other activities that appear still to be achieving economies of scale and are moving from formerly local markets to strategic places like New York, which is geared to national and even international markets.

External Economies and Activity Location

A factor encouraging concentration in a few areas is external economies. This simply means that where large concentrations of other activities are found, particularly those that are similar, many advantages accrue to a business enterprise. First, such firms receive better service with regard to obtaining a skilled labor force and find it easier to use all kinds of business aids, including legal, educational, financial, and municipal services. In many instances, these are services such firms would have to provide for themselves if they were not in an area that afforded such agglomerative or external economies. More concentrated areas, particularly metropolitan areas, also contain an *infrastructure* of public facilities and private services that is not available in less fortunate areas. In the United States, the large cities now seem to have the advantage in this regard. Consequently, the large cities are getting even larger as more employment opportunities develop in them, but other territories also have such external economies — for example, parts of the industrial belt of the United States, the "Western Triangle" in Northern Europe, and the petrochemical industrial complex among the Gulf States of the United States. In fact, most activities found in large industrial complexes benefit from such economies.

Perhaps the classic example is the automobile industry in Michigan. The automobile assembly plants benefit by the proximity of all types of parts plants that manufacture special items and sell their products to the automobile manufacturers. Such a large service component nearby makes it difficult for the automobile assembly plants to move. After a time it is difficult to tell which is the dog and which is the tail; at any rate, it appears that the external economies' tail is wagging the dog in many industrial complexes. Where the manufacture or assembly of an item runs in spatial contradiction to the manufacture of parts, however, these two functions can be widely separated.

Some Transportation Pricing Systems

Several of the ways in which a firm may reduce its on-site costs have been demonstrated under the principle of economies of scale and external economies, but a firm can also adopt strategies to increase its price, thereby making greater profit by manipulating the transportation cost variable. Three procedures are widespread: (1) F.O.B. [Free On Board] pricing system, (2) the postage-stamp pricing system, and (3) the basing-point pricing system.

The *F.O.B. system* is simply a system where the price of the item at any given location is a function of the costs of production at plant site, plus transportation costs to the consumer, plus some markup or profit margin. This system creates a spatial configuration that makes prices smaller for those nearer the source of production than for those further away. According to the supply and demand principles discussed earlier, those people further away who are being charged higher prices will demand less of the item. Thus, the density of coverage will decrease outward from the source. From a manufacturer's point of view, this may not be a very beneficial system inasmuch as it may not enable the plant to achieve the quantity of output, and hence the economies of scale, that it might under another price-distance system (Figure 4.5).

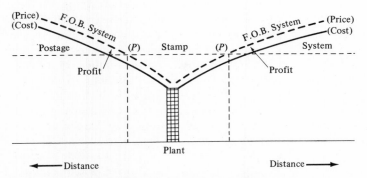

FIGURE 4.5 The Postage-Stamp Pricing System versus an F.O.B. System.   Note that customers near the plant (*P* to *P*) pay more than they otherwise would, whereas customers beyond distance *P* from the plant pay less. This system is commonly used to boost volume of production and hence achieve scale economies.

Another pricing procedure, referred to in Chapter II, is the *postage-stamp rate system* (Figure 4.5). Under this system all consumers are charged the same price regardless of location from the source of production. Thus, those closest to the source pay more for the item, and those beyond a critical distance (*P*) pay less for the item than under the first method. Here the producer location strategy would be to locate nearest to the highest number of potential consumers. In this way the producer should save the most on transportation costs and hence make a greater profit than if he located in an area of sparse demand. (Incidentally, under the F.O.B.-plus-transportation system, the plant would make equal profits from each consumer no matter where the consumer was located.) The postage-stamp method is heavily practiced by national firms where national price advertising is important and where increased production volume gives scale economies that outweigh transportation cost considerations.

The third method, the *basing point system,* is constitutionally illegal, but still practiced in modified form by a number of large firms (Figure 4.6). Under this system, various places are designated as basing points. Consumers near these points then buy the item as if it had come from this basing point. One result is that prices are much lower at these selected points than they are in the surrounding area. For many activities, therefore, lower prices at these points make for considerably lower production costs. One basing point system practiced by the steel industry, until it was declared unconstitutional, was *Pittsburgh Plus.* At that time, all steel purchased in the United States was priced as if it had been made in Pittsburgh, even though it often came from steel plants much closer. This generated tremendous profits inasmuch as transportation that was not being used was being paid for by the consumer. The automobile industry bases its prices on transportation from Detroit, even though the cars are assembled in local plants. In this case, however, most of the component parts are indeed shipped from Michigan, but at a rate lower than that charged for a completed automobile.

An interesting geographical aspect of such a pricing system is that transportation costs appear to drop just before they get to the basing point. Thus, here is a case where transportation charges are less for further distances than for closer distances. Again, however, it must be cautioned that in practice and principle such a system is no longer legally acceptable in the United States. It still operates somewhat, however, in modified form.

It is difficult to gauge whether such a modified F.O.B. system is beneficial or detrimental to the consumer. Those consumers who live near basing points undoubtedly benefit. Those who live outside of basing point ranges, points *Q* on Figure 4.6, are perhaps just paying their fair share. Such a system, however, does favor those areas that are designated as basing points, as well as those areas near them.

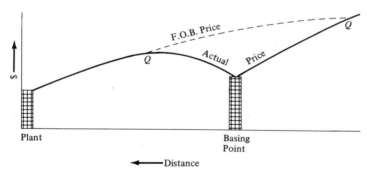

FIGURE 4.6 The Basing-Point of Pricing versus an F.O.B. System. Customers near basing points (*Q* to *Q*) pay less than under an F.O.B. system. Such a situation, however, results in those persons to the left of the basing point to *Q* paying more for the item even though they are progressively closer to the plant.

Conclusions

The economic principles discussed above are aimed primarily at the entrepreneur rather than the state. Regional concerns relative to economic development have been ignored. Instead, simple profit maximization over the short run has been the guiding principle.

It is quickly evident, however, that goals which may achieve maximum profits over the short run (say, several decades) may not be the same goals that would achieve maximum accumulated profits over the long run. This bias of the models presented is especially critical from a locational analysis standpoint inasmuch as the placement of a factory, say, in one location may be the most profitable thing to do for the present, but not for the future. In fact, focusing on current profit maximization might allow opportunities for injurious competitive responses in other territories to occur and thereby may jeopardize the future profitability of the operation. A wise locational strategy might even be to operate at a loss for a few years in a new and expanding territory, in order to ensure future competitive strength in that area.

It is difficult to find many activities that are based solely on short-run maximization procedures. For example, a farmer might plant his total farm to the most profitable crop, but in so doing he might deplete his soil. Most crops require rotation to maintain soil fertility and avoid soil disease. This means planting a crop that is less profitable over the short run. Likewise, a timber company might make high profits by cutting all its available timber in one year, but then what will they do in the future? Of course, for most companies, taxes and other factors mitigate against making excessive short-run profits. A grower of beef animals could sell his entire herd and keep nothing back for animal propagation, but he would be foolish to do so. Instead, he generally tries to maintain a satisfactory profit, to operate at the least cost possible within a set of goals, and to improve his competitive position.

In other cases, profit maximization is further reduced in importance by other, perhaps noneconomic goals. Many case studies show that industrialists seek out the more amenity-laden areas for their plants, other things being somewhat equal. They place high value on an attractive community, good schools, public facilities, and especially on those areas that offer a good physical environment and recreational opportunities. Likewise, some farmers could probably obtain a greater profit by switching crops or location. But these farmers like and understand the crops they grow. They consider themselves potato farmers, or wheat or cotton farmers, and they don't want to switch. They like the area in which they live; they know people there, and they have become attached to the land and to the region. It would take more than just the possibility of greater profit to get them to move.

The economic bases are critical in the understanding of man and his activities. Nonetheless, they must be used with great caution. A *ceteris paribus* must be kept in mind constantly if one is not to be accused of being a geographical ignoramus. In fact, it was possibly the empirical knowledge of the earth that kept geographers so long from accepting and using more of the economist's concepts and tools. The principles discussed do have validity when used with proper restraint and qualifications; when used properly, they are indispensable to geographical understanding.

BIBLIOGRAPHY

Dean, Robert D.; Leahy, William H.; and McKee, David L. *Spatial Economic Theory.* New York: The Free Press, 1970.

Losch, August. *The Economics of Location.* New Haven: Yale University Press, 1954.

McCarty, Harold H., and Lindberg, James B. *A Preface to Economic Geography.* Englewood Cliffs, N.J.: Prentice-Hall, 1966.

McKee, David L.; Dean, Robert D.; and Leahy, William H. *Regional Economics: Theory and Practice.* New York: The Free Press, 1970.

McNee, Robert B. "The Changing Relationships of Economics and Economic Geography." *Economic Geography,* July 1959, pp. 189–198.

Samuelson, Paul A. *Economics: An Introductory Analysis.* New York: McGraw-Hill, 1967.

Smith, Adam. *The Wealth of Nations.* New York: Random House, 1937.

V

Institutional Bases of Economic Geography

    This chapter focuses on the differing human characteristics of mankind as they are reflected within an institutional context. The diversity of religions, ethnic features, languages, and general attitudes demonstrates how greatly people vary in their social and cultural characteristics. Moreover, these diversities are ofttimes crystallized into institutional frameworks that can be examined with reference to their spatial impact on man and his distribution of economic activities.

    It is through his institutional frameworks, such as national governments, that man's sociocultural values are translated into actual production, consumption, and occupancy patterns. Man communally develops various governmental policies toward production and trade, has distinctive monetary systems, forms national alliances, and uses his institutions in many other ways to determine economic policies that affect the placement of man.

    This chapter will not attempt to explain *why* the institutional characteristics of man vary from place to place. Instead, our attention will be placed on exploring the effects of these institutional forces on the location of man and his activities.

    It is evident that we see ourselves becoming progressively engaged in circular reasoning and explanations. On the one hand, the places where man is located are understood from the foundation of where his activities are best placed. Inasmuch as man is a producer and constitutes the labor force, he must be located near where he must work. Thus the discussion dealing with the placement of production-oriented activities provides considerable explanation for the placement of man himself.

    But in another context, man is the market for all production. His location will strongly influence the placement of the productive activities and, of course, the services.

    Finally, man, through his cultural eyes, decides on the nature of "usable" land and resources; his attitudes and values are reflected in the nature and extent of his resource-related activities; and his decisions determine the kind of spatial response, if any, to be made. Thus, man is the final judge and arbiter of what he will and will not do in any given place and in any given situation.

The most evident manifestation of how man views the resources about him is reflected in the distribution of world population. Observation of any world population distribution reveals a tremendous concentration of man in a few limited parts of the earth and a tremendous paucity of man in other parts. Most of the earth is very scantily populated.

Two great blocks of population are at once noticeable: (1) an enormous massing of population in Southern and Eastern Asia, and (2) a sizable concentration of population in Western Europe. Almost one-half the world's population is found in such nations as China (over 700 million), India (500 million), Pakistan, Japan, and Indonesia (each over 100 million). Another one-fifth of the world's population is found in the Western European countries. The imminency of the "United States of Europe," therefore, represents the largest Western "nation" and, given its technological superiority, potentially the world's greatest power. The coalescence of these ten European nations, each with about fifty million persons, is one of the most important production and marketing blocs in the world. Thus, these two clusters of population contain almost three-quarters of the earth's population in an area which comprises no more than 5 percent of the land's surface.

A third important cluster of population, although much smaller (about 120 million persons), is the northeastern quadrangle of the United States and the Ontario peninsula of Canada. Together these areas account for another 3 percent of the earth's inhabitants.

The remaining one-quarter of the earth's population is widely scattered. However, the more densely populated nodes are represented by cities near littorals, for example, along the Pacific Coast of the United States, in the southeastern part of South America, the southeastern part of Australia, and West Africa. Other small nucleations are found inland, as in Central Mexico and the East African highlands, or sporadically situated near major river estuaries.

The primary implication of such an uneven pattern of population distribution is that man has been very selective, in part for reasons advanced in Chapters 3 and 4. Simply put, some areas of the earth are just better places for supporting sizable populations than are others. Regardless of the reasons, however, the spatial fact is that such a distribution sets the stage for understanding man's needs within an areal context. For some of these areas, the heavy population might be considered largely within a negative context; employment and food resources do not appear to be adequate for the existing population. Thus the large concentrations in China and India may reflect a deficit inasmuch as the population size severely taxes the ability of the land to support it. But for most areas such population importance is indicative of considerable advancement in industrialization and urbanization; such populated areas are also indicative of the physical prosperity of the land either through especially good soils or through profitable trade opportunities.

National States as Institutions

The most important single institutional factor affecting the placement of differing activities is the creation of national states or countries. Each country can, and usually does, set its own economic policy, decide on the priorities and allocation of its resources, and can, in short, set the stage for progress or decline in its territory.

The importance of understanding the role of national states in the arrangement of things on the earth is apparent when one realizes that there are almost 200 different independent nations. About one-quarter of these nations, mostly in Africa, have emerged during the past several decades. Thus, many nations are still novices in the governing of activities and in the setting of policy.

Nonetheless, many governments of the world are the prime decision-makers with regard to the placement of various activities. This is especially true in countries with Communist governments and in many newly emerging nations vitally concerned with economic development and the priorities of resource allocation. It is also much the case in dictatorships and in capitalist democracies alike. First, most governments actually own or control certain economic activities — for example, railroads, postal services, banks, power plants, major factories, roads and highways, parks, and air systems. (Communist governments control all economic activities.) Thus the extent and the placement of such activities is strictly a government decision made within the value system of each national state. Another way in which government affects the placement of things is through national taxation systems. Government channeling of resource use results in different distributions of man and his activities among various countries. Government policy and government works thus are often first-order factors in any such explanation.

For example, the government of Venezuela, a country rich in petroleum, has decided that it will offer favorable conditions for petroleum exploitation to foreign companies. By using this money properly, the Venezuelan government plans to build up a wider and more diversified range of activities. Oil is similarly used as a basis for economic development in the Mideast. Thus, in these countries petroleum is perhaps deliberately used, and possibly depleted, in hope of achieving something better in the long run. On the other hand, Mexico also has rich oil resources. Several decades ago, it supplied half the world's oil, but today its government has deterred foreign companies from entering. Because of this government policy, its oil production has dropped markedly during the past several decades. In the United States, too, there are strict controls on the amount of petroleum that can be taken from any given area or well.

In short, the decision as to whether a particular resource in a country will be used now, in the future, or not at all is often made by the government, mainly through its export policy, regardless of the political form of that government. Thus, more important to the economic geographer than the political nature of a country is the nature of its policy with regard to particular commodities and activities. An easy measure of such policy would be a country's trade relations with other countries as they might affect the distribution of people and activities. Such relations can perhaps be covered most simply by an examination of the formal political and trade alliances among countries of the world.

Regional political alliances among nations

In an area having similar cultural features — language, race, religion, and technological stage — and sharing common aspirations, the formal national policies of states will often reflect these common values. In the context of world regions, the national associations, expressed through various political, military, and trade agreements and alliances, are most revealing.

Six major formal political-military alliances are worthy of note: (1) the *Warsaw Pact*, which ties the Soviet Union politically and militarily to its satellites in Eastern Europe; (2) the *Organization of African Unity* (OAU), which links some thirty-five African nations having common interests in regard to development; (3) the *Organization of American States* (OAS), which contains some twenty Latin American nations and the United States in a collective arrangement to settle disputes and to render mutual military support against Communist interference; (4) the *North Atlantic Treaty Organization* (NATO), a defense alliance of some thirteen European nations, the United States, and Canada; (5) its counterpart in Asia, the *South East Asia Treaty Organization* (SEATO), which includes some eight countries in that area; and (6) the *Central Treaty Organization* (CENTO) composed of Great Britain, Iran, Pakistan, and Turkey, for purposes of mutual defense. These political associations, though primarily defense-oriented, clearly set the stage for furthering economic interests and forming world-wide economic blocs.

Two types of alliances are evident: (1) those which are primarily compacts among culturally similar countries for mutual defense (OAU, OAS, and the Warsaw Pact), and (2) those which involve patronage support from outside areas and cultures (SEATO, CENTO, and NATO). In addition, there are a number of less formal pacts, such as the general United States sympathy with Israel, and the Soviet support of the nearby Arab nations.

National trade groups

The political-military associations are further brought into focus by an examination of formal trade associations of nations. Here the general attempt is to facilitate trade among certain selected nations — generally those having strong social and cultural similarities. Thus, paradoxically, trade, which presumably best occurs among different types of areas, is molded through such arrangements to include primarily those countries which are culturally most alike. As might be expected, therefore, many have not been very successful, particularly those in South America, Africa, and Asia where most nations have more trade demands with nations in other areas than with their nearby neighbors. Nevertheless, these trade advantages undoubtedly encourage more trade among such similar cultural areas than would otherwise be the case. By the same token it discourages trade among areas which otherwise might logically appear to have need for interaction.

Historically the most territorially extensive trade alliance in the world has been the British Commonwealth of Nations (Figure 5.1). These twenty-nine independent countries and about forty dependencies cover almost one-quarter of the earth's land surface. Foremost among these nations are former colonies such as New Zealand, Australia, Canada, India, Pakistan, Kenya, Nigeria, and many other African countries. The commonwealth nations are given preferential treatment with Great Britain whereby for many commodities no tariffs are charged. With Great Britain's entry into the Common Market, some preferential treatment is also extended to some of her commonwealth countries' exports — for example, New Zealand dairy products in Europe. (Rhodesia is an exception and is currently being censured for its racial policies, among other things.) The success of this commonwealth system, which includes a tremendous diversity of physical, political, and economic systems, is demonstrated by the fact that about one-quarter of all non-Communist world trade occurs within this bloc — a bloc in which Great Britain, especially England, is still the kingpin. Nevertheless, each associated country maintains its own foreign policy independently and has its own form of government. Lately, however, the British Commonwealth of Nations has had less impact because of the declining importance of England. Commonwealth countries have found it increasingly profitable to trade with other countries rather than with the "motherland." Historically, however, this system has operated much to the advantage of the leader nation. Great Britain (England, Scotland, and Wales, and Northern Ireland) has received industrial raw material and food from commonwealth members and traded them finished products in return. Lately, however, as some of the member nations have become more industrialized — for instance, Canada and Australia — they have responded less and less to this arrangement because they, too, prefer to import raw materials and export finished products; or, as in the case of India and Australia, they have placed high import duties on manufactured products from other areas, including England, in order to encourage local manufacturing production (Figure 5.1).

Since the Treaty of Rome in 1957, six European nations — Italy, France, West Germany, and the Benelux countries — have been formulating various "unions" in order to form eventually an economically and politically integrated new community or nation. This European Economic Community — or Common Market, as it has become known — has reached significant agreements

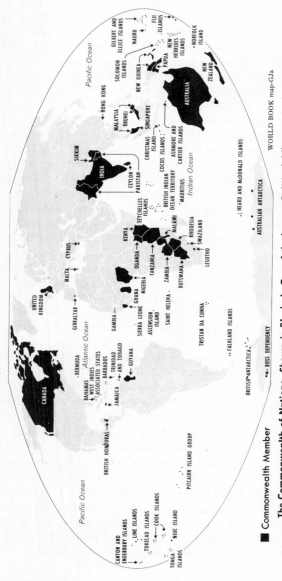

■ Commonwealth Member

The Commonwealth of Nations, Shown in Black, Is One of the Largest Political Alliances in the World.

WORLD BOOK map-GJa

FIGURE 5.1 The British Commonwealth of Nations. From the World Book Encyclopedia, (C) 1970. By permission of Field Enterprises Educational Corporation, Chicago, Ill.

on the flow of industrial materials and labor and is now endeavoring to achieve a fully integrated economic union. Such things as a common monetary system, a single taxing policy, and integration of agricultural production are currently being developed. In 1972, four other nations — the United Kingdom (England, Scotland, Wales, and Northern Ireland), Norway, Denmark, and Ireland — were admitted. (The citizens of Norway, however, declined admittance.) The ultimate hope is that these nations will be able to form a political union leading to the emergence of a new "United States of Europe."

Thus the European Economic Community represents a most significant economic and political bloc in world affairs. This nine nation union contains a population of over 260 million as compared with slightly over 200 million for the United States. Economically, it is the richest in the world. In terms of import and export dollars and in terms of gold reserves and other measures, such as steel output, these ten "Common Market" nations are superior to any other nation on earth. Only in overall gross national product does any nation, the United States, exceed the European community. There is no question but that this combine of nations, in conjunction with vast earth-circling arrangements with still other countries, represents the most impressive world economic and political force since the times of the Roman Empire.

The Soviet-bloc countries have also set up an Eastern European "free trade territory," which includes the Soviet Union and eight of its East European satellite nations, under the *Council of Mutual Economic Assistance* (COMECON). This, according to some member countries, has proven highly successful.

In 1961, a trade arrangement similar to the Common Market, the *Central American Common Market* (CACM), was formed in Central America. This included the countries of Costa Rica, El Salvador, Guatemala, Honduras, and Nicaragua. The purpose was to stimulate mutual trade through reduction and elimination of tariffs. However, as might be expected, most trade is outside this area.

The world's largest free trade association is the *Latin American Free Trade Association* (LAFTA), which includes some eleven major Latin American countries. However, since its inception in 1961, progress has been extremely slow. First, there is the problem of adequate transportation among the many countries (the Pan American highway is still not complete). Second, the products each has to offer have more demand outside of Central and South America than within it. Finally, there have been problems of governmental disorder and general disagreements on the extent to which tariffs should be lowered. Perhaps the greatest hope for Latin American countries came when President Kennedy called the *Alliance for Progress* meetings in 1961. In 1967, an agreement was made by some nineteen Latin American nations and the United States that a common market would be established. Already, the LAFTA common market has changed production and trade patterns. For example, Chile is now buying cotton from Mexico rather than from the United States, Mexico now sells steel to several Latin American countries, and Brazil continues to industrialize and to sell manufactured items throughout Latin America.

Commodity agreements

Commodities that move heavily in international trade are usually controlled by commodity agreements among the affected nations. Whereas the trade agreements discussed above are regional in nature, these are topical. Wheat, coffee, and sugar are examples of internationally controlled commodities. Such controls are developed in order to stabilize prices, to ensure continuity in production areas, and to gain some commitments of various types from consuming areas. A multitude of crops are protected and given special treatment by reciprocal trade agreements between any two countries. Such favored treatment is often characterized by guaranteed quotas, lowered or discontinued custom duties, and various forms of price support. In other instances, unilateral action is taken by a single country, as in the case of sugar, discussed below. The end result of such agreements is that certain areas are given preferential and protected status with regard to particular commodities, and other areas are discriminated against.

In 1948, more than forty countries signed the *International Wheat Agreement*. These wheat-growing nations agreed to share the existing world market for wheat rather than for any one of them to glut the market during a highly productive year. Theoretically this agreement was to protect the world price of wheat. It has been only partially successful. The Soviet Union withdrew as early as 1949 because it thought its quota too low — it had a good wheat crop in 1949. Great Britain dropped out in 1953 because it thought the import price was pegged too high. The United States usually has stockpiled its surplus and has maintained two price systems, one for domestic consumption and one for world trade. Of course, those wheat-growing nations that did not sign the wheat agreement have had a field day, periodically selling at below the pegged world prices. Consequently, nations like the United States have adopted price support and various other plans to control domestic production. The end result is that the production and price of world wheat is highly distorted by such national self-interest and general commodity agreements.

Coffee is another crop that has gone through various periods of surplus a deficit, and is likewise highly controlled, at least among certain countries. The stockpiling of coffee in Brazil and the initiating of artificially high prices had encouraged coffee production in other places, such as the Ivory Coast and Mexico. As a consequence, in 1963 in the United Nations an *International Coffee Agreement* was signed whereby exporting countries accepted export quotas and importing countries accepted a lower limit on coffee prices and further agreed to limit purchases from those nations not signing the coffee agreement.

There could be no more controversial commodity than sugar, which can be produced from a number of sources but comes primarily from sugar beets and sugar cane. The latter is presumably a more efficient source, particularly as grown on large plantations outside the United States, but national interests have long protected beet sugar production. Any any rate, those midlatitude nations which grow sugar beets have suffered a continual dilemma over the importation of sugar cane. (There is no basic difference in the sugar made from each.)

The problem has become especially thorny in countries such as the United States, where some states (for example, Hawaii and Louisiana) produce cane sugar and other states (for example, California, Idaho, and Colorado) produce beet sugar. Consequently, the federal government has arbitrarily controlled the production and price of both types of sugar within the United State. In addition, it has set up import quotas in dealing with other countries.

A classic example of trade restrictions preventing general fulfillment of the logical transportation, physical, and economic features is the sugar embargo imposed on Cuba by the United States. Cuba is considered to have the comparative advantage over most other sugar producing areas of the earth. This is certainly the case with regard to shipment of sugar to the United States. In fact, before the United States imposed its embargo on Cuban sugar, Cuba supplied over one-third of all sugar imports to the United States. The consequences of this action was that other, less efficient sources, both foreign and domestic, increased their production. Other things being equal, this would have had the effect of increasing prices drastically, but inasmuch as United States prices were already pegged artificially high, the increase was small. Almost every country, through tariff duties, taxes, subsidies, and other means, has exerted some controls over sugar pricing and hence over the location of sugar producing areas. Sugar is not an isolated example, however; most crops moving heavily in international trade are controlled by some of these methods.

Thus, these cases demonstrate ways in which national policies can neutralize certain areas that are otherwise favorably endowed or provide advantages and encourage activities in areas that otherwise could not complete. Such policies are clearly injurious to the best use of the land from a physical and economic sense and constitute one of the major arguments presented by economists and geographers in favor of free trade. Nevertheless, from the standpoint of an individual nation in competition with the rest of the world, some of these policies make a great deal of sense.

Cultural Influences of Institutional Arrangements

The foregoing discussion of various alliances and arrangements among countries requires some augmentation. We can no longer be content to take all of these as givens; some general considerations as to "why" must now be entertained. The affinities and disaffinities among nations are, of course, highly complex; to understand them fully, they must be placed within a historical and economic context. Much information can be gained, however, simply through an examination of the general cultural features of various nations as these might affect their relationships. In particular, it is instructive to examine three great ecouragements and/or encumbrances to cooperation among nations: (1) religion, (2) language, and (3) stage of technology.

Religion

Religion is one of the most pervasive factors affecting the nature of governmental policies and the general welfare — though often in a subtle fashion. First, religion affects people's way of life and hence their values in regard to social, economic, and legal institutions and systems. The difficulties engendered by the caste system in India, which is still operative to a certain extent, and by that country's custom of considering the cow a sacred animal are well known. Religious restrictions with regard to food occur in many groups: Catholics usually eat fish on Fridays, Jews and Moslems may not eat pork, Hindus may not eat beef. Some groups, such as Mormons and Catholics, place high value on large families and believe it is their religious duty to "multiply and replenish the earth." Thus seemingly simple and pat solutions to some of the economic problems of the earth (for instance, instituting birth control, ending the plethora of unused cattle in India, reducing the consumption of fish, or raising the consumption of milk) are not applicable in the face of religion-based customs.

Some argue that religion plays a less dominant role in the more economically advanced nations, but this is a questionable thesis. For example, even though formal religion has been conscientiously separated from state government in the United States, the Protestant ethic is still strongly reflected in governmental policies. The tax-free status accorded to religious institutions is a case in point. The pervasive influence of religion can also be demonstrated with regard to the work pattern and holidays. Sunday is considered a "day of rest" — clearly a Christian work taboo. Although not as limiting as the Hindu caste system, in which each person has particular economic functions to perform, the restriction nonetheless has tremendous import for productivity and the nature of the economy. Incidentally, this system is probably much better suited to an urban-industrial economy than to an agricultural one, where uninterrupted periods of intensive planting and harvesting are required; yet it was more pervasive when the United States was predominantly rural. Consider, too, the various religious holidays such as Easter, various "feast days," and Christmas.

The effect of religion is also evident on the landscape itself. Both Protestant and Catholic institutions own or use tremendous amounts of territory. First, they own and directly control a great deal of land for the placement of churches, schools, and various other religious or religion-based activities. In fact, in many communities the cathedrals, churches, mosques, and temples are perhaps the most distinctive structures. Perhaps religious structures of today do not match the pyramids of Egypt or the buildings of the Aztec civilization or of the Buddhist kings in Cambodia, but they are impressive indeed. Second, a major land use in the Christian world (and in China, incidentally) is for cemeteries — clearly a need based on religion. Other cultures, such as the Hindu, Buddhist, and Japanese, commonly cremate rather than bury their dead. The number of associated activities required for such religious practices are considerable. In fact, one might reach the conclusion that only economically advanced nations can afford to put so much emphasis on economically non-productive structures and activities without seriously overtaxing the economic system.

There are hundreds of different religions in the world, but the eight major ones are Christianity, Islam, Hinduism, Confucianism, Buddhism, Shintoism, Taoism, and Judaism. On a world basis, the first six of these constitute the main religious blocs. The "Western" countries of Northwest Europe, the countries of North and South America, and the European outliers of Australia and New Zealand are Christian in general philosophy. So, too, are many other areas such as the Philippine Islands, Hawaii, and other Pacific islands — largely as a result of missionary work during the last century. The Middle East, North Africa, and Pakistan are primarily Islamic (Moslem), and the other Asiatic areas are strong in the tradition of Buddhism and its associated religions.

Many serious conflicts in the world today are based on religion. The initial separation of Hindu India from Moslem Pakistan was effected for religious reasons and the continuing conflict between them mirrors such differences. The mounting crisis between Jewish Israel and the Islamic Arab counties is also in large part fanned by religious differences. Religion-based conflicts are also evident among Christian and non-Christian nations and even between Christian peoples of different sects. For example, difficulties between the French Canadians (Catholic) and the remainder of Canada (largely Protestant) continue to brew. Differences here, of course, also relate to different European national bases and languages, but religion is by no means unimportant. The recent eruptions in the long-standing conflict betwen the Catholics and Protestants in Northern Ireland are representative of still another religious difference that has permeated national political life. Thus, it is easily seen that religion is reflected — more than most people realize — in politics and in national policies, which, in turn, affect locational decisions among and within countries.

In some areas, religious disagreements are so strong that separate facilities have been set up for each religious group. Where several religious groups live in close propinquity, there is a tremendous duplication of facilities — not only churches, but schools, stores, and "public" facilities. Thus there are many more establishments in these areas than would be expected on the basis of population demand alone.

Finally, many religious groups have set out to settle their own colonies and, in some cases, to found their own nations. In Israel, a classic case in point, the occupancy of the land and the character and placement of settlements are determined largely by a religion-based policy. In such cases, the manner in which cities will be laid out and built and the manner of rural land ownership are also determined from a religious base.

Ethnic groups

Another feature generally affecting the institutional arrangements among and within nations is what is popularly termed "race." In point of fact, biologically all peoples belong to one common pool of genes and form one mating circle. There is no scientific basis for distinguishing among the earth's people racially. All evidence points to one family and one origin. Nonetheless, there are vast outward variations among the population in kinds of skin color, types of hair, facial features, and other characteristics.

The most generally recognized crude categorization consists of three types: (1) the Caucasoid (white-skinned), (2) the Mongoloid ("yellow"-skinned), and (3) the Negroid (dark-skinned). There are many subtypes and many other classifications, but these will suffice as a broad framework. In fact, major differences in world patterns of trade and general conflict in resource use appear to be among the Caucasoid, Mongoloid, and Negroid. Where these differences also tend to coincide nationally with religious and language differences, the implications for world activity patterns are direct and potentially violent.

Unfortunately, much of the trouble within countries is also of a racial nature, and where racial differences are strongly evident, this likewise leads to discernibly different spatial patterns among the groups. Again, the result is often a duplication, although certainly not an equal provision, of equal functions. Perhaps the most notorious case is that of South Africa, where the Caucasoids (Europeans) have forced the Negroids (Bantus) to live in special areas. Such an *apartheid* policy is ostensibly based on the assumption that the white-skinned population is currently so advanced relative to the Bantus that separation is necessary for the protection of the Bantus. South Africa is not alone in discriminating against peoples with ethnic backgrounds quite different from the ruling group (in the case of South Africa, a ruling minority). Most Caucasoid nations discriminate against Mongoloid and Negroid peoples. Certainly the immigration policies in Great Britain, Australia, and the United States are racially based. The Mongoloids also practice discrimination (China is a case in point), against the Caucasoids, or "barbarians" as they are commonly called. Moreover, it is unquestionably true that national states have been formed primarily on the basis of ethnic traits. The division of Hispaniola into two nations, "black" Haiti on the west and relatively white Dominican Republic on the east, is a good case in point.

Finally, one would be delinquent not to mention a major land-use feature in the United States that is based primarily on ethnic backrounds — namely, the extensive Indian reservations. Whereas Australians early hunted the Tasmanian peoples for sport and thereby exterminated them, the United States placed its indigenous population in territorial prisons. Most other countries have not taken such drastic action, and considerable intermixing has occurred. Still, racial conflicts are visible on the landscapes of many areas of the world. The characteristic Indian settlements in Alaska, the ghettos and "Chinatowns" throughout much of the Western world are other cases in point.

Language

Language, religion and race constitute an important trinity in cultural distinction among peoples. Its importance in Balkanizing various peoples of the earth is evident. Lack of communication presents barriers not only to trade but to general understanding. Language differences in particular present a barrier to the transmission of technological innovations and to economic development and progress. Not uncommon are the examples of different languages among upland and lowland peoples in the same general area, and a consequent disparity in their economic development. Generally, those groups able to comunicate with the wider group are the most prosperous and the most economically developed. Groups that find themselves isolated linguistically as well as geographically are often the most economically backward. (These peoples are discussed in Chapter 7.)

A people whose language is spoken only in a very limited area can communicate with the outside world or with other small groups nearby through what is termed *lingua franca* — a simplified, generally understood trading-language used over a wide area by people of varying native tongues. The need for lingua francas becomes evident when one realizes that there are hundreds of different languages, belonging to more than twenty major language families, spoken on earth. Furthermore, even people whose languages belong to the same family cannot understand one another.

The Indo-European language family alone (whose languages are spoken by one-third of mankind) is divided into several branches, each of which, in turn, includes several languages: the Germanic branch includes English, German, most of the various Scandinavian tongues, and others; the Italic branch includes Spanish, Portuguese, Italian, French, and others; the Slavic branch includes Russian, Polish, Czech, and others. In addition to these three branches, there are the Celtic (Gaelic and Welsh, for example), the Iranian (Persian and Kurdish, for example), and the Indic (Hindu and Urdu, for example). Of these, English is the most widely used — it is spoken by about 300 million persons. But Chinese, a branch of the Sino-Tibetan family of languages, is used daily by some 550 million persons. Other families of languages, each accounting for about a hundred million persons, are the Dravidian (spoken in various parts of India), Japanese, the Hamitic-Semitic (Arabian), and the Austronesian (Indonesia).

As with religion and ethnic characteristics, when languages differ within and between countries, difficulties and conflict often result. The obvious exception to this is Switzerland, which has consistently been one of the most peaceful of nations although German is spoken in the northeast, Italian in the south, French in the west, and Romansch in the far southeast.

That language affects the location of economic activities can perhaps best be appreciated by comparing the relations of the United States with Canada and Mexico. Both countries are friendly to the United States. Canada is highly industrialized and prosperous. United States firms have large investments in Canada, and most products move quite freely across the border, which is one of the freest in the world. Thus the United States and Canada are closely tied. On the other hand, the nation of Mexico has had very little but trouble with the United States. The Mexican-American war was but one evidence of this, and other difficulties still exist. American firms have been reluctant to invest in Mexico. Although that government's recent policy undoubtedly is one cause of this reluctance, the language barrier has also contributed to the problem. Few Americans speak Spanish, and this presents difficulties in all kinds of transactions between the two countries. Recently, however, because of the presence of cheap labor in Mexico, a number of border-based American firms have opened outlets in Northern Mexico. At any rate, despite its rich resources, Mexico is a poor country compared with Canada. Cearly this is in part due to language difficulties. It would be interesting to speculate on how Mexico would look today if the people in the United States and Mexico spoke the same language.

Stage of technology

In practice, the stage of technology is often interrelated with the religious, ethnic, and language patterns discussed above. With regard to current and future economic activities, stage of technology is undoubtedly the critical item. Here again, it is like a two-edged sword: On the one hand, we will take it as given in order to gain some understanding of why people and activities are distributed as they are on the earth; on the other hand, this entire text is geared to provide some further explanation as to why there is such a differential in the level of technology and economic well-being among the various parts of the world. Hence we are discussing stages of technology here only in a preliminary context — a context that will prove valuable in the analysis of certain activities to be discussed later.

There are many measures that might be used to separate the levels of technology and stage of economic development among areas and nations. These include per capita consumption of goods, services, and energy; per capita production of goods and services (gross national product); and, of course, per capita income. Other measures might include productivity per worker and occupational characteristics. Regionalization of technology levels depends on the number of regions desired. For example, under a twofold division, one would need to distinguish only between the have and the have-not nations, between the poor and the rich, or between the developed and the under-developed. It is pointed out, however, that such a twofold division does an injustice to the wide differences among the so-called underdeveloped areas — some are intensive agricultural systems, whereas the economy of others is based on the most rudimentary forms of hunting and gathering. Thus under a threefold division the countries with "primitive" economies are differentiated from underdeveloped and overpopulated countries.

First, let us examine the level of development among nations on the basis of the primary, secondary, tertiary, and quaternary breakdown discussed earlier. Remember, however, that this is on a national basis and must necessarily ignore anomalies within any given country. Therefore the information for those countries with large territorial boundaries might be considered the most unreliable in this regard. About three groups of countries emerge:

1. Countries in which most of the labor force (over 60 percent) is engaged in primary activities, with few workers in the secondary, tertiary, or quaternary sectors. In this category are found China, India, and the countries concentrated in Southeast Asia.
2. Countries in which there is a mixture of all the employment activities. In this category are found the U.S.S.R. and many smaller countries.
3. Countries, generally considered advanced, in which there is high employment in the tertiary and quaternary sectors, fairly high employment in the secondary sector, and very little employment in the primary sector. Such countries include England, the United States, Canada, Australia, New Zealand, and certain other countries in Western Europe (Figure 5.2).

Slightly different arrangements of countries are possible, depending on the criteria used. No matter what criteria are used, however, the countries that emerge as very urbanized, industrialized, and rich are always the same, as are the countries that show up as extremely poor.

One approach to the differentiation among nations as based on a multiplicity of criteria is that by Broek and Webb.[1] In their study a fourfold breakdown is presented: (1) advanced; (2) intermediate; (3) underdeveloped, upper group; and (4) underdeveloped, lower group. As might be anticipated, the nations in the advanced group include the United States, Canada, most of Western Europe, Australia, and New Zealand; these are the most urbanized of the

[1] Jan O. M. Broek and John W. Webb, *A Geography of Mankind* (New York: McGraw-Hill Book Co., 1968), pp. 326–327.

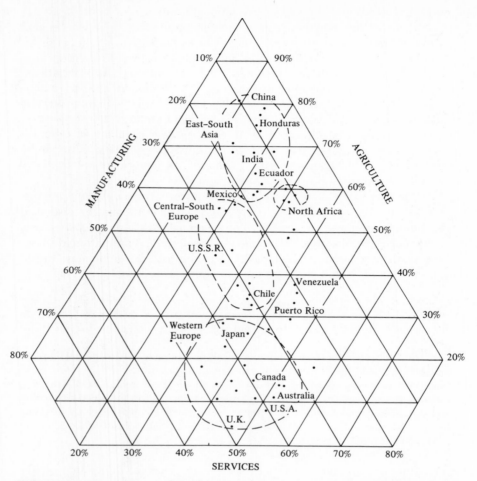

FIGURES 5.2 Percentages of Working Population in Agriculture, Manufacturing, and Services in Selected Countries. Based on Jan O.M. Broek & John W. Webb, *A Geography of Mankind*, (C) 1968. By permission of McGraw-Hill Book Co., New York.

world's nations aside from Japan. Japan is listed by Broek and Webb as an "intermediate" developed nation along with the U.S.S.R., South Africa, Argentina, Chile, Uruguay, Venezuela, Panama, Cuba, Spain, Portugal, and Israel. The "underdeveloped" countries in the upper group include the remainder of Central and South America, Southern Rhodesia, most of North Africa, most of the Middle East, Pakistan, India, China, Korea, Malaya, and the Philippines.

Such a static classification, although useful for general orientation purposes at any one time, places some very different countries in the same category.

For example, Japan is considered an "intermediate" country by the criteria used, but is otherwise quite different from the U.S.S.R., South Africa, and Argentina. In many respects, Japan is highly developed. Likewise, India and China may have living standards somewhat similar to those of the Arabs of Northern Africa and the Middle East, but are otherwise so culturally and occupationally different that we would not generally group them together.

World "cultural" blocs

If one considers the combined influence of the features discussed above — religion, race and language and stage of technology — some notion of the differences in attitudes, values, and economic characteristics of various peoples can be placed in a spatial context. Certainly, these are not the only factors making up culture in the anthropological use of the term, but these factors do provide a fair approximation of how one might visualize the world in terms of the human bases.

From these bases, six broad types of cultural territories can be readily distinguished: (1) Western-Christian, (2) Communist, (3) Islamic-Arab, (4) Indian, (5) Southeast and Maritime Asian, and (6) tribal and other (Figure 5.3). Each of these could be further subdivided, but in general such culturally based regions are also fairly closely correlated with general stage of economic development and general ethnic, religious, and linquistic characteristics. Thus the Western-Christian portions are generally industrialized, whereas the tribal and other areas are characterized by primary economic activities. Nevertheless, there is mixing in a number of places, but only the predominant culture type is shown. For example, about 10 percent of the United States population is not Northwest European, but African. However, it is largely Christian in religion.

In all but the Southeast and Maritime Asian and the tribal cultural regions, such similarly classified areas can be thought of as having strong economic and political ties. Thus these areas often coincide with trade patterns and certainly with the formation of trade agreements. Where trade crosses the first-order cultural realms, it is only because of strong complementarity among areas. Such interaction, however, is often tense at best. Some heavy world flows of this type include petroleum from the Islamic Middle East to Northern Europe, tropical products from Africa to Western countries, and the shipment of Canadian wheat to the People's Republic of China. Even the reciprocal trade between Japan and the United States, two highly industrialized nations, is not without certain culturally based difficulties. Perhaps because of such cultural differences, the general rule is for most trade to occur within these blocs rather than between them. Nonetheless, the most urbanized and industrialized areas require the most material and have greater interaction with other dissimilar places than those at the less developed part of the scale.

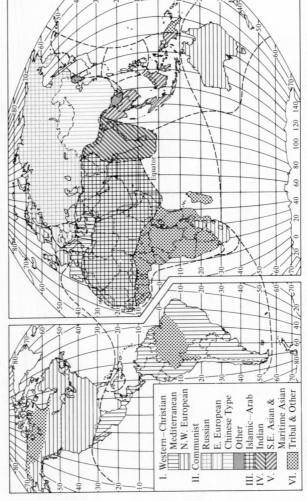

I. Western—Christian
   Mediterranean
   N.W. European

II. Communist
    Russian
    E. European
    Other

III. Chinese Type

IV. Islamic—Arab
    Indian

V. S.E. Asian &
   Maritime Asian

VI. Tribal & Other

FIGURE 5.3 World Cultural Areas as Based Primarily on Religion, Language, and Racial Characteristics (generalized).

Conclusions

This chapter has presented but a few examples of the way in which human factors and national policy affect the location of production. It was shown how the human bases can play a far more important role than the transportation, physical, or economic bases discussed in Chapters 2, 3, and 4.

Despite the importance of these human and institutional bases, they are not the be all and end all for the distribution of the earth's activities. For some things, they may be dominant and crucial; for others, they are major modifying ingredients; but for many things, particularly the distribution of activities within nations and cities, they play a small role indeed. Thus the key to geographical understanding is knowing when to draw upon the various bases of economic geography and how to combine these in an effective way for spatial analysis.

Finally, there is no doubt that the national states are regionalizing and fortifying themselves into large political, cultural, military, and economic alliances. Thus the forces of national groupings are seen here only in embryo stage; the future world units will be even more dominant and evident. Certainly the trend and the intention are clear. For example, many African nations are trying to cooperate for mutual political and economic benefit, the Latin American countries and the United States are attempting to develop an integrated territorial and industrial complex, and Western Europe is working toward the creation of a new nation — the United States of Europe. These trends, coupled with the already highly integrated Soviet bloc, will be major factors in determining the geographical reality in the future.

BIBLIOGRAPHY

Alexander, John W. "International Trade: Selected Types of World Regions." *Economic Geography*, April 1960, pp. 95–115.

Benson, P.H. *Religion in Contemporary Culture: A Study of Religion Through Social Science.* New York: Harper & Row, 1960.

Downs, Anthony. *An Economic Theory of Democracy.* New York: Harper & Row, 1957.

Isaac, Erick. "Religion, Landscape, and Space." *Landscape*, Winter 1960, p. 14.

———— "The Influence of Religion on the Spread of Citrus." *Science*, January 23, 1959, pp. 179–186.

James, Preston E. *One World Divided: A Geographer Looks at the Modern World.* Waltham, Mass.: Blaisdell, 1964.

Meinig, D.W. "The Mormon Culture Region: Strategies and Patterns in the Geography of the American West, 1847–1965." *Annals of the Association of American Geographers*, June 1965, pp. 191–220.

Shanks, Michael, and Lambert, John. *The Common Market Today – And Tomorrow.* New York: Praeger, 1962.

Smith, Howard R., and Hart, John Fraser. "The American Tariff Map." *Geographical Review*, July 1955, pp. 327–346.

Soja, Edward W. *The Political Organization of Space.* Commission on College Geography, no. 8. Washington, D. C.: Association of American Geographers, 1971.

Sopher, David. *Geography of Religions.* Englewood Cliffs, N.J.: Prentice-Hall, 1967.

Tawney, R. H. *Religion and the Rise of Capitalism.* New York: Harcourt, Brace & World, 1952.

Towle, Lawrence W. *International Trade and Commercial Policy.* New York: Harper and Brothers, 1956.

VI

The Urban Bases of Economic Geography

The placement of cities over the earth is a critical and paramount base from which other activities can be understood. In fact, with cities as a "given," the distribution of many other activities can, in crude fashion, be ascertained. Hence in later chapters the placement of cities will be treated much as will be transportation routes, physical features, and various national and institutional features. For example, the location of agriculture will be partly explained by the necessary proximity of certain crops to markets. Thus when accessibility to markets is under discussion, what is really being discussed is the spatial relationship of particular activities to cities — the places where most of the people are found. As a further example, cities are both a cause and an effect of manufacturing inasmuch as they are the places that have the available labor force and the channels of transportation so necessary for the acquisition of raw materials and the distribution of finished products to various other markets. In most cases, it is difficult to ascertain which is the cause and which is the effect. In practice, both are simultaneously interrelated. For purposes of graduated understanding, however, it is deemed wise at first to treat each activity separately and as if it were locationally flexible, while treating its associated activities as if they were spatially fixed.

In this chapter the location of cities will not be taken as a given feature; rather, an attempt will be made to provide explanation for the abundance of cities in some areas and their paucity in others. Nonetheless, the patterns of cities, although treated early in this text, are not a simple locational problem. It is necessary that they be treated at this point so that the nature and location of the activities discussed in the immediately forthcoming chapters may be more meaningful and more easily understood. Only the more simple explanations for the distributions of cities will be presented now. Many of these principles will be augmented in later chapters.

Thus the approach throughout much of this book appears to be highly circular as we proceed to unravel a truly complex spatial problem. In truth, all activities are functionally and spatially interrelated. To explain one thing fully, everything else must be explained. For pedagogical purposes, however, it is most prudent to focus on only one activity at a time and to treat it within a "pure" spatial framework. In terms of exposing the full subject matter, it might be possible to start almost anywhere and commence the unraveling procedure, much as with a great ball of yarn. The approach taken here is to proceed from the more simple to the complex. However, what is often considered a simple locational problem can be so considered only within the context of the assumptions that enclose it.

In order to "understand" the location of cities, five major items are considered: (1) the distribution of rural population; (2) the location of man's extensive space-using occupations such as agriculture, forestry, and mining; (3) the location of transportation routes; (4) the industrial structure of government needs as reflected in geographical space; and (5) the functions that cities generally perform. However, it must be quickly pointed out that these things are also, in turn, much contaminated by the placement of cities.

This chapter will approach the study of cities in four ways. First, an attempt will be made to demonstrate why cities are important — indeed, why in many respects they are the key to geographical understanding. Inasmuch as cities are the focal points around which the earth is occupied and utilized, it is evident that cities are also one of the bases of geographical understanding. Although this chapter is called "The Urban Bases of Economic Geography," the title is not entirely appropriate since we are not treating cities in all their geographical aspects but only as points on the surface of the earth. The internal arrangement and placement of activities within cities will be covered later.

The Importance of Cities

The importance of cities for spatial understanding will become fully evident in the forthcoming chapters, where cities will often be treated as the prime controlling force in the placement of any given activity. Much of the discussion of the extractive activities, agriculture, and industry will use cities as the fixed locational element in providing explanation of patterns. In fact, once cities are given, it is possible to explain most of the geography of the world.

Cities are also important as a bellwether for the degree of specialization over the earth's surface. They can occur only in areas of territorial and occupational specialization. Thus the more territorially specialized an area, the greater will be the urban response. In this regard, cities offer the best reflection of technological and economic progress in an area. Those areas with no cities (discussed in Chapter 7), which are therefore the least economically advanced places on earth, have not yet met the basic prerequisites for cities.

Cities are also important because of their control over the territory around them — that is, their tributary areas. They are important out of all proportion to the areas they occupy. First, they contain over one-third of the world's population (generally from 60 to 85 percent in industrially advanced countries). Yet the land actually occupied by cities accounts for less than one percent of the earth's surface. The sheer concentration of population in such limited space, in itself, makes cities important places of geographic interest. But most important, cities contain those decision-making functions that set the stage for the use of the earth. It is from them that government and law radiate; they contain the commodity and stock exchanges, the financial institutions and capital reserves, the major concentrations of manufacturing and industrialization; they also contain the major libraries and institutions of higher learning and the arts; they are the centers of innovation, brainpower, and communication. In short, they include the controlling elements for the use of earth space.

The above comments are not meant to imply that cities can operate independently of rural areas. To the contrary, it is the activities in these areas that give cities their *raison d'être*. Because cities fundamentally are important only in conjunction with such territory, however, does not mean that they are in an inferior position. Here is a case where logic might suggest that the country should control the city, but in practice it is the other way around. In a geographical context, however, the country and the city are intertwined in one complementary system; both are critical parts of a highly complicated whole.

Unfortunately, there are no hard-and-fast rules as to just what is rural and what is urban territory. In fact, such criteria vary widely among specialists in urban studies and must be modified to fit various areas of the world. Nonetheless, several criteria are commonly used to differentiate urban from rural land. First, there must be a certain amount of incorporated population. In the United States, such places must contain at least 2500 persons. In many European countries, an incorporated place is not considered to be urban unless it has 5000 or more population. Second, population is an almost universal measure for urbanization. In the United States, the general breaking point between rural and urban is 2000 persons per square mile.

However, some of the "farm villages" in China and elsewhere in Asia often have populations of 10,000 or more and have population densities exceeding 5000 persons per square mile. Nonetheless, this hardly strikes a Westerner as meeting the essential criteria of a "city" inasmuch as most functions characteristic of cities are missing. A third measure often concerns the occupation of the inhabitants. For an area to be considered urban, the majority of its nucleated population must be engaged in nonagricultural pursuits. This is a highly arbitrary criterion, but it does solve the knotty problem of Chinese farm villages. Finally, a city's functions and road pattern, as well as the amount of land covered by its structures, will be discernibly different from such features in the surrounding "rural" area.

But perhaps the easiest way to visualize and delimit the kinds of urban areas, or cities, we will be discussing is simply to examine an aerial photograph of an urban place. The outer edge will be ragged and somewhat indefinite, but the general outline of such "urban" territory will be clear. The formal municipal boundaries have very little effect on the territorial extent of urban development in an urban area. We might thus term this built-up area, this urbanized complex, the true or geographic city, as distinct from a municipality. In this work, the term "city" will be used as a synonym for geographic city.

In the United States, the nearest formal delimitation of a geographic city is the designation *urbanized area* used by the 1970 U.S. Census.[1] Such an area includes all municipalities with 50,000 or more population, plus surrounding territory that meets certain political, demographic, and density criteria.

Types of City Patterns

Most satisfying to the geographer are definitions of cities that include an explanation of their spatial pattern. Why are cities placed where they are? Why are some larger than others? Why are some growing and others declining? How is it that some parts of the world have many cities and other parts none?

The first approach to this is to categorize city types within such a framework. In one sense, there are hundreds of different city types. Some specialize in making airplanes, some in making steel; others are state capitals, university towns, resorts, ports, and so forth. From a geographical viewpoint, however, there are four major types that make spatial sense: (1) those that respond to transportation; (2) those that respond to territory; (3) those that respond to resources on site; and (4) those that respond to the institutional needs of man. Each of these types has a particular locational pattern that is readily identifiable on a map.

It should be evident also from the above that cities do not just happen, nor are their locations and particular functions accidental. Where a city is placed and what it does are directly affected by the demand for such functions as based on transportation, territory, or resources, and by the demands of man for the placement of his institutional functions such as governmental, educational, religious, and military activities. These latter institutional demands have far more latitude in placement and hence are far more difficult to understand locationally than are those activities which respond more in light of the transportation, physical, and economic bases.

Cities that respond to transportation

Cities affect the placement of transportation routes possibly more than

[1]An *urbanized area* is different from a *standard metropolitan statistical area* (SMSA) of the U. S. Census. The SMSA includes a central city and the county in which it is found, plus nearby counties that meet certain criteria. The SMSA is thus a much broader designation than *urbanized area*, and may include territory that is actually rural.

any other single feature of the earth. In fact, they create the demands for movement. The major things a city needs are contact, communication, and connection with the outside world. A city without transportation cannot exist. But cities also respond to transportation conditions. Such transportation opportunities may be reinforced by building a city at a port or junction. In the following discussion, various transportation conditions are taken as given. The placement of cities is examined in terms of the opportunities made available by such facilities.

There are several spatial responses that a city might make with regard to transportation features. First, cities are needed where breaks occur along a transportation route. The most spectacular of these is the break between land and water. Here a change of transportation mode is necessary. Workers are required for such a transfer, and this further creates opportunities for adding value, through manufacturing, to the commodities being moved. Thus, all port cities are, in part, transportation cities of this type. As such, port cities are also strategic transfer points that serve the land area behind them (their hinterland) and bring in or ship out produce to and from areas in front of them (their forelands). Inasmuch as ocean water transportation opens up numerous trading possibilities in different parts of the world, the port city is possibly the most numerous type of city; it is clearly the most numerous kind of large city (Figure 6.1).

But break of bulk also occurs along transportation routes on smaller scales, as between a plains area and a mountainous region, or where land routes cross major rivers. Such topographically based breaks create new kinds of transportation responses. Thus cities have developed in many of these places to serve such transfer needs. River towns are an extremely common example of this type. Where river transportation is the dominant route, cities develop at barriers along this route (for example, the waterfalls at Cincinnati) or at strategic places (for example, where a change from large craft to small craft has to be made, or where an ice-free river becomes a periodically frozen river, as at St. Louis). Changes in topography also result in transfer adjustments. Perhaps extra diesel engines will be required before a mountainous area is traversed, or people will wish to rest before engaging in a difficult portion of a route. Consequently, cities often locate at such topographical breaks.

Finally, cities respond to transportation-induced opportunities at strategic points created by routes. The best known is the crossroads, or junction, position — a break-of-bulk opportunity. Here, transfer of people and freight from one route to the other might be required. Consequently, this is a good place for railroad consolidation yards or like functions. Such centers are really transportation hubs where a number of transportation routes converge. Atlanta, Salt Lake City — in fact most large cities in the interior — have some activities based on these needs.

Cities also respond in a periodically spaced fashion along routes that have no physically based differences (type *B* in Figure 6.1). At intervals along the

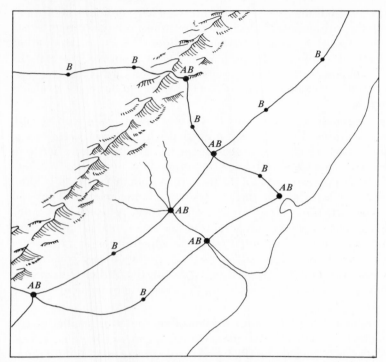

FIGURE 6.1 A Pattern of Transportation-Type Cities. Type *A* cities are break-of-bulk "hits," and Type *B* cities represent service centers designed to aid the flow of movement along the routes.

route, stops are required for rest, food, repairs, or other services. The spacing required varies from one mode to the other, but generally increases as one proceeds from highway to railway to air. Spacing has also tended to increase over time as improvements are made among the modes. Thus coal-burning railroad engines needed many watering stops (whistle stops) as compared to diesel engines. Road transportation needed far more stops with horse-powered than with gasoline-powered vehicles. It needs even fewer today in countries that have developed extensive freeway systems. Consequently, a number of former transportation service cities, beaded along major transportation lines, have been abandoned.

Other questions are also raised. Why, for example, should cities be on one side of the river rather than on the other? Generally, the reasons for such site features are multiple and are based on the direction of the traffic and the direction from which the route was built, on physical factors such as a high and low side of the river, or on institutional factors such as the advantages of one county or state versus another. The precise location of the port and the routes themselves are also the result of a combination of factors such as the time at which the routes were constructed (that is, sequence in construction), the physical conditions affecting route alignments, the best place to cross streams and mountains, the best place for a port, and the external regional requirements that dictate the position of the routes within the "study area." It is evident that the reasons for the exact placement of transportation routes and cities are indeed multifaceted, and each city must be treated separately.

Once these cities, derived initially for transportation purposes, are developed, other functions also find it advantageous to locate there. Some manufacturing plants, for example, reap considerable benefit by locating at break-of-bulk points. Others find that locating at strategic crossroads positions gives them real advantage in assembling raw materials and distributing products to a wide market area. Thus, manufacturing of these types (discussed in Chapters 8 and 14) might be thought of as transportation-induced manufacturing as distinct from other manufacturing types.

Note in Figure 6.1 that even among transportation cities, there is an overlap of different kinds of such cities in various places. Thus, Type *A* and *B* cities are sometimes found separately, sometimes together. They may also be duplicated. The larger the city, generally the more "hits" by such types. Note for example that the port city shown has five "hit" conditions and hence is the largest city in the area: first, it is a break-of-bulk between land and water for two different routes (2 hits); second, it is a periodic service center for two different routes (2 hits); and third, it is a crossroads point for three routes — two land and one water (1 hit). Therefore its symbol of importance might be symbolized AAABB as compared with the next largest cities, which are classified as AAB centers. On the basis of transportation response alone, we would expect cities of different sizes to develop.

The overall pattern is one of alignment and linearity along routes. The general feature to look for in such a pattern, aside from periodically spaced centers, is the general absence of clustering of cities in any one location.

Cities that respond to territory: central places

Another common characteristic of cities is their relatively evenly spaced pattern, generally most prominent in agricultural areas or in places where people are spread somewhat evenly over the countryside in some occupational pursuit. Cities in this kind of area locate centrally to this rural market in order to provide the goods and services needed by the people in the surrounding area. This centralizing location principle is one of the more general features in the placement of all activities. It is particularly critical with regard to the site of certain kinds of cities, namely, those formally labeled *central place cities*.

The general characteristics of agriculturally based central places are fairly easy to visualize. First, farmers and their families need various goods and services they cannot provide for themselves. These include such things as food and clothing, and legal, educational, governmental, and social services. Second, the farmer needs a market in which to sell his farm commodities. Thus grain elevators, warehouses, and the like are often adjunct features of such central places. Moreover, when farm commodities are perishable or otherwise difficult to ship, opportunities often exist in the city for manufacturing. Thus processing and other nondurable manufacturing are also often characteristic "services" of a central place city. With the money the farmer gets for his crops, he not only buys the goods and services mentioned above, but often requires machinery, seed, and other things critical to the operation of his farm. Thus a typical central place is not simply a location for providing retail and service items, but is a complex reflection of and response to a multiplicity of demands in a surrounding area. As such it is a reflection of the opportunities for economic activity that the production of farm commodities affords. These things all combine to create jobs in the central place city and thus support people in that city.

Finally, the people who are directly engaged in central place activities within a city also require goods and services. Thus a "second round" of demand functions occurs. In some cases, these people merely augment the number of customers otherwise available for an establishment and hence increase profits; in other cases, the number of customers is raised sufficiently to justify new stores — stores otherwise not possible with only the rural area customers.

As might be expected, there is a formal theory that pretends to explain the number of cities, their distribution, hierarchy of sizes, and the territory controlled by each place in the hierarchy, given such a dispersed market. This theory is called *central place theory* and was originally formulated by Walter Christaller and published in German in 1933.[2] The theory is based on three primary principles: (1) centralization as a principle of order, (2) economic distance and the range of a good or service, and (3) the nature of complementary regions — that is, trade areas of different order, or size, of places.

Given an even spatial distribution of customers and given the inability to locate a business adjacent to each customer, the best locational strategy is to locate centrally with regard to those customers who accumulatively will constitute a viable market. Cities will therefore locate at the place that minimizes transportation costs and time to the potential customer market. If the people are scattered over an even surface and if transportation is equally free in any direction, then such businesses (and hence urban places) will be evenly spaced over the landscape, with each one serving an equal number of surrounding customers. The territory each serves cannot, of course, be a circular one, inasmuch as circles would create uncovered or overlapping spaces. Such space

[2]Walter Christaller,*Central Places in Southern Germany* (Englewood Cliffs, N.J.: Prentice-Hall, 1966). This is a translation by Carlisle W. Baskin, of Christaller's *Die Zentralen Orte in Sud-deutschland.*

would therefore result in competitive zones. In exercising their options to minimize transportation to each market, the consumers would re-create zones of a hexagonal nature — the geometric from nearest to a circle — which work in such a fashion as to leave no unused spaces.

But what size is necessary to support any given function, such as a service station, a department store, a grocery store? Clearly, there is a different-sized minimum market necessary for each activity to carry on a viable business. The number of persons required will also depend on consumption patterns, incomes, and other variables, but we shall assume these to be homogeneous over the rural surface. In this case, the minimum number of persons, the *threshold* level, for each function can be estimated. Thus there are establishments that can be maintained with very few customers — for example, service stations, grocery stores, barber shops — and hence are labeled *lower order functions*, and establishments offering goods or services that require a large number of customers and hence are labeled *higher order functions*.

According to this theory, there are about seven levels, a hierarchy of seven places (or cities) of different order, that result from these differing market sizes. By thinking about these functional levels in terms of such concrete things as hamlets, villages, towns, cities, and metropolises, we can better visualize this hierarchy. Such functions locate together in a central place as a result of certain linkages and aggregation economies mentioned in Chapter 4 and explained in detail in Part E.

Thus if there are groups of establishments, each having similar threshold levels, a hierarchy of places should occur over space. But the settlement pattern would still be one based on the original, even spacing of farmers and hamlets. What happens is that those higher order functions will locate at an already established lower order center, again in a way central to the market, and the result will be the creation of the next higher order center. For example, if town functions centralized at a former village (V) site, then that village would now move up the hierarchy to town (T) status. However, it will continue to contain all the functions of a village (although the number of establishments would be much greater) as well as those of the town. Hence, we might label such a center a *VT* center — that is, a town but with the reminder that it also has extensive village functions.

At this point, the distinction between number of *functions* and number of *establishments* should be clarified. For example, a village may have two service stations, three food stores, two barber shops, and one drugstore. In this case, it has only four functions, but eight establishments. Thus, a town might have five service stations, four food stores, four barber shops, and three drugstores, but it has the same number of functions as the village above; it has more establishments, however, because of a greater market area. Hence a typical town (VT) has more V establishments than a village (V).

A hypothetical distribution of central places is shown in Figure 6.2, for

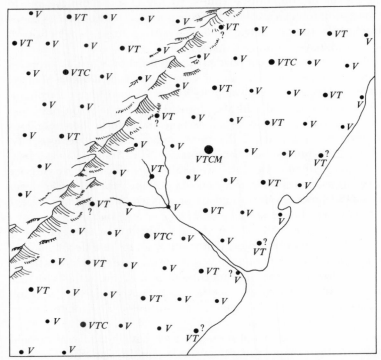

FIGURE 6.2 A Possible Pattern of Central Places.   Note the even spacing in the "plains" area. The hierarchy level is designated by the last
letter given — for example, *VTC* is a "city," and *VT* is a "town."

the same area used for the analysis of transportation cities. Several things
are quite different from the transportation city pattern. First, the distribution
of places is highly regular; an even spacing prevails, although disrupted by
physical features. (Transportation routes for the moment are assumed to be
different from those shown in Figure 6.1). Second, there are many more central
place nuclei than there were transportation cities. Third, there is a definite
order in the number of different-sized places. There are 57 villages (*V*), 20
towns (*VT*), 4 cities (*VTC*), and only one metropolis (*VTCM*), or 82 places
in all. Even so, the physical factors are somewhat distorted from the ideal.
If we had a completely uniform plane, there would be a progression in number
of places by threes — for example, 1:3:9:27:81 — whereby there would be
one metropolis, 2 cities, 18 towns, and 54 villages, thus making 81 places
in all. The reason this area has more cities and towns is because we are not
dealing with a single, uniform region. Some of the places are dominated by
higher-order centers outside the area shown on the map. It should be cautioned

that only a hierarchy of three different-sized places is shown. Nonetheless, this should suffice to demonstrate the manner in which territory is divided.

The second major spatial principle of this theory involves the range of a good or service. The notion of range is based on the assumption of threshold level, identical with the *inner range of a good,* and the central placement of various activities to serve this customer level. It is also based on the competition with other nearby centers of equal order of importance. Given this arrangement, the area from which each similarly sized center will draw customers would be halfway between each (Figure 6.3). Note that in the example, customers to the left of the ideal range travel to Town A in order to get the item at lowest cost; those to the right of the ideal range will travel to Town B for the same reasons. Thus the breaking point for customers is precisely halfway between the two centers, if both towns are identical in price of goods and in size. According to the pure central-place system, the breaking points will always be halfway between all similarly labeled places.

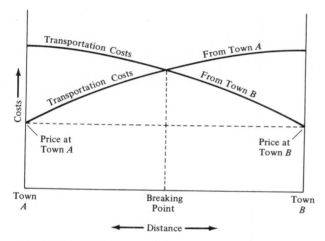

FIGURE 6.3 Breaking Point between Two Towns. This assumes that customers will shop in the town that offers goods at least cost when the customers' travel costs are taken into consideration.

The three aspects of range are illustrated in Figure 6.4. Note that each central place has an *inner* and an *outer* range for each good or service. The inner range is the ideal empirical range and is identical with the concept of threshold, or minimum customer requirements, discussed above. A smaller number of customers will not allow a business to operate at a profit. The outer range is the limit of territory from which customers would theoretically come to any given center. The empirical range is the actual range of customers as determined by competition among central places.

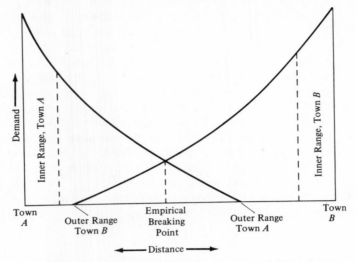

FIGURE 6.4 Inner and Outer Ranges of Goods and Services. Note that the outer range is the farthest distance people will travel to purchase an item in a community. The inner range is the farthest distance people would have to travel to constitute the minimum market population for a particular good or service.

Careful examination of Figure 6.5, however, which illustrates town trade areas, indicates that all towns are not the same in terms of their potential trade areas. Many towns along the coast and near mountains have less trade area and hence fewer customers than towns further inland. This means that they are not able to achieve customer levels to the ideal limit (as shown in Figure 6.3), but perhaps only to a level slightly beyond the threshold. Thus in competing with with full status towns, they are not going to fare very well. Other areas have "no man's lands" near them (shown with question marks) which may logically fall to them. For example, the breaking point between A and B, for instance, will not be the hypothetical dashed line of Figures 6.3 and 6.4 but will shift to the right, so that Town A will become more important and Town B will become less important. Both towns may have the same number of functions, but they will vary greatly in number of establishments and hence in territory controlled.

One empirical way to compute the breaking point on the real earth is to use population of the town as a surrogate measure for number of functions and establishment importance. (Researchers also often use measures such as retail floor space.) A gravitational formula, often called *Reilly's Law*, is a very useful calculatory device in this regard. Only two pieces of information are needed: (1) the general size, or mass of any two places, and (2) the distance

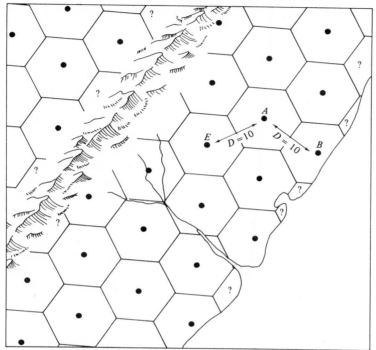

FIGURE 6.5 Breaking Points between Towns. Breaking points equidistant between towns result in a hexagonal tributary-area network. Partially developed tributary areas, however, may not be of adequate size to support the full services of a town, and the breaking point might be expected to shift toward the smaller center.

between them. From this, the breaking point (D) from the smaller center (P_1) can be computed as follows:

$$D = \frac{d}{1 + \sqrt{\dfrac{P_2}{P_1}}}$$

where d is the distance between places, $P_2)$ the size of the larger place, and P_1 the size of the smaller place. Thus, for example, if Place A in Figure 6.3 has a population of 20,000 persons and Place B has a population of 5000, and the distance separating A and B is thirty miles, then D, the breaking point from B, will not be fifteen miles as shown by the dashed line, but only ten miles. This formula works for all kinds of trade area estimations and is also of considerable value for computing the territorial domain of centers within cities.

In fact, the trade areas of cities are much more complicated than shown above. First, there are different threshold levels, and hence range characteristics, for each good or service offered. This means that there are many different service areas of a central place. The trade area discussed above is merely a composite average (one kind of tributary area) for a number of similar types of goods and services. In practice, each establishment has its own competitive territory. Second, the trade areas will not be pure, as shown, but distorted to the extent that various "no man's lands" are picked up. This makes even similarly ranked places slightly unequal in population and importance. Finally, transportation routes, not yet considered, will cause serious distortions in the actual placement of the central places. The general effect is for centers to be located at accessible positions along transportation routes, that is, centrally in terms of time accessibility to customers but not in terms of the physical geometry. Such deviations from pure, even distributions cause still further deviations in the trade area patterns.

It must also be pointed out that even with the constraints mentioned above, there are many possible patterns of regularly spaced cities. Simply by starting at another place or by rotating the even pattern of city distribution, other patterns emerge. Clearly, time is involved in the development of any particular pattern. The fully developed pattern of central places does not occur simultaneously over an area. The places that first develop contaminate the placement of the ones that come later.

Cities that respond to on-site resources

Figure 6.6 shows the kinds of cities that develop at sites of, or very near to, a particular resource — for example, a mineral deposit, physical environment suitable for recreational purposes, or some other equally distributed feature. For example, in order to make use of minerals, the mining activity must be at the source of minerals. Inasmuch as many minerals contain impurities, it is usually advantageous to remove the waste material at the site. In the process of removal, it is also often most economical to carry on various other activities such as smelting and refining. Thus, this activity becomes the main economic base of a town or city. The location of such cities is, of necessity, governed by the placement of some mineral resource.

Resorts and recreational functions also must, of necessity, be placed where such resources are found. Thus, places at a sandy beach or near good mountain recreational land are selected and urban settlement occurs.

Cities and institutionally based functions

A fourth type of settlement is related to the functions that are located in particular places for a multitude of institutional purposes. County seats, state capitals, universities, prisons, military bases, and a wide variety of other government functions are examples. In many respects, such functions would

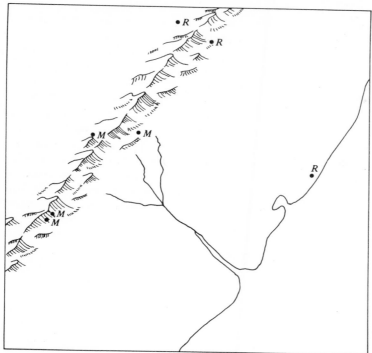

FIGURE 6.6 A Pattern of Cities Based on On-Site Resources. Such cities occur where a local resource is found — at the site of mineral deposits where mining centers (M) develop, or at ocean beaches where resorts (R) occur.

be located anywhere, inasmuch as they are not tied to resources, to surrounding areas, or to transportation (they often create their own route responses). Thus, the location of these functions and the kind of cities that characterize them are perhaps the most difficult to understand because of the multitude of factors and uncertainties involved.

The placement of state capitals in the United States is a case in point. In one sense, a state capital could be anywhere, and indeed they are found in just about all possible locations — in isolated, undeveloped areas, in large cities, and in small. One might logically think that the strategy for the placement of state capitals would be on the basis of geographic centrality, and some are clearly so located. Another strategy might be to locate the state capital in the center of population, but population centers change. Some states put the capital on the "frontier" at the time, in order to encourage state settlement. In short, because of the myriad different strategies, the time element, and the sheer politics of it all, it is difficult to arrive at a clear understanding of the specific placement of these functions. Perhaps the closest locational explanation relates to the human and institutional bases described in Chapter 5.

The same difficulties are encountered in understanding the placement of state universities, state prisons, and various other government functions. Political considerations, difficult to generalize about, also underlie the location of many military bases. All this does not mean that there are no locational principles. In fact, this is the difficulty. There are so many specifics required to explain each case that one is plagued with trying to explain unique placements. Figure 6.7 illustrates one possible arrangement for our study area. Note that the government center (G) is placed near the center of the land mass east of the mountains. It might be assumed that this is a state capital. For many government activities, accessibility to the general population is a primary concern. Many state capitals in the United States are centrally situated within states, or were in the center of the population mass when designated. The university (U) is assumed to be situated in an area somewhat remote from the major population center. Nonetheless, depending upon the spatial philosophies of the time, such governmentally placed centers might be located almost anywhere.

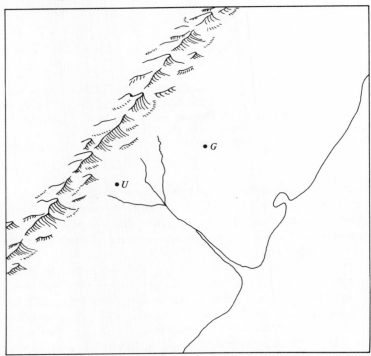

FIGURE 6.7 A Pattern of Institutionally Based Cities. These types of cities are located in particular areas for institutional reasons — for example, a government center (G) in the middle of the territory, or a university (U) in a more peripheral position. Such types of cities may occur in many different locations depending on the policies at the time of initiation.

Interpretation of a Hypothetical Urban Landscape

Given these four patterns of city placement, one can begin to see the complexity of interpreting an actual landscape of cities. Rarely is one city formed in response to only one of these factors. Most likely a number of functions combine to produce a settlement. Hypothetically, the more "hits" that occur — that is, the greater the number of overlapping functions — the larger any given place will be. Thus any given city might be a state capital, a transportation center, and a central place, and might have some local resource feature as well. The patterns that one looks at on the earth, therefore, are contaminated by this juxtaposition of various locational responses.

Patterns are also contaminated by time, or sequence, in settlement. If an area developed primarily as a central place pattern and later as a response to transportation routes, its pattern will be quite different from that of an area developed primarily on the basis of on-site resource responses.

Figure 6.8 shows one possible hypothetical pattern as based on the assemblage of all four types of cities in the study area. In this case, the general sequence over time is (1) transportation, (2) central places, (3) resources, and (4) institutionally based patterns. In other words, Figure 6.8 represents the consolidation of patterns in Figures 6.1, 6.2, 6.6, and 6.7. Note that some smaller places that entered later in the sequence have been consolidated with previously existing centers. You can confirm this by making a composite map of Figures 6.1 and 6.6 and comparing this with the pattern shown in Figure 6.8.

The composite pattern, however, is composed primarily of "hits" of the various functions. In this regard, the largest city to emerge is that near the center of the map. This city, labeled *ABVTCMG*, has been "hit" seven times: (1) as a periodic service center along transportation routes (A); (2) as a major break-of-bulk point at the crossroads of two transportation routes (B); (3) as a central place village (V); (4) as a central place town (T); (5) as a central place city (C); (6) as a central place metropolis (M); and (7) as an institutional center (G). These combined functions create employment, thus making this place larger than those around it. Not shown or anticipated on the composite map is the probability that manufacturing would also find such a large and strategically placed city to its advantage and thereby create another factor of growth in the city's economy.

This composite map deserves very careful reading. Note the comparisons between this pattern and patterns on other maps. Observe how the mountains have created a concentration of cities near them. Note also the relative absence of large cities in certain areas. Make a composite pattern of your own by using the central place map, Figure 6.2, as a first base. Then look at some actual patterns of cities and try to estimate their main *raison d'être* in each case.

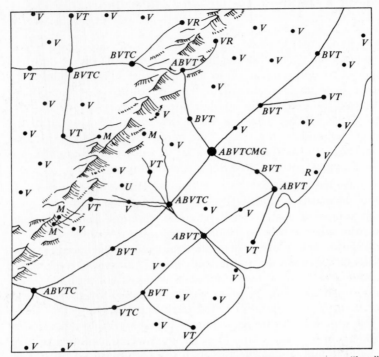

FIGURE 6.8 A Composite Pattern of Cities. When the various "hits" of city types in Figures 6.1, 6.2, 6.6, and 6.7 are combined, a composite pattern of cities results. Note that in this example it is assumed that the transportation routes and the urban responses came first in time and that the institutional cities came last. Thus the institutional city functions are located at the sites of formerly existing cities.

Toward an Understanding of Actual Patterns of Cities

It should be evident from the above discussion that the interpretation or understanding of any real pattern of cities is difficult indeed. First, each pattern is in process of change. Most important, it has evolved out of past conditions in a veneerlike fashion. City types that arrived on the scene first have affected the placement of functions that followed. Thus the actual city pattern in any area is a composite of the sequence of city occupancy over time. On a world scale, understanding the present pattern of cities can best be approached from the standpoint of hearth areas for the initial development of cities as these spread to other areas. By far the most important factor in this spread has been the development of cities from hearth areas of Europe through the colonization process.

Second, the pattern of cities can be understood on a detailed basis only by careful attention to what cities do. For example, inasmuch as cities are focal points for the control of the earth, they may be located strategically. They are also portals of interchange and hence would be greatly affected by transportation routes.

Third, cities reflect various features in the surrounding area. Some are service centers for agriculture and some are convenient places from which to assemble and distribute materials for manufacturing.

Finally, the pattern of cities reflects in their interconnection. There is a general hierarchy involved — few large places but many small ones. There may also be clustering of cities either for site reasons or because of the agglomerative economies to be derived in manufacturing or retailing.

One way to demonstrate further how cities reflect their surroundings is to examine an actual pattern of cities. The pattern of cities in the United States in 1930 (Figure 6.9), rather than a later date, is chosen in order to demonstrate that the interpretation of any pattern must be made within a particular time and that there is spatial contamination involved in past and future patterns. Also, the pattern was far simpler and purer in 1930 than it is today.

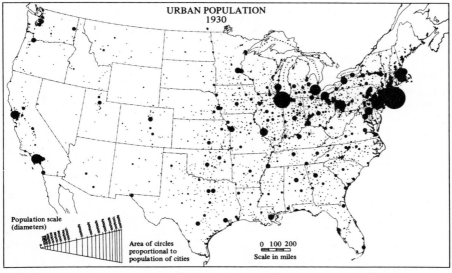

FIGURE 6.9 The Pattern of Cities in the United States, circa 1930. Source: National Resources Committee. *Our Cities: Their Role in the National Economy*, 1937, Figure 8.

The first thing you will note about the distribution is the tremendous unevenness in city densities over the area. The density is extremely high in the manufacturing belt, but relatively low in other areas. Your first goal, therefore, might be to regionalize the United States by its various city patterns. Your criteria might focus on similarity of pattern as based on the previous discussion. Thus, places with transportation-related, agriculture-related, and resource-related city patterns might be identified. A major regionalization could also be on the basis of city densities as they correlate with physical bases. Of particular note in this regard is the humid-arid distinction at about the one-hundredth meridian. On the humid eastern side, cities are numerous, particularly where there is a productive agricultural area such as in Iowa, Illinois, Indiana, and Ohio. On the arid and semiarid western half, the pattern of cities is sporadic. Here, cities are mostly concentrated in places that have possibilities for irrigation and in places where resources are found. The physical bases are also evident in the eastern United States, where city densities are extremely low in upland and mountainous areas like the Ozarks, the Adirondacks, and most of the Appalachians, as well as in low and swampy areas like those found in much of Florida.

A second regionalization or spatial generalization stems from the effect of transportation on city concentration. In this regard, the break-of-bulk opportunity in coastal areas has resulted in major concentrations of fairly large cities. Transportation routes have also exerted tremendous influence on pattern alignments, for example, in the Mohawk corridor of New York, in many places in the Midwest, in the South, and particularly in Utah, Idaho, and Colorado. In most such places, cities form beaded patterns along the major transportation routes.

Finally, clusters of cities have occurred in a few strategic places. In areas where manufacturing flourishes, a definite irregularity or clustering is evident, as in North Carolina, in much of New England, and in eastern Pennsylvania. Clustering is also much in evidence near Detroit, Cleveland, Pittsburgh, and Chicago — in fact, around many large cities.

A careful evaluation of such a pattern would require book-length treatment in itself. The historical stage would have to be developed in detail, as would the ways in which cities may have responded to particular conditions in past times. In addition, very careful buildings of "hits" of various city-forming functions would have to be derived on the basis of pure patterns and empirical data. A useful exercise at this stage, however, is to compare the 1930 pattern in Figure 6.9 to the 1970 map of the U.S. census. Make note of all major pattern changes and try to provide some explanation for them. Be sure to note how the 1930 pattern has contaminated the 1970 pattern — that is, in what ways the patterns are similar. How closely might you have been able to predict the 1970 pattern?

Conclusions

We have only begun to understand the nature and placement of cities over the earth. Full and comprehensive understanding would involve careful presentation of historical, functional, and theoretical information detailing the ways in which cities have responded and functioned at various times. What should now be clear, however, is that a full appreciation of city placements must be grounded on the four bases previously presented: transportation, territory (central places), on-site resources and institutionally based functions. Thus an understanding of these bases and their various combinations, interactions, and ramifications provides the key to appreciating what is perhaps man's greatest artifact — the city itself.

This chapter should have demonstrated that cities are no simple locational problem. They are, in fact, so complex that for the purpose of understanding other activities, we must use cities as givens. Cities are thus one of the many bases for understanding the distribution of many of man's other activities.

Finally, the intent of this chapter was to provide only certain exploratory insights into the nature, function, and locational characteristics of cities. As you progress through the book, future insights should be gained.

BIBLIOGRAPHY

Berry, Brian J.L. *Geography of Market Centers and Retail Distribution.* Englewood Cliffs, N.J.: Prentice-Hall, 1967.

———; Barnum, H. Gardiner; and Tennant, Robert J. "Retail Location and Consumer Behavior." In *Readings in Economic Geography*, edited by Robert H.T. Smith et. al., pp. 362–384. Chicago: Rand McNally, 1967.

Christaller, Walter. *Central Places in Southern Germany.* Translated by Carlisle W. Baskin. Englewood Cliffs, N.J.: Prentice-Hall, 1966.

Fielding, Gordon J. "Los Angeles Milkshed: A Study of the Political Factor in Agriculture." *Geographical Review*, January 1964, pp. 1–12.

Getis, Arthur, and Getis, Judith. "Christaller's Central Place Theory." *Journal of Geography*, May 1966, pp. 220–226.

Gottman, Jean. *Megalopolis.* New York: The Twentieth Century Fund, 1961.

Harris, Chauncy D., and Ullman, Edward L. "The Nature of Cities." In *Readings in Urban Geography*, edited by Harold M. Mayer and Clyde F. Kohn, pp. 277–286. Chicago: University of Chicago Press, 1959.

Hoyt, Homer. "The Utility of the Economic Base Method in Calculating Urban Growth." *Land Economics*, February 1961, pp. 51–58.

Johnson, James H. *Urban Geography.* New York: Pergamon Press, 1967.

Mayer, Harold H. "Urban Nodality and the Urban Economic Base." *Journal of the American Institute of Planners*, Summer 1954, pp. 117–121.

Murphy, Raymond E. *The American City.* New York: McGraw-Hill, 1966.

Putnam, Robert G.; Taylor, Frank J.: and Kettle, Philip G., eds. *A Geography of Urban Places.* Toronto: Methuen Publications, 1970.

U.S. National Resources Committee. *Our Cities: Their Role in the National Economy.* Washington, D.C.: U.S. Government Printing Office, 1937.

part b

Locational Problems with Production Sites Fixed— Noncommercial Economies and Extractive Activities

"Under the general term 'Destructive Occupation' should be classed all kinds of exploitation of the earth whose object is to take raw materials from it — mineral, vegetable, or animal — without restitution of any kind. . . . Among the various forms of destructive occupations some are of a normal and systematic character, while others, on the contrary, are carried out with an unrestrained intensity that makes them well deserve the German name *Raubwirtschaft* — 'robber economy,' or more simply, devastation. Destructive, or robber, economy is in a way a special form of wild-fruit picking, but it makes a far more violent attack upon nature. . . . It seems strange that this devastation should be the particular accompaniment of civilization, while so-called savages know it only in its less extreme forms.

Jean Brunhes, *Human Geography*. Translated by Ernest F. Row (London: George G. Harrap, 1952), p. 147.

VII

Locational Features of Noncommercial Economies

The noncommercial economies are the exceptions to the rule. Most of the world's people are engaged in serving other people (tertiary and quaternary pursuits) and in manufacturing — in short, in producing things that can be traded or exchanged. Moreover, most people of the earth are specialists in that they do not directly provide their own food, shelter, clothing, tools, or other material items. Each person is highly dependent on the other for his existence. This is not the case, however, in the noncommercial, largely subsistence economies, which are extremely inefficient by comparison.

In some respects, the noncommercial or primitive economies mirror in present-day terms the plight of the entire world population in prehistoric times. Physically and economically isolated from the mainstream of world development, the people living in primitive economies represent a residual population. They are often left in the foreboding environments that provide few opportunities for a technologically poor people and thus offer little latitude for experiment and no grace for failure. In almost every respect these people live on the margins of the good earth. Those in the high latitudes and desert areas are fortunate to eke out a subsistence living from the meager table that Mother Nature has provided.

Although explanations of why these primitive peoples are found in such unfortunate locations vary greatly, most contain the implication that they have been treated unfairly. One rather popular explanation for the advanced peoples is that general cultural and economic progress has resulted in those places offering an optimum environmental challenge to man. The primitive peoples, therefore, have been treated unfairly in terms of physical environment. If the challenge is too harsh, however, man can do little but remain relegated to a hand-to-mouth existence, as are many primitive peoples today. If the challenge is too easy, as perhaps it is in some tropical areas where food is readily available, then man again fares poorly with regard to economic and technological progress; instead, he focuses on superstitutions, taboos, ceremonies, and general shamanism — activities fascinating to the anthropologists but in other ways a tragedy of opulence.

A second theory suggests that the ancestors of today's primitive peoples were the most adventuresome of the world's prehistoric peoples. These were the people who ventured the farthest from the heartlands of population and, as it turned out, civilization. Thus the primitive peoples of today may have been the great frontiersmen of yesterday who pushed — or were squeezed — farther and farther outward until they found themselves more and more on the margins of the good earth and trapped into a stagnant existence.

The more verifiable theory, however, is that of acculturation. Evidence demonstrates that the more contact a group has with other peoples, the greater will be its technological and general economic progress. Thus the peoples of the Western world, heavily engaged in exploration and trade, learned many things of value through the resulting contacts. The noncommercial peoples are, by definition, those who have long been isolated from contact with other peoples of the earth.

One might wonder why primitive peoples do not move to other, better lands. This did occur in the past, and considerable economic progress was made. Most such movements, however, were forced; it seems that where man can eke out a living, he is fairly firmly placed. Aside from this, there are several factors that discourage such movement. First, these peoples are isolated and unknowledgeable about the nature of the earth. They are not aware that they are occupying the least productive parts of the earth. Second, the lands on their peripheries are already occupied by other peoples. Inasmuch as most of these primitive peoples prefer to avoid contact with outsiders, such occupation stands as a major barrier to migration. Finally, they have so little surplus in food or resources and are consequently so tightly tied to the resources of the land, that they have no latitude for experimentation or territorial exploration. One might say that they must keep their noses to the grindstone to such a degree that they are not free to seek out better opportunities in better areas.

Some Micro Locational Principles

The primitive peoples are fairly easy to understand from a micro locational standpoint; they are found at or very near the source of their food. (In "advanced" economies, the food sources are usually found at great distances from the consumers.) Thus, food is a dictating element in their locational arrangement. For example, in simple gathering societies, food is consumed where it is taken, or in fishing-oriented societies, for example, the village is near the body of water supplying the fish. In simple gathering societies, the people go to the food, not vice versa. In herding societies, the nomads move their camps with their herds in search of new pastures. In primitive agricultural systems, the villages are found close to the fields. Perhaps the only locally challenging aspect of noncommercial economies is the choice the people make among alternative food sources.

These people are almost totally involved in obtaining sustenance for their daily existence. There are few specialists among them; all are involved to some degree in providing the basic necessities for survival. Thus primitive economies tend to be highly cooperative and communal in nature — the individual works not for his own benefit or that of his immediate family, but for the clan as a whole. These noncommercial economies tend to favor homogeneity among individuals more than do the commercial economies.

Another characteristic of primitive economies is the small number of people generally found in any given camp, village, or gathering. The general rule is for assembly in small bands. This is perhaps a reflection of the limited nature of food in many areas, where the land is unable to support large numbers of people in a single cluster, given the nature of the economy. Although such people are nominally part of some national state, they are little affected by political boundaries. Most of them know little, if anything, about plant or animal domestication, soil characteristics, or specialization and trade. Since nature dictates the location and locational responses of these peoples, they are almost entirely at her mercy.

Yet peoples living in primitive economies are clever and resourceful in ways that modern man is not. First, they use nature's resources, whether animal or vegetable, to a much fuller extent than does modern man. The Eskimos' ingenious use of all parts of available animals — for food, fuel, clothing, tools, and shelter — is a case in point. Certainly, little is wasted in these primitive economies. By contrast, modern man undoubtedly throws away more than these people use. Equally inspiring is the balance with nature that many primitive peoples, like the early American Indian, have achieved without scientific knowledge. They do not upset their resource balance, nor do they overuse or overkill their food supply. Again in contrast, modern man, with his tremendous misuse of many resources and his eradication of many wild animals, shows little conservation skill. Primitive peoples, on the other hand, can little afford to abuse nature. The penalty for such abuse is often death.

Primitive man carefully protects the resource that is the mainstay of survival. If he is a herder of animals, he avoids killing them, but concentrates on using renewable features. If he is a paddy rice farmer, the preservation of the soil is paramount for survival, and all other resources, including man himself, are bent toward this goal.

Nonetheless, scientists now believe that primitive man in the past has modified much of the natural vegetative and animal landscape. He has done this through ignorance, by burning, by migration paths, and in other ways. Many of these changes have not been beneficial and have resulted in major territorial migrations. Yet, ironically, such forced migrations may have proven beneficial in that he discovered much better areas and became sedentary.

Absence of Cities: A Key to Understanding

By understanding why primitive economies have no cities, we understand much about their nature, and also gain further insights into the nature of commercial economies. In this regard, there are at least five prerequisites for cities: (1) an agricultural or food surplus; (2) a means of transporting such surplus to a city and a method of distributing this food to people in the city who are involved in food production; (3) a technology beyond the neolithic, so that housing, water, and other necessities can be provided; (4) a culture amenable to accepting and protecting the city; and, perhaps most important, (5) a purpose for the city, or a function for it to perform. Clearly, cities exist for a reason. They cannot have any economic base they wish or be located just anywhere. Economies having no cities are, therefore, lacking in these basic prerequisites.

The satisfaction of these prerequisites leads, in turn, to other characteristics associated with cities, for example, literacy, law, an exchange medium, and a division of labor beyond mere family job allocation. In fact, these latter features are attributes of the term *civilization*, which has the same Latin root as the term *city*. By Western criteria, places without cities are uncivilized or barbaric.

The difficulty of obtaining a dependable and permanent food surplus that could be given to "nonproductive" people is undoubtedly the first barrier to the building of cities in primitive economies. Inasmuch as a city is also permanently placed, such surplus must be available to that place — an impossibility for a migratory economy. It is estimated that even with the development of agriculture, under very favorable conditions in ancient times, it took about one hundred farmers to provide enough food surplus to support one person in the city. Today, only about one-twentieth of a farmer's effort in the United States is needed to feed one city person. Given the fact that only the most "advanced" primitive economies have agriculture and that their agriculture is primitive indeed, even by ancient Tigris-Euphrates standards, it is obviously impossible for them to achieve the first prerequisite for cities.

Equally difficult to obtain is a means of acquiring such surplus for city needs. The earliest method of acquisition was religion-based taxation, or tithes. Some surplus was also extracted by force, but military force requires specialization of labor — a feature generally lacking in primitive economies. They do have a strong religious framework, but it is based on each person's providing directly for his own needs. The system that has endured longest and is most used today is taxation by the state, which was perfected by the Romans.

Once acquired, food must be physically transported to the city. The easiest method is by water. In the very early cities on the Euphrates, for example, food was moved to the city through an elaborate canal system not unlike that in Southeast Asia today. Yet, most primitive economies are land oriented. And although fishing is practiced, the rivers are not used for irrigation or for the growing of crops nearby. In fact, under a migratory system, a river suitable at one time of the year would not be suitable at another time.

But perhaps most significant, people in a primitive economy, as will be demonstrated, have no real need for cities. Until such a need is evident, cities will not emerge, nor will these economies emerge from the primitive stage.

Types of Noncommercial Economies

The truly primitive economies include, in ascending order of economic advancement: (1) primitive gathering — characterized by hunting, fishing, and the gathering of materials close at hand and supplied by nature; (2) primitive cultivation — characterized by the practice of a rudimentary, domestication type of agriculture in an attempt to improve nature's offerings; and (3) primitive herding — various nomadic economies in which selected indigenous animals are "domesticated" and aided in their survival. All three types are migratory and nomadic over the long run and are limited to a level of subsistence barely above the minimum for survival. In order to supplement their main food activity, all engage at times in simple gathering of things that nature provides.

As primitive, subsistence-type activities progress to highly specialized activities, more and more people are generally found in each group[1]. For example, while there are only a few thousand primitive gatherers and about one hundred million primitive agriculturists, there are almost a billion persons engaged in "paddy"-type, intensive subsistence agriculture. Finally, there are almost two billion persons directly involved in commercial-industrial economies. In fact, about one-third of the world's population resides solely in urban environments. Thus it is evident that in terms of the world's peoples, the primitive economies are the exception to the general rule. In terms of the amount of area utilized by each, however, the less specialized activities are comparable to the more advanced commercial economies.

If the various economic activities were to be discussed on the basis of

[1]A notable exception to this progression occurs in the case of herding, or the nomadic sector. Although herding is generally considered to be a more advanced activity than primitive agriculture, it has considerably fewer people — only a few million herders as compared with about one hundred million shifting agriculturists.

the numbers of people involved, the primitive economies would hardly receive mention. Studying them is important, however, in differentiating commercial systems from others and, consequently, in understanding the locational patterns of man and his activities in the advanced economies. Charles Lindbergh summed up this attitude in the July 4, 1949, issue of *Life* magazine as follows:

> Wilderness expeditions in Africa, Eurasia and the American continents brought me to an appreciation of nature's extraordinary wisdom. I found myself in the fascinating position of moving back and forth between the ultracivilized on the one hand and the ultraprimitive on the other, with a resulting clarity of perspective on areas between — a perspective that drove into my bones, as well as into my mind, the fact that in instinct rather than in intellect is manifest the cosmic plan of life . . . in wildness there is a lens to the past, to the present and to the future.

One way to demonstrate this comparison is to classify economies according to the proportions of the population directly engaged in the various economic sectors (see Chapter 1). In primitive economies, almost the entire population is directly engaged in primary activities (Figure 7.1). Practically absent as full-time occupations are such sectors as manufacturing, trade, and personal services. In other words, there is little specialization of labor among activities except for male-female distinctions in jobs. (Incidentally, in the hunting and herding economies, males secure the food, but in the primitive agriculture economies, females have this job.) In contrast to primitive economies, advanced commercial economies usually have less than 10 percent of their population engaged in the primary sector. The largest occupational category is the quaternary or service category. In the United States, even the number of persons employed in the secondary production sector is dropping as machines replace labor.

The items that the primitive economies lack, therefore, constitute the critical differentiation between noncommercial subsistence economies and commercial economies. The nature and purpose of such things as cities, specialized agricultural areas, and industry can thus be better understood by examination of the reason that some peoples of the earth are not able to obtain these.

The reader should note that the very intensive paddy-agriculture economies characteristic of much of Southeast Asia are not considered to be truly primitive economies. This rice-dominated system accounts for about one-third of the world's population, is sedentary, and occupies a considerable portion of the earth in an intensive way. It is my contention, however, that this kind of agriculture-based society is (1) not as primitive as usually supposed, although admittedly such peoples are largely ignorant of characteristics associated with civilization, and (2) not fully subsistence oriented. Moreover, these economies support large cities where considerable trade occurs. Although they are discussed in this chapter as noncommercial economies, rice-dominated systems really

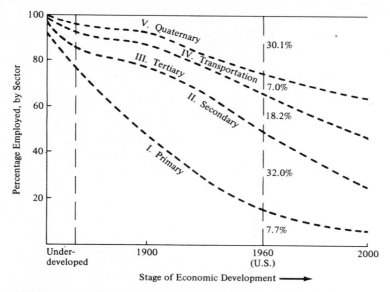

FIGURE 7.1 Relationship between Stage of Economic Development and Percentage of Labor Force Employed by Economic Sector. Note that there is a tendency over time for the primary sector to contain a smaller proportion of the labor force whereas the quaternary sector takes an increasing share. Based on the United States from about 1850 to 1970.

lie somewhere between the truly subsistence and the truly commercial economies. A distinction is thus made between the primitive, noncommercial and subsistence economies of herding, gathering, and rudimentary agriculture — hereafter labeled *primitive economies* — and the intensive, rice-dominated economies, hereafter called *traditional economies*.

Primitive gathering economies

The primitive gathering, hunting, and fishing economies are becoming more and more of a rarity on earth. At most, they account for only a few tens of thousands of persons, who are limited to small groupings in the vast areas where they are found. These are the peoples who are restricted largely to the more difficult environmental areas: (1) the far northern latitudes; (2) the central tropics of the Amazon and Congo basins; (3) the harsh margins of certain desert areas such as the Kalahari (home of the Bushmen) and the Australian deserts; and (4) isolated parts of certain Pacific islands, namely New Guinea and various Melanesian islands. In many of these types of areas they are not the dominant people, nor are theirs the dominant economies. As such, these people occupy but small pockets of the earth and engage in the most rudimentary economic practices.

It is often said that such people, while limited in number, occupy at very low densities vast areas of the earth. This is probably an exaggeration. In fact, such primitive peoples are huddled together in small bands over widely scattered areas. They do not truly occupy even small areas of the earth except in a very transitory way. The vast areas on maps generally labeled "occupied" by these primitive economies — the northern high latitudes, many parts of the tropics, and the fringes of vast deserts in Africa and Asia — are not really so occupied inasmuch as they contain only a few small bands of people wandering about a vast, empty place. Moreover, since there are large seasonal movements, most areas are void of population during most of the year. In this regard, these peoples represent true residual populations now occupying areas long ignored by the remainder of the earth's population. On the other hand, as "civilization" grows, it does encroach on some of these areas and peoples, thus making such types of economies even smaller and less significant on a world basis.

Detailed anthropological studies of peoples in primitive economies have focused on their social structure, their customs in regard to courtship, marriage, birth and death, and their religious practices. As residual populations, these peoples have provided anthropologists with much valuable data and many important insights about prehistoric societies.

In the far northern environments, hunting and fishing are the mainstay of economic survival, but the predominant economic activity in these environments is primitive herding — a more advanced system. In the tropical areas, gathering of a fairly abundant assortment of foodstuffs, supplemented by hunting, is the main activity, but the predominant economic activity in the tropics is the more sophisticated "slash-and-burn" type of migratory agriculture. On desert margins, food gathering has been replaced by the herding of animals from place to place in order to increase animal yield. Thus the primitive gatherers (whether of plants, animals, or fish) represent those peoples who have made the least progress, even within a primitive framework.

From a locational standpoint, however, the gathering economies are fairly easy to understand inasmuch as they are so closely tied to the natural food resources. These economies seek fulfillment only of man's simplest and most basic needs: food, shelter, and tools. In this regard, people living in such economies are the true scavengers of the earth. They merely assess the bounty of nature lying before them and work out the locational strategies that will best allow them to partake of this bounty.

An example taken from the far-northern tundra areas in Canada makes the locational strategies clear. In this area, animals migrate from the forest lands in the south to the tundra area in the north during the several months of summer. Fish are most easily caught in winter. This means that to enjoy these resources, man must move with the resources at various times of the year. Second, no one area provides a year-round food resource. Therefore, man here is at the mercy of these animal paths. His locational strategy is therefore to locate in those places affording him maximum interception of the range patterns and trails of animals. (In the fall and winter he leaves the marshy tundra area in favor of coastal locations where he can partake primarily of fish.) He does not domesticate or herd these animals; he merely takes, in a sensible and renewable way, the animal resources at hand. His only domesticated animal is the dog, which is useful for hunting, a good scavenger, and helpful for transportation and protection.

Such peoples are diminishing in number as a result of their plight when they meet more advanced peoples. For example, the Alaska Eskimos have not been able to maintain their old way of life after the coming of the white man. The Eskimo has become more sedentary, has begun to use guns and various other hunting methods, and has overkilled much of the animal resource. More and more he is finding himself at the mercy of both "civilization" and nature.

It has been argued that because of their culture, such gathering peoples reject many opportunities available to them. However, given the foreboding environments in which these people are found, it is difficult to find much that they are overlooking or are treating as taboo. The general framework appears to be based on a highly rational survival instinct. In very meager areas, such as the desert regions of Africa and Australia, these people are eating just about everything humanly possible — for example, lizards, frogs, snakes, ants, all manner of roots, eggs, and game. Perhaps the surprising feature is the large number of things that are not considered taboo, as they are in "civilized" places. It is difficult to think of any other way so primitive a people could survive in such a harsh environment.

Primitive herding economies

Primitive herding is carried on in two of earth's major physical environments: (1) the far northern areas of Europe and Asia, and (2) the margins of many Old World deserts. The best-known people in the first area are the Lapps, who herd reindeer — or at least provide protection for them — and who attempt to increase the reindeer yield over that which might occur naturally. The best-known people in the second area are the desert nomads, such as the Bedouins in North Africa. The people in the second area are in many ways more advanced than those in the first and are many times more numerous. In fact, the nomads of Saudi Arabia, Afghanistan, Mongolia, and parts of North Africa number some ten million persons.

Both herding economies, however, attempt to increase animal reproduction by protecting the herd from enemies, leading them to new forage areas, and otherwise attempting to work in cooperation with the animals. Both economies are also based on an extremely sparse and only seasonally adequate vegetation for animals. In both cases, therefore, seasonal migration is involved.

Inasmuch as the forage is extremely scanty in both environments, a considerable overall area, estimated at more than 100 acres, is needed for each animal. In most desert areas, ten days is about the maximum length of stay before nearby forage is depleted. Because of such sparse vegetation and the great loss of energy consumed in the seasonal migrations, only a very small percentage of the world's animals (certainly less than 5 percent) are so herded. The herds are generally small, as are the groups who herd them.

Such environments also largely dictate the kinds of animals chosen for herding, which are those indigenous to the area and most easily "domesticated." In the dry areas, animals that can survive on little water and that can forage on scanty and short vegetation are chosen for herding. These include the sheep, the goat, and the camel.

The distances to which such animals are followed or herded vary greatly in different areas. In Eurasia, such distances may amount to hundreds of miles in a year. In desert areas where mountains are nearby, the horizontal distance traveled may be only forty or fifty miles, and the vertical distance a few thousand feet. Obviously, if the mountains provide an excellent opportunity for the seasonal migration of animals over a small area, possibilities for permanent settlement occur. Where such settlement does take place, the economy changes to a more diversified type and emerges from a primitive to a more modern kind. In fact, much agriculture in Europe and in the western part of the United States is based on seasonal migration of domesticated animals — a process called *transhumance*.

An important characteristic of primitive herding peoples is the care with which they use their animals. In most cases, animals are not killed except on special and ceremonial occasions. Instead, renewable resources are used, such as wool, hair, milk, and even blood, which (among the Bedouins and others) is tapped from the live animal. The diet of such people is supplemented by the gathering of available plants and nonherded animals. Unlike the primitive gatherers, however, the gathering done by herding peoples is somewhat incidental to their herding. They are therefore somewhat more specialized and thus more dependent on a single food source than are primitive gathering societies, which have a diversity of foods.

Because of their greater specialization, many herding peoples also engage in limited barter and trade. Thus, theirs cannot be considered a strictly subsistence-level economy. In fact, the nomads of much of Asia are far less subsistence-oriented than are the rudimentary agriculturists — the next higher order of primitive economies.

Primitive agriculture economies

A surprising two hundred million persons, a population equal to that of the United States, are involved in a primitive agricultural economy in tropical areas. Such primitive agriculture includes the shifting of fields and villages over time and a general method of clearing the natural vegetation called *slash and burn*. Crops are grown on the basis of the simplest notions of plant and animal domestication. The surplus is so limited, however, that crops must be grown the year around, thus limiting this type of agriculture to tropical areas.

Very simply, the practice is as follows. Small bands of people gather in tribal villages from which they go forth to clear fields for planting by banding and burning. The ash-laden fields are then planted in the most rudimentary fashion by use of crude sticklike "hoes." No field preparation other than this is involved. Soon the natural vegetation takes over again or the soil is depleted, and new fields must be found. Nonetheless, careful study of such field rotation systems has revealed a conscious and rather structured pattern of field rotation. Consequently, many of these people are sedentary over the short run and are able to carry on an exchange with nearby tribes. Those who have been most fortunate also have time for nonfood pursuits such as making pottery, carvings, and various religious and prestige items.

Even so, this rudimentary agriculture is just a step above the herding of animals as practiced by the Lapps. The primary difference between this primitive economy and others occurs in the division of labor. Women do practically all the field planting and field work in the primitive agricultural system, whereas men do most of the hunting, fishing, herding, and gathering in other primitive systems. The former system frees men for other pursuits during certain parts of the year and has resulted in the development of considerable cultism and ceremonialism — perhaps certain innovations as well.

One result of partially cleared fields is the ability to "farm" on extremely steep slopes. Thus the need to be highly selective in land is diminished. On the other hand, slope farming creates some spatial disparity in resources between land and stream so that spatial juxtaposition does not occur. Consequently, the primitive agriculturalist spends much of his time traveling from village to fields, village to stream, and village to various hunting and gathering places. His village location is, at best, a compromise among these uses.

Traditional economies: intensive agriculture

A number of names have been applied to the paddy-type agricultural economies in much of Southeast Asia. They have been referred to as primitive or rudimentary agricultural systems, as subsistence or noncommercial economies, as *sawah* (rice field) agriculture, as traditional economies, and as overpopulated and underdeveloped areas. In one sense, this system is a little of all of these, but in another, it fits none of them perfectly. First, it is not the most intensive agricultural system in terms of yield, perhaps not even in terms of intensity of use per given unit of land (certainly the vegetable-garden agricultural system and the factorylike poultry, dairy, fish-farming, or hydroponics operations of advanced countries are far more intensive). Even the rice yields are higher in such commercial economies as Australia, Egypt, Japan, Italy, and the United States than they are in most of the paddy-type agricultural economies. Furthermore, this agricultural system is neither rudimentary nor simple. It is fairly complex in its interconnections between man, animals, crops, and the soil. It is, of course, highly labor and land intensive, but one might counterargue that much of American production is capital intensive. Moreover, the paddy system is not strictly a subsistence one. Trade occurs and surpluses are sent to markets in exchange for other items. Finally, it is not strictly a rice economy inasmuch as other crops, as well as animals, are involved. In short, this is a particularly difficult activity to categorize. Perhaps the most fitting statement is that it is a high-density, sedentary, soil-based economy, lying between subsistence and commercial systems.

Perhaps something should be said about the general choice of crop grown. Rice has been justified as the logical crop, but the popular reasons are not the valid ones. First, it is not the most productive crop in the world (manioc, potatoes, and several other crops produce more calories per acre). Second, it is not an easy crop to grow inasmuch as it requires considerable labor for planting, diking, and soil renewal. Third, it is one of the most water-demanding plants found; the major species used is actually characteristically found in a swamp environment. Even in the subtropical areas, irrigation is required to obtain reasonable yields.

Rice has other characteristics, however, that outweigh such deficits and make it an ideal crop for sedentary settlement. First, as a grass, it depletes the soil very little. With annual soil renewal through composting, manure, nightsoil, ash, and other renewing elements, such soil is little affected by use. Certainly the longevity of the sedentary system amply testifies to this. Second, the flooding of the flat land required for rice growing, necessary during much of the growing season, prevents the land erosion that so often occurs with many other kinds of crops. These two factors alone make for a continued food resource whereby sedentary settlements can be maintained. Third, rice keeps extremely well, as do most grains, so that it can easily be stored for winter use or held in reserve in case of crop failure. Finally, it is a crop with many food uses so that a reasonable diet, based on rice as a staple, can be developed. For example, it can be eaten whole kernel in various forms and used as flour for various purposes. In fact, rice has become a whole dietary way of life for many peoples in the subtropical areas where it can be grown.

(In contrast, the bread grains have formed much of the staple diet in Western Europe.)

Rice is so deeply entrenched as the main staple in much of the Asian diet that it is grown even in areas to which it is not physically suitable. For example, rice is planted in many "upland" areas where flat land and humid conditions are absent. Ranking with some of the most impressive landscape features on earth, terraces have been built in mountainous areas. Here elaborate irrigation and soil-renewal procedures have been developed. Even so, these two forms are the exception to the general rule of paddy rice farming.

The nature of the paddy system is understood by noting the biotic interconnection among man, the soil, crops, and animals. These form a solidly linked system whereby soil replenishment is the key to survival. First, rice and other crops are planted that diminish soil productivity very little if nonedible material is returned to the soil in compost form. Second, animals are used to eat various crop and household residuals, and manure is returned to the soil. In this regard, many of these animals are best classified as scavengers — for example, the chicken, pig, duck, and fish. These animals eat the scraps of various vegetative, human, and animal components. They also provide the farmer with a supplement to his rice diet. Consequently, paddy farms commonly have ponds in which various kinds of vegetable matter and garbage are placed to feed carp and ducks. Man himself is also tied to the biotic cycle. The most well known practice is the carrying of nightsoil to the fields — nothing beneficial to maintenance of the soil is overlooked. Fortunately, rice has another very admirable characteristic — it is largely disease proof. Very few crops could withstand nonrotated and heavily contaminated cycles such as this and remain viable.

One result of the close biotic tie between man and the soil is the effect the proximity of man's residence has on field fertility. Inasmuch as the soil renewal material comes from the homesite of the paddy farmer and directly from human wastes, there is a tendency for him to renew those fields closer to him more heavily than those farther away. This is particularly noticeable around many farm villages — soil fertility and the resulting rice yields tend to decrease as one proceeds from the village outward. This occurs despite the fact that every effort was made initially to place homes on the land least valuable for rice farming. Here, proximity to settlement actually improves the soil rather than diminishes it, as is more commonly the case.

To the Western observer, the major detriment of the system is its buildup of "population." Given a system in which the land is fully occupied, migration or expansion is impossible, and primogeniture does not operate, the tendency is for an extended family system to develop so that more and more people must make do with less and less land. In fact, the average size of "farm" in much of the paddy farm area is one acre or less. This means that there is a labor glut.

Being economically rational, the paddy farmer attempts to conserve those items in smallest supply — that is, land and capital — and to maximize use of that resource in greatest abundance, namely, labor. Consequently, man does most of the things done by draft animals or machines in commercial economies. Moreover, he tends his land so meticulously and in such detail that many of the jobs could not possibly be done by machines, even if they were available. As long as no other occupational outlets exist, there is no incentive to substitute machine labor for that of man. Consequently, people in such areas are caught in a vicious circle. Children are needed to supply labor, yet the abundance of labor makes for little incentive to find substitutes for it.

One place in which the vicious cycle has been partially broken is Japan, where mechanized garden cultivators are rapidly coming into vogue. In Japan, where industrial jobs are plentiful and where other jobs exist in the cities, people are leaving the crowded farm areas for nonfarm work. In such cases, farm labor is becoming more scarce and mechanization can thus logically proceed. Of course, the use of mechanization also means more cash farming so that crops can be traded for items manufactured in cities.

Conclusions

This chapter has provided a scenario of how man may have progressed from a subsistence to a commercial economy and, particularly, how direct reliance on nature today restricts some people to particular locations and to particular types of economies. Here are cases where what man does is directly tied to the nature of the physical bases in his area. Here also is demonstrated the restricted nature of economic advancement in places where man must exert almost his entire effort to the provision of food for living. Without a surplus of goods in this pursuit, man's advancement appears to be permanently restricted. Thus, this chapter has provided an example of man's inability to choose where he will live: he is clearly at the mercy of nature.

In such primitive systems, man must be at or very near the site of his food. Inasmuch as the source of his food changes seasonally, he must also move. Here is the simplest type of locational problem wherein the place of acquisition, production, and consumption are all at the same point. Without spatial separation of such functions, there can be no territorial or occupational specialization and consequently no advancement made toward the four hallmarks of a commercial economy — trade, cities, the rise of various services, and specialization.

In summary, this chapter has painted a dismal picture for many peoples of the earth — a picture that should serve as the basis on which man can evaluate his progress and his future.

BIBLIOGRAPHY

Harris, David R. "New Light on Plant Domestication and Origins of Agriculture: A Review." *Geographical Review*, January 1967, pp. 90–107.

Jen, Mei-Ngo. "Agricultural Landscape on Southeastern Asia." *Economic Geography*, April 1948, pp. 157–169.

LeClair, Edward E., Jr., and Schneider, Harold K. *Economic Anthropology: Readings in Theory and Analysis.* New York: Holt, Rinehart and Winston, 1968.

Lewthwaite, Gordon R. "Environmentalism and Determinism: A Search for Clarification." *Annals of the Association of American Geographers*, March 1966, pp. 1–23.

Mead, Margaret. *Cultural Patterns and Technical Change.* New York: New American Library, 1955.

Redfield, R. *The Primitive World and Its Transformation.* Ithaca N.Y.: Cornell University Press, 1953.

Sauer, Carl O. *Agricultural Origins and Dispersals.* New York: American Geographical Society, 1952.

VIII

Fishing, Forestry, and Mining: The Extractive Activities

Fishing, forestry, and mining constitute the extractive activities. However, in terms of numbers of people, all combined they are minuscule in comparison with agriculture, the other primary sector component. At most, the extractive activities employ only 2 or 3 percent of the world's working population. Agriculture alone accounts for over one-half of the world's employment force. Nonetheless, the extractive pursuits are fundamental to the maintenance of any commercial economy. In fact, these activities are the first step in a long ladder of processing, manufacturing, and distribution activities, which would otherwise be nonexistent without the extractive commodity inputs.

The extractive activities, although only a small segment of the primary sector, are treated separately for at least two reasons. First, they are distinctive in their production characteristics. For example, the production of extractive commodities merely consists of harvesting the fruits of nature. Man does little to augment this bounty, although in the case of forestry and fishing he may work in cooperation with nature. Nonetheless, such commodities are not much augmented by man — a situation quite unlike agriculture, in which man enlarges the natural offerings tremendously — and in places he himself chooses.

A second and more important reason for separating agriculture from extractive activities is the difference in the degree of locational complexity between the two. The extractive activities are by far the simpler to understand. Obviously, such activities must occur at the location of the resource — that is, fish can be caught only where the fish are, mining can occur only where the minerals are, and timber must be cut where the forests are found. Thus, one of the locational elements is given — the place where an extractive commodity is produced is at the location of the resource as fixed on the earth.

Variables Affecting Resource Use

The major variables affecting these resources to be used, however, are based on a number of considerations. The first is the location of the market. Clearly, other things being equal, those resources located closest to the market will be used first. The extent of resource use will therefore be determined by market demand. If the demand, is small, only those deposits close to the market will be utilized, but if the demand is large, then production may occur outward to great distances. Of course, this must be tempered by the distributional characteristics of the resource. For example, if mineral deposits are plentiful, as in the case of sand and gravel, then even great demand can be satisfied locally. If the resource is parsimoniously distributed, then it will often be transported at great distance from markets.

A second variable is the quality of the deposit — its size, purity, and value. If the deposit is such that it can profitably be used — that is, it has met the accessibility conditions mentioned above — then this particular deposit will be considered in competition with others. The determination of deposit usability is subject to clarification based on quality. Conversely, extremely large deposits can cancel out some aspects of purity and value. Likewise, a high-value commodity, such as gold or diamonds, can be profitably worked in small deposits. Similarly, low quality ore can be made usable only by large-scale production, thereby requiring a large deposit. Thus the factors that determine the quality of a deposit, and hence its usability, are somewhat substitutable one with another.

To complicate the problem further, accessibility to the market and quality of the deposit also often run counter to each other and are therefore often played off against each other. Hence, a high-quality resource located some distance from the market may be as usable as a lower-quality resource located close to the market.

The manner in which these two variables might operate is demonstrated in Figure 8.1. Let us assume that there is only one market. Radiating from the market there are three distance-cost zones: T_1, T_2, and T_3. Within this territory the qualities of particular deposits are graded from A through D on the basis of overall quality features, excluding accessibility. Now assume that between the market and T_1, deposit types A, B, and C are profitable, that between T_1 and T_2 only deposits types A and B will do, and that beyond T_2 a workable deposit must be of type A quality. Thus the two variables of accessibility and quality are intermeshed in order to create the actual pattern of resource use in a region. Poorer quality deposits are often used close to the market, T_1, but are not usable farther away, say in zones T_2 and T_3. Yet there is a quality limit required near the market also, as shown by the fact that deposit type D remains unused even when in zone T_1. Likewise, in the second zone, T_2, there are many deposits of equal quality to those in use in zone T_1, but because of accessibility, these are unused.

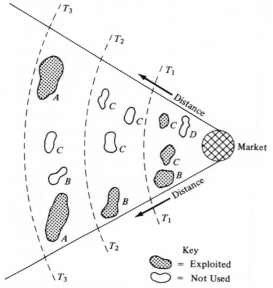

FIGURE 8.1 Generalized Relationship between Quality of Resource and Distance from Market. Note that the greater the distance from the market, the higher must be the quality of the resource.

Thus it is evident that considerable locational choice remains. A map of forest, fishing, or mining use reflects varying qualities of deposits in conjunction with considerations of accessibility to the market — not to mention various controls and regulations so characteristic of these types of activities. Nor are the contaminating effects of time removed from the actual pattern. It is very evident that all similar-quality resources are not being equally utilized. A challenging geographical problem is to determine the critical points at which accessibility and quality features are being equally played off against each other. For example, what ore content and deposit size must be found to balance out a particular distance cost from the market?

As indicated in Chapter 5, there is a strong relationship between the scarcity of a resource and its price. Inasmuch as price is one of the factors affecting the "quality" of a resource and hence its use, this must be explored in greater detail. Given price or value differences, how are they likely to affect the pattern of resource use? As a general rule, the more widely distributed the resource, the lower its price and the greater the number of production sites. Consequently, the more widely distributed an extractive resource, the smaller will be the average distance it is shipped to market. Thus, the lower the value, the shorter the haul and, paradoxically, the more important the consideration of accessibility becomes.

Because some commodities are produced close to market and are fairly widespread over the earth does not make them any the less important. For example, sand and gravel operations rank among the most important types of mining by almost any measure: volume, total value, and employment. Yet, because of their wide distribution, production occurs relatively near the demand source. Consequently, their value per unit of weight is also very low; therefore they presumably cannot "stand" long-distance transportation costs. Yet if they were parsimoniously distributed over the earth, their value would certainly increase, as would their average distance of shipment to markets. On the other hand, gold and diamonds are restricted to very few areas and consequently have a very high value relative to transportation cost. Because of this, such resources can be sought out and utilized almost without regard to distance from markets. Thus the factor of acccessibility must be carefully interpreted in terms of resource value, which, in turn, generally, reflects the degree of spatial scarcity. Moreover, it must be appreciated that the price of any item will thus vary from place to place, depending on spatial proximity of that place to the resource.

Unfortunately for our purposes, most extractive resources are neither as cheap nor as ubiquitous as sand and gravel, nor as expensive and scarce as diamonds and gold. They fall somewhere in a highly compromised and highly complicated middle. For most of the extractive resources, the location of production involves a fairly complicated and rather subtle interplay among three variables: (1) *proximity to market,* (2) *quality of the resource,* and (3) *price of the resource* at the market place.

As if these three factors did not make for sufficient complication, most extractive activities are also highly regulated and controlled in their nature and place of production. One reason they are so restricted is because of their exhaustible, or potentially depletable, nature. Another reason for tight control stems from the fact that many extracted commodities move in international trade or, as in the case of fishing, are obtained from international waters. Minerals in particular move heavily in international trade inasmuch as no one nation appears to have the full range of mineral resources it requires; at least, most nations find it more profitable and wiser to import some minerals than to exhaust their own or to use lower-quality domestic resources at higher costs of production. For national defense purposes, for example, many minerals are carefully kept in reserve as long as they can be obtained elsewhere. Fish, too, are increasingly caught in international waters. To protect this resource from depletion, international agreements and territorial water rights are common. Such characteristics add still another variable necessary to spatial understanding of production.

A final contaminating factor is the location of the market itself. We have already noted in the discussion above, where market location is taken as given, how it exerts an influence through accessibility. However, the location of the market also plays an important role, far beyond that of accessibility, in the determination of resource use. This is clearly revealed by examination of any world resource reserve (exploitable, but not used). The nature of mining and fishing is such that the existence of resources must be discovered. The exact nature of reserves is, therefore, not precisely known; indeed reserves increase drastically from time to time. But the major effect of markets is shown by the fact that, logically enough, man tries to find resources close to markets and relatively neglects the more distant potential resource areas. Consequently our knowledge of the extent of reserves is heavily biased by the location of the market and especially by proximity to those areas already in profitable production. Perhaps this is one reason why we have generally found that those areas which are heavily industrialized and are utilizing resources in abundance also appear to have the greatest number of usable extractive resources. In fact, this may be an illusion inasmuch as the remainder of the world has been examined only in a sporadic and often fleeting manner.

Depletability Considerations

The extractive resources are especially distinctive from most others in that their commodities are subject to depletion. In the case of mining, minerals are clearly fugitive — once they are used they are exhausted insofar as a particular site is concerned. Minerals are created over geologic time — a time of such length that the present distribution of mineral resources over the earth is fixed. Because minerals are depletable, numerous questions arise as to which resources should be used where and when and in what quantity in any given country. Questions of short-run versus long-run needs, reserves for national defense, and ways to achieve maximum use are often critical.

The general rule has been that the highest-quality resources are used first (that is, those with the highest ore content, of greatest size, or greatest ease of acquisition). Man generally works from the top downward on the resource pyramid thus formed. To date, this has proved satisfactory isasmuch as new methods to make lower-quality resources increasingly usable have been perfected. In this regard, the question of what is a workable deposit changes with time. For example, a hundred years ago only "pure" metallic copper, such as that found in northern Michigan, was deemed minable. Several decades ago, copper oxides with more than 15 percent copper were considered usable. Today, through large-scale mining methods and improved processing techniques, copper sulphide ore deposits of one percent copper or less are being worked.

A similar transition has occurred in iron ore. Several decades ago it was assumed that rich Mesabi iron ores would soon be exhausted and production would have to occur elsewhere. Ores having 50 percent or more iron ore content did indeed become scarce, but few foresaw the technological development that would permit low-grade taconite ores to be used. (Taconite, which contains about 30 percent iron, is the mother rock from which the richer iron ore came.) This has been made possible through the process of *beneficiation*, by which otherwise worthless material can be efficiently removed. Similar stories could be told about many other mineral resources. The point is that in deeming a resource usable, the general trend has been toward reduced deposit richness but increased size in the deposit; consequently, many small mines formerly worked are no longer considered profitable — they do not contain enough total deposit to make the investment worthwhile. Geographically, this means that more and more production is coming from larger but fewer sources. Thus many small but very rich mineral resources are currently considered non-workable.

Forestry and fishing are also potentially depletable resources. Numerous examples are available to show where such resources have been destroyed — the cut-over forested areas of upper Michigan and Minnesota, the demise of the sperm whale in the North Pacific, the ruin of Great Lakes trout (initially caused by the sea lamprey, which first entered the Lakes thru the Welland Canal in 1829, and later by water pollution), the demise of the Arctic fur seals, and most recently, the declining catch of Pacific Ocean salmon. Although more attention is being paid to making such resources available on a sustained yield basis through careful control and management, the general pattern is one of depletion rather than continuation. Certainly in the United States annual use exceeds growth in both fishing and forestry. The obvious fact is that without careful control, such resources could easily be exhausted in many areas.

One major economic difficulty in the deliberately controlled or slowed-down use of such resources is the problem of short-run profits versus long-run public gains. The general desire of the typical entrepreneur is to get as much as possible of the resource now, while it is in demand and while he has access to it, rather than later, when perhaps demand has shifted or he has lost out to a competitor. This is particularly the case in the fishing activities, where if one fisherman or nation does not get the resource, another fisherman or nation might. Hence strong controls on use have been placed on forestry through regulation and especially through the placing of many forested areas in the national sector under the control of the United States Forest Service. Use is controlled in the fishing sector by regulation.

Another important geographical implication of depletable resources is that activities connected with their extraction have little lasting impact locally. First, these activities employ few people. Second, the commodities are usually shipped to distant markets so that few connected activities generally occur in the area. Finally, and most important, such operations are often transient. About the only contribution made by earlier mining operations has been the ghost town.

Fishing operations have resulted in many abandoned fishing villages. Even more dramatic is the detrimental effect on the natural environment from large-scale mining operations — for example, copper, iron ore, coal, and even sand and gravel. Because of the negative aspects of the extractive activities resulting from the depletable-resource framework, they are of dubious value for purposes of economic development. Yet these are the activities that are highly prominent in underdeveloped parts of the world — for example, petroleum from Venezuela and the Middle East, and iron ore from Eastern Quebec in Canada, and from Chile. These extractive activities provide the raw materials of industry and are hence on the periphery of the industrial and urban complexes characteristic of the advanced economies.

Extraction Considerations

Because extractive activities generally represent depletable resources, their aim must be to maximize the resource take. In the case of mining, the goal is to obtain all usable minerals in a particular deposit. In the cases of fishing and forestry, the goal is to harvest only the "ripe" resource and to extract it in a manner that ensures a sustained future supply. Full take, however, is sometimes impossible in mining because of the inability to extract minerals from low-grade ores that may be part of a worked deposit; or in the case of underground mining, considerable ore must be left to support shafts and similar structures. Often, too, ore must be left because seams become so small that it is uneconomical to work them. In other instances, only the higher-grade deposit is considered economical to work, yet lower-grade material may be adjacent. In working the higher-grade deposit, the residual lower-grade deposit is often contaminated in such a way as to make it more difficult to use in the future.

In the cases of fishing and forestry, the problem is often one of overuse rather than full use. The optimum extraction framework would, of course, be to harvest only those ready resources in such a manner as to ensure a sustained yield. In case of fishing, only the mature fish would be caught, preferably after spawning. In net fishing, the net size would be geared to allow smaller fish to escape. In the case of forestry, only trees that have reached their full growth would be cut. These are logical goals but are often difficult in practice. Basically, such selectivity costs money and takes away from profits.

In fishing, such goals are difficult to practice, not only because net and other techniques have not been fully developed, but because of the nature of the resource. Fish, being a water resource, are not directly owned by any one party until caught. Given a number of fishermen in common waters, the incentive is to catch all one can before someone else does. Thus, without restraints on catch, the supply of many types of fish would soon be exhausted.

Most fishing is therefore highly regulated. Elaborate international agreements have been made with regard to national fishing water rights and quantity and time taken. This is particularly the case with regard to whale fishing in the Antarctic Sea, salmon fishing in the Pacific, and cod fishing in the North Atlantic. Many nations control the fish catch near their coasts by imposing twelve- and even fifty-mile territorial fishing limits. Despite all such attempts, many kinds of fish are rapidly being depleted as large-scale fishing techniques become more developed.

In forestry the goal to achieve maximum extraction has been hindered by several considerations. First, timber has historically been looked upon as a nuisance; most settlers wanted farm land rather than forest land. There is still much of this frontier attitude among many owners of timberland who look upon the timber as merely a short-term and one-shot affair — that is, the timber is removed in order to prepare their land for other purposes. Second, the growth of timber takes a considerable number of years. Compared with fish, which often have a three- to five-year cycle, timber growth in most areas takes upwards of thirty years. This length of time is beyond the "farming" time limits of all but the giant corporations. Hence, forests are not something an individual is likely to plant as a future crop. Even large corporations have been reluctant to practice tree "cropping" rather than tree "mining." Finally, it is often difficult to utilize only the mature trees because of the difficulty of getting such trees without injuring others. This can be accomplished only in a labor-intensive environment, such as in much of Northern Europe, where large-scale machinery is not involved. In much of the United States, particularly in the Pacific Northwest, the practice is to clear off cleanly all vegetation in a particular area. In this way, the area can be replanted to trees. Since they would all be the same age and be ripe at the same time, the area would be cleared once again at the next harvest time. The strategy here seems to be that of achieving both short- and long-run economies — short-run economies are achieved because large-scale machinery can be used to harvest the trees indiscriminately; long-run economies are achieved because of standardization in the age of trees the next time around.

This sounds pretty good in theory, but in practice it presents many problems. Replanting of these areas has often been delayed, and the denuded landscape causes serious problems. Erosion occurs in many areas inasmuch as many timber operations are on steep ground. The full cleaning of the vegetative landscape also ruins the area for many other associated uses, such as recreation, wildlife, and watershed purposes. Moreover, such a cleared area is shockingly ugly in comparison to the original treed landscape.

The difficulty in achieving satisfactory extraction practices in forestry is perhaps best demonstrated by the existence of the national forest reserves in the United States, Germany, and many other industrial nations. Thus, considerable portions of the forest lands were placed in the public sector and carefully managed in order to ensure their continuation.

Full Utilization Considerations

Even if forestry, fishing, and mining resources were extracted perfectly, according to the principles cited above, there would still be questions as to full use. For example, a tree used only for timber has considerable waste in the form of bark, small branches, slab cuttings, and sawdust. Fish used only for human food involves considerable waste in terms of the removed portions that could be utilized for pet food, fertilizer, and various oils. Ores often contain more than one mineral.

The general trend has been for fuller utilization of these former waste products by turning them into by-products. In the western part of the United States, for example, bark is being used to beautify urban gardens, sawdust is being pressed into small logs for use in fireplaces, and small, otherwise unutilized wood pieces are being pressed into flakeboard and used in the making of various compressed-board surfaces. (In fact, the outdoor burning of sawdust is now prohibited in many areas.) The very low copper ore deposits in Bingham Canyon, Utah, contain quantities of gold and silver which, it is said, support the cost of removing the copper from waste material. Natural gas associated with oil wells has become a major fuel.

Much waste, however, still occurs in areas where there is little demand for such by-products. Certainly, the selling of pressed fireplace logs in the vicinity of many forest areas would make little sense, and such logs cannot bear the cost of transportation to distant markets. Thus the further from the market that production occurs, the less likely is it that such extracted material will be fully utilized.

Substitutability Considerations

Most extractive activities are plagued by substitution possibilities with other commodities. Such substitution may occur both within and between production components. For example, stone may be substituted for lumber as a building material. Petroleum may be substituted for coal as a fuel. Indeed, energy may be obtained from coal, petroleum, natural gas, nuclear fuels, wood, and hydro and solar power. Likewise, in many cases metals may be substituted for wood, and vice versa; and aluminum may be substituted for steel. Of course, there are many food substitutes for fish. Hence, the demand for these activities may vary greatly from place to place as various substitutable items are in greater or lesser supply.

Thus each commodity is in competition with a number of others for the market. Most do not have a monopoly position (uranium, kyrolite, and certain rare minerals are exceptions). The production of these commodities, therefore, fluctuates greatly as the demand mix changes. For example, the use of petroleum is on the rise relative to coal both as a fuel and as a base for making chemical derivatives. The use of trees for pulp and paper is on the rise relative to their use as a fuel. Beef is on the rise relative to fish, although fish consumption is rapidly increasing in many underdeveloped countries.

Such slippage makes the analysis of any given extractive activity difficult. In fact, salmon fishing cannot be understood except in competition with other types of fish and other kinds of food. Many minerals have substitutable counterparts, nor are forest resources unique in terms of the roles they serve. Such substitutability allows spatial patterns to shift from one extractive activity to the other, thus creating a complex pattern of use. If timber becomes too expensive, mineral resources might be substituted. If steel becomes too high, other metals might be used.

Further Notes on Fishing

Simply stated, fishing must occur where the fish are — but where are they? What are some of the locational conditions? How does accessibility and proximity to markets specifically affect fishing areas? Which areas will be used and which will remain unused? How can one type of fish be substituted for another, or for other food? These are some of the questions that arise because of the discrepancy between where particular kinds of fish are found and where fish are taken.

Location of fish relative to the market has always exerted a tremendous effect on where fish were caught. Because fish are highly perishable, they must be delivered quickly, whether to the market for fresh consumption or to canneries for preservation. Consequently, most fishing has occurred near the major markets, which have traditionally been in Western Europe and the Eastern United States. Lately, Japan has also become a major market, and fishing has become most concentrated in the North Atlantic and the Pacific oceans.

As it turns out, fortuitous circumstances have also resulted in the great concentrations of fish in these midlatitude and northern ocean areas in the northern hemisphere. It seems that fish are mostly found, and certainly most easily caught, in shallow (that is, continental shelves and banks) cool, mixed waters, near forested continents. Here, plankton-forming materials are built up from the nearby rivers flowing from forested areas.

There are more than 30,000 kinds of fish, and they are found from the equator to the poles and at most depths of the sea. In fact, most salt water areas contain fish. What we are talking about here are those places where man has found fish to be most easily caught, most usable, and most accessible. That we are still in a hunting stage, rather than in any stage of aquaculture, is demonstrated by the fact that this potentially rich 70 percent of the earth's surface to date provides only about 3 percent of the earth's food.

In fact, a great number of fish, and certainly some of the largest, are found in tropical waters. Unfortunately, tropical fish rarely run in schools, whereas midlatitude fish generally do. Clearly where schools are found, the resource is purer and more profitable. In fact, almost all fish caught commercially are found in schools or, like the shrimp, the oyster, and the sponge (which are technically not fishes but which, for our purposes, will here be treated as such, as will the whale), in highly concentrated conditions.

There are also large numbers of fish in the Southern Hemisphere, but until recently, because of lack of accessibility to the markets, they were largely unknown and untouched. With the development of floating canneries and nationally owned fishing fleets such as those of Japan and Russia, fishing at greater distances from the markets can be developed. One major fishing area is off the coasts of Peru and Chile, where (even off a desert coast) the mixing current area has provided a major deposit of valuable fish. In fact, Peru has taken advantage of this deposit to the extent that it is now the leading fishing nation in the world in terms of tonnage. Major fish caught in this area include the anchovetta, tuna, cod, and many others. A similar new area is just developing off the southwest coast of Africa (another desert area), in which anchovy, flounder, herring, red snapper, and sardines are caught in great abundance. Today almost one-quarter of the world's fish tonnage is in the Southern Hemisphere, yet only a small portion of the tonnage was found here a decade or so ago. Perhaps the importance of the deposits in the Southern Hemisphere has been greatly underestimated. Although employing only a small percentage of the world's population, fishing is increasingly becoming the domain of large corporations using large-scale operations. One spatial implication of these large-scale and technologically advanced fishing operations is to allow fish to be taken at greater distance from market areas. This condition must be greatly responsible for the rising importance of fishing ground on the west coastal areas of South America and Africa. Another consequence is that the many small fishing villages and isolated canneries are disappearing. The general trend is to trade with larger ports closer to markets. The prime exception to this trend is the case of the American salmon industry, to be discussed below.

In order to understand the location of fishing, it is necessary to differentiate among the various kinds of fish. The first critical breakdown would surely be between fresh-water and salt-water fish inasmuch as this has obvious geographical implications. Fresh-water fish are relatively unimportant, however, and amount to only about 3 to 5 percent of the world's commercial catch, and about 10 percent of the world's fish consumption.

As might be expected, there are a number of ways fish can be classified. It might at first seem most logical to use their biological classification, which tends to break fish into two major types: the clupeoid, or herring family, accounting for about one-third of the world's catch; and the scombroid, or mackerel family. However, this classification provides little geographical understanding inasmuch as it includes both very sought after and very unpopular fish in each category and has little relationship to where or how such fish are extracted.

A much better classification for geographical purposes is according to general location and movement habits. Here, four types of fish might be distinguished: (1) *pelagic*. This includes all fish that feed on the surface of the water and roam widely. Such ocean life includes mackerel and herring, menhaden, tuna, and the whale (which, as stipulated earlier, for our purpose will be included with fish and fishing). (2) *demersal-mobile*. These are fish that live near or on the bottom of the ocean floor. Only those that prefer shallow bank waters would be commercially exploitable. Such fish include the cod, haddock, halibut, hake, sole, and flounder. As a general rule these fish are caught by trawlers rather than seiners, in contrast to pelagic types. (3) *demersal-sedentary*. These fish live near the bottom and remain pretty much in the same general area throughout their lives. They include oysters, lobsters, shrimp, and sponges. As a general rule the demersal fish cost much more than the pelagic because of the different costs in acquiring them. (4) *anadromous*. These fish spawn in fresh water, usually rivers, but spend most of their lives in salt water. The most important fish in this category is the salmon. As might be expected, these are some of the easiest fish to catch inasmuch as they run in schools and return to rivers to spawn. Consequently, many simple ways of catching them have been outlawed, and control is exercised over when and where they may and may not be caught.

Finally, a very useful classification is according to eating habits. The simplest breakdown is between those that eat plankton, which include the herring, menhaden, and mackerel, and those that eat other fish. The latter group includes the tuna and bluefish, which are usually caught by trolling with hooks rather than by snaring, as is the first group. The whale, on the other hand, is usually caught by an attack method, such as electric and explosive harpoons.

Most fish are caught for food, but several are used for other purposes and amount to sizable tonnages. These include the menhaden and hake. Menhaden are found in the Atlantic Ocean from Nova Scotia to Brazil but are concentrated in schools near the East Coast of the United States. Here, these plankton eaters are easy prey for fishermen and are caught in large numbers; in fact, they are by far the largest groups, in terms of tonnage, caught in the United States. These fish are used for a variety of purposes: as livestock feed; as fertilizer; as bait for mackerel, cod, and tuna fishing; for their oil; in the manufacture of oil, paints and varnishes; and even in the tempering of steel. The hake has also become popular as a bottom "scrap" fish, where it is taken in large numbers by Russian and Japanese fleets for use in making fertilizers, fish flour, and in the manufacture of glue.

These fish demonstrate a current trend in fishing products. More and more, resources formerly considered useless are being used in large numbers for industrial purposes. In fact, industrial use now amounts to one-third of the world's tonnage, in contrast with only 10 percent or so several decades ago. Undoubtedly many other uses for sea life will be found in the future.

Some fish types, however, are perilously close to extinction. The most notable example is the Pacific salmon, an anadromous fish. Because it is easy to catch, it has been subject to overfishing; because it must spawn in fresh water, it has been particularly injured by land-based conditions. Wastes from industries and cities have polluted many streams. Dams have destroyed the runs of many salmon. Soil erosion and the like have ruined lakes and streams that were formerly important spawning grounds. The present catch is only one-quarter of what it was several decades ago. The case of the Pacific Northwest salmon is even more critical inasmuch as the Russians and Japanese, with their large-scale floating cannery operations, have also found ways to catch the salmon successfully in the open ocean. In order to preserve the salmon, the United States has limited the types of fishing gear that can be used and the times at which fish may be caught, and has attempted to stock salmon by means of fish hatcheries. This has relegated the American salmon-fishing industry to primitive and relatively obsolete fishing equipment. Moreover, there are so many salmon fishermen that very few make much money from the operation.

This condition has led to a continuing controversy between the United States, Canada, and Japan over the salmon catch. The Japanese, by international treaty, agreed to restrict their catch to areas west of the 175th West Longitude, supposedly restricting them to Asiatic salmon. But with the ability of the Japanese to catch American-based salmon on the open ocean, new controversies continue to arise. What the future holds for the salmon industry is therefore quite controversial.

Whaling is a resource that would have been wiped out without international agreements. In 1946 the whaling nations of the time set up the International Whaling Commission, which tightly regulates almost every aspect of the industry in the Southern Hemisphere. (Incidentally, there is no such control in the Northern Hemisphere, and whales are quickly becoming extinct in this area.) Japan and Norway are the leading whaling nations, and about 60,000 whales are killed annually. Basically, the regulations restrict whaling to certain areas for individual countries and prohibit whaling in warm-ocean regions. They also forbid outright the killing of white whales and gray whales. For others, the regulations specify size, forbid the killing of calves or of cows nursing their young, limit the total amount of oil that can be taken, and restrict the operations of shore whaling stations to six months of the year. Nevertheless, certain types of whales, such as the blue whale, have been officially declared extinct.

Further Notes on Forestry

Forests cover about one-quarter of the earth's surface — about the same area as does agriculture. However, only about one-third of these forests are now considered productive enough to warrant exploitation. This means that only about one-twelfth of the earth's surface is favorably endowed for commercial forest operation. Nevertheless, two-thirds of this one-twelfth are dismissed as being inaccessible for use. Thus only about 6 percent of the earth's surface contains favorable forest lands. This raises three questions of paramount geographical importance: (1) What must a forest be like to be classified as productive and hence commercially exploitable? (2) What does the pattern of inaccessible forests look like and how is this pattern derived? (3) How are the potentially exploitable forests utilized?

Before these questions are answered, however, it might be well to note that some of the world's best forests in terms of productivity and accessibility have been destroyed. These former forests account for about 10 percent of the naturally forested areas of the earth and, as might be expected, were primarily located in highly populated and industrialized areas. Major denuded areas include vast parts of the midwestern states such as northern Michigan, southern Indiana and Ohio, most of Western Europe, and most of China and India. In the United States over one-third of the original forest acreage has been converted to other uses, and much higher proportions have been converted in other areas. In all areas but India the forests removed were of mixed coniferous and deciduous types. It is debatable whether such forests should have been preserved inasmuch as more profitable uses were made of the land, but surely much could have been done to maintain forests in certain of these areas. In fact, reforestation is occurring at great time and expense in many parts of Europe and China at the present time. Afforestation, the planting of trees on land not formerly covered with forests, is also occurring in many places.

Three major factors determine whether a forest is of sufficient quality for commercial use. The first is the general density of the particular type of tree desired. In far northern and high mountain areas, tree stands are generally quite thin because of climatic conditions. Here, scrubby trees are characteristic. Consequently, the board feet of lumber per acre in such areas is considered too low to be harvested. The same factor operates in many tropical forest areas inasmuch as the tree desired, for example, mahogany or teak, is often widely interspersed among many other tree varieties. Thus a thick forest alone does not necessarily ensure a profitable forest resource. However, the lack of stands in tropical areas is somewhat counterbalanced by the size of trees. On the other hand, some trees are so dense that they will not float and must be hauled overland or in barges to reach ports. Yet large trees tend to compensate somewhat for thinness of stand or generally lower densities. Third, trees that are more scarce, and thus in shorter supply, bring higher prices than do those more widely found. Again, value is a major factor in the determination of whether a deposit is profitable for use. The general size of the forest in terms of area covered is a final factor. A pure stand of good and valuable trees will nonetheless be considered unprofitable if such a group is not of sufficient size to justify the equipment and other features necessary for their removal.

The determination of accessibility to the market, or lack of it, is based on the same general features discussed above. Generally, areas are "inaccessible" if they are distant from major rivers that can be used for transportation and if they are not served by roads and railways. Thus many forests in tropical areas, those in high mountains, those in nondeveloped continental interiors, and those located in very hot or very cold lands present accessibility problems. Lack of transportation facilities in an underdeveloped area raises costs inasmuch as the timber company must bear the expense of providing them. To define something as inaccessible is thus another way of saying that the area has not been found profitable for other uses and therefore basic transportation facilities have not been provided.

For example, before the transcontinental railroads came to Washington and Oregon, forests in those states were considered inaccessible. The costs of building railroads for forest purposes alone were clearly too high. But after railroads were built on a subsidized basis, great amounts of timber from that region became profitable to use. In fact, Oregon is today the largest lumber producer in the United States.

Undoubtedly the reason so much otherwise usable forest land is considered inaccessible is that forests are generally found on land unfavorable for agriculture, industry, and other uses. Thus forests truly support frontier activities.

The limitation of inaccessible forests thus provides some measure of the urban-industrial intrusion boundary into underdeveloped lands. This area and associated frontier lines are shown in Figure 8.2.

It should be apparent from the above, however, that questions of deposit quality and accessibility are interrelated; moreover, a certain degree of substitutability exists, as was demonstrated in Figure 8.1. This is evident from the fact that so much otherwise marginal forest land in and very close to major markets has been exhausted, while inaccessible but otherwise excellent forests remain unused today.

In terms of future supply of forests, the picture looks fairly good. Certainly, the inaccessible forests will increasingly become more accessible and therefore more usable. Moreover, with increasing scales of operation many deposits now considered unprofitable may soon be usable. These two factors, coupled with a general philosophy of sustained yield in many parts of the world, make the future outlook for forests rather bright.

Classification of trees and forest types are also numerous. There are over one hundred kinds of trees commercially used in the United States alone. Many of these types have very specific and nonsubstitutable uses. For our purposes, however, we might recognize three main groups of trees: (1) coniferous evergreen, (2) deciduous broadleaf, and (3) broadleaf evergreen. The coniferous trees are generally softwoods, and the deciduous and broadleaf evergreen are usually hardwoods. Among the softwoods are such trees as fir, spruce, pine, hemlock, cedar, larch, cypress, and redwood, which are heavily used in the lumber industry, in the pulp and paper industry, and for general fuel use. The hardwoods include a wide variety of trees. In midlatitude areas, oak, maple, poplar, chestnut, beech, birch, elm, ash, hickory, walnut, cherry, and sycamore are used. In tropical areas, the hardwoods that are commercially exploited are mahogany, teak, ebony, and rosewood. With the exception of these, most tropical trees are used more for forest products than for lumber purposes.

Geographically, four types of forest areas can be noted: (1) tropical or broadleaf evergreen, (2) coniferous evergreen forests of far northern areas, (3) midlatitude mixed coniferous and deciduous forests, and (4) montane forests, which are generally coniferous. Of these, the softwoods account for about twice the lumber volume of hardwoods. However, the hardwoods are more expensive and are used for higher use purposes, such as tool handles, furniture, and various sports equipment. Softwoods are primarily used for lumber and in the pulp and paper industries.

These four forest zones are strikingly different in terms of the use to which the forests are put. In fact, there are a number of forest uses such as recreation, wildlife reserves, watersheds, and the like, but only the following uses will be discussed here:

1. forest products
2. lumbering

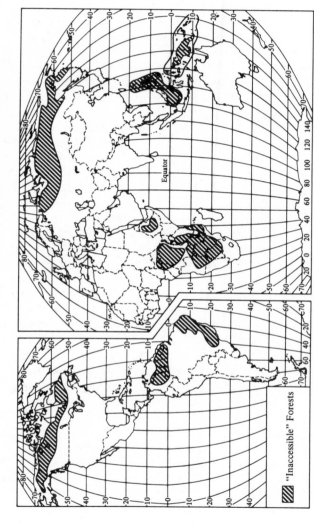

FIGURE 8.2 Generalized Boundaries of Inaccessible Forest Lands. Such "inaccessibility" is in part based upon better forest lands closer to the markets.

"Inaccessible" Forests

3. fuel
4. pulp and paper
5. chemical products

Forest products are particularly important in tropical forest areas. Here, such products include nuts (copra, oil, palm, ivory, kapok, and coir), leaves (coca), bark (abaca, quinine, and cinnamon), and sap (rubber). In midlatitude areas, forest products include naval stores from the loblolly pine of the southeastern part of the United States, where turpentine, tars, and pitches are used; bark (cork) and tanning materials; and such items as molasses. Aside from these items, a number of chemical products are derived from trees.

Both hardwood and softwood trees are used in lumbering. Softwood is used primarily for construction purposes and, like timber or roundwood, in the building of homes, bridges, piers, and so forth. Hardwood is used primarily for items of a more manufactured nature, such as baseball bats, bowling pins, furniture, pencils, railroad cars, and shoe heels. Tropical hardwoods are used for very fine furniture, for carvings, and for highly valuable items.

Fuel use accounts for about half the wood used from all the forests of the world, in terms of volume. However, in terms of value, fuel accounts for only about 10 percent of world wood use. Much of the wood used for fuel is inferior or is characteristically used in many underdeveloped parts of the world, where coal, petroleum, and other fuels are absent. Some major uses of wood for fuel in the United States and elsewhere include vast quantities of charcoal (hardwood). In much of Latin America, Japan, and other parts of Asia, charcoal is very inefficiently prepared as a supplement to coal. Another growing use is in the manufacture of compressed logs, primarily made from sawdust and scraps, for fireplaces. Perhaps the most distressing use of wood for fuel is along some of the major rivers in tropical areas. Many steamboats in these areas use wood, and giant mahogany and rosewood trees — trees of great value — are burned as fuel. Along many of these streams deforestation has become a major feature of the landscape. This was also the case along the Trans-Siberian Railroad when wood-burning engines were used.

In highly industrialized countries, full of "paperopolises," the demand for paper is increasing very rapidly. Newsprint, magazines, books, and vast new uses for packaging materials have caused the pulp and paper industry to flourish. Such activity is most concentrated in the coniferous softwood areas of the Pacific Coast and in Canada. Spruce, pine, hemlock, and fir are all heavily involved.

Many chemical products, such as rayon and various plastics, are so different from wood or other parts of the tree that it is hard to believe they are derived from wood. Some of the main chemical products include acetic acid (perfumes, plastics, rayon, solvents), acetone (solvents, acetylene, explosives), butadiene (synthetic rubber), charcoal (explosives, fuel, medicines, feeds), methyl alcohol (antifreeze, paints, shellacs, varnishes), ethyl alcohol, and various oils, tars, and solvents. One product, lecithin, is a by-product of softwood that is used for a wide variety of purposes. Most of the above products are really by-products of wood, being used primarily for other purposes, but there is a growing wood chemical industry quite akin to the tremendous revolution in petrochemicals.

Thus the "mining" of the world's forests represents the raw material for many different products. In many cases, the site of such raw materials exerts an important locational impact on the next stages of use. Hence an understanding of the major areas of forest commodities provides insights into the location of all related, raw-material-oriented activities. Furniture making is particularly affected in its position by the location of hardwoods in Michigan, North Carolina, and other areas. Paper-making industries are also found fairly close to the forest raw materials. With the use of recycled paper, however, market location may prove more important for the future. Even the tanning industries were at one stage locationally affected by proximity to oak and hemlock trees. Today, tannins are made chemically by chromium compounds or from the bark or extracts of certain tropical and subtropical trees.

Further Notes on Mining

While important as a raw material base for industry, forestry is nonetheless small compared with mining. There are well over 200 different minerals in use today, and each has special locations and uses. At least eight categories of mining resources are generally specified: (1) iron ore, (2) fuels such as coal, petroleum, and natural gas, (3) nuclear energy fuels such as uranium, thorium, radium, plutonium, and lithium, (4) construction materials such as clay, granite, sandstone, slate, gypsum, asbestos, and limestone, (5) ferro-alloys, which include manganese, chromium, tungsten, nickel, cobalt, molybdenum, and vanadium, (6) nonferrous metals such as copper, tin, aluminum, magnesium, zinc, and lead, (7) mineral fertilizers such as nitrates, phosphates, and potash, and (8) chemical resources such as salt and sulphur. It can readily be seen that a discussion of all these mining resources would require a book in itself. We will be content to develop some spatial generalizations.

Mineral resources are extremely widespread over the earth. To the casual observer, it might appear that minerals can occur almost anywhere. Nonetheless, mineral deposits are closely associated with particular geological features. For example, mountainous areas such as the Urals, the Appalachians, and various European ranges are outstanding in their abundance of minerals. In the United States, the Appalachians, particularly in West Virginia, are noted for coal. Minnesota and upper Michigan are important for iron ore, although it is also found at Birmingham, Alabama, and in many parts of the Rocky Mountains. The Gulf states, particularly Louisiana and Texas, are notable for the mining of petroleum, natural gas, and related chemical products. Bauxite is found in the Ozarks. The Rocky Mountains contain a vast assortment of ferrous and nonferrous minerals. By contrast, the Great Plains, the Midwest, Florida, and much of the Pacific Coast show little mining activity. In terms of total number of employees, Pennsylvania, West Virginia, and eastern Kentucky are the leaders. A second important mining-employment area is Texas and Oklahoma, followed by southern Illinois and Indiana (Figure 8.3).

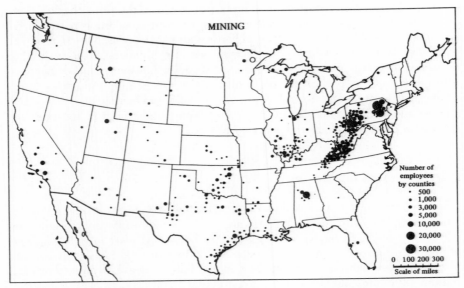

FIGURE 8.3 Number of Employees Engaged in Mining in the United States by Counties. From John W. Alexander, ECONOMIC GEOGRAPHY, (C) 1963. Reprinted by permission of Prentice-Hall, Inc., Englewood Cliffs, New Jersey.

On a world scale the most striking picture is presented by the great profusion of mining resources in the advanced industrial countries in the Northern Hemisphere, especially in the United States, Canada, and countries in Northwestern Europe. Practically any mining resource one can mention is found somewhere in this area. A possible explanation is that this concentration of resources merely reflects the fact that man has more closely explored nearby areas than those in more remote locations. Such superabundance of mineral resources in the industrialized nations does not appear to fit any neat, logical, physical explanation. If man has primarily found minerals where he has looked the most — that is, in areas near him — it would follow that there are considerably more mineral resources on earth than one would imagine simply by looking at present distribution maps.

That this is probably the case is evidenced by periodic discoveries of extremely large and rich mineral resources in other parts of the world. Petroleum exploration has been very successful in many areas outside industrialized countries. In fact, some of the most productive fields in the world are in places like the Middle East, northern Venezuela, and more recently, in southern Nigeria and Northern Alaska. Vast mineral resources, including copper, tin, zinc, manganese, cobalt, and others, have been found in the African areas of Katanga, Zambia, and Rhodesia. In short, it appears that to date vast areas of the earth have received little exploratory attention.

Nevertheless, most advanced nations import a number of minerals from other areas. This occurs either because outside resources are richer and more economical to use than are natural resources, or because of an outright scarcity of minerals locally. Most imports are the result of the former condition, in which it is more profitable to use foreign mine commodities than perhaps less-accessible or lower-quality resources at home. This is particularly the case where the local resource is in the interior of continents. For example, for steel production along the East Coast of the United States, it is cheaper to bring iron ore from Nova Scotia than to use Minnesota iron ore. On the other hand, Canada finds it more advantageous to import American iron ore, via the Great Lakes, even though the iron ore in Eastern Canada is richer. Thus, both Canada and the United States import and export iron ore, a practice illogical to an accountant but sensible to a geographer.

In fact, most advanced countries today could survive on their local mining resources, but at a higher cost. Only a very few resources are not available without imports. Nevertheless, various countries have certain critical resources, which make local supply almost, if not completely, impossible. Even if the resource is available somewhere within a country, it can still be quite inaccessible and clearly less economical than importing the resource by water. Some classic cases include the relative lack of coal in much of South America and Africa. Although coal is found in a few places there, it is not in a good location relative to iron ore deposits, which, by contrast, are impressive. Large deposits are accessible to the sea in Venezuela, Peru, and Chile. In fact, considerable iron ore is exported to the East Coast of the United States where massive steel production is occurring. Second, Western Europe appears to be highly deficient in petroleum, yet has most other mineral resources needed for industry. (Petroleum discoveries in the North Sea area may change this.) It is, therefore, highly dependent on the closest major source, the Persian Gulf area of Southwest Asia, for its supply of petroleum. The United States, although having great oil reserves, is a heavy importer of Venezuelan petroleum.

Some rather critical deficiencies of mineral resources in the United States are nonetheless apparent. Such resources include cobalt, nickel, tin, and possibly columbium and bauxite. Nevertheless, discoveries are continually being made so that these shortages can change to surpluses in short order.

Conclusions

The extractive activities are, spatially speaking, in one sense among the easiest to understand — fishing, forestry, and mining must, by definition, occur where these resources are found on the face of the earth. Man selects the resources he will use on the basis of proximity of the resource to the market, quality and size of the resource, and price of the resource in the marketplace.

In another sense, however — that is, in dealing with questions of *when* and *how* a resource is to be taken — the extractive activities are made more difficult to understand because of the numerous public-policy questions with which they are plagued. Inasmuch as most of the extractive activities are depletable, especially if abused, questions often occur as to whether or not the resource should be used now or in the future. Moreover, if the resource is not taken carefully, waste often results. Thus questions of how best to extract the resource are highly relevant. Finally, since most extractive activities occupy considerable territory, they are in conflict with nonextractive uses of the resource. Often the overriding concern is what might loosely be labeled *conservation* — that is, the wisest and best use of resources.

BIBLIOGRAPHY

Gillespie, G. J. "The Atlantic Salmon." *Canadian Geographical Journal*, June 1968, pp. 186–199.

Gonzalez, Richard J. "Production Depends on Economics — Not Physical Existence." In *Readings in Economic Geography*, edited by Howard G. Roepke, pp. 353–361. New York: John Wiley & Sons, 1967.

Helin, Ronald A. "Soviet Fishing in the Barents Sea and the North Atlantic." *Geographical Review*, July 1964, pp. 386–408.

Marts, M. E. "Conflicts in Water Use and Regional Planning Implications." In *Regional Development and the Wabash Basin*, edited by Ronald R. Boyce. Urbana: University of Illinois Press, 1964.

Minghi, Julian V. "The Problem of the Conservation of Salmon with Special Reference to Bristol Bay, Alaska." *Land Economics*, November 1960, pp. 380–386.

Smith, David M. *The Practice of Silviculture*. New York: John Wiley & Sons, 1963.

Smith, Guy-Harold, ed. *Conservation of Natural Resources*. New York: John Wiley & Sons, 1958.

part c

Agricultural Location

All materials for a living come directly or indirectly out of the soil or crust of the earth. The man in a ship at sea or in a steel skyscraper in a modern city gets his sustenance from the soil just as surely as does the farmer who takes potatoes from the furrow.

J. Russell Smith, *Industrial and Commercial Geography* (New York: Henry Holt & Co., 1925), p. 4.

IX

The Bases of Agricultural Location

The locational understanding of agriculture ranges from the simple to the difficult. In some respects, agriculture can be treated as a simple locational problem much as were the extractive activities discussed in Chapter 8. For example, some crops are highly restricted to particular locales because of such physical restraints as climate. A valid differentiation can be made between agricultural activities that require a tropical environment, such as growing bananas, and those that require a cool climate, such as dairying. The potential areas of cultivation for highly selective crops like cotton, rice, bananas, and coffee can thus be reasonably determined on the basis of physical requirements alone. To find places of production, man merely searches through the suitable environments. In this manner, as with the extractive activities, the location of the resource areas are given.

Another simplistic approach to agricultural location is to assess crop potential in terms of accessibility to the market. This procedure applies remarkably well to regions that have fairly homogeneous physical features, such as similar climate, soils, and topography. In this manner, a delightful morsel of spatial understanding can be achieved by simply ranking agricultural types according to the intensity with which they occupy the land. This provides a fairly reliable clue as to their potential bidding power for land relative to market location. Simply put, those crops which have the highest profits per acre, or which for reasons of high cost transportation due to perishability must be close to the market to survive, bid highest and thereby get the land closest to the market. Activities with less rent-paying ability are squeezed outward from the market in a series of zones of decreasing intensity.

We will proceed to dissect the agricultural location problem in this manner. As we progress into the discussion, however, these simplifying assumptions will be systematically removed until a fairly realistic approximation of actual patterns of agricultural use is mirrored by the theories. At this latter phase, the true difficulty of the agricultural location problem will emerge.

Such a progressive approach serves two purposes. First, the early *ceteris paribus* process used with regard to agriculture should also augment considerably the locational theories pertaining to the extractive activities. In fact, the initial theories can be fruitfully applied to fishing, forestry, and mining. Second, this approach should enable us to gain a rather complete grasp of the components of agricultural location theory inasmuch as each will be examined in connection with its locational consequence.

Such a building-block approach is also judicious because the spatial understanding of agriculture is in reality much more difficult than that of the activities previously examined. Specifically, one more degree of freedom in locational choice is evident in agricultural location than was previously the case. In agriculture, there are two possible questions rather than one. The familiar query is, given the land (resource), what crop, or crops, will best be produced on it? (In the extractive activities, the question is merely whether or not the resource should be used.) A second question is, Given a crop (resource), where is the best place to produce that crop? This choice is not available to extractive operations; thus there is considerable interplay in the agricultural location problem among land, crops, and location. Different crops can be and are produced on similar kinds of land. Conversely, similar lands are often used for different crops. By contrast, in the extractive activities, the resource and the place of production are always bound together. With agriculture, no such geographic determinants can be confidently taken as given.

There are three major locational determinants in agriculture: (1) inputs, or procurement costs, (2) outputs, or distribution costs, and (3) on-site production costs. The input costs include items not available on site, such as seed, fertilizer, machinery, and other items required to produce a crop. These inputs involve capital outlay as well as transportation costs necessary to get the "raw material" items on site. Fortunately, these costs are often of such a nature that they do not exert much locational significance within any given region. For this reason, the problem of agricultural location is more simple than that of industrial location. The inputs, or procurements, can be largely ignored in the locational decision. Even though machinery, tools, fertilizers, and other items that must be assembled to produce any agricultural crop vary greatly from place to place, these are not decisive in the determination as to whether any given crop will be grown.

Market Accessibility and Agricultural Location

The major locational determinant of the type of agriculture practiced in any given area is proximity to market. Unless the farmer can get his produce to market, that area is useless for commercial agricultural purposes. Some parts of the earth that might be physically suitable for a particular crop remain unused simply because of their remoteness from markets. The development of land transportation and the opening up of farm lands have always occurred together. The technical name for such market-accessibility needs is *distribution costs* and will be symbolized by the letter *T*.

The other major cost, and hence locational determinant, with respect to agriculture is the *on-site* production costs. These relate to the physical quality of the land, to labor costs, and to general operating costs during the production period. Since most of these are variable because of differing physical environments, in the following analysis they are labeled *on-site costs* and are symbolized by the letter *E*.

In order to see how these two costs *(T and E)* relate to crop production patterns, the *ceteris paribus* technique will be used. Initially, all costs associated with production, except *T*, will be held constant. After this effect is presented, the on-site costs *(E)* will be allowed to vary spatially in an attempt to see how site and transportation costs affect the profitability of various lands. Such relaxed assumptions will also set a more realistic framework by which actual agricultural patterns can be nominally assessed.

The analytical procedure discussed below is usually referred to as a *Von Thunen Model*. It is named after its originator, Johann Heinrich Von Thunen, a member of the German landed gentry, who in 1826 developed a number of simplistic models of agricultural crop production patterns primarily on the basis of differential transportation costs for concentric zones around a single market. His assumptions, which will be used here initially, include first of all a single market (city) in an isolated, isometric planar surface. Thus all surplus commodities from the surrounding areas must go to this one market. In addition, the tributary area is considered to be homogeneous in terms of environment and in terms of productivity per unit of land for any given crop. Von Thunen's second assumption is an agricultural hinterland traversed only by a single mode of land transportation. All areas within a particular distance zone from the market have equal accessibility to it. In other words, all transportation lines are radially focused on the market town. Moreover, transportation costs, which are directly proportional to distance, are to be born directly by the farmers, who must ship all commodities to the city in "fresh" form. Von Thunen's final assumption is that we are dealing with rational, economic man who desires to maximize his profits and is completely flexible in the type of crop he produces so that he can change production immediately in order to maximize profits.

The above are, of course, assumptions or premises that do not hold in the real world. Nevertheless, the importance of market accessibility is of such great significance for many crops that if one looks for them within the framework of this kind of model, examples of such influence can be seen in the actual crop patterns of the world.

The general result of applying these premises in such a landscape laboratory is that the number of profitable crops which can be grown decreases as distance from the market increases. Thus there is an outer limit beyond which a crop cannot be grown because it would be unprofitable, and there is an inner limit for a crop because more choices of profitable crops exist. In Von Thunen's study the inner zones were devoted to market gardening and fresh milk production. These uses were primarily located here because of perishability considerations (high transportation costs) and the consequent need to get these commodities to the market fresh. Of course, with today's refrigerated transportation, fresh milk can be brought to centers from distances of 300 miles or more, and fresh vegetables can be brought in from across continents. The second zone also reflected the technology of the day and was occupied by farmers specializing in producing firewood — then the main type of fuel for heating homes. Its bulky nature made transportation costs high, thus putting heavy emphasis on production in the inner zones. Also, the heavy demand kept the market price fairly high so that silviculture yielded greater returns to the farmer than did any other crop except fresh vegetables and milk. The third, fourth, and fifth zones were occupied by grain-type crops of decreasing profitability. Zone six was used most profitably, according to the premises above and the prices at that time, for livestock production. Von Thunen considered the transportation costs of livestock to be quite low inasmuch as cattle could be driven to market. Another activity in the sixth zone was cheese production — a commodity not highly perishable and one that could easily stand the high transportation costs. Finally, the zones beyond were considered unprofitable for crops and remained unused wilderness areas. It should be apparent from the above discussion that three variables show up as decisive: (1) price or value of the commodity at the market (V), (2) cost of producing the commodity at the farm site — in this case, assumed to vary only among commodities and not among areas, and (3) cost of transporting the commodity to the market in fresh condition.

The method in which these operate is demonstrated in Figure 9.1. These three variables are considered as follows. The on-site production costs (E) are assumed to be equal throughout the market hinterland inasmuch as the physical environment is presumed to be homogeneous. The price at the market (V) is given on the basis of going prices. And the distribution or transportation costs (T) are assumed to increase for any particular crop in a linear manner with distance from the market. (In Figure 9.1, the distribution costs are shown in an exponential fashion in order to make the example more realistic.) It is evident that the crucial variable in this model is transportation costs, or proximity, to the market. The variation over distance of this variable thereby makes the profitability for producing any one crop decrease with increasing distance from the market location. Thus, all crops would be more profitably produced in zone 1, but inasmuch as some crops are more profitable than others, less profitable crops are squeezed out to less advantageous locations.

Note that for the example crop shown, the limit of profitable production is at d_3. Beyond this distance, the production of that crop will lead to a deficit — the farmer will lose money by growing it. The extent of this loss in any given location is shown by space Q.

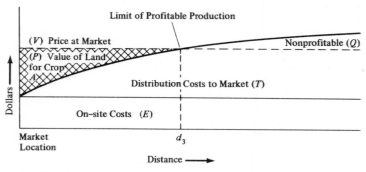

$$P = V - (E + T)$$

FIGURE 9.1 Profitability of Cropland in Relation to Distance from Market. Note that the value of land for crop (P) decreases with increasing distance from the market because of increasing distribution costs (T) to market. On-site costs (E) are considered equal for all locations.

The critical curve is the line enclosing space P. Note that this space shows decreasing profitability as distance from the market increases. Such a curve is called a *rent gradient* and is a spatial representation of the profitability of any given crop for any given area. The rent gradient is generally presented in the manner shown in Figure 9.2. Note that the rent gradient (P) is merely that curve which has been derived from two constant features $(E$ and $V)$ and receives its distinctive shape from the transportation cost line (T). In formula form, therefore, $P = V - (E + T)$, where E is held constant.

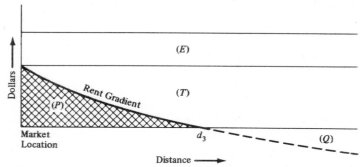

FIGURE 9.2 Developing an Agricultural Rent Gradient. Based on Figure 9.1.

The application of this in the Von Thunen context is shown in Figure 9.3. This model contains one market and three crops: A, B, and C. Note that crop C is the most profitable crop at the market, but that it also has the steepest rent gradient. Thus its maximum limit of profitable production is at distance Qc. However, it is not produced outwards to that distance inasmuch as crop B is a more profitable crop at distance d_1 before Qc is reached. Therefore, crop C will be produced to distance d_1 and crop B beyond that point to distance $d2$, where crop A becomes the highest potential rent-payer. This ranking of territorial profitabilities among crops leads to a series of concentric zones outward from the market as shown.

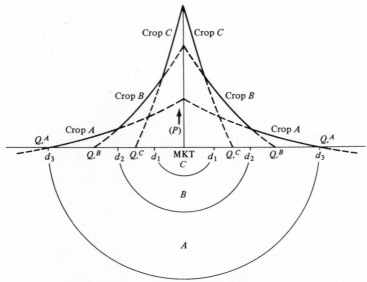

FIGURE 9.3 Agricultural Rent Gradients for Three Crops around a Single Market Place and the Territorial Result.   Note that Crop C would be grown outward to distance d_1 to dominate Zone C, Crop B would be grown between distance d_1 to d_2 and would dominate Zone B, and that Crop A would dominate the area from d_2 to d_3 in Zone A. Crop A would not be grown beyond d_3 because it becomes unprofitable beyond that distance (Q^A).

This same procedure can also be applied to multiple markets, as shown in Figure 9.4. Note that the crop with the highest rent-paying ability gets first choice for production in any given area. Thus the crops to be grown along a traverse connecting markets are along the top rent gradient lines. Other possible, but less profitable, crops are shown beneath this line in dashed form. Such subterranean rent gradients, in reality, represent those crops next in line for production should the market price decrease for the crop currently most profitable, should transportation costs for it increase, or should the next-order crop increase its rent-paying position. The markets for the most profitable

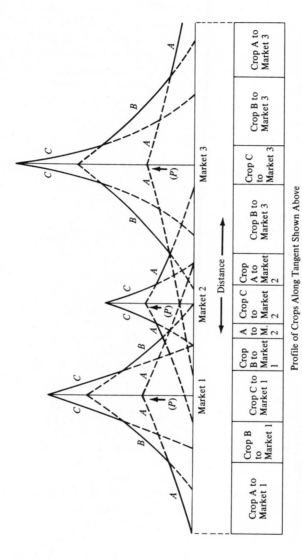

Profile of Crops Along Tangent Shown Above

FIGURE 9.4 Agricultural Rent Gradients for Three Crops around Three Markets. Note that the subterranean lines (dashed) are ignored in the determination of surface crop responses as shown for the profile of crops along tangent based on the rent gradients above.

crops are demonstrated by the extension of the rent gradient to its highest point at a particular market place. The profile of crops and markets is shown directly below the rent gradient curves. Note that it is possible that some markets may not be markets for all crops. For example, a town may purchase wheat, but have no stockyard. Thus it is possible that crop C might be shipped to market 3 even though markets 1 and 2 are closer. This principle begins to approach reality in those areas which are fairly physically homogeneous. Thus, this model, despite its *ceteris paribus* assumptions, provides a fairly good first-order approximation of the distribution of many actual crop patterns.

On-site Costs and Agricultural Location

Perhaps the most blatantly questionable premise of the model above is the assumption that we are dealing with a planimetric environmental surface. This is a particularly serious variable to hold constant inasmuch as agriculture is so much affected by on-site factors like climate and soil. Therefore, in Figure 9.5 the on-site costs (E) have been allowed to vary concomitantly with transportation costs. In this case there are two zones of profitability, P_1 and P_2. Thus, as with many actual agricultural patterns, particularly on a local scale, environmental features cause an otherwise smooth rent gradient to become spatially disrupted. An example of how this works is demonstrated by going outward from an imaginary town where the land near the town is relatively flat and fertile, but the land slightly farther out is hilly and rocky. Beyond this zone is a recurrence of the fertile soil like that near the town. Crops might be found in the good soil lands, but perhaps grazing, or some less intensive use, will be found in the hilly and rocky areas. Nonetheless, the general gradient affected by transportation still exerts some effect inasmuch as the profitability further out (say, at P_2) is much less than otherwise identical land would be closer to the market. Likewise, the second zone of unprofitability, Q_2, is much greater than the nearer zone, Q_1.

The same method of assessing highest and best use of the land can nonetheless be used with this model, as shown in Figure 9.6. Note that crop A is identical to that shown in Figure 9.5. Two other crops with their respective rent gradients are also introduced. The principle of determining which crop is best produced in an area is identical to that used earlier. In the case shown, crop C appears to be least affected by the hypothetical hilly and rocky land and thus is able to use such land at a profit. However, there is some land, perhaps swamp land or very rough land, which is not profitable for any crop. Thus, despite its proximity to the market, this land is left unused for agriculture.

It is apparent that to assess the potential for agriculture on the real surface of the earth, detailed and factual information must be obtained relative to the E variables. Thus, those characteristics discussed at some length in Chapter

3 become highly significant when one examines the actual pattern of agriculture. It is also apparent that to understand the spatial pattern of agriculture, one must have a fairly good classification of levels of intensity — that is, bidding- or rent-paying abilities — among different crops and among different farming systems.

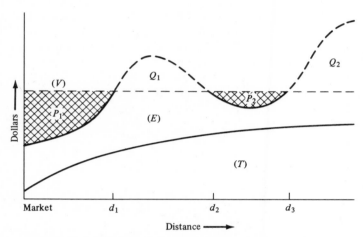

FIGURE 9.5 Profitabilities of Land for a Single Crop with Variability in On-Site Costs *(E)*.   This is but one of many possibilities inasmuch as the on-site costs *(E)* are based on peculiar topography, soils, farm and field size, and many other variables not directly related to distance from market. Compare with Figure 9.1.

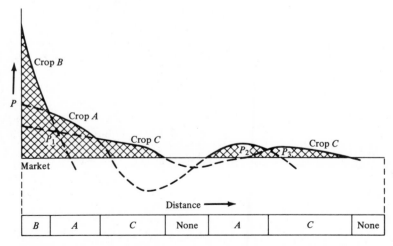

FIGURE 9.6 Hypothetical Rent Gradients around a Single Market with On-Site Costs Considered.   Compare with Figure 9.5.

Types of Agricultural Patterns

By now you may have noticed some confusion with regard to the terms "crops" and "agricultural activities." This occurs largely because agriculture is a highly diverse economic pursuit. Not only are there hundreds of different crops, localized in various parts of the earth, but these are intertwined with different farming systems. In some places, a single crop may dominate the system (monoculture), whereas in others such a crop may be but one of a complex combination of crops. In fact, the question of agricultural classification is surely one of the most perplexing in geography.[1]

Indeed, the first question to be answered is, What is agriculture? Technically, agriculture should refer only to "cropland" pursuits, but in popular usage it has come to refer to any kind of "farming" activity. This is the way it is referred to here, but of course in this chapter agriculture will include only commercial farming activities and will encompass *bioculture* (the husbandry of animals, best described by the term "ranching"), *pisciculture*, also termed *aquiculture* (fish farming and the "farming" of ocean areas as, for example, the oyster beds in Chesapeake Bay), *silviculture* (timber cropping), and *horticulture* (the raising of flowers, fruits, and vegetables). The primary focus, however, will be on crop and animal farming and various combinations of each.

One system for classifying farming types is according to their general degree of land use intensity (that is, rent-paying ability) as shown in Figure 9.7. This diagram shows the following trend of agricultural activity extremes: (1) areas dominated by a single crop such as wheat or cotton, (2) areas dominated by animals such as ranching and dairying, and (3) mixed animal and crop farming. Note that the intensity of land use also generally increases as one moves from the ranching and single crop types to mixed farming types. Intensity also increases, however, as crop- or animal-oriented farming activities become more heavily dependent on proximity to urban markets. Thus garden-type agriculture, primarily vegetables, demands a more intense use of land than does cotton farming; dairying is a more intense, animal-based crop than is ranching; and the newly emerging factory-type production of chickens, milk, and beef on very small areas is perhaps the most intensive of all rural activities. It should also be noted that several "agricultural" types (that is, those still somewhat reliant on land resources) such as nurseries, kennels, and horse stables, are found within cities.

It should be evident also that there is a slippage among land, labor, and capital within the animal-crop dichotomy shown here. Generally, as agricultural types move diagrammatically toward the more intense urban realm, they become more parsimonious users of land. However, the "crop only" functions

---

[1]For an excellent article on the many agricultural classifications, see David Grigg, "The Agricultural Regions of the World: Review and Reflections," *Economic Geography*, vol. 45 (April 1969), pp. 92–132.

appear to change most with regard to labor, and the "animals only" functions appear to become more capital- than labor-intensive. By contrast, intensity is achieved in the mixed crop and animal combination through an elaborate fusion of these two activities. In the case of Mediterranean agriculture, however, such efficiencies are also achieved through irrigation and especially by a system that capitalizes on different crop and animal combinations at different seasons of the year. Thus the mixed systems appear to have been able to achieve a certain amount of efficiency through careful combinational mixes that provide flexibility over space and time.

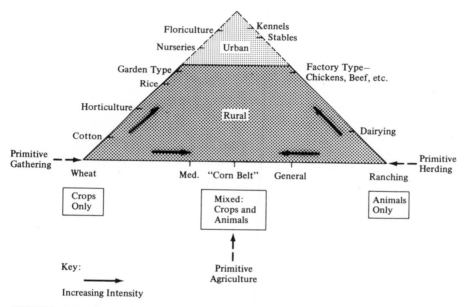

FIGURE 9.7 Schema of Agricultural Intensity Rankings according to Types of Crops and Agricultural Systems.   Note that the most intensive crops are those found closest to cities.

A general, ranking summary of the intensity of land use is shown in Table 9.1. Intensity generally refers to the degree of profit derived per acre of land. As will be demonstrated in Chapter 10, this does not directly correlate with the extent of total profit made per farm. In fact, some of the less intensive land uses, such as ranching and wheat farming, are among the most profitable on a per farm basis; by contrast, their profit per acre, and hence their ability to bid for land on a unit area basis, is of a very low intensity. Another measure of intensity, therefore, is reflected in size of farm — the larger the farm, generally the less intensive the land use. However, with the development of large-scale irrigated lands, there are increasing exceptions to this rule.

TABLE 9.1
COMPARATIVE INTENSITY OF LAND USE AMONG SELECTED TYPES OF AGRICULTURE IN THE UNITED STATES

Farming Type	*Degree of Land Use Intensity* High	*Medium*	*Low*	*Very Low*	*Estimated Average Farm Acreage*
Garden	X				*20-150*
Mediterranean	X	—			*300-600 plus*
Mixed	X	—			*160-350*
Irrigated	X	—			*80-1,000 plus*
Rice	—	X			*300-600*
Cotton		X			*300-600*
Dairying		X			*160-350*
Horticulture		X	—		*40-150 plus*
Wheat			X	—	*640-1500*
Ranching				X	*Over 2,500*

Of course, Table 9.1 is very crude. The exact degree of intensity varies greatly from place to place. The general variation from the average figures (X) is shown by the hyphen (—). Nevertheless, if physical factors are generally ignored, this seems to be a fairly reliable approximation.

Agricultural pattern of the United States

The importance of crop intensity in providing spatial understanding for the distribution of crops is demonstrated for the United States (Figure 9.8). Although this map is highly schematized, the general decrease in crop intensity with increasing distance from the major United States "market" is most evident. Note that with the exception of Mediterranean agriculture, all high-intensity crops appear near the major American market. In fact, the rise of Southern California as a major supplier of vegetables and citrus products for the main market of the United States is a marvel in large-scale production and marketing efficiencies, and strongly reflects the general revolution in transportation. The medium intensity areas are next farthest removed, except that dairying, an activity dealing with a highly perishable commodity, has in some areas been able to occupy land close to the market. It is also an activity that fares well in the climate to the north, with its shorter growing season — an area generally unfavorable for many other crops. Finally, the low-intensity agricultural pursuits of wheat farming and ranching have been squeezed to outlying areas relative to the market. These very low intensity-activities also occupy the land that is physically less desirable for other kinds of agriculture. In the Far West, either because of accessibility problems or environmental difficulties, most of the area in agricultural production is limited to irrigated areas. The primary activities in this most distant zone are forestry, silviculture, and general grazing — even lower-intensity uses than ranching. However, where irrigation is practicable, quite intensive production occurs; these areas are thus able to compete with much closer-in areas. In fact, Idaho is the largest potato producer in the United States, yet potatoes are a highly bulky and perishable commodity.

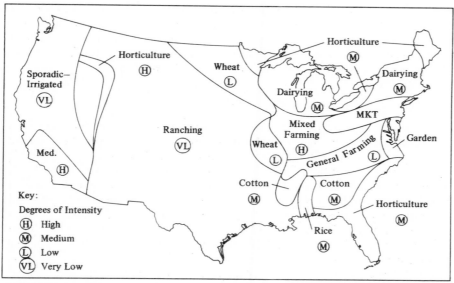

FIGURE 9.8 Schematic Map of Various Farm Types and Farming Systems within the United States. Compare the proximity of these types and systems to their levels of intensity, shown in Figure 9.7, as these relate to proximity to the major United States market.

Thus proximity to markets is clearly a powerful force. But there are several conditions that militate against accessibility being the be-all and end-all. First, most types of agriculture are affected by physical conditions. Obviously, Mediterranean-type agriculture can occur only in a Mediterranean climate. Even if areas with so favorable a physical environment are far removed from the market, they still have potential for fairly intensive production. On the other hand, such areas may be so distant that accessibility problems largely prohibit their intensive use, as is the case with the Mediterranean climate belt in central Chile. Second, some areas close to the market are so difficult to use for high-intensity agricultural purposes because of climates, slope, or soil conditions, that only very general types of agriculture can be practiced. Such is the case in much of the Appalachians and the Ozark plateau.

Finally, a dilemma in interpretation is posed. For example, is wheat farming an extensive use of the land because it is in a poor bidding position for land closer to the market and hence must occupy land farther away, or because it can do better in more difficult lands than most other crops? Certainly, wheat does fairly well in dryer areas and is a commodity that is relatively less perishable than most others. Undoubtedly, both conditions are involved. However, a more likely explanation is the latter — the less physically attractive lands are used extensively for environmental reasons rather than because the crop has been squeezed to a position less accessible to the market. This is demonstrated by the fact that the Mediterranean agricultural practices in Southern California are highly intensive, whereas other nearby areas are used in an extensive way. In fact, one might use a reverse argument: in order to use good lands far removed from the market, they must be used more intensively than otherwise to compete with similar crops grown closer to the market.

Agricultural pattern of the world

The world pattern of selected agricultural types is shown in Figure 9.9. Note that a pattern similar to that for the United States emerges. Those agricultural types most associated with the urban-industrial heartlands — especially the northeast part of the United States and Northwest Europe — are characterized by mixed farming. This type of farming activity is complex and, in fact, is a tightly intertwined system — somewhat akin to the traditional paddy farming activities. In this case, it is similarly based on a profitable blend of crops and animals. The major food and animal feed crop in the United States heartland is corn, but wheat and other grains are also grown. Lately, soybeans, an industrial and feed crop that enriches the soil, has become widespread in the Midwest of the United States. In Europe, sugar beets and potatoes are important crops, but the general crop-animal mix is somewhat similar to that in the United States. Such crops are fed to animals like beef cattle, pigs, and poultry in a manner that provides a year-round income and work pattern for the farmer. In this regard, farmers in midlatitude areas are feeding animals in order to give them some of the same advantages that farmers enjoy in subtropical areas where multiple cropping is possible. Thus animals provide a major source of profit during the off-growing season of the year. It must also be stressed that such mixed crops are also the result of rotation. Of special interest too are the broad bands of dairying activity. This activity, close to the major market source for reasons already mentioned, is primarily associated with advanced industrial and highly urbanized economies. Very little massive development of this activity occurs in South America, Africa, or Asia.

Dairying is not a homogeneous activity; the commodities produced change relative to distance from the market. Hence, areas nearest the market produce primarily fresh milk. The next zones are engaged in the production of butter and cheese, which are commodities less valuable than milk. This arrangement into dairying bands also occurs because such areas are beyond the milkshed

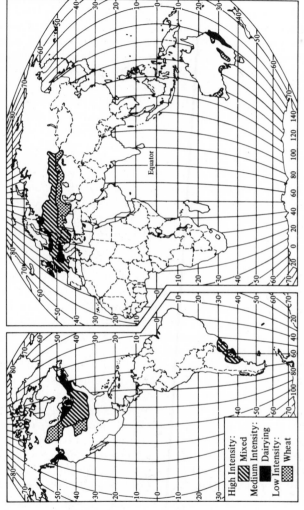

FIGURE 9.9 Selected Commercial Farming Types by Intensity over the World. Compare with level of intensity, shown in Figure 9.7, as these relate to proximity to the European and U.S. markets.

zones and because butter and cheese are less perishable than milk. Butter and cheese are also made from the surplus milk in any area, but a surplus is more likely in an outlying area.

These conditions have created a differing pricing system that is bothersome to many people. For example, let us assume the relative retail prices per pound of milk, cheese, and butter to be $0.12, $0.45, and $0.63 respectively. It takes about ten pounds of milk to make one pound of cheese or one half-pound of butter. Those not familiar with the geographical factors discussed above might thereby conclude that both butter and cheese are highly underpriced. They might assume that cheese should cost $1.20 a pound and butter $2.40. The reason this does not occur is basically connected with the availability of surplus milk and with the fact that most butter and cheese is made in outlying areas. Another reason for butter being much cheaper than might be expected is, of course, competition from margarine.

The extreme market orientation of dairying is also shown by the fact that milksheds are found within overnight commuting distance of almost every large urban center in the world. In fact, less than one-fifth of all the world's milk comes from the dairying regions as delimited in Figure 9.9. Dairying is carried on in conjunction with many other farming activities. Perishability keeps dairying very close to even small markets as does the great weight and volume of dairy products. Despite such market proximity, dairy products account for more millions of tons than does the output of any other "crop." In fact, dairy products amount to almost 400 million tons annually as compared with some 250 million tons of wheat and about 200 million tons of corn. (However, wheat ton-mile volume is greater than that for milk.)

As one moves outward from the various world markets, the pattern progresses, as anticipated, into less intensive agricultural pursuits. First, various crops of medium intensity are encountered. In the United States these include commodities like tobacco, cotton, and rice, and in other areas of the world, various other general-type crops. These medium intensity crops are followed first by wheat farming and then by ranching, a progression that is particularly orderly in the United States, Argentina, and Australia. Regarding cattle production, it should be noted that nomadic herding and the raising of cattle in conjunction with other farming activities is not specified on the map in Figure 9.9. Thus India, which has over one-sixth of the world's cattle, is not included inasmuch as cattle play a role of little commercial importance there.

Two classes of agricultural activity stand out as peculiar in Figure 9.9. One is the potentially high-intensity Mediterranean system, found only rather near the market in Europe. The other is the medium-intensity plantation system, which appears to be located in some of the remote places of the earth. Such spatial peculiarity is obviously the result of highly restrictive physical features. However, Mediterranean agriculture located nearest the European and United States markets is by far the more developed, thus perhaps showing somewhat the effect of accessibility.

The physical features of the Mediterranean climate are perhaps the best on earth for agriculture. First, the temperature in the Mediterranean climate is generally above freezing the year around. This allows it to produce crops the year around and, more particularly, to grow crops that other temperate areas cannot grow. Its full-year growing season also allows it to capitalize on the production of crops calculated to enter temperate markets during the high-price winter period. Finally, through irrigation, the land can be worked in a more intensive fashion than in almost any other area of the world. Consequently, its three major crop types include: (1) those which do well on the winter and spring precipitation, such as grains, (2) those which can withstand the hot summer drought (primarily tree crops, such as oranges, olives, grapes, figs, and nuts), and (3) specialty irrigation crops, such as garden vegetables and fruits, which are grown at strategic times of the year to yield the highest market prices. Thus, the Mediterranean agricultural system represents a monumental commercial symbiosis with nature and is a year-round endeavor. As might be expected, animals are subordinate to crops here, although in some areas they are involved—much as they are in the mixed farming areas.

The main problem with agriculture in Mediterranean climates appears to be oversuccess rather than failure. The climate is considered so attractive for urban settlement and recreation that considerable invasion of agricultural land has occurred, particularly in California. The urban intrusion, however, has also had its sparking effects on extremely intensive gardening, dairying, and factory-like operations. Paradoxically, one of the big problems in the animal-type factory farming systems, where much is produced on very little land, is the problem of getting rid of manure. Of course, the other Mediterranean agriculture areas have not been as successful as California in developing factory farming, but the basic agricultural system is similar.

The other physically contaminated system is plantation agriculture. It should be noted that this system is limited to tropical areas where Western man, primarily European, has attempted to augment tropical commodities through a commercial farming system. Most plantations are thus islands of Western intrusion into a primitive and underdeveloped world. All commodities are heavily dependent on indigenous labor, based at first on slavery-type conditions in many areas, and all commodities are prepared for export to developed countries. Typical commodities include rubber, coffee, tea, bananas, sugar, pineapples, and cocoa. Initially, such plantations were made possible by the development of the steamship, railroads, and other improvements in transportation which, when used in conjunction with cheap water transportation, opened many tropical areas to commercial agriculture.

Plantations are characterized by large-scale production under a centralized management corporation. One of the largest is the United Fruit Company, whose operations are so extensive in Central America that countries in this area are often derisively referred to as "banana republics." Some plantations are of such an extensive corporate nature that they are almost completely *vertically integrated*. These integrated plantation-based companies, therefore, control not only the production of the commodity but its transportation, manufacture, and distribution to commercial outlets.

Despite the large-scale nature of plantations, they occupy only small portions of the tropics. In fact, the location of plantations is highly generalized on the map, and only a small part of most territory so indicated is actually covered by plantations. They are thus mere pinpoints of commercial agriculture in a vast sea of subsistence economies and largely unoccupied territory.

In fact, small-scale indigenous farming is on the increase in tropical areas. Farmers there are preparing many plantation-associated commodities for export. Of particular note are cotton from Uganda, cacao bean's from Ghana, rubber from Malaya, and bananas from Ecuador. With Ecuador the awakening of many countries of Africa and Asia, the future role of plantations, at least Western-controlled plantations, is much in doubt.

Confronting Reality: An Individual Crop Approach

The true difficulty, and perhaps delight, of the locational problem in agriculture is manifest when one examines the distribution of a particular crop. An individual crop is usually not limited to a single area or farming system but is found in a wide variety of agricultural settings. Thus, explanation for its distribution is challenging indeed and provides an exploration into the intricate workings of the farm operation itself — intricacies to be discussed in Chapter 10.

The examination of a particular crop reveals many other locational factors crucial to full distributional understanding. These include: (1) seasonality, (2) changing market demand, (3) problems of disease and crop pestilence, (4) particular varieties within a crop type, (5) possibilities for mechanization and for achieving economies of scale, and (6) many other variables like the spread of such a crop over the landscape and the residual patterns left from former times of profitability. Principles like this are perhaps most clearly and easily demonstrated with regard to the changing pattern of the common, or Irish, potato in the United States. Here is a crop that must be raised in combination with other crops (because of rotation needs) and one that is commercially produced in every state (see Figure 9.12 later in the chapter). Moreover it is a high-intensity, highly perishable, bulky, and disease-plagued crop that, despite expectations to the contrary, has moved farther and farther away from the major markets. It thus presents a fascinating example of the way the above principles operate and provides an inkling into the real nature of the agricultural location problem as well.

Nor are potatoes an insignificant crop. Over the world some 250 million tons of potatoes are produced annually. This tonnage compares evenly with that of rice, and is superior to wheat and corn tonnages. In terms of acreage, it ranks some 60 million acres as compared with some 500 million acres in wheat. It is a high-calorie crop and one which provides the staple diet for many Europeans and Americans. Within the United States, it accounts for more ton-miles than does any other agricultural crop except dairying. This is partly the result of distance from the market, but also the result of the tremendous bulk produced.

The spatial dynamics of potato production and acreage patterns in the United States from 1900 to 1964 are shown in Figure 9.10. Note that potatoes were heavily market oriented in 1900 but have since shifted to outlying areas. In 1900 there was almost a perfect correlation between state population and the relative amounts of potato acreage and production in each state. By 1964, some of the least populous states accounted for sizable productions — for example, Idaho, Maine, Washington, and North Dakota.

Also evident in the pattern change is the tremendous decline in acreage, despite the fact that production has remained almost constant. Clearly, fewer acres are doing more of the producing through an increase in yields per acre. In fact, average yield has increased from 60 hundredweight per acre in 1900 to well over 200 hundredweight today. However, inasmuch as population has grown tremendously over this time, annual per capita consumption has dropped from over 200 pounds in 1900 to slightly over 115 pounds today. The rapidly rising potato-chip, processed-potato, and frozen-potato industries are largely responsible for recent gains in per capita consumption, but fresh weight consumption is still dropping and is now about 80 pounds annually per person.

Three major factors are behind the shift in production patterns away from the market. First, transportation has improved to the point that this highly perishable commodity can be shipped to distant markets. Second, vast irrigation areas have been developed in the western part of the United States and have been put into intensive potato production. The effect of irrigation on California and Washington production is clearly evident in Figure 9.11. Inasmuch as the potato yield of irrigated lands averages more than twice that of most nonirrigated acreage, the former areas have a tremendous advantage. Finally, the newer areas are the most mechanized and generally the most efficient because of large-scale production. Many of the older areas have been unable to mechanize — either the fields are too small or the ground too rocky or cloddish — and have consequently gone out of production. Potatoes are a heavy-labor crop, especially without mechanized harvesting, so that the scarcity of this kind of labor has been a critical factor in many areas.

In the realm of increased production, Idaho has been the agricultural wonder. As shown in Figure 9.11, Idaho was an extremely small potoato-producer in 1900 but has increased its production steadily until it is now the major producer in the United States. As will be made clear in Chapter 10, the development of new, irrigated lands has produced economies of scale rarely obtained in horticultural pursuits.

Concentration trends are, however, offset by seasonality (Figure 9.12). Particularly significant is the late spring and early summer production response from areas in the southern parts of the United States, namely Southern California. This response, in fact, amounts to some 15 percent of total production. These areas capitalize on their climatic advantages in a manner calculated

IRISH POTATOES

Average acreage

Average production

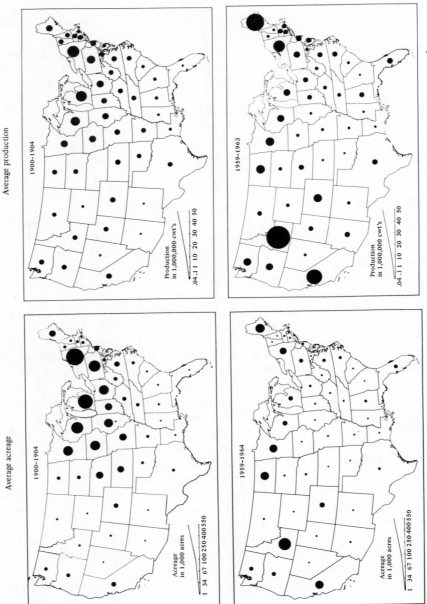

1900–1904

1900–1904

Acreage
in 1,000 acres
1 34 67 100 250 400 550

Production
in 1,000,000 cwt's
.04 .1 1 10 20 30 40 50

1959–1964

1959–1963

Acreage
in 1,000 acres
1 34 67 100 250 400 550

Production
in 1,000,000 cwt's
.04 .1 1 10 20 30 40 50

FIGURE 9.10 Changing Acreage and Production Patterns of the Irish Potato, 1900 – 1964. Note the general proximity of potato production and acreages to the United States market in 1900, but the great lack of proximity to market today.

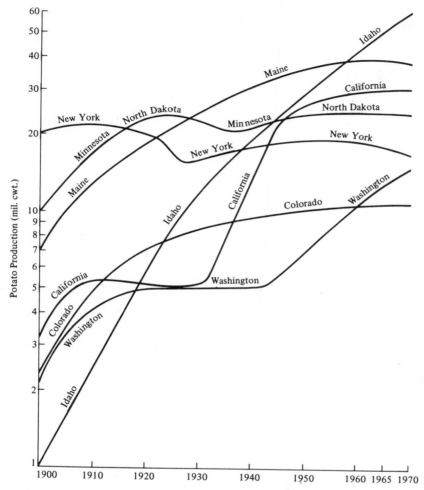

FIGURE 9.11 Potato Production by State, 1900–1965. Note the tremendous long-term rise of Idaho potato production throughout this century.

to enter potatoes in the market at a time of highest price. These "early" potatoes, however, are not ripened by frost and are hence highly perishable and short-lived. Finally, the pattern is made possible by the development of particular varieties of potatoes. Some are good, all-around potatoes, such as those produced in northern areas (for example, the russett of Idaho and the katahdin of Maine). Others are "early" potatoes, developed to mature in a short growing season (for example, the white rose of California and the sebago of Florida). Still other potatoes, such as the kennebec, are grown primarily for the potato chip industry. Of course, everyone is aware of the continuing preference battle

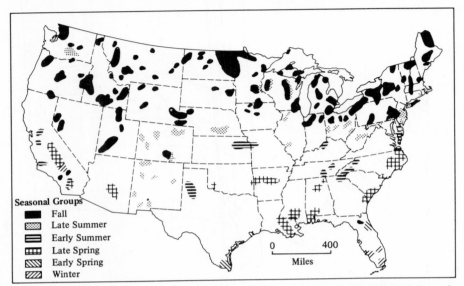

Seasonal Groups
- ◼ Fall
- ▦ Late Summer
- ▤ Early Summer
- ▥ Late Spring
- ▨ Early Spring
- ▧ Winter

FIGURE 9.12 Major Potato Producing Areas by Seasonal Groups.   Adapted from the U. S. Census of Agriculture, 1963. Note the widespread nature of potato production. Every state has some commercial production. Note also the latitudinal effect on seasonal groups.

between the red-skinned potato (produced mostly in the Red River Valley of Minnesota and North Dakota, and in the San Luis Valley of Colorado) and brown- and white-skinned potatoes. This battle is reminiscent of the great white-egg versus brown-egg controversy, but it is nonetheless important in setting demand patterns.

Perhaps enough has now been said to demonstrate the complexities involved in an analysis of individual crop patterns. At this stage we have really just opened the door to full spatial understanding — an understanding that cannot be provided in any one book or, for that matter, in a whole encyclopedia of books.

Conclusions

This chapter has explored some of the major factors that affect the location of agriculture on a macro scale. It has attempted to specify those bases which are most vital to the interpretation of broad agricultural activity patterns. We have progressed from a fairly simple and abstract approach to a place where some of the major complexities in the geography of agriculture have been exposed.

To appreciate these bases fully, it is necessary to spend considerable effort applying them to new areas and to new patterns. We have attempted only to provide frameworks for analysis — not much of the actual analysis itself. Thus you should experiment with the models in various ways. You should also now hungrily pursue locational facts about farm activities with the goal of interpreting them within a theoretical context. Finally, the goal is not so much to understand the present distribution of things but to anticipate and make inferences about probable future patterns, given new developments in transportation and farming technology as well as changes in demands among commodities. This predictive quality is clearly one of the hallmarks not only of a specialist in geography but of any educated citizen.

In apologia, however, the specific nature of those variables which affect the profitability of an agricultural undertaking at the on-site or farm level have remained obscure indeed. The discussion in this chapter has been on a fairly general and rather high level. To appreciate the agricultural location problem fully, it is necessary to get right down to earth at the farm-scale level.

BIBLIOGRAPHY

Baker, Oliver E. "Agricultural Regions of North America." *Economic Geography*, April 1931, pp. 109–153.

Blumenfeld, Hans. "The Economic Base of the Metropolis." *Journal of the American Institute of Planners*, Fall 1955, pp. 114–132.

Boyce, Ronald R., ed. *Regional Development and the Wabash Basin*, pp. 22–39. Urbana: University of Illinois Press, 1964.

Dunn, Edgar S., Jr. "The Equilibrium of Land-Use Patterns in Agriculture." In *Spatial Economic Theory*, edited by Robert D. Dean, William H. Leahy, and David McKee, pp. 233–250. New York: The Free Press, 1970.

––––––. *The Location of Agricultural Production*. Gainesville: University of Florida Press, 1954.

Durand, Loyal, Jr. "The Major Milksheds of the Northeastern Quarter of the United States." *Economic Geography*, January 1964, pp. 9–33.

Garrison, William, and Marble, Duane F. "Spatial Structure of Agricultural Activities." *Annals of the Association of American Geographers*, June 1957, pp. 137–144.

Gregor, Howard F. "The Changing Plantation." *Annals of the Association of American Geographers*, June 1965, pp. 221–238.

Harvey, David W. "Theoretical Concepts and the Analysis of Agricultural Land-Use Patterns in Geography." *Annals of the Association of American Geographers*, June 1967, pp. 361–374.

Higbee, Edward. *American Agriculture*. New York: John Wiley & Sons, 1958.

Highsmith, Richard M., Jr., and Jenson, J. Granville. *Geography of Commodity Production*, pp. 3–87. New York: J. B. Lippincott, 1963.

Hoover, Edgar M. *The Location of Economic Activity*. New York: McGraw-Hill, 1948.

Johnson, Hildegard Binder. "A Note on Thunen's Circles." *Annals of the Association of American Geographers*, June 1962, pp. 213–220.

Ullman, Edward L., and Dacey, Michael F. "The Minimum Requirements Approach to the Economic Base." *Proceedings of the Regional Science Association,* 1960, pp. 175–194.

Whittlesey, Derwent, "Major Agricultural Regions of the Earth," *Annals of the Association of American Geographers.* December 1936, pp. 199–240.

X

Spatial Characteristics of the Farm

In the preceding chapter the general effects of on-site production costs and transportation costs to markets were related to agricultural patterns. It was found that proximity to market, when interpreted in light of differential site productivity among crops, provided a fair approximation of general location patterns. Nonetheless, on-site production cost variables were taken pretty much as given within any climatic or physical environment. Moreover, the procurement costs, or costs of getting needed material to the farmsite, were largely ignored.

In this chapter, these costs will be examined in some detail. For example: Why should production costs, and hence intensity of land use, be higher for potatoes than for wheat? Under what conditions do procurement costs affect relative productivity of the same crop grown in two locations? These questions will be answered from the vantage point of five factors: (1) factors that affect ownership and occupancy patterns, (2) determinants of farm site, (3) determinants of field size, (4) rotation characteristics, and (5) possibilities for achieving farm efficiencies through farm cooperatives and vertical integration.

These features are vital to the full understanding of how on-site production costs vary among crops and among agricultural regions. In fact, knowledge of these factors provides the basis for determining the intensity of uses among crops and farming systems; this treatment thus provides the foundation material necessary for more than superficial use of the models in Chapter 9. Knowledge of these on-site procurement and production economies thus separates the novice and overconfident student from the more mature and solidly confident scholar.

As will be demonstrated, many site costs are primarily spatially based — for example, on size of farm, shape and size of fields, and rotation patterns. However, we will not attempt to understand fully all the various on-site production costs but only those derived from geographical factors. The other costs will still be, for the most part, accepted as given.

This approach raises a long-standing debate about how much a geographer should know about the subject he studies, whether it be agriculture, manufacturing, or cities. What should he take as given and what should he try to explain? Of course, he should know something about those factors which affect spatial distributions, but how much? Should he know what causes the factors that cause the patterns to exist? Undoubtedly, his geographical understanding should penetrate to some knowledge of phenomena one step removed from the item on which he is focusing. Beyond this, however, things become more uncertain. Of course, for full understanding, all things may have some relevance; in knowledge, there are no arbitrary cutoffs.

The above argument is perhaps best put in methodological terms. In statistics there are often one dependent and many independent variables. The dependent variable represents the phenomenon one wishes to understand. The independent variables include those factors which correlate with the dependent variable in a meaningful manner and thus provide understanding of it. This procedure is shown in Figure 10.1 with regard to an understanding of agricultural location. Note that our approach through Chapter 8 has been to take the independent variables as given. However, the independent variables can also be studied as dependent variables in another context, so that explanations for their characteristics might also be pursued. Thus the procedure results in a series of explanations that are ordinally removed — that is, explanations of the first order, the second order, and so on. Of course, if the investigator continues to work backward, he will ultimately arrive at the eternal question — the nature of the universe itself.

More formally, the order of removal with reference to agricultural location can be shown as follows (see Figure 10.1): Assume C to be the dependent variable, the spatial pattern of agriculture. This pattern would then be a function of procurement and on-site production costs (E) as well as distribution costs (T), both of which would be labeled the independent variables. But T and E can also be individually treated as dependent variables — just as A_1 (transportation cost variables) was treated in Chapter 2 and as E is treated in this chapter. In this chapter it is assumed that procurement and on-site production costs (E) is a dependent variable and that such things as farm and field size, rotation systems, and vertical integration (A_4) are the independent variables. Moreover, we are attempting to explain variation in such things as farm and field size. Now working forward sequentially, much more can confidently be said about the relationships discussed in Chapter 9.

Determinants of Farm and Field Size

Few variables affect farm production costs more than do the general pat-

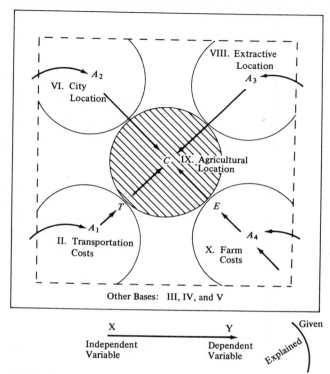

FIGURE 10.1 Explanation for Agricultural Production. Roman numerals refer to chapter numbers. Note that in Chapter 9 the purpose was to explain the general locational principles affecting crop placement. Placement was explained by such things as location and distance of farm from market, on-site costs, and other variables that were taken as given. In this chapter farm costs shift to the center (the dependent variable), and other variables are held constant.

terns of farm ownership and occupancy inasmuch as they correlate with farm and field size. Most cultures have developed standard procedures for settling the land for agricultural purposes. Four basic strategies are evident. First, there are the large-scale government-owned patterns evidenced in Communist countries. Second, there are patterns, characterized by large-scale estatelike private holdings, in which only a few persons own most of the land. Third, there is the strategy of allowing the maximum individual ownership of land through a freehold system. Finally, there is the tenant system, a compromise that is becoming more and more prominent.

In all but the government-owned patterns, agricultural settlement forms have generally resulted in a single farm being composed of noncontiguous units. One such fragmented field system was practiced in much of medieval Europe, where the farmers settled on fiefdoms. The basic pattern there was the three-field rotation system, whereby one field was allowed to lie fallow every third year. According to the prevailing philosophy, each farmer should have a plot in each of the three major fields. This caused no great difficulties in medieval times but has resulted in a diffusion of plots for each farm — a highly inefficient system when the plots are of similar physical characteristics.

Another widely practiced land-allocation system was the long-lot farm system practiced by the French along many rivers in North America, particularly in the eastern part of Canada. It was rationally thought that each farm should have access to the river, the only reasonable form of transportation at the time, and that each farm should comprise various types of land, including river bottom land, upland, and others. To implement this thinking, strips of land perpendicular to the river were plotted. This system, however, prevented any one farmer from being able to achieve the scale necessary to specialize in any one crop. In fact, today these long lot farms have been split into several parcels, subdivided along roads that have since paralleled the river at various distances. This has further reduced farm size. Because of the initial ownership pattern, it is difficult for one farmer to acquire just one physical type of land (say, bottomland) in any contiguous pattern. Consequently, most large farms here are composed of widely spaced fields.

A strategy similar to that of the French was characteristic of initial Mormon settlement in Utah during the 1850s and 1860s. Here, too, it was deemed most appropriate for each farmer to have some of each kind of land. Inasmuch as diverse physical land types were situated in various places around the farm village settlement, each farmer ended up with disjointed fields. This was of no great problem in pioneer times, when the village was located centrally to most of the different fields and each field was of an economic size. Today, however, any one field is of such small consequence that much cost is involved in moving from field to field. Because of the initial ownership pattern, here, too, it has been almost impossible for any one farmer to assemble a contiguous farm unit. Consequently, he is generally left with a diversity of land potentials. Many of these farming areas have practically disappeared today as a result of such inefficiencies. With a new farm pattern, many of these former farming areas might once again become profitable.

Even seemingly foolproof agricultural settlement patterns have proven to be inefficient over time. Perhaps the most sensible basis of settling an agricultural area was the system of homesteading used in the United States, in which land parcels were highly compact and of sufficient size for an efficient operation at the time. This compactness was primarily the result of the rectangular grid land-survey system, in which the land was divided into square-mile sections that could be combined or subdivided into half sections and quarter sections. The size of the homestead was modified in various environments so that it amounted to a full section in many areas, but only a quarter section (160 acres) in many areas the government thought irrigable. Nonetheless, the farm was of more than sufficient size initially, was compact, and had the potential of being a viable farm pattern arrangement.

Subsequently, two conditions arose that have caused difficulties even in these areas. First, as many farms have become more specialized in crop types, and as mechanization has allowed greater acreages to be farmed by a single farmer, many of the original homestead plots have proven too small. Perhaps this difficulty could have been overcome by the purchase of nearby farms — if the scourge of subdividing homesteads among the offspring of the pioneer could have been circumvented.

At this point in our discussion, a brief look at the laws governing land inheritance would be helpful. In much of Europe today (and in England until 1925), the law of primogeniture, under which a man's entire landholding passes to his eldest son, still applies. This law, designed to keep a nobleman's holdings intact after his death, has kept farms at a viable size and has allowed for considerable response to changing times. In the United States, however, Thomas Jefferson sponsored a bill making illegal the rule of primogeniture and entail (limiting the passing of property to a specified line of heirs). Jefferson was primarily concerned about the large slaveholdings in Virginia, which he wished to break up so that the land might be distributed to a greater number of owners. His bill was thus called a "land reform" bill. Another reason for repealing the rule of primogeniture was that in those days only men who owned land (freeholders) had the right to vote. Thus Jefferson acted to broaden the suffrage and make the country more democratic.

The long-term result of this law in the United States, as will be further illustrated, is the "share and share alike" principle whereby all offspring of the landowner hold equal land-inheritance rights. Consequently, over time, homesteads and many other farms of viable size were cut up among the children. Fortunately, this worked well initially, inasmuch as the homestead plots were perhaps too large until about 1930. Then inefficiency in farm size became prevalent. Such cutting up of the land also largely prevented any one ambitious inheritor from assembling the homestead in its original, compact form. Instead, fields and farms have become widely separated, a situation that causes considerable wasted effort and creates serious farm inefficiencies.

These inefficiencies are reflected in several forms. First, many farmers who inherited their plots soon found them uneconomical. Unable to assemble more land, they soon sold or rented their plots and left the farm for the city. As a consequence, a major rural migration occurred, but only after much hardship and many futile attempts to survive on the part of would-be farmers. Second, many farmers found their income to be marginal. In this position many survive today, at a level not much above the poverty level. Many of our traditional "family farms" — the so-called backbone of America — are of this type. In farming areas near cities, however, or near other employment opportunities, part-time farming is the rule. With off-farm work, the farmer is able to achieve a semblance of continuous employment and a slightly higher level of income. Nonetheless, as far as farming is concerned, these people are underemployed and their farms are, at best, marginal operations. The economic result has been for vast farm acreages to be used very inefficiently in terms of current possibilities.

The plague of farm fragmentation, however, is not peculiar to the United States. In fact, in most areas occupied by Catholics, Buddhists, Muslims, and Hindus, primogeniture is rarely practiced. Consequently, in some parts of Asia a five-acre holding may be subdivided into some twenty different strips. Undoubtedly, the emergence of smaller and smaller farms (and the farm fragmentation resulting from the attempt to assemble larger holdings) is one of the major problems in agricultural production today.

Paradoxically, problems of inefficiencies can also result when large landholdings are somehow kept intact. The *latifundias*, or estates, in much of Europe well demonstrate the difficulties caused by large landholdings. Here, many estates have been piece-rented to farmers. But in many other parts of the world, the large landowner is in about the same moral position as the typical large-city slumlord; he milks the land for all he can and gives very little in return. Moreover, the tenant farmer is often in a very precarious position inasmuch as he can rent only on a year-to-year basis. Such uncertainty hardly encourages the tenant to improve the land.

Even so, where tenants' rights are carefully spelled out, the system can be a fairly beneficial one for the tenant farmer. Tenancy is particularly high in England, perhaps because tenants' rights are so well protected and so fairly established. But tenancy is not just the result of scandalously extensive lands controlled by an absentee landholding class. In the United States large holdings have resulted in vast regions worked by sharecroppers, as in the cotton areas of the Mississippi Valley and Eastern Texas, and tobacco areas along the east coast Piedmont. Tenant farming is also particularly prevalent in the Midwest of the United States. In fact, about one-third of the farmland in the United States is tenant-operated. Here some of the richest and most profitable land in the world has gone into tenant status. The reasons for this appear to be primarily social in nature. Farmland holds great status among urban Midwesterners — perhaps because of their rural upbringing and because of their general tendency to stay in the Midwest even when they leave the farm. Consequently, it is common for city people who have absolutely no intention of becoming farmers to invest in farms. Their land is leased to tenants, who provide the landowner with "outside" income. Strangely, much prestige among city people in the Midwest is achieved by having "just purchased another farm." Similar tendencies characterize much of the American urban population, but not to the same degree as here.

The most successful farms appear to be those which have reached a size large enough to permit economies of scale. Such farms have been assembled in many areas of the United States, particularly by family corporations or by certain farm entrepreneurs. Some of the largest assemblies in the world include the King Ranch in Southwestern Texas (almost one million acres) and, of course, the banana and rubber plantations owned by large corporations. But other very profitable farms have been developed in most kinds of crops, such as cotton, wheat, and potatoes. In the latter case an extensive, irrigated farm might be only a few thousand acres in size, but it is massive in comparison with the very small farms nearby.

Other large-scale farms occur in Communist countries and in those places which have nationalized much farm land. The *sovkhozes* (collective farms) in the Soviet Union often amount to over 50,000 acres each and several are well over 100,000 acres in extent. Nevertheless, perhaps for political and social reasons, many of these farms have not been as productive as might be expected. Other variations on the communal tenure patterns include the *ejido* of Mexico, the *kibbutz* of Israel, and the *kung-she* (collective farm) of China. Ironically, many of these countries initiated collective farms as a reaction against the ills of large estates and latifundia. Other collectives, of course, are attempts to consolidate multitudes of small landholdings. It is estimated that in many parts of Southeast Asia where paddy agriculture is prominent, the total land in cultivation could be increased by one-fifth with the removal of property "fences," cemeteries, and other land lying unused because of multiple ownership.

Determinants of field size and shape

The determinants of field size are somewhat different from the determinants of farm size. One of the primary determinants of field size is natural or physical features such as small streams and variations in soil and topography. Such physical features cause irregularities in shape but do not reflect an ideal pattern. Nonetheless, small and irregular fields are often put to uses lower than those in nearby fields.

Other, more functionally related factors that determine field size and shape are the nature of the agricultural system and the degree and type of mechanization. The nature of the farming system is strongly correlated with field size. For example, the medieval system was based on cumbersome plows pulled by oxen — plows that were difficult to turn around or to turn at corners. Consequently, in the typical three-field system, each man's property was in long, narrow fields. Each field was about one furlong (220 yards) long. Thus in this system, the length of the field — not its width — was the critical factor. Fields were rectangular, with a height-to-length ratio of about fifteen to one. By contrast, grain farming requires large machinery, which is best used in a circular fashion. Inasmuch as circles leave unoccupied land between fields, the next best thing, the square, is commonly found. Here, the plowing and harvesting is done by going about the field in a series of smaller and smaller "circles."

The major problem in the use of machinery, however, is fields that are too small. Such machinery is often difficult to turn around and requires much space to be operated efficiently. Consequently, many farms with small fields have been placed at a cost disadvantage, inasmuch as hand labor or less efficient machinery must be substituted for the more mechanized operations.

On surface irrigation farms, the size of field is particularly critical. If the fields are too small, potential cropland will be taken up with numerous irrigation ditches. If the fields are too long, the soil near the irrigation sources will be soggy wet before the water reaches the far end of the field. Another problem, largely the result of increasing field size, is the deterioration of the soil through the buildup of alkalinity. Vast areas in the West have been made largely unproductive for this reason alone.

Rotation: Asset or Deficit?

Rotation is another characteristic of farming that affects the cost of production considerably. Basically, it is practiced in order to build up nutrients in the soil that have been lost through cropping. Inasmuch as many cash crops are particularly hard on the soil, some way must be found to restore lost elements. The traditional restoration procedure is to plant crops that replace removed materials. Today, however, these lost elements can be resupplied by the use of fertilizers. It might thus seem that rotation is an archaic system and no longer need be practiced.

Certainly it is an old system. As indicated above, it was practiced in the medieval three-field system where one-third of the land was left fallow each year. The fallow land was largely left to grow back its natural vegetation, which was then plowed under in order to restore lost ingredients to the soil. A rotation system was also postulated by Von Thunen in his third, fourth, and fifth rings outward from the market (see Chapter 9). With each outward ring the intensity of use decreased, as did the number of years between fallowings. Thus in Zone three, the land was made fallow only every six years, whereas in Zone five the land was fallowed every three years, much like the medieval three-field system.

Today, leaving the land fallow as part of a rotation system is practiced primarily among less intensive crops like wheat. In this case, land is left fallow every other year, or sometimes every third year, not necessarily to restore nutrients lost in grain growing (actually grain is a grass-type crop not too hard on the soil), but to clean-cultivate in order to eliminate weeds and to restore moisture content. Wheat, unlike row crops, cannot be cultivated during growing season; therefore, under yearly use, weeds tend to squeeze out the grain. Moreover, grain growing usually occurs in dry areas (often having less than twenty inches of rainfall annually) so that the renewal of moisture content in the soil is vital. Thus the fallow procedure in wheat production appears to have less to do with the nature of the crop's demand on the soil than it does with other characteristics involved in growing the crop and with physical features.

The more common practice is to maintain a rotation scheme that provides for some crop on all fields each year. Thus crops like corn, tobacco, or potatoes, which remove vital nitrogen from the soil, are followed by crops that tend to restore nitrogen — for example, various hay crops (alfalfa, clover, timothy), peas, or beans. For many crops, nutrients and trace elements like iron, manganese, boron, copper, zinc, iodine, and cobalt, which occur in very minute but critical amounts, can be fed directly back into the soil through fertilization.

Nevertheless, there are two major reasons for continuing the common rotation practiced with many crops, namely, (1) the disease dangers inherent in the growing of the same crop year after year, and (2) the dangers of extensive erosion. Some crops, like potatoes, are very disease-prone. With continued cultivation, many of the disease organisms build up in the soil. The continued growing of this crop on the same field, therefore, will result in serious blight, in root and tuber problems like wireworm and nematodes, or in various potato skin diseases such as warts.

Even with a rotation system as careful as the one practiced in Southeastern Idaho, discussed below, soil and blight problems are widespread. In many areas of the United States certain crops have had to be eliminated because of disease organisms. Examples include the Colorado potato beetle in Northern Colorado and the boll weevil in much of the South.

Crops that are open-tilled and grown on sloping land must also be rotated in order to prevent extensive erosion. Cotton, tobacco, potatoes, and corn are examples. In such cases, other crops must be grown periodically in order to hold the soil in place. In some places like the Great Plains in the United States and the steppe areas in the Soviet Union, vast areas have been set aside as "shelter breaks" in order to keep the wind from blowing topsoil during parts of the year. In other places, strip farming and contour farming are practiced.

All rotation schemes, though necessary, add up to a considerable cost factor or an overall lowering of productive intensity. First, rotation requirements prevent ultimate specialization in any one crop. Inasmuch as other crops must also be grown, separate machinery must be purchased for these often less profitable crops. Rotation requirements also prevent farmers from taking maximum advantage of high market prices. Thus field rotation patterns are fixed; the penalty for not rotating is often serious. For example, during the high potato-price period of World War II, some Idaho farmers planted all their fields to potatoes. The thought was that fertilizer could be scientifically applied so that soil fertility could be maintained. This worked splendidly for about three years, but on the fourth, the plants grew about six inches high, then slowly wilted and died. This so impressed neighboring farmers that even today they are reluctant to try out any revolutionary new scheme to intensify production that is not based on a fairly tested rotation system.

Farming Cooperatives and Production Costs

One way in which small farmers affected by high production costs can greatly increase efficiency is by forming cooperatives.

Consequently, cooperatives are widespread in those agricultural areas that have achieved distinction in a particular commodity. Cooperatives are found in wheat, cotton, dairy, livestock, tobacco, wool, citrus, and poultry areas, to name a few. The system operates through joint ownership of critical off-farm facilities by cooperating farmers. Such farmers may cooperate in the marketing of crops, the consumption of goods and services, or in making available farm loans through credit unions. Marketing co-ops, in which the farmers attempt to set grading standards for their crops and to process and sell produce, are the most widespread. Some marketing co-ops are heavily involved in packing, storing, trucking, advertising, and even in testing activities with regard to the crop in question.

In this way, such areas hope to penetrate greater and more distant markets. Three outstanding examples of cooperative success are evident in the western part of the United States. First, cooperatives in the Yakima Valley of Washington have made the Washington Delicious apple marketable throughout the United States. The Idaho Potato Growers Association, along with cooperatives, has set quality grades on potatoes such that the product has made Idaho famous throughout the nation. Finally, the many cooperatives in California are largely responsible for the impact California vegetables and citrus crops have had on the national market.

In extending the demand for his crop far beyond what otherwise would be the case, cooperatives have enabled the small farmer to receive prices higher than those likely to prevail in a free market economy. He has also achieved, through his communal entry into the processing and marketing channels, a reduction in the costs of delivering his produce to market. Moreover, he is able to procure his tools of production (fuel, feed, seed, machinery, and so forth) at less cost than otherwise. He is also able to get loans at a lower interest rate than that obtainable through normal financial channels. Finally, as a shareholder in the cooperative, the small farmer may even make some money on his investment. These benefits all have importance in reducing procurement, production, and distribution costs for the farmer so that he is able to achieve higher profits under this system than he would by working independently.

The importance of cooperatives, however, should perhaps not be exaggerated. Much agricultural production still occurs outside any cooperative sector, and in most areas, cooperatives are somewhat loosely run organizations that many farmers do not join. Undoubtedly, such organizations could make even greater impact than they now do, but the typical farmer tends to be a rather obstinate and individualistic fellow whose attitudes toward cooperative effort make this an unlikely eventuality.

The Farming Principles Exemplified: The Changing Character of an Idaho Potato Farm

The general principles affecting procurement and production costs are perhaps best illustrated by a real case history. A study of the changing features of a surface-irrigated potato farm in the southeastern part of Idaho provides an excellent illustration of these principles. This study admirably exemplifies the principles of ownership and settlement-pattern contamination, change in size of farm, and the competitive challenge of new large-scale farming. In the last-named case, the formidable and perhaps futile task confronting the small farm operator is made abundantly clear. Large-scale production has placed the traditional, surface-irrigated farm at a distinct competitive disadvantage and bodes ill for small farming operations of other types elsewhere.

General settlement pattern and changing farm size

Southeastern Idaho was homesteaded by Mormon pioneers about 1880. Unlike the Mormon settlements in Utah, this area was allotted according to the Homestead Act, which dictated that each farmer residentially occupy the land. In this potentially irrigable but sagebrush-covered territory, each homesteader was deeded one quarter-section — 160 acres — as shown in Figure 10.2.

This was more land than could actually be used for crops for some time to come. Consequently, only small portions of it were made suitable for cropland irrigation. The remainder was extensively used for grazing by drawing primarily upon the natural vegetation. It was thus a generous grant and one which held good promise for ultimately very successful farming.[1]

The first herculean task of the pioneer was to bring surface water to the land. To do this, canals were channeled from some dozen miles to the east,

---

[1]The homestead in question was also one of the better ones in the immediate area. This pioneer arrived shortly after the small vanguard of founding settlers and had fairly good quarter-sections from which to select. The homestead chosen, although it had a slough on its southern part, was mostly potentially usable. By contrast, the quarter-sections to the south and west were affected by lava intrusions and the hilly land of the knolls. Those sections immediately to the north were largely wooded — something to be avoided because of clearance problems. The land immediately to the east was already taken for village use as were other good sites in the vicinity.

where water could be obtained from the Great Feeder River (now called the Dry Bed), a branch of the Snake (see Figure 10.3). In the quarter-section in question, two major canals were brought in: the North Parks Canal (named after the man who guided its development) and the Missionary (referring to the proselytizing nature of the Mormon Church). Along these canals, headgates were built to carry water to the new fields. The manner in which these small ditches traversed the fields was largely dictated by natural topography, and many ditches were curved about in order to maintain proper gradient. Consequently, they were extensive and took up considerable land, but land was in abundance and little concern was paid to this situation at the time.

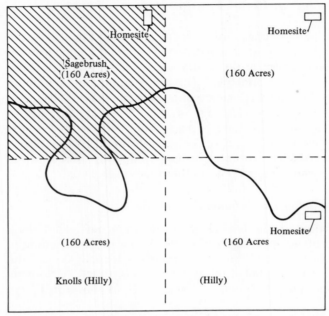

FIGURE 10.2 Typical Homestead Pattern in Southeastern Idaho. Note that each homestead consists of only 160 acres but that homesteads vary somewhat in quality because of physical features and proximity to market centers.

The farming operation generally prospered during the next thirty years as more and more land was brought under cultivation and as experimentation in various crops occurred in order to find the best crop combinations. Such crops as sugar beets, potatoes, wheat, corn, hay, and all manner of vegetables and feed grains were attempted.

However, with the premature death of the male pioneer about 1910, and the maturing of the large family of children, questions began to be raised about inheritance and birthrights. In conformance with general custom, each child, male and female, was given equal parcels of land. Some parcels were slightly larger than others because of differing land quality, but every attempt was made, within the then-developed pattern of fields, to allocate the land equally among the seven living children. This pattern is shown in Figure 10.4, and might appropriately be labeled Stage 2 in the general process of changing farm size. This resulted in only slightly over twenty acres to each, but was adequate for the time when such land would be improved and used intensely.

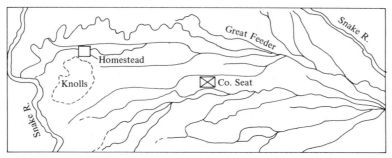

FIGURE 10.3 Irrigation Canal System near Rigby, Idaho (Jefferson County). Note that, unlike natural stream patterns, the canal system branches out with distance from water source. Canal flow in the case above is from east to west.

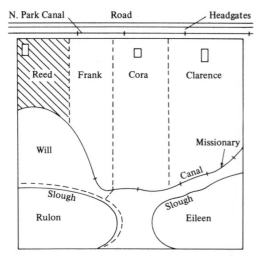

FIGURE 10.4 Typical Inheritance Pattern from 160-Acre Homestead, circa 1880. Note that females were also given land inheritances. The differing size of parcels allocated was largely determined by soil quality and topography.

Nevertheless, only three children remained on the farm — Clarence, Reed, and their sister Cora, plus their respective wives and husband. Noticeably, those staying to occupy the land had inherited property adjoining the main road. Other parcels, although somewhat larger, were more isolated. Consequently, the other three brothers and one sister (Frank, Rulon, Will, and Eileen) rented their land to Clarence and Reed. (Cora's husband was an "outsider" and, primarily for this reason, was not considered a suitable renter.)

During the 1930s and early 1940s, Clarence and Reed began trying to buy back the family homestead. Clarence, who had the original homestead site, had the best chance of success, but Reed won out and finally was able to consolidate all land except that owned by Clarence and Cora. The latter two, embittered perhaps at losing out to Reed, spitefully sold their lands outside the family despite high price offers from Reed. Clarence sold his original plot to a neighbor, much in the same land position as Reed. Cora, much to the disgust of others in the family, sold her land to the Mormon Church. This was a particularly bitter pill for the others to swallow, for it meant that the land could never again be consolidated into the original homestead territory — a sentimental wish on the part of most of the children.

During the period of consolidation of fields and the purchasing of parcels elsewhere, the land was made considerably more productive. There was an attempt to increase field sizes and to put into better production all land used marginally, as in the case of "permanent" pasture land. First, willows and other material that had grown along canal banks were cleared in hopes of making better pasture land for cattle. Second, many of the fields were resurfaced by leveling and scraping so that various ditches could be removed and fields could be combined. Specifically, Frank's and Reed's fields were fused into one long field. Eileen's and Rulon's fields were leveled so that only one ditch was needed where formerly several had weaved through them. The Missionary canal was moved so that it ran straight east through Frank's field and then south along Cora's plot, where it joined the original channel. This enabled the southern portion of Frank's plot, formerly used mostly for pasture, and all of Will's to be combined into another single large field — a major undertaking.

Scraping and leveling of land was largely done through Federal subsidy. This was necessary not only because capital was scarce, but because there were also some risks involved. Heavy removal of topsoil usually resulted in poor crops for several years. Sometimes the removal of soil revealed unsuspected deposits of gravel, which permanently rendered the scraped land much less productive than formerly. There were also some unsuspected risks. This became apparent later when, because of the long surface irrigation of the fields, alkalinity became a problem.

This was also the period in which the farm converted from horses to tractors. Consequently, land formerly used for oats, hay, and pasture was made available for other use. For many of these pasture lands, there was no alternative use, and Reed found himself with more pasture than he could use. Like many farmers in the same happy predicament, he decided to focus on dairying. After a few years of hard work and fairly low returns, however, he decided that dairying was not the answer. Because his barn and his milking equipment were not up to standard, the milk could be sold only for use in making butter and cheese. It took more capital to reach Class A dairy standing than most farmers were willing to provide. Consequently, the raising of beef cattle became the supplemental animal crop.[2]

The fourth stage continued the demand for farm land. Such demand was primarily the result of the need to use the new tractors and machinery more efficiently. Thus began the search for nearby small farms that could be rented or purchased. Several were found and purchased, but at some miles distant. Meanwhile, the price of land had reached the scandalous heights of $1000 or more per acre, and most land could not be bought at any price. In fact, paying such prices could be justified only if the land were bought as an increment to an already existing farm. Once again, many small farmers sold out and left the area. The demand for such acreages was so great, however, that land prices remained extremely high.

Two discouraging factors loomed large on the horizon. First was the recurrent problem of granting inheritance to children (about every fifty years). Certainly, subdivision today would create unworkable units for farming. Second, a veritable revolution in potato farming, by then the main cash crop, broke out on formerly dry farm grain areas adjacent to the fertile irrigated lands. Here, deep well irrigation began to emerge and the rush was on to the new land frontier. (These new lands will be discussed at greater length below.)

The general cycle in average farm size in the area is summarized in Figure 10.5. Note the four main stages in farm size: (1) the initial 160-acre homestead, (2) the fragmentation of the farm because of inheritance, (3) the consolidation of fields by the lucky few in their long climb toward a viable farm unit, and (4) the current period, in which additional farms have been assembled. Note also the lurking problem of refragmentation due to inheritance. Despite its dramatic form, this pattern is not atypical of farm areas in much of the United States, albeit at a slightly different time and on a different scale.

The changing rotation patterns

It is well to pause here to examine closely the emergence of the present

---

[2]The decline of animal raising in general is evident in the landscape. Several decades ago all fields were elaborately fenced, and it was an almost unforgivable error to leave a field gate open. Today, most of the old fences are in disrepair, and some farmers have even removed fences between their property and public roadways. One of the most noticeable features of earlier farmsteads was also a reflection of animal raising — the barnyard, the impressive barn, and the granaries. Today, the machine shed has usually replaced the other structures in visual and functional importance.

system of crops and the patterns of rotation. These, too, pass through about four main stages, as do the farm size changes noted above. Generally, such crop patterns have progressed from fairly extensive to highly intensive production during the period discussed.

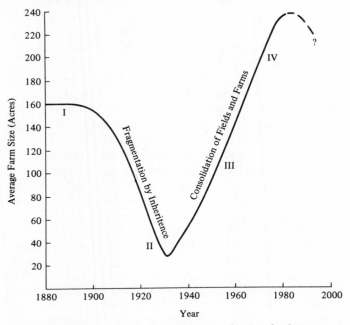

FIGURE 10.5 Typical Farm Size Change as the Result of Fragmentation by Inheritance and Reconsolidation of Fields by the More Successful Inheritors.   This example is based on the farm shown in Figure 10.4.

In the pioneer period most of the land was, in general, grazing land or pasture. Cultivated cropland was used for experimental crops such as peas, sugar beets, corn, and potatoes. These cash crops were heavily supplemented by nitrogen-building legumes in such a way that a typical rotation pattern on cultivated land included a cash crop about once every four years.

A number of rotational patterns were practiced during the remaining stages. In order of intensity, these included: (a) sugar beets, potatoes, feed grains, alfalfa, alfalfa, alfalfa, and (b) wheat, alfalfa, alfalfa, peas, potatoes, potatoes. Another common pattern was wheat, alfalfa, alfalfa, potatoes, wheat, and potatoes. In stage four, potatoes had become *the* crop and the pattern was highly intensified, as illustrated by the following rotation scheme: wheat, potatoes, potatoes, wheat, potatoes, potatoes, wheat, alfalfa, alfalfa. Note that all but the last rotation pattern covered a six-year cycle.

The most prominent sequence is from a grain crop like wheat to a hay crop like alfalfa. This occurs because alfalfa takes one full year to reach maturity. Consequently, it is usually seeded along with a grain crop. Thus a harvest of grain is received during the first summer. Also, the eight- to ten-inch-high alfalfa after grain harvest is excellent for pasture purposes. The grain stubble is cut high so that the alfalfa is left on the land. In fact, alfalfa is not so extensive a crop as it might first appear. It does triple duty. First, it returns needed nitrogen to the soil during growth and when, as green manure, it is plowed under to prepare the soil for a cultivated crop. Equally important, inasmuch as the hay is fed to animals, alfalfa is indirectly valuable as barnyard manure. Finally, alfalfa is not just a one-crop harvest during the summer. In fact, two and even three hay crops are common.

Another alteration is quite evident in the changing rotation patterns — sugar beets and peas were discontinued as crops. Sugar beets were the first to go because of the tremendous amount of labor involved on the one hand (they were tremendously unpopular with children, who were assigned the backbreaking chores of thinning and weeding them), and mechanization on the other. When children could more profitably be used as tractor chauffeurs, they would naturally be less and less used for menial hoeing tasks. Also, in about 1950, the mechanical beet toppers and other special equipment came to the fore. First, the big toppers were very expensive (then about $10,000), but even more decisive was the fact that they could not operate effectively on such small fields.[3]

Sugar beets were nonetheless a valued crop for the farmers and one which was not immediately eliminated. First, of course, sugar beets were a cash crop of no small importance compared even with potatoes. Moreover, sugar beets were much easier on the soil. But perhaps most important, the farmers could contract their crop to the Utah and Idaho Sugar Company and thus receive payment immediately after thinning and weeding. This payment supplemented summer income greatly. Inasmuch as the labor, done by children, was unpaid, sugar beets were a lucrative crop indeed.

The demise of pea production is primarily and simply due to the finding of more profitable crops. A major incentive for raising peas was the presence of several pea canneries nearby and the sure market thus provided. Peas were a fairly reliable cash crop (although weather sometimes caused ruin), one that was especially good for the soil as well. Moreover, after it was harvested,

[3]It is notable that the need for large and expensive machinery for beet harvesting did not result in the use of communal labor and rotated machinery, as it had in the grain industries. In the latter case, a traveling thresher-owner contracted to do each farmer's crop, and the large crew needed to feed the thresher was supplied by exchanged labor among the farmers. This communal threshing was actually a gala event at each farm, with each farm wife attempting to outdo the next in the elaborateness of the meals served. Most midday meals (called "dinner" in Idaho) were veritable banquets. A somewhat similar but far less elaborate work festival occurred during the haying season, when farmers pooled their horses and wagons as well as their labor to provide a meaningful operation for one another. Both of these practices have disappeared. The combine has eliminated the threshing festival, and the mechanical hay baler and mechanical loaders have largely destroyed the excitement of haying days.

the crop provided excellent forage for pigs. Indeed it was during the intensive pea period that pigs were most widespread. However, peas required special machinery for their production — machinery that was becoming more mechanized and that the farmer was reluctant to buy. Since there were more profitable crops he could raise, the farmer left peas by the wayside. As a consequence, almost no pigs are raised today.

It can therefore be seen that rotation is not just a simple matter of keeping the soil at constant fertility. It is a fairly elaborate system that is subject to change and greatly affected by the market prices for various crops. Moreover, it reflects fairly well the potential demand for the land. In places where the land is extensively used, rotation appears to be more leisurely; but in places and times that present great opportunities for profit in cash crops, the rotation pattern — indeed the whole system of farming itself — can be drastically changed.

The impact of large-scale potato farms on traditionally irrigated agriculture

As was mentioned above, in the early 1960s much formerly dryfarm wheat land suddenly became potentially irrigable. This was the result of enough capital being available in the area for well-drilling and pumps so that deep-well sprinkler irrigation could be attempted. The farmers in the valley had long known about the potential, but had not possessed sufficient risk capital to undertake the experiment. By the early 1960s several of the larger and more prosperous potato farmers met the challenge. Although the first few faced disaster, in a few years the large-scale sprinkler-irrigated farm was a reality and a major threat to traditional small-scale surface-irrigated lands.

The new lands that had been converted from dryfarm to "wetfarm" had several obvious advantages. First, inasmuch as such wheat dryfarms were of extensive size, having more than several thousand acres each, the land was ready-made for large farm and field use. Second, with the development of sprinkler irrigation, which relies on pipes rather than ditches to distribute the water, levelness of the fields made little difference. Hence no extensive field preparation was involved in converting the land to irrigated use. Third, the soils in much of the dryfarm and desert areas were a lighter, more calcareous, and very fine sandy and silty loam. The Bannock silt loam had excellent drainage characteristics and was perfectly suited for mechanical harvesters. Moreover, these lands were tremendously fertile and, for the first few years at least, had higher yields than did the traditional potato farms nearby. Finally, during the first year or two the entire farm could be put into potato production. Inasmuch as the land formerly had been entirely in grain use, it was ready for potatoes. Thus the new farmers had tremendous opportunities for making a killing the first few years, and several of them made over a million dollars annually.

By contrast, the traditionally irrigated farms had many disadvantages. Not only were the farms and fields small, but the land was not amenable to mechanical harvesters. The soil is a heavy calcareous loam, often rocky, and has a tendency to be cloddy. In fact, if such soil is plowed too wet in the spring, it may remain cloddy for years.

Strangely enough, however, reliable figures show that the traditionally irrigated farm still has the advantage on a cost-per-acre basis. These costs are shown below in Table 10.1. Average procurement and production costs per acre amount to only $149 for traditional, surface-irrigated farms versus some $174 for the new large-scale sprinker-irrigated farms. The clue to the competitive advantage of the sprinkler-irrigated farms, however, is seen in their scale of production.

TABLE 10.1
COMPARATIVE COSTS: SURFACE-IRRIGATED VERSUS SPRINKLER-IRRIGATED POTATO FARMS IN SOUTHEASTERN IDAHO

Type of Cost	Traditional, Surface-Irrigated Farm (per acre)	New, Sprinkler-Irrigated Farm (per acre)
Procurement Costs		
Seed	$44	$44
Water	2	20 (includes power)
Fertilizer	10	16
Machinery	8	20
Pipes and pumps	None	10
Subtotal	64	110
Production Costs		
Seed-cutting labor	4	4
Planting and soil preparation	6	4
Irrigation labor	3	3
Cultivation	3	3
Harvesting labor	50	10
Ditch maintenance	1	None
Digging	9	35
Taxes	3	1
Subtotal	85	64
TOTAL	149	174

The profit to be made on a traditionally irrigated farm with 160 acres is only about one-seventh of that on a sprinkler-irrigated farm. The latter is about 1000 acres in size and has some 300 acres in potatoes (during the first several years all of the 1000 acres are in potatoes). By contrast, the traditionally irrigated farm can support only about 40 acres in potatoes in any one year because of its rotation pattern and because of heavy labor requirements at harvest time. If it is assumed that the average yield is 300 hundredweight per acre in each case and the field run price is $1.80 per hundredweight, then the traditionally irrigated farm will clear $1.30 a hundredweight, or $15,640 in all, whereas the sprinkler-irrigated farm, although making only $1.10 per hundredweight, will clear some $82,500. Thus, the sheer profitability of the land on a per acre basis is not always a reliable measure as to the ability of various crops to pay rent or to prosper.

However, the real advantage of the sprinkler-irrigated potato farm over the small-scale surface-irrigated potato farm lies in the farmer's access to economies of scale in production and to possibilities for vertical integration. Neither of these were figured in the above calculations.

Economies of scale are achieved in two ways. First, as discussed in Chapter 4, a large producer can use his machinery more effectively and can generally save in ways not open to the small producer. Second, the large-scale farmer often gets discounts on the basis of volume for most of his procurement inputs, such as machinery, fuel, seed, and fertilizer. Of course, the small farmer can fight back somewhat against such preferential treatment through his cooperatives, which offer him discount purchases.

The economies achieved through vertical integration, however, are formidable indeed to the small farmer. Such integration is possibly the most effective way in which the large-scale operator truly makes his operation pay. Vertical integration for a large-scale sprinkler-irrigated farm is shown in Figure 10.6. In this case, such a large-scale operator controls both forward and backward costs associated with his potato-producing operation. He controls backward items by sharing heavily in the profits of machinery, pipe, fuel, and seed companies — even of financial institutions. He controls forward items by having his own storage cellars and warehouses for shipment to markets, but he also attains considerable benefit by making use of those potatoes for which the small farmer receives little or no payment — namely, the culls (potatoes that do not meet Class 1 or 2 inspection criteria). These include knotty, too small, and otherwise damaged tubers, which are sent to a processing plant for dehydration and shipment to extensive markets throughout the United States. The wastes from the processing plant are then largely used as feed for beef animals kept in large feedlots. The large-scale raising of beef cattle in this manner affects even Midwest beef growers in a competitive way. Finally, as if this were not enough, the beef operation is sufficient to support a separate meat-packing plant. With such a system, it is a mystery that the traditionally irrigated farms have survived as long as they have — but complete vertical-integration systems are just beginning to gain full steam in Idaho, and perhaps it will not be long before the older system fades into oblivion. At any rate, the demand for small farms will surely decrease and a new method of agriculture will have to be developed. Given this latest challenge, coupled with the imminent need for sharing the farm among the offspring, the future looks bleak indeed. Thus one of the more interesting revolutions in land tenure and pattern will probably occur in this area soon. Indeed, such changes will occur in many areas throughout the United States as large-scale and integrated farming becomes more and more entrenched.

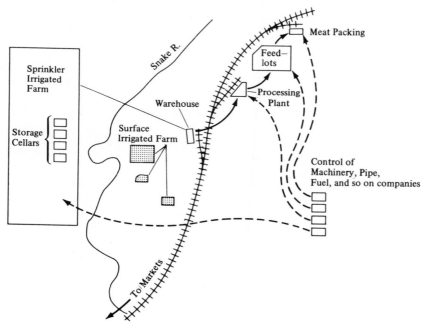

FIGURE 10.6 An Example of Vertical Integration in Potato Farming. Note the small size and fragmented nature of the older, surface-irrigated farms on the east side of the Snake River in comparison to the sprinkler-irrigated farms on the west side.

Conclusions

We have now arrived at the conclusion of our first major attempt at a comprehensive understanding of one activity. It is perhaps unnecessary at this point to repeat that the agricultural location problem is indeed multifaceted, interconnected, and difficult. Moreover, it is an activity that is spatially highly dynamic (albeit not nearly so dynamic as the distribution of activities within cities) so that an emphasis here on present-day facts and statistics would be of little use to the student. What *is* important is acquiring the framework for spatial understanding, inasmuch as that framework can be applied, with prudence of course, to any distribution at any time. More important, such a framework should aid the economic geography student in the interpretation of new patterns as they rapidly emerge on the rural landscape.

BIBLIOGRAPHY

Gregor, Howard F. "Farm Structure in Regional Comparison: California and New Jersey." *Economic Geography*, July 1969, pp. 209–225.

————. *Geography of Agriculture: Themes in Research*. Englewood Cliffs, N.J.: Prentice-Hall, 1970.

————. "The Large Industrialized American Crop Farm." *Geographical Review*, April 1970, pp. 151–175.

Hawkes, H. Bowman. "Irrigation in the United States." In *Conservation of Natural Resources*, edited by Guy-Harold Smith, pp. 90–115. New York: John Wiley & Sons, 1958.

Highsmith, Richard M., Jr. "Irrigated Lands of the World." *Geographical Review*, July 1965, pp. 382–389.

Lambert, Audrey M. "Farm Consolidation and Improvement in the Netherlands: An Example from the Land Van Maas en Waal." *Economic Geography*, April 1961, pp. 115–123.

Lewthwaite, Gordon R. "Wisconsin Cheese and Farm Type: A Locational Hypothesis." *Economic Geography*, April 1964, pp. 95–112.

Vermeer, Donald E. "Population Pressure and Crop Rotational Changes among the Tiv of Nigeria." *Annals of the Association of American Geographers*, June 1970, pp. 299–314.

part 8

Manufacturing Location, Regionally Considered

The problems connected with the vast changes that can now be foreseen in manufacturing distributions on the global and national scenes are a matter of importance not only for the small group of people classified as professional economists, geographers, businessmen, or politicians: They are of direct concern to the man in the street. A factory worker in a wealthy nation may be retrained for new jobs several times in his active life span, and move from a stagnating town to one with rapid growth industries: As a citizen he may have to face the demand from less fortunate countries that the tariff behind which his factory works be lowered to allow industries in the poor countries to enter the market. Global thinking will be required as modern technology shrinks all distances.

Gunnar Alexandersson, *Geography of Manufacturing* (Englewood Cliffs, N.J.: Prentice-Hall, 1967), pp. 1–2.

XI

Principles of Manufacturing Location

The three basic components in industrial location are analogous to those contained in our discussion of agricultural location: (1) procurement costs of raw materials — generally, transportation costs required to assemble the raw materials on site, (2) on-site or processing costs, and (3) distribution costs — that is, costs of transporting the finished product to market. However, unlike agriculture, all three costs may be independently dominating or all may be intermixed to bring about a particular locational response. Especially different is the fact that for a number of industrial firms, procurement costs are of extreme importance. It will be recalled that in the location of agriculture, these costs (for example, seed, machinery, and fertilizer) are of small importance.

Thus the location of manufacturing is a much more complex subject — and more difficult of understanding — than is the location of agriculture. This is also due to the myriad of locational possibilities and the host of variables that may play a significant role in manufacturing location. Any one of the three types of costs enumerated above may dominate the locational decision. Thus for many types of manufacturing, an additional locational choice occurs — affording a degree of choice not available to activities previously examined. This additional variable is one of the primary ingredients that tend to make locational understanding of manufacturing more complex than that of the primary activities.

There is also much more flexibility and substitutability in the major factors of production — land, labor, and capital — than there are in factors of the other activities thus far studied. For example, labor and capital are highly interchangeable in that machinery can be substituted for labor, and vice versa. Thus a factory situated in a low-cost and relatively unskilled labor area may opt for using much labor and little machinery in the production process. The degree to which such substitution possibilities can operate, however, as with

205

agriculture, is highly dependent upon the type of manufacturing. In comparison with agriculture, however, most manufacturing is highly machinery-oriented. However, furniture and apparel manufacturing are to a certain extent atypical in that they use heavy labor inputs.

Land is likewise a rather flexible item. Certainly, land costs vary greatly; centrally situated metropolitan sites often cost more than $100,000 an acre while suburban sites are generally under $20,000 an acre and rural sites still less. This, of course, is important in differentiating among industry types in terms of their rent-paying needs and abilities. However, it is land costs in the broad, regional context that most interest us here. Manufacturing plants are not prohibited in extremely hot or cold areas. Operation costs in such environments are simply higher. Thus processing costs might be increased because of the need for air conditioning, insulation, or heating. Mostly, however, other factors are more dominating so that these costs are often not critical.

Manufacturing is more complicated than agriculture for other reasons as well. First, possibilities and practices of integration are more widespread and more extensive. Many industries are involved in controlling, through *vertical integration*, activities that are linked in both a forward and backward direction to their production processes. Unlike agriculture, *horizontal integration* is also possible in manufacturing. Here, an industry, through amalgamation or mergers, can control that sector of production in which it specializes. Thus it has much more influence on the competitive framework than does agriculture. For example, no matter what is done in Idaho, farmers there cannot control the price of potatoes in the United States — too many other areas are also involved and would independently move in to take advantage of any strategies Idaho farmers might adopt. If it were determined that production should be curbed in Idaho in an attempt to raise prices, other areas would increase output and reap most of the price benefits. But in industry, oligopoly (control of the market by only a few major producing firms) is common in many activities so that one firm can have considerable possibilities for manipulation and be far more able to control the destiny of its own undertaking. In fact, the number of firms involved, that is, the extent of competition, has very clear locational implications.

This is evidenced by the fact that most manufactured products, unlike agricultural commodities, are known to the consumer by brand name. Thus a given firm can encourage consumption of its product primarily through advertising, service, and general reputation of quality. This likewise provides greater possibilities for dominating markets than are open to other activities.

Manufacturing is also distinctive in that it is heavily affected by *agglomerative economies*. This is one of the major reasons for the clustering of manufacturing firms in an area. Agglomerative economies result from three general features: (1) the fact that the manufacturing process of many products occurs in an extensively linked system wherein one firm's "finished product" becomes another's "raw material," (2) the development of plants for the manufacture of by-products from waste materials, and (3) the complementary advantages manufacturing firms achieve by being close to one another — for example, drawing upon a large common pool of skilled labor. Use of the various business services that result from the concentration of plants, and particularly from the development of large cities, is another agglomerative advantage. This latter feature is particularly instrumental in causing those manufacturing firms which otherwise have the choice to locate in or very near large cities.

The effect of a highly linked system, in which one firm supplies another with raw materials, is regional concentrations of such feeder-related industries. One well-known system has developed in Michigan and upper Ohio. Here, various firms manufacture parts for the automobile assembly plants in Detroit and the surrounding area. In fact, thousands of different factories are involved in producing items for the manufacture of a single automobile. Such plants are scattered over a wide area in the Midwest. Less well known feeder manufacturing systems include the petrochemical concentration in and around Houston (sometimes called the "spaghetti bowl" because of the elaborate interconnections among firms); the textile industries in Birmingham, England, and the North Carolina Piedmont; and the apparel industries in Manhattan. Less elaborate systems, however, occur in many other parts of the world, particularly in Northern Europe.

Other agglomerations are somewhat similar, but in these cases a major firm(s) may be feeding "parasitic" industries that utilize by-products of the parent industry. In many such cases, one firm may achieve tremendous economies through vertical integration. In most instances, these by-products must be processed fairly close to the main plant so that the locational pull is extremely direct and strong.

The combination of all these possible conditions clearly makes manufacturing a more complicated locational problem than are the other activities studied so far. Nevertheless, there are wide differences in the complexity of the problem among industries. Within the secondary sector, the location of some plants is rather simply dictated by the necessity of being adjacent to raw materials; other plants must locate at the market. The most complex problems, however, are presented by those diversely located activities which may be found in a variety of places for reasons not evident by the dominance of any single factor such as procurement, distribution, or on-site processing costs.

Procurement Costs as a Location Factor

The major factors in industrial location are shown diagrammatically in Figure 11.1. Any one of these components may be a determining factor. The procurement costs primarily represent the costs of transporting the raw material resources to the factory. For those industries which use a single raw material — for example, the mineral and petroleum processing industries — maximum adjacency to the raw material resource results when a firm finds these costs to be most critical. However, most manufacturing involves multiple raw materials from a number of different sources. Each raw material has its own weight, volume, value, and transportation cost characteristics. Thus, even if the best location for such a firm is a place where its raw material costs will be minimized, the determination of that place is no simple matter. Consequently, a number of rather elaborate techniques for minimizing transportation input costs, to be discussed later, have been developed.

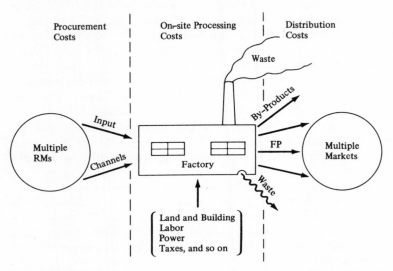

FIGURE 11.1 Locational Contaminants for Manufacturing. Note that each cost may exert a decisive locational pull on the placement of a factory.

This becomes an especially knotty problem inasmuch as there are usually possibilities for substitution among raw materials. Thus, wood can be replaced by plastic or metal in the manufacture of an item. Instead of purely high-grade coal being used for coking (in the manufacture of steel), lower grades can, by beneficiation, be mixed with it in a way that lowers total raw-material transfer costs. Instead of iron ore being used exclusively, scrap can be inserted. And even gas can be used as a fuel in place of coke in some parts of the operation. The same kinds of possibilities are apparent in most manufacturing so that, unless the raw material sources and costs are given, even a determination of the location that minimizes procurement costs is fraught with uncertainties.

Processing costs on-site include not only labor, land, building rent, and machinery costs, but also taxes, power, water, and costs associated with waste disposal, all often critical. Any one of these might be a critical item in the locational decision. Labor is clearly one of the major costs in production, and for many labor-intensive industries, this may be the overriding factor. Small differentials in wage rates among cities and regions may make large differences in terms of production costs. Of course, most industry is limited in its ability to take advantage of such wage rate differentials among nations, but some international movement does occur. Clearly, wage rate differentials between the United States and Japan are giving Japan a major advantage in the manufacture of many items. This model assumes that wage rates and labor are immobile, but in reality this is hardly the case. European workers are free to move among Common Market countries for employment purposes.

Within the United States, wage rates have traditionally been lower in the South than in the North, thus encouraging certain firms to relocate. The textile industry's migration from New England to the Piedmont area in North Carolina is a classic case of how wage rate differences have affected locational patterns. Today, some plants are setting up production along the southern border of the United States, in or near Mexico, in order to take advantage of lower labor costs.

Even so, lower wage rates alone do not tell the full story; productivity of the workers for wages paid is a better measure. Skilled workers are usually more productive and consequently worth higher pay than unskilled workers. More and more are manufacturing plants requiring greater training and skill on the part of the workers. Thus, not just any labor will do. The labor must be capable of doing the job. If the labor is unskilled, the wage rates will be lower, of course, but the factory might have to emphasize labor rather than mechanization. In much of the industrialized world the general trend has been for more mechanization to occur concomitantly with increasing skills and wage levels of the workers. Extremely high wage rates thus force industry to substitute machinery for labor. In fact, in terms of actual numbers of workers it employs, industry has been declining slightly in the United States over the past several decades.

For other industries, power might be the big cost in the production process. In this regard, industries like aluminum seek out those locations which have the cheapest power rates. Until recently, the Pacific Northwest, because of its abundant and cheap power, was able to pull considerable aluminum production away from market locations. During World War II, in fact, alumina (the second stage in aluminum production) was shipped by rail from the Gulf States to the distant Pacific Northwest — one of the longest ton-mile hauls in the world at that time — in order to capitalize on power savings. The finished aluminum was then shipped to the industrial belt for fabrication and for use in the manufacture of a multitude of items. Today, a segment of the aluminum industry has shifted to the Ohio River Valley, where it is able to obtain reasonable power costs by use of natural gas and thus save on transportation costs to the market.

In still other industries, the need to dispose of waste products may dictate locational requirements. For example, on a micro scale, slaughter yards have been relegated to outlying areas of metropolises. Other obnoxious industries include the pulp and paper industry, which pollutes both air and water, and the iron and steel industry. In many areas such industry is severely discouraged because of these effects. Thus a general principle might be that the more obnoxious an industry, the more it might be prevented from moving into certain urban areas, which would otherwise be optimum locations.

Finally, a number of industries, which otherwise have considerable locational choice, have been lured to areas offering lower taxes. A classic case is the heavy industry discrepancy between New York and New Jersey. New York has much higher industrial taxes than its neighbor, with the result that industry abounds on the side of New Jersey near New York but is scarce by comparison in New York proper. Many small communities in the South and elsewhere have also offered tax advantages for new industries in order to bring in employment. Some firms are even given free land and are offered leases on ready-built structures. The success of these latter efforts, however, is much in debate as far as the quality of the community itself is concerned. (This will be discussed at greater length in Part E of the text.)

Another on-site "cost" or asset that has strongly affected industrial location has been the movement of certain kinds of plants to places offering the best overall community amenities. Manufacturing activities whose products can stand high costs of transportation and require a highly skilled, high-priced, and fairly particular labor force are apt to locate in places where such a labor force would like to live. Of particular notice has been the movement of electronics and space industries to places with desirable climates (California, for example) and to cultural centers, especially those with prestigious universities. Thus a new trend is being set for this footloose type of industry that has a highly mobile labor force and a fair latitude of choice among production areas.

Distribution Costs as a Location Factor

Another major transportation cost component is the distribution of finished products to market. Inasmuch as transportation rates are usually more per ton-mile for finished products than for raw materials, these costs can be considerable. In fact, if there is no reduction in weight between the raw material inputs and the finished product outputs, other things being equal, the plant will invariably be best located at the market.

Market location is also critical where perishability is involved. Examples of highly perishable products include baked goods, candy, and newspapers. This factor thus dictates that the manufacturing outlet be close in time, if not in space, to the consumption outlets. On the other hand, as is the case with many agricultural commodities, sometimes the raw material inputs are more perishable than the finished product. In this case, the plant will be raw-material-oriented in order to preserve the longevity of the product through freezing, packing, dehydrating, canning, or the like.

These relationships are shown in Figure 11.2. Note that inasmuch as raw material transportation costs *(PC)* are lower than finished product costs *(DC)*, the lowest aggregate transportation costs *(TC)* will be at the market location. (Costs are less than four at market versus more than five at raw material location.) However, in places where a break-of-bulk operation is necessary in the shipment process, an intermediate location between raw material source and market may occur in order to save the costs of such an operation. Inasmuch as raw material transportation costs have been decreasing faster than finished product costs over the past several decades, this also makes a market location more advantageous for many activities. It is particularly critical where procurement and distribution costs are not too different between the raw material and market locations.

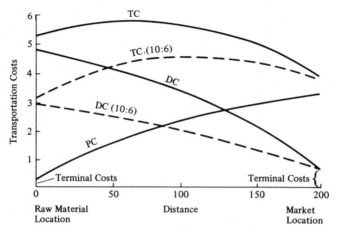

FIGURE 11.2 Procurement Costs *(PC)* versus Distribution Costs *(DC)* to Markets As Industrial Locational Determinants. Other things being equal, the manufacturing plant will locate where total transportation costs *(TC)* are the least. In the case above, the manufacturer would be located at the market. The dashed lines show a changed weight-loss and its effect on best plant location. See text for discussion.

But most manufacturing processes generally result in a reduction in bulk between the raw material and finished product stage. This can be calculated as a *weight loss ratio*. Products that lose more than 30 percent of volume between input and output stage might be labeled as having high weight-loss ratios, in which case the location of the plant, other things being equal, will be at the source of raw materials. The general formula for computation is to divide the finished product volume by raw material volume and then subtract the quotient from 100 percent. Thus, if it takes ten units of raw materials to produce six units of finished product, the weight-loss ratio would be forty $(100 - 6/10 = 40)$.

Now, note that with a raw material to finished product ratio of 10:6 (dashed lines), the total aggregate costs *(TC)* are lowest at the raw material location. The total costs remain about the same at the market source but are considerably lowered at the raw material source. Thus the effect of weight reduction is to favor a raw material location. Note also that the highest cost point has shifted, closer to the market. Nonetheless, the least profitable point in this example, that is, the place of highest total transportation costs, is still intermediate between raw material and markets.

Territorial implications

It should be evident from the above discussion that a change in any one of the costs of production may affect the location best suitable for a given activity. Such changes might include the costs of transportation, a change in the mix of raw materials, or an increase or decrease in output. These, in turn, very much affect the territory from which a manufacturing plant might receive its raw materials and to which it might send its finished products.

The ability of any firm to compete for the marketing of its products in a territorial context is based on its general costs of production as these are accumulated at the place of consumption. As an example, let us assume the existence of three different plants, each producing the same product and competing in the same region. Let us also assume that, for reasons associated with the necessity of being near the source of raw materials, three plant locations are feasible. But each of the three plants has different processing costs because of different on-site costs such as labor, power, and the like. Because of these varying on-site production costs, they also have differing abilities to bid for customers over a given territory. As a result, the plants will be of different sizes and hence will achieve different scale economies. In turn, this will result in second-round effects whereby the more advantageously situated firm will obtain an even larger market.

This principle of territorial control and territorial progression is illustrated in Figure 11.3. First, assume that the three firms are raw-material-oriented and fixed in location, but that they have varying on-site production costs. Plant A actually has the lowest on-site costs, but the closeness of Plant B prevents it from dominating much territory. Its limit of price advantage is at distance d_1. Plant C actually has the highest on-site costs, but because of its isolation from the other competitors, it dominates a much wider territory (from d_3 to the right side of the figure). This means that Plant C will have a greater volume of output and hence can achieve greater economies of scale (see Chapter 4) than can either Plant A or B. This advantage will enable Plant C to reduce its on-site production costs considerably so that its costs are now lower than those of its nearest competitor, Plant *B*. The spatial result is that Plant *C* now has a price advantage in the area from d_2 to d_3 — territory in which Plant *B* formerly had the advantage.

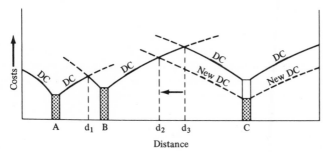

FIGURE 11.3 Effect of Distribution Costs *(DC)* from Manufacturing Plants A, B, and C on Territorial Dominance. The vertical bars at each plant represent procurement costs (PC) and on-site costs. For clarification, see Figure 11.1. Should on-site production costs be lowered as shown at Plant C, then the new distribution cost curves (DC) would allow Plant C to shift its zone of territorial dominance toward Plant B from distance d_3 to distance d_2.

However, it must be cautioned that because of the brand name features of most manufacturing, these plants are not homogeneous in terms of the consumer market. Some customers may prefer to buy from a particular company even though another company actually has a price advantage in the area. Thus, even in those cities where a major plant of a large manufacturer is located, the local population will buy many products from other companies. Price is not a definitive measure of territorial control with regard to manufacturing. Nevertheless, it does indicate which firm has the advantage and which should, with equal competitive spirit and service, provide the product for the majority of customers in an area.

Minimization of Production Costs

As might be anticipated, there are a number of partial solutions to the manufacturing location problem. Most such "solutions," however, are based on keeping several components fixed and given. Basically, the problem can be dissected in three different ways: (1) finding the point of minimum transportation costs for the procurement of raw materials, (2) finding the minimum transportation costs for distribution of the product to markets, and (3) finding that location at which on-site production costs are minimal. In the overall sense, the best location for a given plant is the one that minimizes all these factors.

However, it is soon apparent that such costs can be minimized by merely producing nothing. Therefore, when we talk about minimizing production costs in terms of a locational optimum, we really mean minimizing such costs, given certain levels of output. Perhaps an even better way to state the problem is to find that location which will maximize profits.

When the problem is put in this latter framework, all kinds of factors emerge that are not covered by the theories discussed above. Such variables include notions about plant size, growth potential, long- versus short-run profits, competitive strategies, and pricing systems — all of which will, in turn, increase output and perhaps allow greater scale economies. These factors are complex indeed and will be covered mostly by examples in forthcoming chapters.

A simplified, transportation-based location model

The nature of the transportation aspect of the manufacturing location problem is perhaps most easily seen by examining a hypothetical situation involving one market and two raw materials. (The case involving one market and one raw material was covered above.) From this slightly more realistic vantage point, several major axioms can be developed.

Figure 11.4 shows such a situation. This is modeled after the famous locational triangle solution of Alfred Weber, a German economist who in 1909 formulated locational principles for industry along the lines developed by von Thunen for agriculture at a much earlier period.[1] Given are two raw materials, *RM1* and *RM2*, and one Market. In this example, all three are fixed points 200 miles apart. Quite simply, the question is, Where is the best place to locate an industrial plant, given these fixed points and the various distance-cost relationships?

First, if the raw materials are pure — that is, if there is no weight-loss incurred between raw materials and finished product — the plant would be best located at the market *(M)* at a "transport cost" of 400 unit miles. However, if the weight-loss ratio is 0.50 — that is, if two units of raw materials are required to make one unit of finished product — then the location that will use fewer distance units can be found. The point which minimizes raw material transfer costs is located halfway between the two raw materials at distance *X*. If the plant is situated here, then the raw material distance units would amount to only 200 distance units (for example miles) and the finished product units would amount to some 164 distance units, or some 364 distance units in all. However, some quick students of trigonometry might have discovered that location *Y* is the best place inasumuch as it is the center point between all places. Some calculation shows that total distance units of only 344 (115 distance units for each raw material and 114 distance units for the finished product to market) are needed to serve this location.

---

[1]Alfred Weber, *Theory of the Location of Industries,* translated by Carl J. Friedrich (Chicago: University of Chicago Press, 1929).

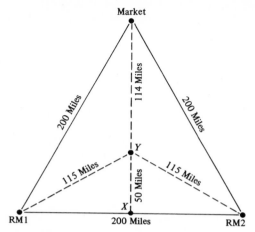

FIGURE 11.4 A Locational Triangle for Manufacturing Plant Location Given One Market and Two Raw-Material Sources. The minimum cost solution depends not only on mileages involved, but upon weight-loss estimations.

As another variation, let us assume that different raw material inputs are required for production. Let us further assume that the weight-loss ratio remains the same, but that it takes one and one-half units of *RM1* and only one half-unit of *RM2* to produce one unit of finished product. In this case, it is seen that the best place to locate the plant would not be at *M* or *X* or *Y*, but at the source of *RM2*. Here, the total distance units would be only 300. Thus, where raw material mix is involved, the best location is strongly pulled toward the most dominant raw material source.

This example could be greatly expanded, but it should now be evident that when one says "raw-material-oriented," he is describing a multifaceted problem. In fact, solution of actual problems of this type require high speed computers. Nonetheless, there are mechanical devices, such as the *Varignon frame* devised by Weber, that can provide some solutions. (See Bibliography.)

A more realistic model

Now let us apply this logic to an even more realistic situation (Figure 11.5). In this case, we shall keep the schema of two raw material locations and one market but introduce variable transportation costs among raw materials and finished products, different costs between water and land, and break-of-bulk considerations. To keep the mental calculations simple, we shall assume that the weight-loss ratio is still 0.50, but that it takes one and one-half units of

RM2 and one-half unit of *RM1* to produce one unit of finished product *(FP).* We shall further refine this by introducing actual transportation cost figures:

A. *Transportation Costs on Land:*

RM1	$2/unit mile
RM2	$3/unit mile
FP	$5/unit mile

B. *Transportation Costs on Water:*

RM1	$2/unit mile
RM2	$2/unit mile
FP	$3/unit mile

C. *Break-of-bulk Costs at Portston*

RM1	$10/unit
RM2	$10/unit
FP	$15/unit

At this stage, the problem may seem rather complicated. However, using the principles discussed above, it is simple enough to be figured out with mental calculation. For confirmation purposes, the correctness of your thoughts can be easily verified. The important technique, as with most geography problems, is to focus on the map (Figure 11.5) rather than stare at the figures.

Inasmuch as the total market is at Macropolis, the location problem can be approached in a simple and logical way. First, it is clear that neither Coalville nor Middleton would be the best place for a plant. The transportation cost for finished products from a plant at Coalville amounts to some $300 via the southern route to Macropolis, whereas such cost would be only $205 from a plant at Ironton via the northern route. Moreover, Coalville would not be chosen because the heavy-mix raw material *(RM2)* is at Ironton. For this same reason, the plant would not be located at the intermediate point of Middleton, which is also ruled out because there is no way to find a shorter distance to the market from Middleton than from either Coalville or Ironton. Thus, because of the actual transportation route system, there are no possibilities for intermediate strategies, as was the case with the more abstract example shown in Figure 11.4. The best location from a raw material standpoint would thus be at Ironton.

However, the best location from a market standpoint would be at Macropolis inasmuch as the market is at this location. The second major question therefore is, Which is cheaper: a plant at Ironton or a plant at Macropolis? By a little quick calculation it is found that Ironton has some $45 per unit advantage ($245 versus $290 for a plant at Macropolis).

But before one hastily concludes that the best plant location is at Ironton, he should take note of a possible intermediate point, Portston, located between the raw-material-oriented production site at Ironton and the market-oriented-site at Macropolis. This intermediate point is also at a break-of-bulk place and might be significant in reducing land-water transfer costs. A plant at Portston would save such break-of-bulk charges inasmuch as raw materials could come in by land at the back door of a plant and finished products could go by water out the front door. Hence, if the saving is $45 or more below that for Ironton, Portston would be the best location. This is clearly the case inasmuch as such break-of-bulk costs amount to some $15 from *RM2* (one and one-half units at $10 per unit) and $5 for *RM1* (one-half unit at $10 per unit). A plant located here also saves the differential in costs over the shipment of two units of raw materials by water ($120) versus one unit of finished product ($90), an advantage for finished product shipment of some $30. Total savings thus amount to $50. Hence the plant at Portston costs only $240 as compared with the one at Ironton at $245 and the one at Macropolis for $290 per unit.

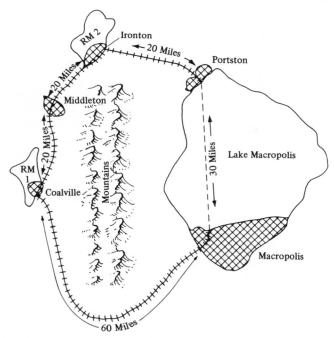

FIGURE 11.5 Schematic Demonstration of the Effects of Variable Production Costs on Plant Location.   See text for assumptions.

   Having seen how this model operates, you can now insert other costs and considerations of your choosing. For example, you may wish to specify different labor costs at various production points as a reflection of different on-site processing costs. If you really want to create a more realistic problem, you might add other raw materials, other markets, and new transportation routes.

Conclusions

The concepts discussed above provided a framework by which the various locational factors for industry can be identified and particular spatial patterns can be anticipated. In summary, two types were emphasized: raw-material-oriented and market-oriented. Raw-material-oriented firms were characterized as those whose products (1) have a high weight-loss ratio, (2) contain a highly perishable raw material, (3) are less perishable than the raw material, or (4) are less bulky or breakable than the raw material. By contrast, firms whose products show the opposite characteristics were commonly market-oriented.

However, as will be demonstrated, these abstract concepts become difficult to apply to any particular manufacturing type. In fact, most types of manufacturing are likely to have several spatial patterns — some plants will be located near their raw material, some at the market, and others at various intermediate locations. Thus an examination of the distribution of any particular industry leaves one with the feeling that something is wrong; the pattern is not pure, but a mixture of various locational positions.

Nonetheless, firms are not scattered haphazardly over the landscape; there is spatial order, but it requires a multifaceted and dynamic approach, which will be presented in Chapter 12, to reveal it. Those uninitiated in the application of locational principles to pattern interpretation will therefore find the distributions of manufacturing perplexing.

There are a number of reasons why the pattern of any particular industry might not be as pure as the theoretical assumptions discussed above would indicate. First, the above models are static and therefore do not take into account the dynamic nature of location. The locational pattern of any function is developed over a period of time; and as a result some firms are found in places that are no longer optimum while others are located in areas that hold promise for the future. Tabulation of the majority of firms in a particular locational situation may merely reflect the major growth period in that industry. At any rate, there is always a lag effect inasmuch as firms often cannot make an immediate and detailed response to new or short-term locational opportunities. Inasmuch as opportunities for manufacturing continually change, there is always some residual effect whereby some industries remain in suboptimal locations. Once investment is made in a particular plant, this plant will often remain in operation long after its full usefulness and perhaps even its geographic rationale have departed. In fact, the investment in buildings and other nontransferable items may be so great that it prevents any spatial response whatsoever, even though another location may now be optimum. For such reasons, any given distribution will usually contain plants developed at different times under different technological, monetary, and competitive conditions.

To the geographer, the most obvious reasons for expecting a particular industry to have several different pattern components lie in the peculiarities of the areas themselves and their distorting effects on firm placement. Territorial features may actually cause an inherently raw-material-oriented firm to be located at the market, or vice versa. Thus ports are often prominent as manufacturing centers, both as out-shippers near the raw material source and as in-shippers near or at the market. In order to understand a particular distribution, one must understand the particular nature of the territory where the pattern occurs — its transportation routes and costs, raw material source possibilities, differences in on-site costs such as labor, and the distribution of the producer's consumers. This is, of course, a big order. Nonetheless, without territorial knowledge, only limited interpretative application of the principles discussed above is possible.

BIBLIOGRAPHY

Alexandersson, Gunnar. *Geography of Manufacturing*. Englewood Cliffs, N.J.: Prentice-Hall, 1967.

Greenhut, Melvin L. "Integrating the Leading Theories of Plant Location." *Southern Economic Journal*, July 1951, pp. 225–228 and April 1952, pp. 526–538.

————. *Plant Location in Theory and Practice: The Economics of Space*. Chapel Hill: University of North Carolina Press, 1956.

Harris, C. D. "The Market As a Factor in the Location of Industry in the United States." *Annals of the Association of American Geographers*, December 1954.

Hoover, Edgar M. *The Location of Economic Activity*. New York: McGraw-Hill, 1948.

McGregor, John R. "Water As a Factor in the Location of Industry in the Southeast." *Southeastern Geographer*, vol. X, no. 1, pp. 41–54.

Miller, E. Willard. *A Geography of Industrial Location*. Dubuque, Iowa: William C. Brown, 1970.

Smith, D. M. "A Theoretical Framework for Geographical Studies in Industrial Location." *Economic Geography*, April 1966, pp. 95–113.

Tornquist, Gunnar. *Transport Costs As a Location Factor for Manufacturing Industry*. Lund, Sweden: C. W. K. Gleerup, 1962.

Weber, Alfred. *Theory of the Location of Industries*. Translated by Carl J. Friedrich. Chicago: University of Chicago Press, 1929.

Will, Robert A. "Finding the Best Plant Location." *Chemical Engineering*, March 1, 1965, pp. 87–92.

Zelinsky, Wilbur. "Has American Industry Been Decentralizing? The Evidence for the 1939-1954 Period." *Economic Geography*, July 1962, pp. 251–269.

XII

Regional Patterns of Manufacturing

The substitutions that occur among the factors of production (that is, procurement, processing, and distribution costs) makes the analysis of any given type of manufacturing difficult. Detailed information as to the nature of the firm is generally required in order to make any good assessment of location decisions. Even with detailed data and intimate knowledge of the firm in question, the task is arduous and the results are not always correct. Peculiarities of regions, for example, the peculiar distribution of raw materials and transportation routes, cause deviations to occur among the factors of production even for identical firms located in different areas. Hence good territorial knowledge, as well as manufacturing-firm knowledge, is a requirement for sound understanding of locational variables. Of utmost importance, however, is the identification of the cost characteristics in the more recent locations so that trends can be ascertained. Fortunately, an approximation of the importance of the various factors of production can be made by careful analysis of the various patterns. The focus of this chapter is to make the nature of such pattern interpretation explicit.

Another major pitfall in interpretation of the factor of production costs results from the fact that one cannot merely add up the components of each of the three major production costs (that is, procurement, processing, and distribution) to ascertain which of the three is most critical in determining location. In general, if a firm is located near raw materials, then the raw procurement costs may be very low relative to finished product costs. Thus one might erroneously conclude that such a firm is there because of otherwise heavy raw-material transfer costs. But nontransfer cost considerations may be the dominating factor. In fact, on-site costs (labor, taxes, power, water, and other processing features) may outweigh all transfer cost considerations. Nonetheless, such firms will still try to use as little transportation as possible and will seek out strategic places — where transportation costs are minimal — whenever possible. On the other hand, a particular industry may be located at the market, but its location there may have little or nothing to do with distribution cost considerations. Rather, the determining factor may be that such market area is the key labor area for that industry. Thus, unlike many raw-material-oriented and market-oriented patterns, industries dominated by such processing costs often do not reveal the real reasons for their location.

A further contaminating agent is differences in institutions and economic-social systems from place to place. This is especially the case for those industries which are distributed, as in the Soviet Union, on the basis of variations in on-site features. Labor can be moved easily to particular localities. In the United States, taxes are often made a major inducement — or deterrent. Differentials in power costs, a function often controlled in the public sector, can also cause decided distortions in some industrial location patterns. Inasmuch as on-site costs are the prime locational determinant for many industries, power cost differentials make for considerable variation in industrial pattern for a single industry type. Even so, for many types of industry the locational components discussed above are so strong that institutional considerations cannot easily override them. Thus, when one looks at an industry that is typically raw-material-oriented or market-oriented on a global scale, he will note little basic difference in pattern. Communism, socialism, or capitalism have little major effect upon the placement of types of industries tightly controlled by transfer costs considerations.

Finally, the models in Chapter 11 are somewhat limited in that they are based on the assumption that each firm location is an independent entity. In fact, this is rarely the case. Branch plants of major corporations are the rule today. Thus the viability of any particular location can often be fully understood only in light of the total distribution of plants in any particular corporate structure.

A simple but operationally meaningful way to better understand the locational characteristics of a particular type of manufacturing is to study its broad regional pattern. Despite certain pitfalls caused by peculiarities of time and place, the examination of a particular industry's pattern of location is often highly fruitful and yields accurate data. Admittedly, it would be helpful also to have detailed cost information for the various components of production, but such information is rarely available. This is particularly the case in areas outside the United States.

Two basic pattern types will be examined in some detail: (1) market-oriented patterns, and (2) raw-material-oriented patterns. In most examinations of industrial location, the distribution seen on a map provides the primary input for locational understanding. The following discussion, therefore, should aid considerably in such pattern diagnosis in two ways. First it will aid in the positive identification of patterns by pointing out the critical features that need to be identified in any particular pattern before any conclusions are reached.

Second, it will aid (in a somewhat negative manner) by demonstrating certain common fallacies in pattern analysis. Nonetheless, these operational devices are by no means foolproof. Only after long and patient studies of the trial-and-error type and great knowledge of particular activities and territories will students become comfortable and sure in their diagnoses.

Other labels for market-oriented firms commonly include both *ubiquitous* and *city-serving* industries. A ubiquitous firm is not one that is found everywhere but one engaged in an activity that is found in about the same distribution pattern as the market, which in most cases means the urban population distribution. Thus, a map of the United States, or the world, that shows the distribution of cities by population size and a map that shows the distribution of a market-oriented activity, such as soft drink bottling, would look very similar. Nevertheless, ubiquitous firms are not found in any city of a particular size until the threshold for a suitable market has been reached, much as is the case with retailing establishments. To support a viable plant, some manufacturing firms, such as soft drink bottling plants, need a city of only a few thousand people, whereas a brewery requires a city with a much greater population. Part of the reason is that not everyone drinks beer, whereas people of almost all ages drink soda pop. These city-serving manufacturing types generally include printing and publishing, construction, and many food industries.

In contrast, raw-material-oriented industries are usually *sporadically distributed* and are labeled *city-forming*. Sporadically located manufacturing firms are simply located unevenly with respect to the market. In most instances, they are raw-material-oriented. A major difference between city-serving and city-forming industries is that the product of sporadically located firms is generally sold to consumers outside the urban area in which they are found. Thus the city-forming types are important for urban growth. Such workers are hence labeled *basic* workers, whereas workers in the ubiquitous pursuits are called *service*, or *nonbasic*, workers. Inasmuch as a good deal of industry is of the sporadic type, it is not difficult to see why chambers of commerce and similar organizations the world over try to bring in more industry. It is postulated that the workers in such industries indirectly support other people in the community and hence create new jobs and new population growth for the urban centers. This idea is a crucial part of the *economic base concept* and hence of theories concerning the growth of cities.

Another dual classification in much use distinguishes between durable and nondurable manufacturing types. Durable manufacturing includes most of the sporadic industries such as iron and steel, the metal industries, machinery, chemicals, and mining. Strangely, even the industries with such truly temporary products as apparel, paper, tobacco, fur, leather, and textiles are also classified as durable manufacturing types. The nondurable types are mostly market-oriented and include printing and publishing, construction, and most kinds of food processing such as meat, bakeries, soft drink bottling, and the manufacture of dairy products. Nevertheless, there are a number of exceptions to this generalization inasmuch as such nondurable manufacturing types like meat packing, flour milling, and canning are raw-material-oriented and are hence sporadically distributed in conformance with their raw materials.

The extent to which each of the major industrial categories is associated with cities is shown in Table 12.1.

TABLE 12.1
UNITED STATES EMPLOYMENT IN MAJOR MANUFACTURING CATEGORIES ACCORDING TO DEGREE OF URBANIZATION

			Percentage Employed by Type of Area	
Manufacturing Type	*# Employees (mils)*	*Urban**	*2500 to 10,000 Population*	*Places over 1,000,000 Population*
Mining	0.9	35	15	5
Furniture, and so on	1.2	44	10	10
Primary metals	1.2	82	5	36
Fabricated metals	0.8	84	5	40
Machinery, excluding electrical	1.3	82	5	30
Electrical machinery	0.8	85	3	45
Motor vehicles	0.9	83	1	45
Textiles, and so on	1.2	68	15	15
Apparel	1.1	83	6	51
Printing, publishing and so on	0.9	89	5	40
Chemicals	0.7	78	5	35
For comparison purposes:				
Retail sales	8.5	80	10	30

* An "urban place" is defined by the United States Census as any incorporated place having more than 2500 population.
Source: **United States Census of Manufacturing, 1963**

Note that manufacturing types least associated with large urban places include mining, textiles, and furniture making. These are characteristically found in small and isolated areas and are clearly raw-material- or resource-oriented. Only one-fifth of all mining-related manufacturing in the United States is found in places over 2500 population, and only slightly higher urban percentages are found for textiles and furniture making. By contrast, several manufacturing types like primary metals, fabricated metals, machinery, motor vehicles, apparel, and printing have a higher percentage of their work force in urban places than does the hallmark of urban employment itself, retail sales. In fact, a few industries of this class are highly concentrated in the largest metropolitan areas; these include particularly metals, machinery, apparel, printing, and chemicals.

Market-Oriented Patterns

Overall, market locations are becoming more common in industrial location patterns. This occurs primarily because considerable improvement has been made in the movement of raw materials, but relatively few improvements have been made in the handling of finished products, containerization being an exception. Because of bulk shipments and special handling procedures, the costs of raw material movements have been greatly reduced relative to finished products over the past decade.

A market-oriented manufacturing pattern is to be expected if one or more of the following conditions are met: (1) The raw material inputs and finished product outputs are similar in bulk and weight. This is the case because raw materials are generally easier and less costly to transport than finished products (see Chapter 2). (2) The finished product is more bulky, more perishable, or more fragile than the raw material. Such manufacturing types include most kinds of bakery items, candymaking, and glassmaking. (3) The product is augmented with a rather ubiquitous raw material during the manufacturing process. One common example is water, used, for example, in making beer and soft drinks.

A market location is particularly prominent in the manufacture of products that actually gain weight as processing occurs. In beer production and soft drink bottling, for example, water is added to the imported raw material. Inasmuch as water is a fairly ubiquitous commodity, it makes little sense to pay transportation-to-market charges on it in the finished product. However, where water of a different quality is important in the manufacture of the product, as is claimed in the case of the beer brand that advertises, "It's the water," the weight-gain factor may exert considerably less influence in favor of choosing a market location than it ordinarily would.

Products that become breakable or more bulky in the manufacturing process are likewise also often made near markets. Examples include dishes and glasses, pots and pans, metal fabrication, furniture manufacturing, and the assembly (construction) of machinery, and automobiles — but not airplanes. However, because of other locational factors, not all of these activities are found at the market. For example, transportation costs to markets of these more bulky items can be reduced through "breakdown" shipment. Thus furniture is shipped in a breakdown fashion and simply reassembled at the site of retail purchase. In this case, one might say that the manufacturing process is bifurcated: finished elements are made at one site and assembled at another. This is increasingly the procedure used in the manufacture of automobiles, whereby many regional assembly plants have developed.

Nonetheless, two types are most prominent: (1) Type A, in which distribution coincides almost perfectly with the general urban population, (2) Type B, in which only higher order centers contain the firm, or in which a point of minimum aggregate transportation costs for the finished product is the chosen location.

In this latter case, the plant may be located in a small community or even in rural territory, yet its main locational force is still proximity to markets.

The Type A market-oriented pattern, one which coincides almost perfectly with the distribution of urban centers, is shown diagrammatically in Figure 12.1. Thus a map showing the relative size of urban centers is almost identical with one showing the general extent of this manufacturing activity in those centers.

(Type A Pattern)

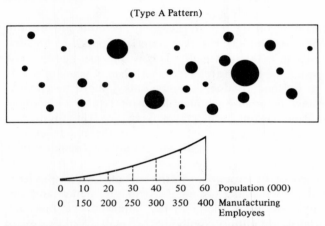

| 0 | 10 | 20 | 30 | 40 | 50 | 60 | Population (000) |
| 0 | 150 | 200 | 250 | 300 | 350 | 400 | Manufacturing Employees |

FIGURE 12.1 A Market-Oriented Industrial Pattern, Type A. Note that all markets contain industrial employment in conformance with their relative populations.

Various quantitative measures of deviation from the base population distribution can be developed. One method is shown in Figure 12.2. City population is plotted along the X axis and some measure of manufacturing importance in that city is plotted along the Y axis. Thus, given the population of City X and the number of employees in Manufacturing Type Y, a direct relationship is obtained if this kind of market location pattern is prominent.

In the example shown, note that there is a population below which a firm cannot operate because of market size limitations; thus cities below 10,000 population will have no manufacturing of this type. Such centers will then be supplied with the product from larger nearby centers, causing the latter to have a larger number of employees than their population would indicate.

Note also that there is rarely an equal increase in industrial employment with increasing population. For example, in this case a city with 20,000 population is expected to have 200 employees in a particular market-oriented industry. But a city twice as large, at 40,000 population, is not expected to have 400 employees (twice as many as the center half as large) but only about 300 employees. The reason for this exponential relationship relates to economies of scale as well as other on-site efficiencies.

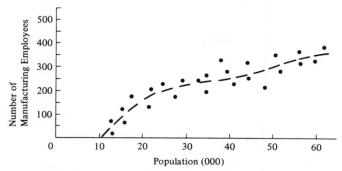

FIGURE 12.2 Graphic Presentation of a Type A Industrial Location Pattern.   See Figure 12.1. Note that there is a direct, albeit not linear, relationship between the amount of population a place contains and the number of employees in manufacturing.

Given a higher threshold level for various manufacturing activities, only the larger city or cities will contain the industrial function (Figure 12.3). Examples in the United States are regional capitals such as Denver, Atlanta, Saint Louis, Los Angeles, Seattle, Minneapolis-Saint Paul, and Chicago. These regional centers develop because of scale requirements that enable only one plant or one location to best serve the entire area. In most cases, this plant will be found at the largest city because the latter will contain the largest single market. This large market center also usually has the best access to all other centers in the plant's distribution area. Thus any function that is primarily restricted to New York or Chicago might qualify as a market-oriented activity.

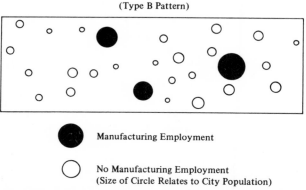

FIGURE 12.3 A Market-Oriented Industrial Pattern, Type B.   Note that only the larger markets contain industrial employment.

This relationship is generally shown by the spatial covariation between the urban population distribution in the United States and the distribution of employees in all kinds of manufacturing (Figure 12.4 and 12.5). The population distribution is almost identical in relative terms with the number of manufacturing workers in each center. Note, as suggested above, that the progression in the number of manufacturing employees does not increase in the same ratio as population size. Instead, it follows an exponential relationship similar to that shown in Figure 12.2. Note furthermore that this demonstrates the general market-oriented pattern of manufacturing as a whole. Thus the sporadic and raw-material-oriented pattern appears to be the exception to the rule. On the other hand, an analysis of each industry reveals a tendency for raw-material-oriented industries to set the initial settlement pattern of cities — a pattern which, in turn, is reinforced by market-oriented industries. From such a crude distribution it is difficult to answer the question of whether industry is the result of cities or cities are the result of industry. In fact, depending on the type of industry, both are correct.

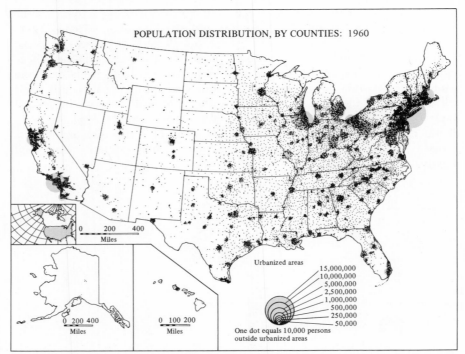

FIGURE 12.4 The Population Distribution of the United States. This distribution can be taken as the "market" distribution for various patterns of manufacturing. A manufacturing pattern that is of Type A (see Figure 12.2) will appear to be identical to this. In a Type B pattern (see Figure 12.3), only the larger cities will contain manufacturing employment. Source: U. S. Census.

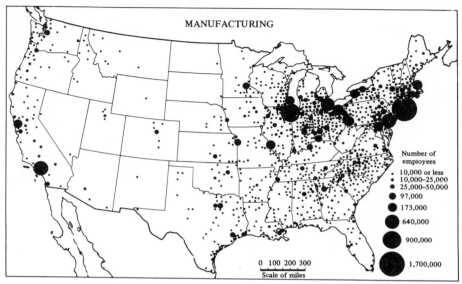

FIGURE 12.5 Total Manufacturing Employment Distribution in the United States. Note the general conformance with Figure 12.4 above. Thus, a Type A pattern is suggested but is imperfectly manifest. Source: John W. Alexander, *Economic Geography*, (C) 1963. Reprinted by permission of Prentice-Hall, Inc., Englewood Cliffs, New Jersey.

As a method of pattern analysis (a method that will be followed throughout this chapter), compare the relative-sized circles representing manufacturing employment with the relative ranking of circle sizes representing urban population (Figure 12.4). In this manner, both positive and negative deviations will become apparent and, once apparent, will suggest meaningful questions as to why such deviations occur. For example, note that there is an overabundance of manufacturing employees in relation to urban population in the industrial belt, but a relative scarcity of them in Florida. One wonders what kind of industry it is that is most prominent in the industrial belt; indeed, what kind of industrial employment is dominant in any one of the regions examined. Examination of the distribution of basic raw materials — for example, timber, vegetables, fruits, and mine products — gives one a first approximation of this answer. In order to gain good insights, however, it will be necessary to examine patterns of individual types of industry.

Three levels of Type A patterns: beer, printing and motor vehicles

The pattern of beer production provides a good example of a Type A market-oriented manufacturing pattern (Figure 12.6). When this pattern is compared with the basic distribution of population, here used as a rough approximation of the market (Figure 12.4), it is at once apparent that while there is a general spatial coincidence, there are also some major exceptions. It is notable that some areas of the United States have almost no beer production. This is in some cases the result of state regulations that prohibit the making of beer. In other cases, perhaps the population is simply too small to support a brewery — a function that appears to require a fairly high threshold of entry. Nonetheless, there are many small towns in Wisconsin and New York where considerable production occurs. A common explanation for this is the large proportion of population of German stock with both a taste for beer and the know-how to produce it. Milwaukee is one of the outstanding centers of production, given its population. Saint Louis is also an extremely large producer. In the Rocky Mountain West, populations having breweries are smaller than are similar populations in other parts of the United States. Perhaps distance between centers is a major explanatory factor here. Nonetheless, the overall pattern is heavily market-oriented and is largely geared to major regional capitals, except for much of the South.

FIGURE 12.6 Beer Production in the United States, by Barrels. Note the importance of the larger centers in any given region for such production. Source: "After N. E. Battist," from John W. Alexander, *Economic Geography*, (C) 1963. Reprinted by permission of Prentice-Hall, Inc., Englewood Cliffs, New Jersey.

Figure 12.7 shows the distribution of employees in printing. The pattern is still a Type A pattern, but the smaller centers have dropped off as compared with the overall pattern of beer production. Most metropolises having over one million population have over one thousand persons employed in printing — a good deal more than would be necessary merely to publish newspapers. Nonetheless, there are some small cities, and a few large ones, that are outstanding relative to their population in this respect. Among these, New York is the paramount center. New York and vicinity accounts for almost four-fifths of all the books published in the United States. Chicago is also outstanding relative to its population; but in proportionate terms such medium-sized centers as Indianapolis, Indiana; Columbus, Ohio; Des Moines, Iowa; Rochester, New York; and Grand Rapids, Michigan, have much more printing employment than their populations, as compared with other centers, would indicate. In contrast, such cities as Phoenix, Arizona; New Orleans, Louisiana; and Miami, Florida, have comparatively little such employment. Thus, even though the pattern very nearly coincides with the market pattern, beyond a certain-sized market level, there are many exceptions. One of the reasons for these exceptions is the mixed nature of the employment category. If it were limited to newspaper publication or to publication of certain types of book (for example, general, academic, or religious), a clearer market pattern might emerge.

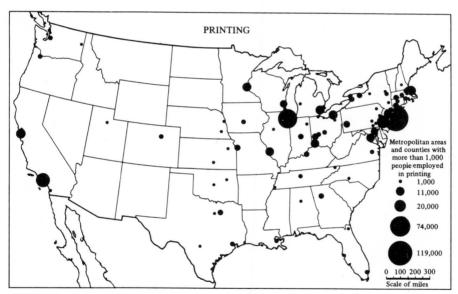

FIGURE 12.7 Employment in Printing in the United States. Note the evidence of a Type B pattern. New York and Chicago loom very large in this activity, but other important regional centers are also evident. Source: "After Sol Levin." John W. Alexander, *Economic Geography*, (C) 1963. Reprinted by permission of Prentice-Hall, Inc., Englewood Cliffs, New Jersey.

The Type B market location

Type B patterns are far more difficult to evaluate (Figure 12.8). Here, industry may be found in a small city or even in a rural area. Even so, if the location of such a firm is the result of an attempt to minimize transportation costs to market, its location is market-oriented. Thus, in the United States a central location is often found in Chicago or in other parts of Illinois, in Michigan, Indiana, Ohio, Missouri, or even Iowa. Transportation networks tend to make such locations highly advantageous with regard to distribution of a product to the entire population of the United States.

(Type B Pattern)

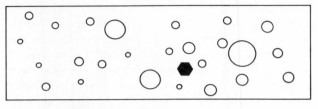

◆   Manufacturing Employment

◯   No Manufacturing Employment

(Size of Circle Relates to City Population)

FIGURE 12.8 A Market-Oriented Pattern, Type B.   Compare this pattern with the Type B pattern shown in Figure 12.3. In this case, the plant is still market-oriented inasmuch as it is centrally situated to serve all markets, but it is situated in a rural area rather than in any market. Certain on-site cost savings may be the cause.

Despite the first appearance of simplicity, it requires careful assessment to determine whether a particular pattern is market-oriented. This is especially the case in the Type B patterns. For example, vegetable canneries are raw-material-oriented. Nonetheless, container-making plants, which are found near canneries and which have a pattern almost identical to theirs, are market-oriented. They are market-oriented because they locate next to *their* market, the canneries. In determining whether a particular industry is market- or raw-material-oriented, specific information about the location and nature of its raw materials and about the nature and location of its customers is required.

Figure 12.9 shows this type of market-oriented pattern. In fact, two subpatterns are evident. In the first instance, the industry, concentrated in and around Detroit, is highly market-oriented and relegated to one general area of production — an area somewhat centrally situated within the total market area of the United States. The heavy number of employees in Ohio, Indiana, and Michigan may work in small towns or even in rural areas. Nonetheless these firms, which produce motor vehicle equipment such as tires, carburetors, and batteries, are market-oriented in that they are clustered about the major motor vehicle assembly plants. Recently, as markets have risen throughout the United States and thresholds have been reached, branch assembly plants have been developed in major regional centers such as Saint Louis, Kansas City, Dallas, Los Angeles, San Francisco, and Atlanta. Thus a newly developing market-oriented pattern is being superimposed over an old market-oriented pattern.

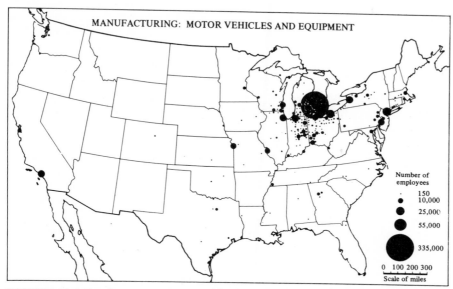

FIGURE 12.9 Employment in Motor Vehicles and Equipment Manufacturing.   Note the tremendous concentration in Detroit and vicinity. Actually, considerable manufacturing occurs in very small towns and rural areas centrally situated in the American industrial belt. Source: "After Donald Hirschfeld." John W. Alexander, *Economic Geography*, (C) 1963. Reprinted by permission of Prentice-Hall, Inc., Englewood Cliffs, New Jersey.

Raw-Material-Oriented Patterns

Just as generalizations can be made about the types of firms that are typically market-oriented, so can they also be applied profitably to types that are raw-material-oriented. Such firms are usually peculiar in one of several respects: (1) the raw material input may contain a major impurity so that there is a high weight-loss between it and the finished product; (2) the raw material is generally perishable or subject to difficulties in handling compared with the finished product; or (3) the raw material sources are diversified or are highly scattered in their location. In this latter regard, an assembly problem is involved. Therefore, the activity will locate at strategic places whereby the costs of assembling the raw material might be minimized.

Nevertheless, there are several exceptions to these rules. One exception concerns the frozen food industry, an industry that generally occurs at or very near the source of raw materials. In such cases the finished product requires special shipment facilities (refrigeration); given proper handling, however, it is much less perishable than are its raw materials. Perhaps the critical factor to be considered is that without some preservation of the raw materials, the finished product could not satisfactorily reach the market at all. Thus foods are frozen at points accessible to farms for much the same reason that foods are canned there. Cattle slaughtering is another case in point. Historically, the finished product (fresh meat) was more perishable than the live raw materials. Therefore, packing formerly occurred at markets, to which the live animals were brought. Today, with refrigeration, the slaughtering industry is moving closer to farm production areas, or most often, production occurs at intermediate locations at strategic break-of-bulk points on the side toward major markets. Consequently, the slaughtering industry has shifted from Chicago to Omaha, and recently, to areas even farther west.

Further distinction should be made at this stage as to what is meant by raw-material-oriented. For example, if the leather industry is parasitically tied to the meat-packing industry, it is raw-material-oriented, regardless of what pattern the meat-packing industry assumes. In this regard, locational understanding within the manufacturing sector is greatly aided when one thinks within a highly linked raw material and market system. Most manufacturing is bound within this chainlike system. Thus we might break down further the secondary manufacturing sector.

A useful framework for thinking about the many types of manufacturing within such a linked system is the connection between the primary sector and the tertiary sector. In this regard, particular attention should be given to the *primary manufacturing* firms as commodities move from the primary sector into the secondary sector. This path should be followed until the terminal portion is reached — the point at which products are prepared for final markets. *Primary manufacturing* is that type of manufacturing whose raw materials are commodities — that is, raw materials obtained directly from the primary sector. This includes most food and agricultural processing, canning, and packing plants as well as most firms that change ores into pure metal and mineral form. *Secondary manufacturing* receives its raw materials as products from primary manufacturing firms. Thus the raw materials of secondary manufacturing firms are the finished products of primary manufacturing. The locational tendency is for primary manufacturing firms to be raw-material-oriented and for secondary manufacturing firms to be market-oriented. Even so, many secondary manufacturing firms are "raw-material-oriented" inasmuch as they are located at the source of *their* raw materials — the primary manufacturing plant.

The simplest type of raw-material-oriented pattern is one that covaries closely with the locational pattern of the raw material used in the manufacturing process (Figure 12.10). Thus this pattern, Type *Y*, is highly analogous to the Type A market-oriented pattern discussed above. If the pattern of raw materials is known, it can be fairly easily determined whether or not the pattern of production coincides with it. For example, if a firm uses lumber as its basic raw material and if similar firms are always found in lumber-producing areas, then one would assume that such a firm is raw-material-oriented. If a firm's raw material is orange rinds and if similar firms are always found near the source of orange rinds, it would likewise be considered raw-material-oriented.

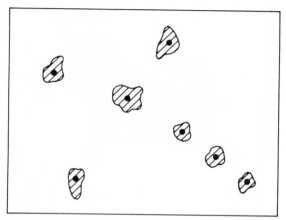

⬭ Raw Material Location

● Manufacturing Plant

FIGURE 12.10 A Raw-Material-Oriented Pattern, Type Y. This pattern is analogous to the Type A market-oriented pattern (Figure 12.1). In this case, each source of raw material contains a manufacturing plant relative to the size of raw material.

The simple correlation type of raw-material-oriented pattern is seen by the covariation of the distribution of forest land and the production of wood pulp in the United States (Figures 12.11 and 12.12). Again, there are some exceptions, such as the relative absence of wood pulp production in the Rocky Mountain states, but this is easily understood given the type of tree required for wood pulp production and the relative inaccessibility to markets. Coastal locations, it will be seen, are highly favored.

A more complicated pattern is demonstrated by flour milling (Figure 12.13). In this case, several subpatterns are evident: (1) a general coincidence of milling areas with grain-growing areas, as in the Great Plains, Montana, and much of the West; (2) the extreme dominance of major assembly centers such as Minneapolis-Saint Paul, Saint Louis, and Buffalo; and (3) the historically older pattern in much of the eastern Piedmont and the Old West. In the first instance, milling centers are centrally situated in the producing areas as based on certain scale requirements. In the second instance, major regional centers dominate large areas. An important exception is Buffalo, which is a major break-of-bulk

DISTRIBUTION OF FOREST LAND IN THE UNITED STATES

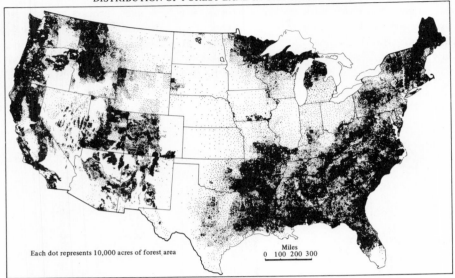

Each dot represents 10,000 acres of forest area

Miles
0 100 200 300

FIGURE 12.11 Distribution of Forest Land in the United States.   Source: U.S. Forest Service.

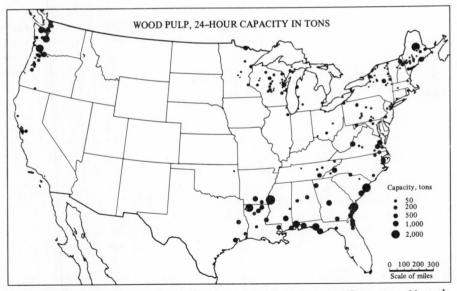

WOOD PULP, 24–HOUR CAPACITY IN TONS

Capacity, tons
· 50
· 200
· 500
● 1,000
● 2,000

0 100 200 300
Scale of miles

FIGURE 12.12 Production of Wood Pulp per 24-Hour Tonnage Capacity.   Note the general correspondence of this manufacturing type with the pattern of forest land (raw material) as shown in Figure 12-11. Source: "After Ray Hargreaves." John W. Alexander, *Economic Geography,* (C) 1963. Reprinted by permission of Prentice-Hall, Inc., Englewood Cliffs, New Jersey.

point for both American and Canadian wheat to international markets. Moreover, that city has been granted special milling-in-transit privileges that have allowed milling to occur with little change in the rates. Buffalo also behaves in much the same way as export ports like Seattle, Portland, and Los Angeles, which are some distance from producing areas.

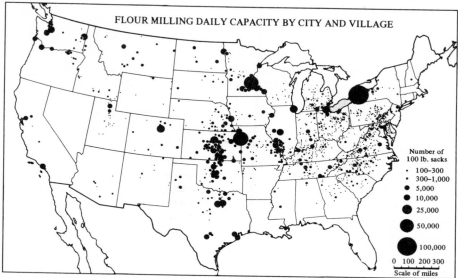

FIGURE 12.13 Flour Milling Production per Daily Cwt Capacity. This pattern of manufacturing production is heavily raw-material-oriented and follows generally the Type Y pattern above (see Figure 12.10). Source: "After Robert Anderson." John W. Alexander, *Economic Geography*, (C) 1963. Reprinted by permission of Prentice-Hall, Inc., Englewood Cliffs, New Jersey.

Yet grain milling might be expected to be market-oriented rather than raw-material-oriented. Certainly milled grain is more perishable than grain kernels. The solution is twofold. First, most of the grain exported is in the whole kernel stage and thus does not show up in the pattern. Second, flour, while highly perishable relative to the raw material, is nonetheless much less perishable than bakery products. Finally, it must be remembered that there is a fair weight-loss between raw wheat and finished white flour. On the average, it takes 100 pounds of wheat to produce 72 pounds of white flour. [The weight-loss ratio is therefore 28 $(100 - 72/100)$.] Moreover, if 28 pounds were of no value, there would undoubtedly be much more milling in remote rural areas than is the case. In fact, the 28 pounds are *shorts* and bran, which are used mostly as cattle feed. Thus there is considerable incentive to mill at raw-material-oriented sites near cattle-feeding areas, and vice versa, there is some incentive to feed cattle near grain-milling sites.

For these reasons any given manufacturing type would not be expected to have just one locational pattern, but a group of patterns. At any one time these firms would be located in a vast number of different kinds of places. One key to decoding such groups is in terms of the size and age of firms in any particular pattern type. As a general rule, the large firms are the newer ones. Thus these might be indicative of the trends taking place in the industry and, more importantly, reflect the future pattern. On the other hand, such firms may be mavericks doomed to extinction. Surely the safest course of interpretation is to discuss the predominant pattern type. Another key to spatial understanding involves the regionalization of the pattern into meaningful territories. A given pattern might have one locational feature dominant in the Midwest, but quite a different one along the Eastern Seaboard or in the West. (Again, note the grain-milling pattern(s) in this respect.)

With most types of manufacturing, however, there are many sources of raw materials (Type Z pattern). In such cases, the determination as to whether or not a firm type is raw-material-oriented becomes much more complex. Obviously, where one firm uses raw materials from several sources, it must make a choice among raw material locations. As noted in Figure 12.10, the firm may be at one raw-material site or at some point in between. Usually the plant will be located at the largest RM input source. In other cases, a raw-material-oriented firm might locate at some place between the various raw-material sources. In fact, a firm could be anywhere within the dashed area shown in Figure 12.14 and still be raw-material-oriented.

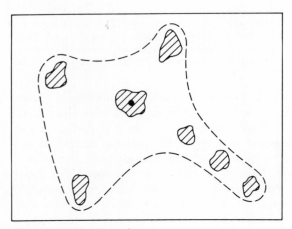

⬭ Raw Material Location

● Manufacturing Plant

FIGURE 12.14 A Raw-Material-Oriented Pattern, Type Z. This pattern is the antitype of the Type B market-oriented pattern (Figure 12.3).

The pitfalls in the interpretation of the Type Z pattern are demonstrated in Figure 12.15(a). Note that a manufacturing activity is shown to be distributed over an area in a fairly even pattern, which coincides perfectly with towns in the area. One's first impression is that such an industrial activity is market-oriented. This would be a logical assumption if one did not know what activity was being discussed. Paradoxically, this is also a classic pattern for Type Z raw-material-oriented plants. Such manufacturing types include flour milling, food canning, food processing, and beet sugar plants. As can be seen by Figure 12.15(b), such plants are centrally located with reference to the farms surrounding each town. The town thus represents a logical place in which to assemble the raw material for processing and shipment to markets. (Here, a change in map scale is most helpful.)

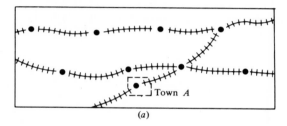

(a)

(Town A and Vicinity)

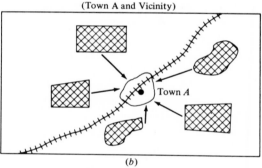

(b)

● Town and Beet Sugar Factory
▨ Beet Farm

FIGURE 12.15 A Raw-Material-Oriented Manufacturing Pattern, Assembly Type Pattern. In this case, the plant is located in a manner that will minimize its total raw material procurement costs. Such a pattern commonly results when several different raw materials are required for production, or where raw materials must be gathered from a number of different areas.

In another respect, however, the town localization might be considered as a distorted form of raw material orientation whereby the town, through its labor force and special transportation facilities, provides a good transshipment point. Thus one might say that the location pattern is skewed toward the most convenient break-of-bulk point.

It should be apparent that each particular type of manufacturing has its own locational peculiarities. Often the pattern is not the pure one that is discussed here but is blatantly multifaceted and distorted. In this limited study, we cannot examine the many types of locational patterns for manufacturing; nor would this suit our purpose, which is to understand the general nature of the industrial location problem.

It is hoped, however, that the student will carefully investigate, on his or her own or with the instructor's aid, other industrial types as they exemplify these locational patterns and principles.[1] Nonetheless, anyone who hopes to understand all types of manufacturing and their patterns has undertaken an almost impossible task. For example, there is a different manufacturing pattern for almost every product, agricultural crop, mineral, and every commodity of forest and sea.

From Raw Material Orientation to Market Orientation:
The Example of the Iron and Steel Industry

Examination of the present distribution of iron and steel production (based on plants with major furnaces such as the blast, Bessemer, and open hearth) reveals some of the complexities and pitfalls involved in pattern interpretation (Figure 12.16). Some production locations are clearly raw-material-oriented in that they are near sources of coal or iron ore. Major world centers of production at sources of coal include the valley of the Ruhr in West Germany; Pittsburgh, Pennsylvania; Karaganda in the U.S.S.R.; Youngstown, Ohio; and the world-famous Midlands area of England. However, on the basis of prominence, one might believe that the source of iron ore is the dominant factor affecting production location. It will be noted that this is primarily the case in the U.S.S.R., France, and Brazil, but is not the case in the United States and Japan. In fact, major iron ore source areas like Labrador, Venezuela, Chile, and Australia have very little or no steel production. In these countries, production appears to be at the market. Thus, as based on the present world pattern of iron and steel production, production is found at just about every conceivable combination.

At Source of Iron Ore	At Source of Coal	At Market	None
Duluth, Minn.	Pittsburgh, Pa.	Japan?	Japan?
Krivoy Rog, U.S.S.R.	The Ruhr, W. Germany	E. Coast of U.S. (Philadelphia, Baltimore)	Cleveland

[1]For a good general discussion of the locational factors for specific industrial groups, see Gunnar Alexandersson, *Geography of Manufacturing* (Englewood Cliffs, N.J.: Prentice-Hall, 1967).

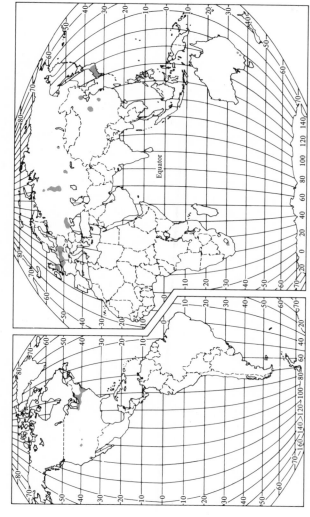

FIGURE 12.16 Major Steel Producing Areas of the World — A Complex Pattern.

At Source of Iron Ore	At Source of Coal	At Market	None
Magnitogorsk, U.S.S.R.	Karaganda, U.S.S.R.		
Lorraine area, France	Midlands area, U.K.	Los Angeles	Detroit
Belo Horizonte, Brazil	Bethlehem, Pa.	Chicago-Gary	Buffalo
An-shan, China	Sambre-Meuse area, Belgium		Geneva Steel Plant, Utah

A glance at the table above and at an atlas might cause one to assume that there is a play-off between a location at either coal or iron ore, depending on which is closer to the market. If the iron ore is closest to the market, then coal will be shipped to the iron ore (as at Magnitogorsk). If the coal is closest to the market, then iron ore will be shipped to the coal (as at Pittsburgh). Production occurs at intermediate locations, such as Cleveland, because these locations are classic break-of-bulk points. Production at the outer extremities of the raw material source is due simply to back-haul possibilities. This all makes sense until it is realized that some of our largest steel centers are located neither at nor between raw materials sources, but are clearly located at markets.

This is easily seen within the United States (Figure 12.17). Note the major production along the Eastern Seaboard. Coal is obtained from West Virginia and iron ore from Eastern Canada, Venezuela, and Peru. Similarly, on the West Coast, the plant at Fontana, California, in the Los Angeles metropolitan area, receives its iron ore from the southwestern part of Utah and its coal from various parts of the Rocky Mountains, especially Colorado. Other centers in the West are likewise not truly raw-material-oriented. In fact, the blast furnaces at the Geneva plant (near Provo, Utah) and at Pueblo, Colorado, were developed during World War II largely for national defense purposes.

This extremely diverse pattern raises questions as to the general importance of the various locational forces. In some areas, markets appear to be most important; in others, coal; and still others, iron ore. In some places, the plant is located neither near raw materials nor in major markets. Thus, careful examination of the pattern leaves one with an enigma.

Examination of actual cost data also reveals contradictions on every hand. Data from some plants "prove" that it costs more to transport coal than iron, while data from other plants "prove" the opposite. Some plants maintain that the costs of delivering the finished product to market are less per ton-mile than the transportation costs of raw materials, while other plants maintain that the opposite is true. How can this be?

The sharp geographer has already reached an answer. He knows that the peculiarities of the resource and market location, and the nature of the transportation available in any given area, will lead to different locational responses for any given steel plant. For example, if water transportation is available, as in the Great Lakes, then that raw material farther from the market (in this case, iron ore) is likely to be transported toward the raw material nearer the market (coal) and toward the market itself. Likewise, raw materials near ocean transportation might be expected to be transported to plants near markets.

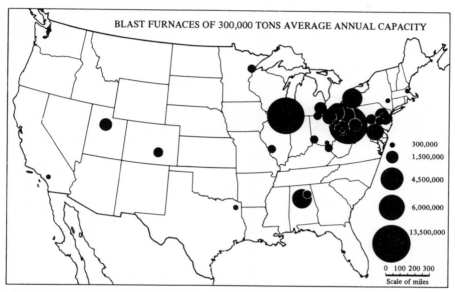

BLAST FURNACES OF 300,000 TONS AVERAGE ANNUAL CAPACITY

300,000
1,500,000
4,500,000
6,000,000
13,500,000

0 100 200 300
Scale of miles

FIGURE 12.17 Blast Furnace Capacity Pattern in the United States.   Note the tremendous concentration of furnaces in the manufacturing belt. Source: John W. Alexander, *Economic Geography*, (C) 1963. Reprinted by permission of Prentice-Hall, Inc., Englewood Cliffs, New Jersey.

As we all know, one cannot make a safe generalization from only a few examples. Based on a case or two, one could prove what one wanted to prove about the locational pattern of the steel industry. The real question, however, is, What is the *predominant* locational pattern? Moreover, by this is meant, What is the predominant locational pattern *today?* Thus it is important to make distinctions appropriate to the age of the steel complexes involved.

In order to answer such questions, the general trends in location over time need to be examined. Historically, the location of iron and steel production has witnessed at least three critical stages: (1) a fuel-oriented stage, (2) an iron-ore-oriented stage, and (3) a market-oriented stage.

During most of the nineteenth century, iron making (the predecessor of steel making, which requires use of ferro-alloys and more advanced production methods) was widely scattered in small plants within forested areas. The source of fuel was charcoal from forests. The relative input was so great that this was the factor determining location. In fact, it took several tons of charcoal (and many more tons of timber) to produce one ton of iron.

By the end of the nineteenth century, coal replaced charcoal as the dominant fuel, and iron and steel production rather promptly shifted to coal fields. Notable in this regard were the Ruhr valley in West Germany, the Midlands of England, and Pittsburgh, Pennsylvania. As late as 1939, it took about one and one-half tons of coal to produce one ton of iron. (This technological condition was perhaps further strengthened geographically, inasmuch as in most industrializing nations, iron ore was more distant from the major markets than was coal. Thus, iron ore was commonly the major raw material to be transported.) One notable exception was in the Soviet Union, where iron was abundant in the Urals (home of the earlier charcoal-based industry) but coal was much farther away. In fact, suitable coal beds could not be found for at least a thousand miles farther east in the vicinity of Karaganda in central Asia. Therefore, in order to achieve steel production in the Urals (the resource closest to the market), the U.S.S.R. undertook the longest massive land movement of coal ever to occur anywhere.

Recently, electric furnaces and other technological advances have permitted the effective utilization of scrap iron as a raw material in conjunction with iron ore. The use of scrap requires less coal for fuel and also, of course, less iron ore. Since scrap is located (as might be expected, given its source) at major consumption points, particularly at most large metropolitan centers, production would be expected to occur there also. Market orientation is further advanced by changing processes and fuel sources. For example, more than one-half of Swedish steel is made in electric furnaces. Distance from coal fields is thus of no concern. Nevertheless, scrap is insufficient in many areas and iron ore is becoming increasingly in greater demand than scrap.

Today, some of the largest and latest major steel-producing plants are located along seacoasts near major markets, as is the case in the eastern part of the United States, Western Europe, and Japan. In fact, Japan is a major importer of both coal and iron ore, and also a major exporter of steel. It has one of the largest and most up-to-date operations in the world and is now one of the two or three largest producers. Undoubtedly, steel production is rapidly becoming market-oriented and, one might add, highly dependent on imported raw materials from underdeveloped nations.

A factor that contributes heavily to the mixed pattern of iron and steel production is the heavy investment involved in developing a major production center. Once production begins in an area, it does not readily shift to new areas despite changes in production-cost components. In fact, the predominant pattern of steel production still reflects decisions made a century or so ago. This discrepancy would be even more noticeable were it not for the fact that markets themselves are likewise quite fixed because of the heavy investments in the infrastructures of cities.

Thus the distribution of most manufacturing types contains crops of the past and plantings for the future. The general age of industrial plants is therefore critical in pattern interpretation for those activities which are experiencing major locational shifts. When viewed within a time sequence and with an appropriate appreciation for local transportation variations, the basic locational conditions and forces usually become evident — steel production is largely market-oriented.

Conclusions: A Linkage Approach

One very useful way to grasp the gamut of industrial locations from the purely raw-material-oriented to the purely market-oriented is in terms of forward and backward linkages among various industrial firms. For example, how might one explain the location of a sports equipment manufacturer who uses calf hide as his main raw material? Let us assume that his product is baseball gloves. Two spatial pulls may be in operation here: (1) the location of his raw material source (a leather tanning operation specializing in calf hide), and (2) the location of his market — the area where baseball gloves are most in demand. By carefully noting these two locations plus certain on-site characteristics, it might be thought that locational understanding of baseball glove manufacturing had been achieved. In fact, the investigation has hardly begun.

If, as is likely, the plant is found in Milwaukee, a good location relative to a large regional market and to the national market, one might too hastily conclude that the plant is market-oriented. However, it is also near its source of raw material, the leather. A helpful approach to this dilemma is achieved by working backwards through a linked spatial system. It will soon be seen that the leather industry (source of calfskin) is, in turn, linked to the veal slaughtering industry. Further, the veal slaughtering industry is spatially linked to the dairy industry in Wisconsin. How, then, does one determine which is cause and which is effect? Common sense tells us it is not the baseball glove plant that is influencing the location of dairying. Thus, it is easily seen that the baseball glove manufacturer is highly linked spatially to his raw materials. Nonetheless, it is entirely possible that an unconsidered force, say the market, may account for the location of both dairying and the baseball glove manufacturer.

By posing such a question, we have gone full circle and are on the threshold of a more complete spatial understanding. Of course, through such a course of inquiry we have also raised our curiosity about all kinds of things. We would especially want to know how the location of each backward-linked plant in the system may be affecting the location of each forward-linked plant. We would also begin to have numerous questions about the specific demand for baseball gloves, the nature of the competition among other plants, and other features as they may be affecting plant location. (Moreover, any detailed study would raise questions about why the baseball glove manufacturer was found in one part of the city versus another — questions that will be considered in Chapters 13 and 14.) Finally, we would perhaps be curious about the reason for the veal industry's close association with the dairy industry, whose main products are milk, butter, cheese, and so forth, rather than meat.[2] Thus, going through this list we would note that each step in the system of manufacturing was based on side products or by-products in the system. Veal and slaughtering are by-products of dairying. The leather industry is a secondary by-product or spin-off of dairying, and the baseball glove plant is but a minor user of the calf leather output.

Following the reasoning above it might prove useful to think about other industry links: in forestry, pulp – paper – printing and lumber – furniture; in fishing, fish canning – pet-food canning; in petroleum, refining – petrochemicals; in pig farming, meat packing – leather – (formerly) football manufacturing. Careful study of such links in a spatial context thus enables us to gain new insights into how places and things are held together to form a regional whole. Such study will also demonstrate that with each additional upward step in the link, the manufacturing pattern tends to become more and more market-oriented. However, with some activities the break in pattern from raw material orientation to market orientation may be sudden — for example, the break between the pattern of pulp and paper manufacturing (raw-material-oriented) and the pattern of printing (market-oriented). Such an exercise will also make us very wary of reaching quick conclusions concerning the locational forces responsible for any given pattern; indeed, it will cause us to hesitate and investigate before proclaiming that a particular pattern is raw-material or market-oriented.

Finally, it has also been demonstrated that the analysis of almost any kind of industrial activity requires solid knowledge of the nature of procurement, processing, and distribution cost elements not only at the present time, but in the past. Likewise, more recent changes in transportation and technology, as these may be affecting such locational factors, require examination. A simple way to see what is happening is to identify the locational characteristics of the newest firms.

Finally, it has been demonstrated that the peculiarities of regions — for example, their distribution of raw materials and transportation opportunities — cause deviations to occur in any given pattern. In many instances, strategic intermediate places are created as "compromise" locations between those that are purely raw-material-oriented and those that are purely market-oriented. Hence, there is no substitute for good locational knowledge about the physical characteristics of any particular territory.

---

[2]The answer to this question is rather simple. In order for cows to continue giving milk, they must be kept "fresh" by calving each year. Since the calves are a way of ensuring the milk supply, there are a great many more calves than are needed to maintain the dairy herd. Moreoever, calves use the milk and feed that is much needed for cows. Inasmuch as these are dairy calves, not beef calves, their main utility is as veal (calf meat) or perhaps as milk cows. Male calves, of course, will almost surely be sold as veal.

BIBLIOGRAPHY

Alexander, John W. "Location of Manufacturing: Methods of Measurement." *Annals of the Association of American Geographers,* March 1958, pp. 20–26.

Alexandersson, Gunnar. "Changes in the Location Pattern of the Anglo-American Steel Industry: 1948-1959." *Economic Geography,* April 1961, pp. 95–114.

————. *Geography of Manufacturing.* Englewood Cliffs, N.J.: Prentice-Hall, 1967.

Estall, R. C. *New England: A Study in Industrial Adjustment.* New York: Frederick A. Praeger, 1966.

Fleming, Douglas K. "Coastal Steelworks in the Common Market Countries." *Geographical Review,* January 1967, pp. 48–72.

Gardner, Clark M. *The Economics of Soviet Steel.* Cambridge, Mass.: Harvard University Press, 1956.

Hurley, Neil P. "The Automotive Industry: A Study in Industrial Location." *Land Economics,* February 1959, pp. 1–14.

Miller, E. Willard. *A Geography of Manufacturing.* Englewood Cliffs, N.J.: Prentice-Hall, 1962.

Pred, Allan. "Toward a Typology of Manufacturing Flows." *Geographical Review,* January 1964, pp. 65–84.

Riley, R.C. "Changes in the Supply of Coking Coal in Belgium Since 1945." *Economic Geography,* July 1967, pp. 261–270.

Sharer, Cyrus, J. "The Philadelphia Iron and Steel District: Its Relation to the Seaways." *Economic Geography,* October 1963, pp. 363–367.

Warren, Kenneth. "The Changing Steel Industry of the European Common Market." *Economic Geography,* October 1967, pp. 314–332.

part e

Intraurban Spatial Arrangement

At first glance, land utilization in an urban area such as New York and its environs appears to be without rhyme or reason, a confused and baffling welter of anomalies and paradoxes . . . . The assignment of the land to the various uses seems to the superficial observer to have been made by the mad hatter at Alice's tea party. Some of the poorest people live in conveniently located slums on high-priced land . . . . Everything seems misplaced. One yearns to rearrange the hodge-podge and to put things where they belong. The confusion, of course, is more apparent than real . . . . Most of the apparent anomalies and paradoxes dissolve into commonplaces when subjected to serious study and detailed examination.

Robert Murray Haig, "Toward an Understanding of the Metropolis." In *Readings in Economic Geography: The Location of Economic Activity*, edited by Robert H. T. Smith, Edward J. Taafe, and Leslie J. King (Chicago: Rand McNally, 1968), p. 44.

XIII

Toward Intraurban Spatial Understanding

Inasmuch as the United States and most other industrialized countries are truly nations of cities and city dwellers, understanding the distribution of man and his activities within cities ranks as one of the most important parts of spatial study. In the United States, Australia, Great Britain, and most other European countries, more than four-fifths of the population reside in cities. In such countries, far less than 10 percent of the working force is engaged directly in agriculture. Moreover, the urban population is heavily concentrated in a few large centers. For example, in France, England, Argentina, and many other countries, over one-fifth of the total population is found in the largest metropolis. Thus in terms of the number and the concentration of people in cities alone, inquiry into the internal placement of things within such centers appears to be fully justified.

This chapter will attempt to provide a basis for understanding the placement of people and functions within cities. Attention will be given not only to *how* the land within cities is used, but to *why* it is so used. It will be demonstrated that the land use patterns of cities are not only quite understandable, but are spatially orderly. These patterns can be understood by using concepts and theories much as they were used in the preceding analyses. In fact, such principles possibly provide more powerful locational explanations for intraurban activities than they did for the activities previously studied.

Intraurban spatial study also includes understanding urban problems like decline of the central business district and the central city, marginal business districts, decentralization, and sprawl. Solutions to these problems and improvements in the quality of the urban environment and the urban fabric must surely stem from a solid base of intraurban spatial appreciation and understanding.

Despite the potential for intraurban spatial understanding, surprisingly little attention generally has been given to the placement of people and things within cities. Such paucity of treatment in economic geography may be related to the small amount of territory occupied by cities. In some respects, however, there is an inverse correlation between the amount of space used by a function and its importance.

Cities, even in highly urbanized nations, occupy only one or two percent of each country's total land area. Yet these microcosms contain over one-third of the world's population. Perhaps more importantly, these small areas are the control centers for much of the occupation and utilization of the earth. It is in these small focal points that much of the world's consumption, production, and services are centered, controlled, and administered.

But the importance of such small territory is even more dramatic than this. A mere few blocks of land within cities often comprise, for a particular activity, the control center for a whole nation or a major part of the world. In New York City, for example, the Wall Street area is the financial center; Broadway, the entertainment center; and other small areas, the fashion, news, and advertising and publishing centers of the United States and much of the Western world. (New York is the world's supreme "headquarters" city.) Chicago's La Salle Street area is a control center for many of the world's commodity prices. London and Paris also have lilliputian areas that loom giant-like in commerce, government, and world affairs. Even small cities may be paramount in some activities. Hartford, Connecticut, dominates much of the insurance world.

The importance of such minute parcels of land is further demonstrated by urban land value relative to rural real estate. Land within cities sells for more than any other real estate on earth (certain mineral deposit areas are exceptions). In most nations, the value of the urban land outweighs the total value of all other land in the country. Prime land within cities commonly sells for well over \$1 million an acre. Buildings, of course, add considerably more value. In fact, urban land is so costly that in business areas its price is commonly calculated by the front foot.

The study of the spatial character of urban land use has in many cases been deliberately neglected under the wishful premise that the placement of things within cities is chaotic, random, or simply the result of a series of peculiar historical events. This is the usual stance of popular writers on the city, many of whom argue that studying the placement of activities within a city is like trying to find order in a garbage can. A well-known planner-architect expressed this widespread but fallacious attitude when he proclaimed, "Cities are nothing but a chaotic accident, the summation of the haphazard, antagonistic whims of many self-centered, ill-advised individuals."[1] This assertion is antipodal to that expressed by urban land economist Richard Hurd: ". . .

---

[1]Quote attributed to Clarence Stein by Jane Jacobs in *The Death and Life of Great American Cities* (New York: Vintage Books, 1963), p. 13.

if cities grew at random, the problem of creation, distribution, and shifting land value would be insoluble. A cursory glance reveals similarities among cities, and further investigation demonstrates that their structural movements, complex and apparently irregular as they are, respond to definite principles.[2]

Still others argue that city land-use patterns are so orderly as to be almost foreordained. Such a simplistic approach to urban land use is illustrated by the too common assertion that the city is an organism. The architect Eliel Saarinen expressed this philosophy by stating, "As long as . . . the expressive and correlative faculties are potent enough to maintain organic order, there is life and progress of life. Again, as soon as this ceases to be the case, and the expressive and correlative faculties are impotent to prevent disintegration of organic order, decline and death occurs. This is true, no matter whether it happens in the microscopic cell tissues of cell-structure where cancer causes disintegration, or in the hearts of our large cities of today where compactness and confusion cause slums to spread."[3] Thus almost every part of the city is presumed to be analogous to some part of the human anatomy — the central business district becomes the "heart," the parks become "lungs," telephone lines become the "nervous system," and the wharves, depots, and warehouses become the "mouth" through which the city is fed. Even residences become "cells," and various other parts of the city are given physiological counterparts.

If such a simile is accepted, the desired outcome and policy is foreordained — the parts of the city, like the parts of the human body, must be kept "healthy." Every function has a purpose and it is to be kept in its right and proper place. Thus a changing city pattern might be viewed as serious; it might be assumed that the city is suffering from some kind of undiagnosed or perhaps incurable "disease." Major "surgery" may even be needed. Clogged streets, or "circulatory systems," are perhaps the result of something akin to arteriosclerosis, and "cancerous" growth and "cell" decay take place. If sales in the central business district are declining, then the "heart" of the city is "sick" and something must be done quickly if the urban "body" is to survive. Major surgery (urban renewal, for example) may be needed. Perhaps even a heart transplant would be considered.

This analogy is fascinating, entertaining — and dangerous. It ascribes far too much order to the spatial matrix and is thus highly deterministic. More seriously, it provides a ready excuse for not studying further the nature of the city. Those who accept this theory in toto have suddenly become wise, their minds are made up, and the "solutions" are self-evident. These people truly have the answer for everything and the solution to nothing.

Although the placement of things within cities is in some respects not nearly so simple as asserted above, the study of intraurban location is largely

[2]Richard M. Hurd, *Principles of City Land Values* (New York: The Record and Guide, 1924), p. 13.

[3]Eliel Saarinen, *The City: Its Growth, Its Decay, Its Future* (New York: Reinhold Publishing Co., 1943), p. 15.

free of one variable that was critical in the study of earlier activities — namely, the physical characteristics of the land. Quite differently from the location of the extractive activities and agriculture, the placement of functions within cities is little affected by the intrinsic qualities of the land. It makes small difference for most urban uses whether the soil is rich or poor inasmuch as most of the land is covered with structures or asphalt. Moreover, low land can be, and often is, filled; hilly land can be leveled; swampy land can be drained. The primary value of urban land therefore is not derived from the quality of the soil but is based primarily on the competition for sites among functions. Simply put, land within cities is such a scarce commodity that it is often "created" in a profitable location.

Nevertheless, in any particular city, topography does affect the general land-use pattern. Hills may provide problems of construction yet are often valuable as residential sites because of the view they afford. Flat land, although subject to flooding, may be held in high preference by transportation and industry. Thus, topography does provide general shaping forces. Nonetheless, these forces are peculiar to particular cities and vary greatly in their importance to different functions and over time.

The General Land-Use Pattern within Cities

Although the specific placement of each land use varies from city to city, depending upon local historical and site conditions, the general arrangement of residential, commercial, and industrial blocks, with respect to each other, is relatively consistent — at least in American cities. Although each city is somewhat unique in its pattern of land use, the degree of similarity among cities far outweighs local idiosyncrasies, and only the similarities make much sense in terms of explanation. Moreover, through such a generalized spatial framework, the truly unique aspects of any particular city can be more fully appreciated.

Even the superficial observer can see the spatial similarity among cities. For example, each land-use type is generally separated from others. Every city has differentiated business, residential, and industrial patterns. As one observes the arrangement of these land uses, a repetition of pattern from city to city is clearly discernible. For example, in the United States, all cities have a high intensity business center, popularly called "downtown"; high intensity residential areas, primarily in the inner zones of the city; and low density, largely single-family residential areas in the outlying zones or suburban areas. Shopping centers and business districts are distributed in a fairly regular pattern and at strategic "crossroads" points throughout the city. Moreover, a definite hierarchy of business centers is noted, ranging downward from the central business center through regional, community, and neighborhood business centers. Most large cities have a recognizable wedge, or sector, devoted to industrial uses. In short, one can hardly avoid being left without the strong impression that the land-use patterns of American cities are indeed orderly and similar.

One composite model of typical land-use patterns in American cities is shown in Figure 13.1. Three major types of land use are shown on the diagram: commercial, industrial and residential land. (Public land uses — streets, for example — are only implied, not directly specified.) Each of the uses shown is spatially separated. Thus for commercial land use, one central nucleus and many outlying, smaller nuclei are noted. Industrial land is broken into three categories: (1) light industry and wholesaling, which category occupies the more central locations; (2) heavy industry, found in a sector further removed; and (3) separate, isolated nuclei of unspecified industrial use. Residential land use consists of homes that are classified according to value as low, middle, and high class (found, respectively, at increasing distance from the central

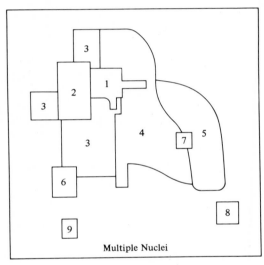

Multiple Nuclei

DISTRICT
1. Central Business District
2. Wholesale Light Manufacturing
3. Low–class Residential
4. Medium–class Residential
5. High–class Residential
6. Heavy Manufacturing
7. Outlying Business District
8. Residential Suburb
9. Industrial Suburb

FIGURE 13.1 The Multiple Nuclei Theory of Urban Land Use. Source: Chauncy D. Harris and Edward L. Ullman, "The Nature of Cities," *Annals of the American Academy of Political and Social Science* (1945).

business district) as well as an outlying nucleus of suburban development. Note that the low-class residential area is near the wholesaling and light industry area, on "the wrong side of the tracks," whereas the high-class residential area is found on the opposite side of the city. High-class residential land is particularly antipodal in position vis-à-vis heavy industry land. The general tendency is for high-class residential areas to move away from the low-class and industrial areas toward places offering more amenities. Ironically, then, it appears that the people least able to cope with the physically most obsolete parts of the city are occupying just those environments.

In summary, several spatial features are evident: (1) centralization or concentration in the most accessible places, (2) general zonation with decreasing intensity and density as one proceeds outward from the point of maximum accessibility, (3) general sectors of land-use similarity along various corridors, and (4) a tendency for similar land-use types to form clusters or nucleations. Thus, the composite land-use pattern of a city is a compromise among a number of opposing forces, some tending to pull functions to outlying areas (centrifugal forces), and others tending to attract certain activities to a more central position (centripetal forces).

It may be surprising to learn that the diagrammatic sketch of major land-use types above is modeled after Salt Lake City, Utah, in the early 1940s. Although more suburbanization and nucleation have occurred in cities since this time, in basic form this diagram still remains accurate. Indeed, it anticipated many of the land-use trends and patterns still current in cities. Most evident in this regard was the recognition of detached clusters of various business, industrial, and residential uses.

Nonetheless, such a model provides a far too simplistic portrayal of general land-use patterns in American cities today. First, there is far more nucleation and sectorization of functions. Second, many of the functions, such as high-class residential areas, were bifurcated when growth could not continue in a particular path. Also, the major influx of Negro population to the central cities, particularly the migration into the formerly low-class residential areas, was not anticipated. Nor could the impact of the federal housing programs and freeway development on urban sprawl and suburbanization be accurately foreseen. Examination of a modern pattern, however, reveals enough spatial consistency with the original model to lead to the conclusion that the basic forces have not been much affected. Thus, as Harris and Ullman postulated, the four major forces at work still seem to be: (1) accessibility and need for special facilities; (2) cluster affinities among like functions; (3) disaffinities among unlike activities; and (4) the inability of certain activities to afford the high rents of the most accessible sites.

Figure 13.2 reflects the continuation of these trends in the land-use pattern of American cities today. Residential land has spread outward at great distance from the central city. Most of this might be considered middle-class, suburban, single-family homes, but there is also considerable representation of high-class residences and multiple-family dwellings in outlying areas as well. High-class housing has been particularly attracted to site amenities like wooded lots and views. Views are particularly prized in Seattle so that most high-value housing runs in sectors along major waterfront areas. By contrast, the industrial land is primarily concentrated in the opposite end of the city in a broad, flat, river valley, which is well served with rail and highway transportation. Also evident is the linear or sector development of commercial activities, particularly along

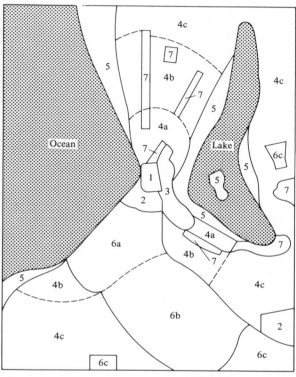

BUSINESS
1. Central Business District
2. Wholesaling–Light Manufacturing
7. Outlying Business Areas–Planned Shopping Centers and Strip Commercial

INDUSTRIAL
2. Light Manufacturing
6a. General Manufacturing
6b. Heavy Manufacturing
6c. Isolated Manufacturing

RESIDENTIAL
3. Black Ghetto
4a. High Density, Mixed High and Low Income Area
4b. Medium–class Residential, Mixed Structures
4c. Medium–class Residential, Suburban
5. High–class Residential

FIGURE 13.2 A Generalized Land-Use Pattern of Greater Seattle, Washington, As Modeled after the Multiple Nuclei Theory of Urban Land Use.

major arterials. Thus the commercial patterns in a metropolis now consist of at least three major components: a central business district, linear commercial strip development, and major nuclei of outlying development mostly in the form of planned shopping centers.

Urban Land Consumption

It is dangerous to make general and unqualified statements as to the amounts of land occupied by different uses in a typical city. First, cities are different. An industrial city will have more industrial land than will a commercial market center. Moreover, different types of industrial uses require differing amounts of land. Such factors as topography, government control, and the like also may play an important role.

Another difficulty in providing information on the proportion of land occupied by different uses among cities results directly from the nature of the classifications themselves. Strange as it appears, industrial land, for example, may be tabulated in various ways, according to the system of classification used. In many cases, industrial land includes not only land occupied by manufacturing plants, but land occupied by warehouses, wholesaling, and even railroads. Other classifications may also include potentially usable vacant sites as industrial land. Similar discrepancies occur among other categories such as residential land. In this category, residential streets, which usually account for almost one-third of the total area, are often included.

The key to understanding such discrepancies lies in paying particular attention to the difference between "net" and "gross" space used. Net, of course, refers to the actual amount of land directly used for the purpose. On the other hand, gross land-use estimates often include vacant land, nondevelopment land, streets, and in some cases even rural land.

The amount of land used by different functions also varies greatly over time. Thus, it is not very meaningful to compare the proportion of land used for a particular function in one city with that in another if the surveys were taken at different times. Generally, the amount of land actually used for any given function has been increasing over time — hence the tremendous spread, or sprawl, of cities. Industry has shifted from a vertical to a horizontal scale and favors large sites that offer parking facilities and other advantages. Likewise, business structures are now one or two stories high, with ample parking space nearby. But perhaps nowhere has the space change been more prominent than in residential land. Not only has the single-family detached dwelling become the dominant residential structure, but larger and larger lots have been the rule. The average size of residential lots is several times larger today than it was just two decades ago.

A word should be said about the comparability of land-use arrangements in U.S. cities with those of other cities of the world. The first difference is primarily one of scale inasmuch as the density of population is higher, and hence the area occupied for any given population is less, in other cities of the world. This is particularly true in cities like Shanghai, Bombay, and Calcutta. Nevertheless, Japanese, Australian, and even some European cities, such as Moscow, occupy space somewhat comparable to American cities. There is also a tendency in non-U.S. cities to mix residential use with commercial and especially industrial use to a much greater extent. In cities like Calcutta, the old home-shop pattern is still much in evidence. Nonetheless, most large cities of the world, such as Buenos Aires and Mexico City, have definite industrial sectors. On a per capita basis, U.S. cities have led the world in intraurban space consumption. By contrast, European and non-Western cities are far more compact and have far higher densities than do their U.S. counterparts. The automobile has allowed great freedom of locational choice and has made possible great horizontal extent. Sprawl and spread and low-lying structures are becoming the rule not only in the United States, but in much of the world.

There is also considerable variation in land uses and their intensities within large and small cities. Large cities have higher densities and taller structures. Therefore, they are far more parsimonious users of land than are small cities. On a per capita basis, more land is used in small cities than in large. Thus, if one's policy were to conserve on land, it would naturally follow that more people should be encouraged to live in larger and larger cities. But the dictum to live in larger cities, as with most urban policies, carries with it negative aspects as well.

Despite warnings about generalizations, some general figures follow. These figures are composite estimates and apply to the geographic or built-up area of the city rather than to the central city only. Regardless of the area taken, however, residential land is by far the largest single land use within a metropolis. More than one-third of all occupied land is taken by this use. By contrast, commercial use accounts for the smallest amount of land occupied by any one function — usually only about 5 percent. However, inasmuch as commercial land use is often the most intensive in the city, most space is found above street level.

Another large user of city space is transportation routes. Streets alone account for one-quarter or more of all urban land. In fact, the aggregate public and quasi-public land — (streets, municipal golf course, hospitals, churches, government buildings, utilities, cemeteries, airports, parks, and so forth) — in a city amounts to well over one-half its total. Since land thus used is generally nontaxable, the concentration of such facilities within the central city of large metropolitan areas adds greatly to the tax revenue problem.

Of all the land uses, industrial land is the most variable within cities.

In fact, some cities — state and national capitals, for example — may have practically no industrial land. On the other hand, cities found in the American manufacturing belt may have more than one-fifth of their total occupied land in such use. Thus the amount of land taken by manufacturing has a considerable range, but as a crude average may be thought of as being about 10 percent of the occupied urban land space.

Accessibility and Land Use Arrangement

The general land-use pattern in any given city appears to be the result of four major forces: (1) centrality or accessibility, (2) competition for sites, (3) interconnections among functions, and (4) public policies. Each of these forces can be best understood within a particular theoretical framework in which other factors are held somewhat constant. It is further understood that such forces operate within a particular economic, social, and political framework and that the examples given below apply primarily to cities in the United States.

Accessibility is generally considered to be the key determinant of the structure and form of the city. This assertion is based on the simple truth that in any given area, one place has greater potential for interaction with all other places than has any other; this is the prime place from which all other locations can be measured. The importance of centrality of location was explicitly noted by Hurd as early as 1924: "As first laid down, the theory of agricultural ground rents emphasized fertility as a source of rent. Later, when it was noted that it was not the most fertile lands that were first occupied but rather those nearest new settlements, accessibility or proximity to cities was recognized as an important factor in creating agricultural ground rent. *In cities, economic rent is based on superiority of location only, the sole function of city land being to furnish area on which to erect buildings.*"[4] While this undoubtedly claims too much for the "standing room only" factor, accessibility is surely a dominating force, giving particular form and shape to cities.

Accessibility is simply a measurement of the degree of potential connection or interaction any given location has with all other parts of the city. Thus "nearness" and "proximity" are often near appositives for accessibility. Accessibility is a reflection of the "friction of distance" among places and is commonly measured in reference to time and/or cost.

The most accessible place in any given city is that place which provides the greatest potential interaction with all other places at least "cost." Such cost is computed by determining the cost of getting from one location to all others, in terms of time-distance. The most accessible point in American cities

---

[4]Richard M. Hurd, *Principles of City Land Values* (New York: The Record and Guide, 1924), p. 1, emphasis added.

is characteristically at the focal point of major arterials. This is generally the central business district.

Once an area has achieved a position of prime accessibility, such as the central business district, it tends to be maintained for a considerable time. In the United States various programs have been and are being initiated to maintain the central business district as the most accessible place within the city. Until recently, these efforts have been successful. As cities have grown outward, however, the central business district has usually become more off-center. Moreover, new crosstown and outer circumferential expressways have given strategic advantage to outlying areas. Ironically, the heavy congestion of routes and traffic in the inner city has also made it less accessible to other parts of the city. As a consequence, the former, almost monopolistic spatial advantages of the central business districts have been lost, and various business and employment functions have decentralized to outlying locations.

The immediate implication of the accessibility concept is that different locations have different potentials for interaction, and hence for development. Thus, for any given activity, all locations in the city can be ranked according to their degree of suitability relative to the prime point of accessibility. In more theoretical terms, any given site can be rated in terms of its degree of substitutability with the chief site. The implication is that the more nearly any particular site approaches the prime site in terms of the accessibility measure, the higher is its potential for that particular use (Figure 13.3).

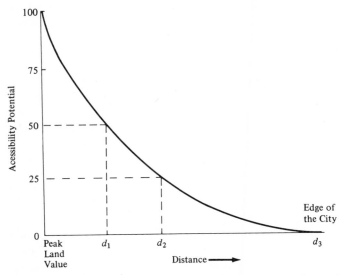

FIGURE 13.3 Accessibility Potential with Reference to the Peak Land Value. Note that at any given distance, some substitution for the prime accessibility site can be achieved until distance d_3 is reached.

The spatial result of this substitutability feature is a drop-off in the accessibility index with increasing distance from the point of highest accessibility. This point will be occupied by the function paying the highest rent and hence will be the place where the city's peak land value is found. Thus a general curve reflecting decreasing substitution capabilities with the peak land value place can be constructed. For example, a site at distance d_1 has about one-half the accessibility value of the prime site. The site at distance d_2 has only one-quarter of the accessibility of the highest point. Finally, at distance d_3 no substitution capabilities exist. Theoretically, d_3 might be assumed to be the edge of the built-up area of a city. Thus it is accessibility that provides the basic explanation for the fact that cities occupy so little area and are so dense and compact. Without the restraint of accessibility, cities could expand outward almost indefinitely.

If accessibility declined outward at an equal rate in all directions from its center, cities would have a circular shape. However, inasmuch as the transportation route system is rarely radial or identical in all sectors of the city, some parts of the city at any given distance from the center are more accessible than others. As a result, the shape of cities is rarely circular but elongated outward along the most speedy routes as, for example, along the major expressways. By the same token, growth is restricted in other sectors because of poor transportation. A crude way to confirm this result is to plot a series of isochronic lines from the center of a city outward. It will be noted that these lines connecting points of equal time generally correspond to similar levels of land-use intensity. In large cities, the outward edge generally conforms with the 60-minute isochrone.

Further evidence of the importance of accessibility can be empirically derived by noting the intensity of land use and its pattern of decrease with increasing distance from the peak land value place. Thus land values, population density, employment density, and the size of lots all reflect the degree of accessibility at any given location. In American cities, the central business district has characteristically contained the highest accessibility site, and all measures of intensity fade off from this center. Note that both the density of population and the density of industrial employees show such a falloff with distance from the center in Philadelphia and Chicago respectively (Figure 13.4). In Philadelphia, net residential population drops from almost 200 persons per acre in the inner part of the city to about 30 persons per acre in its outlying parts. Likewise, in Chicago, the density of industrial employees per net industrial acre falls from a high of more than 300 persons in the inner zone to about 50 in the outer zone. It should also be noted that the density of population and industrial employees is almost nonexistent in the very center of these cities inasmuch as these functions have been squeezed out by the higher-rent-paying business functions.

This decline in intensity of urban land use with distance from the center of the city is a feature characteristic of all cities. Presumably because of better transportation within American cities, however, the density and intensity decline is less steep than in non-Western cities. American cities are therefore lower in overall density and more spread out for any given population than are cities in other parts of the world.

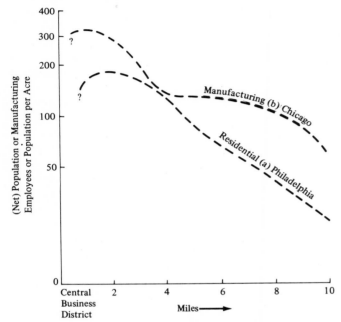

FIGURE 13.4 General Falloff of Manufacturing Employment and Residential Population with Distance from the Central Business District. Source: Adapted from Hans Blumenfeld, "The Tidal Wave of Metropolitan Expansion," *Journal of the American Institute of Planners* (Winter 1954), and Otis Dudley Duncan, "Population Distribution and Community Structure," in *Cold Spring Harbor Symposia on Quantitative Biology* (1957).

Rent-Paying Ability and Land Use Arrangement

The fact that the amount of land acceptable for any given activity is so limited because of accessibility requirements results in a highly competitive bidding for sites among various urban activities. Theoretically, each urban function is in competition with all others for the most accessible — that is, best — sites. Functions that can pay the highest price (rents) will be able to obtain the choicest sites. The functions that are outbid will consequently be squeezed outward to less accessibile sites. This process is made explicit by the concept of *urban rent theory*. The operational process is, in fact, highly analogous to the von Thunen agricultural rent models presented in Chapter 9.

Among the major categories of urban land use — commercial, industrial, residential, and public — commercial activities are the highest bidders for sites. Thus they usually occupy the most accessible sites within a city. Residential land uses are more prominent in the outer parts of a city, but are also represented in the inner and middle parts (Figure 13.5). While some users of residential land, such as millionaires, may be able to outbid commercial functions for land, there seems to be little inclination to do so. In fact, the general rule in American cities is for the highest-income population to occupy outlying sites and for low-income population to occupy fairly close-in sites.

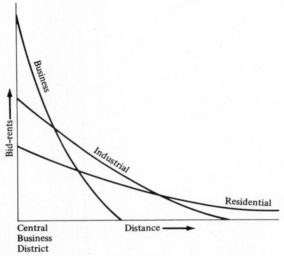

FIGURE 13.5 Variable Bid-Rents among Business, Industrial, and Residential Land Use with Distance from the Central Business District. Note that, as with agricultural rent gradients, the highest bidder for sites prevails. Thus, in this example, business use would be found nearest the most accessible place (the central business district) and residential land use would be found at locations more remote from the city center.

One reason this occurs is that the value and hence the rent-paying ability of the land can be enhanced through the building of taller structures whereby space is occupied more intensely. For example, a four-story building may yield several times as much rent as a one-story building on the same site. In this way, some residential sites when used intensely, as for apartments, may actually outbid single-story commercial uses for that property. Thus the type of structure placed upon a site is a function of its accessibility potential.

For residential land, there is also a play-off between rents and transportation costs. A family may pay less rent in a less accessible place, but will have to pay more for transportation; or a family may pay high rents close in, but incur lower transportation costs (Figure 13.6). Theoretically, as based on these two expenses, both families might be paying the same total "housing" costs.

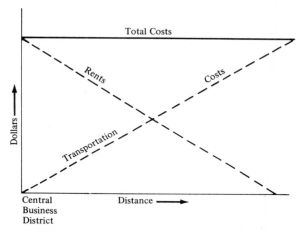

FIGURE 13.6 Relationship between Transportation Costs to City Center and Residential Rents as These Relate to Distance. Note that close to the center transportation costs are low, but rents are high whereas in outlying areas just the reverse situation holds. Theoretically, these should balance out such that total costs should remain about the same throughout the city.

The variation in rent-paying abilities among functions also appears to be related to the range of acceptable sites for that function. The more limited the range of choice, the higher will be the competition for acceptable sites and the higher will be the rents paid (Figure 13.7). Of all functions, business appears to be the most restricted as to viable or acceptable sites. As a consequence, business *must* be located fairly close to highly accessible points in order to operate. By contrast, many locations are acceptable for residential use; hence less value is placed on close-in sites for residential use.

Affinities and Disaffinities as Location Factors

Other important factors in intraurban spatial understanding are the affinities and disaffinities among functions. Some activities are highly interconnected with, or linked to, other establishments and to one another, whereas others have few interaction needs. Thus, in order to understand the placement of any one activity, many others must be simultaneously considered.

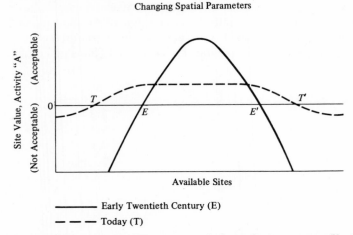

FIGURE 13.7 Changing Parameters of Choice for Sites among Various Urban Functions.   Note that in the early twentieth century there were fewer acceptable sites than there are today when the acceptable sites range from *T* to *T'*. The greater abundance of site choices, however, tends to reduce the monopolistic advantages of any particular site; hence there is less variation in price among sites today than formerly.

Such linkage requirements are more profound than is the case in agricultural or industrial location. For example, people may locate near employment, stores, services, and one another. Likewise, businesses may locate relative to customers, to other businesses, and to various suppliers of goods and services. In short, every function appears to be linked somewhat, and hence somewhat contaminated in its location, by relationships with all others. In contrast, a farm need only be within a profit range from market.

This results in considerably more clustering of similar land-use types than would be anticipated according to accessibility and rent restraints. For example, whole districts of used car dealers, clothing stores, supermarkets, and other activities are common. Business districts, residential neighborhoods, and industrial areas are often found rather pure of dissimilar functions and are separate from one another. The reason, to be more specific, is that like functions generally derive more benefits from being near one another than do unlike functions. In contrast to the law of physics whereby unlike particles attract each other, it is the similar types of urban land uses that are attracted to one another. Activities which are unlike commonly repel each other and are found in separate locations.

Residential uses are particularly affected by intrusions of nonresidential use. People in single-family residential neighborhoods are often much concerned about maintaining their homogeneous residential character. Business and especially industrial uses are commonly zoned out of the higher-income, single-family neighborhoods. Single-family neighborhoods are even at variance with other types of residential use such as renter-occupied units and apartments. First, the age bracket of renters is often quite different from that of homeowners. Thus income and other occupational and social factors are likewise commonly different. In short, the life patterns of the various residential status groups rarely mesh. No doubt there is also a fair amount of snobbishness on the part of many owners of single-family homes, although that is beginning to break down.

From the above it is evident that clustering can occur for different reasons within an affinity or disaffinity framework. Most activities locate in clusters because of the advantages such purity affords them. Some locate near other activities because it benefits both. And some functions cluster together because they are ostracized, discriminated against, or otherwise forced to occupy isolated and cast-off positions relative to other functions. A useful way to understand these various reasons for clustering is according to four linkage types: (1) *competitive*, (2) *complementary*, (3) *commensal*, and (4) *ancillary*.[5]

Competitive linkages are very numerous among business activities and are easily understood. In such cases, like activities cluster near one another in order to compete for a common market. There is usually no direct interaction among establishments; they are simply each trying to get their "fair share" of the same market. Service stations are a good example of this type of linkage. If one service station locates on one corner of an intersection, others are likely to follow on the other three corners. Each station is competing with the others for common customers. The same is true with regard to many other clusters of similar-type stores. In fact, this is probably the most widespread reason for clustering of like functions.

Competitive linkages are beneficial to both customer and function. The duplication of stores in a single area provides the customer with possibilities of comparative shopping, thus enabling him to compare goods and services offered by the various stores. Such competition is so keen that the customer often pays lower prices than he would if there were no competition. Clustering of similar activities also provides benefits to the stores inasmuch as they are able as a group to extend their trade areas and draw customers from a wider territory and in greater amounts than they would individually. The rule is that the whole cluster is greater than the sum of the establishments (its parts).

Complementary linkages result in related functions clustering together. In this case, different establishments supply the same market with different but somewhat similar and interlocking kinds of goods or services. A common example is found among specialty clothing shops where one may sell dresses, another shoes, another hats, and still another purses and various accessories that make up a complete outfit. Another common grouping of complementary

[5]From John Rannells, *The Core of the City* (New York: Columbia University Press, 1956).

store types is found at the neighborhood shopping center level, where a super-market is often found near a drug and variety store.

But nowhere is the complementary linkage more apparent than among industrial land uses. Here, various small manufacturing firms supply bits and pieces needed to manufacture a larger product. Thus the small firms locate nearby the larger one — perhaps an assembly-type manufacturing firm — in order to supply it with components.

Commensal linkages are less common but no less important in spatial effect. In this case two or more establishments may be dependent on a single supplier of materials; or perhaps different types of firms may get their goods delivered from the same warehouse distributor or from the same wholesale area. Thus both firms might be somewhat similarly affected in location but will have little else in common. Similarly, residential areas may be created in a particular place because it affords good opportunities for the residents to get to work.

In another example of commensal linkages, different firms may be found together because of the common use of facilities. Office buildings provide such a common facility to lawyers, real estate firms, physicians, and others. These various office uses are simply found near one another because of similar facility needs.

Ancillary linkages also usually lead to a mixing of unlike establishments in an area. This commonly occurs when a number of different businesses supply a common residential area. Another example is the large office center or employment complex around which cluster small shops, cafes, cigar stores, and other services geared to the nearby work force. These establishments are subordinate to a larger function. In some respects, they are parasitic inasmuch as they live off the customers provided by another firm. This is too strong an indictment, however, inasmuch as most every activity is related in some way to all others. In fact, if such ancillary services were not provided, the parent firm might have to provide them — particularly eating facilities — at its own expense.

Public Policy and Land Use Control

Another feature that strongly affects the placement of activities within cities is public control over land use. This may be in the form of direct measures such as land-use regulation and general zoning and planning, or indirect measures such as taxation and financial policies. In the first instance, the effect is straightforward in that various functions are restricted to specific areas of a city. Such functions commonly include those which are deemed to be a public nuisance; to present a threat to public safety, health, morals, or general welfare; or to be otherwise obnoxious or undesirable except when restricted to special areas. Such publicly regulated activities include many types of business and industrial use; in fact, almost every type of activity in a city is regulated in some way.

Business uses that are often carefully regulated include drinking places, pawnshops, and "honky-tonk" functions. Many of these are regulated by rules that no longer make much sense; nonetheless, the spatial result is profound. This is demonstrated by the case of film distributors, who are commonly clustered in only one block or so of a large city. On the basis of the linkage analysis presented above, it might be assumed that these firms are highly linked to one another. In truth, they are concentrated in one part of the city simply because early film was highly combustible and such firms presented an extreme fire hazard. Consequently, they were restricted to only one small part of the city — generally within a block of the firehouse. Modern film creates little fire hazard, yet the land-use regulation often remains.

In order to protect the public morals, or perhaps its conscience, liquor establishments and various "honky-tonk" functions, which the natives presume are there to cater to tourists, are also often restricted to a small area of the city. Pawnbrokers' shops (sometimes euphemistically self-labeled "jewelry and loan companies") are tightly restricted in most cities to a small downtown area. This is presumably done to enable the police to keep tabs on stolen merchandise that might enter such establishments. Functions regulated for moral reasons — taverns, for example — are also usually restricted to particular sites within the city. Zoning laws usually keep them at a "respectable" distance from "good" residential neighborhoods, schools, and churches.

But regulation of industry is perhaps the most widespread, long-standing, and reasonable of direct governmental controls. Historically, undesirable and highly incompatible industries have been restricted to particular parts of the city. The early zoning test cases in the United States concerned the regulation of Chinese laundries — surely a disagreeable function, given the technology of the time, in the midst of a shopping area. But boiler-factory-type functions, with their ear-splitting sounds, were also early selected for isolation from other activities. And the slaughterhouses, with their putrid smells and waste problems, were commonly relegated to an area outside the city boundaries of the time. Increasingly today, many industries that emit water, land, and air pollutants are being examined critically to determine whether they should be allowed at all in or near some cities. Industries currently being inspected with a jaundiced eye include the iron and steel industries; oil, copper, and other refineries; cement plants; pulp and paper industries; and a large variety of chemical operations.

Conversely, some "clean" industries are now obtaining new-found admittance into residential areas. Many of these campus-like and highly research-oriented industries are even being solicited by some communities. The electronics industries are among the most highly favored in this respect.

Public control of land sometimes imposes restrictions even more severe than those regulating the type of function that will be permitted in a particular area. For example, residential land is commonly distinguished through zoning on the basis of ownership, lot size, and other measures that directly relate to density. Thus, residential areas are of many different types and vary greatly in residential density. It might initially be assumed that municipalities would encourage high densities in order to receive high tax revenues. This is now occurring somewhat in the central city. However, many small municipalities in outlying areas of the metropolis have come into existence primarily to protect and maintain a low density of single-family structures. Minimum lot size in such communities is sometimes one acre or more per single-family residence. Moreover, business and industrial uses are often kept out of such municipalities altogether because of their disaffinities with residential use.

Indirect governmental controls

Surprisingly, the many direct land-use controls discussed above are less important in shaping overall land-use patterns within cities than are the indirect and more subtle measures undertaken as a part of general governmental policy. These indirect controls, which are generally not specifically designed to affect land-use placements within cities, nevertheless trigger tremendous spatial responses. Unlike the direct control measures such as zoning, which can be set aside by variances, the indirect controls are largely unaffected by local governmental manipulation.

Indirect governmental contamination of intraurban land-use patterns occurs frequently and is many-faceted. The two most powerful tools for exercising indirect control in recent years have been (1) governmental financial policies, and (2) general highway and transportation policies. Until recently, the financial policies have favored home ownership and the highway programs have provided the "means" whereby land for such structures could be reasonably assembled. Both have generally favored a sprawled city or, at the least, have favored growth of the outlying and peripheral areas rather than the inner parts of the city. More recently, new financial policies and direct government aid have somewhat reversed this unbalance.

After World War II the federal government, through the Veteran's Administration (VA) made no-down-payment, low-interest, and long-term (twenty-five and thirty years) residential loans available to veterans. The Federal Housing Administration (FHA), in operation since 1933, then responded with a similar policy for the general public. Both favored the construction of new single-family housing units. A significant change in housing ownership patterns resulted. Many Americans who otherwise would have occupied rental housing became homeowners for the first time. The spatial result was that cities began to expand rapidly in area. Suburbanization, or sprawl, was the result. This in turn led to decentralization of business and industry. Thus the present spread pattern was largely triggered by federal financial policies inasmuch as these made construction and purchase loans easy to obtain for new single-family structures.

This spatial spread was augmented even further by the 1956 Interstate

Highway and National Defense Act whereby toll-free expressways were constructed in most large cities. Consequently, agricultural land around cities, now near such expressways, was made accessible and valuable for urban use. With massive residential suburbanization, the outer-circumferential highway, designed initially as an urban bypass, became heavily used as a crosstown feeder and as a major magnet for business and industry.

The combined result of these governmental financial and highway policies was a less intensive utilization of land within the built-up area of cities. Given the growing abundance of "raw" land on the edge of cities now made accessible through improved mobility, and given the VA and FHA financial policies that favored single-family home ownership, the one-story rambler and a subdivided land development system developed. The new policies required lots of seventy or so front feet, almost double the minimum size of city residential lots before World War II. Naturally enough, net residential density dropped drastically.

Business and industry likewise decentralized and used the land less intensively than formerly. Business developed along lines more attuned to the escalator than the elevator and provided several times more area for parking than for ground floor space of buildings. Large shopping centers, a new feature developed during the 1950s, often took more than 100 acres each — an area about as large as the central business district of the city in which the shopping center was located. Industry became more dependent on horizontal, or continuous line, production system rather than on the more intensive vertical system. Thus, 100-acre sites for some industries also became common.

Moreover, the automobile and its related needs resulted in a considerable addition of urban land needed on a per capita basis. First, direct space was needed for parking both at the residence and at work, business, and other sites. This latter requirement alone doubled the land needs of many business and industrial uses compared to the 1930s. Even more important, in terms of lowering overall density of land within cities, was the creation of new and augmented automobile-oriented uses such as service stations, automobile parts stores, garages, and other automotive service establishments. Many other traditional establishments became modified to suit the automobile customer. Drive-in theaters, supermarkets, banks, and so forth sprang up. These functions likewise generally required more space to accommodate the automobile than they did formerly.

It should be remembered, however, that the automobile would not have become so widespread had it not been for the necessity of owning an automobile as the result of suburbanization and decentralization. Residences in outlying locations could no longer be served efficiently by mass transit. First, most suburban developments were located beyond the central city boundaries — the limit of most city bus systems. Second, because of low residential densities and dispersed employment centers, the mass transit was physically unsuitable for assembly and distribution of workers and shoppers in outlying areas. Finally, increased incomes during this period allowed people to spend more on transportation, which meant living farther from work and owning an automobile, or even two. By the 1970s the automobile had become a necessity for the majority of people who lived in cities. Those living in suburban areas and beyond were completely dependent on the automobile for all manner of movement.

However, the new, automobile-oriented life style now found in outlying areas could not be emulated in the older and inner portions of cities. In the inner city, freeways required so much scarce space and were so disruptive to nearby residences that in many cities they were discouraged. Thus a dichotomy was created whereby each city began to consist of a new up-to-date city and an older, perhaps obsolescent city — a dual city and perhaps a dual society had been fostered in large part by indirect governmental policies.

Governmental policies of recent date would appear to have the effect of favoring the central city versus suburban areas. In the late 1960s and early 1970s interest rates, largely the result of these policies, reached such heights that home ownership, especially for low-income families, became difficult. A dramatic shift occurred in favor of constructing apartment and rental housing rather than single-family owned housing as was the case earlier. Thus a reversal in land intensity had begun. Ironically, however, the major change was in the suburban and outlying areas rather than in the older, inner portions of the city, where structures often had to be demolished before new construction could occur. Because of the widespread use of the automobile, even by persons in the inner city, apartments could easily be rented in outlying locations. The "tight money" policy thus led to further suburbanization and a further drop in central city population.

Recently, the federal government has begun to subsidize rapid mass transit for the central city. Theoretically, this should encourage higher densities and limit outward expansion. In this way the inner city might be expected to regain some of its lost population, business, and industry. Whether such transit will be able to reverse the suburban tide, however, is highly doubtful. Certainly those now beyond the central city, for the reasons given above, cannot be served well with a mass transit system. Nonetheless, such a system will surely tend to make the central city less anachronistic than is currently the case.

Conclusions

This chapter has demonstrated that land-use patterns within cities are worthy of study, are spatially orderly, and can be understood within a theoretical framework much like other activities studied. A skeleton framework by which an appreciation of the spatial order within cities can be perceived is achieved by examination of the principles of accessibility, rent-paying abilities among functions, and various affinities and disaffinities among urban activities. Finally, order is seen to be reflected in various direct and indirect governmental policies.

Nonetheless, these principles leave one unsatisfied. This is because they do not jell into a neat and comprehensive model of urban land-use arrangement and form. Instead, each of the principles is a piecemeal explanation. Moreover, because of the *ceteris paribus* manner in which these principles must be treated, they still leave unanswered many questions about urban location. Therefore, each of these principles only illustrates a particular shaping force; other approaches and models are needed before a satisfactory replication of an existing urban-land-use pattern can be achieved.

Particularly needed is a more dynamic approach to urban land use. The placement of things within a city is in constant flux so that the spatial pattern is one of continuous change in location. Therefore, a satisfactory location for an activity at one time may be an obsolete or anachronistic location at another time.

BIBLIOGRAPHY

Alonso, William. *Location and Land Use*. Cambridge, Mass.: Harvard University Press, 1964.

Berry, Brian J. L., and Horton, Frank E. *Geographic Perspective on Urban Systems with Integrated Readings*. Englewood Cliffs, N.J.: Prentice-Hall, 1970.

————; Simmons, James W.; and Tennant, Robert J. "Urban Population Densities: Structure and Change." *Geographical Review*, July 1963, pp. 389–405.

Bourne, Larry S., ed. *Internal Structure of the City: Readings on Space and Environment*. New York: Oxford University Press, 1971.

Clark, Colin. "Urban Population Densities." *Journal of the Royal Statistical Association*, 1951, pp. 490–496.

Dorau, Herbert B., and Hinman, Albert G. *Urban Land Economics*. New York: Macmillan, 1928.

Fellmann, Jerome D. "Land Use Density Patterns of the Metropolitan Areas." *The Journal of Geography*, May 1969, pp. 262–266.

Hansen, Walter G. "How Accessibility Shapes Land Use." *Journal of the American Institute of Planners*, May 1959, pp. 73–76.

Hurd, Richard M. *City Land Values*. New York: The Record and Guide, 1924.

Johnson, James H. *Urban Geography*. New York: Pergamon Press, 1967.

Murphy, Raymond E. *The American City*. New York: McGraw-Hill, 1966.

Newling, Bruce E. "Urban Population Densities and Intra-Urban Growth." *Geographical Review*, July 1964, pp. 440–442.

Putnam, Robert G.; Taylor, Frank J.; and Kettle, Philip G., eds. *A Geography of Urban Places*. Toronto: Methuen Publications, 1970.

Rannells, John. *The Core of the City*. New York: Columbia University Press, 1956.

Ratcliff, Richard U. *Urban Land Economics*. New York: McGraw-Hill, 1949.

Wingo, Lowdon Jr. *Transportation and Urban Land*. Washington, D.C.: Resources for the Future, 1961.

XIV

Patterns of Intraurban Land Use

The industrial, residential, and commercial land-use patterns within cities will now be examined separately. Unlike the preceding chapter, in which the principles of land-use location were discussed in general terms, this chapter will examine particular land-use types and their spatial arrangements. Thus the concepts previously presented will here be applied to fit specific activities. Instead of approaching the question of intraurban land-use arrangement from the standpoint of concepts, particular land-use patterns are viewed from the standpoint of general spatial principles. Such treatment should provide important insights into the variety of land-use patterns within cities and, furthermore, should set the stage for the discussion of urban problems in the forthcoming chapter. Therefore, this chapter complements the preceding one and anticipates the following one. Finally, it provides a further demonstration of the necessity for matching theory and reality carefully to gain satisfactory spatial understanding.

A fundamental purpose in much of geography is to understand the basic differences in spatial patterns among functions. This same goal is applicable to activities within the city. The major uses of the land within the city, therefore, are the building blocks by which such patterns are composed. In this respect, seven basic space needs within cities are noted: (1) living (residential), (2) selling (commercial), (3) making (manufacturing), (4) movement (transportation), (5) governmental, health, and safety, (6) land for the future, and (7) others, such as recreation. Nonetheless, these logical breakdowns may obscure or mix spatial patterns inasmuch as the subcategories of each major type may have different locational forces and restraints. For example, commercial land use does not have one pattern, but several. Second, the value of the classification depends on the purpose at hand — in our case, pattern dissection and analysis. Finally, the purpose here is not to explain all activities, but to recognize a variety of spatial arrangements within cities. Although much time could be

275

spent on land-use classification, for our purposes it seems wisest simply to follow three generally accepted land-use categories: industrial, residential, and commercial. This trichotomy is consistent with the general theories in Chapter 13 and provides an adequate grouping for discussion.

Industrial Land-Use Patterns

In many cities, industry is the triggering agent for urban form and growth. Industry provides the fundamental employment base by which money is brought into the community and by which other people not engaged directly in industry are "supported." This concept is made explicit by *economic base theory*. According to this theory, there are only two types of employment activities in a city: (1) *service* activities or industries — that is, those which locate in a city primarily to serve the existing urban population (labeled *ubiquitous* industries in Chapter 11), and (2) *basic* activities or industries — that is, those which locate at strategic places within cities in order to better serve areas and persons outside the city in question (labeled *sporadic* industries in Chapter 11). The ubiquitous type of manufacturing is generally market-oriented; it occurs in a particular city only after a certain threshold level of demand has been reached. Thus this type of industry is also often referred to as a *city-serving* industry. In contrast, the sporadic types are *city-forming* activities and are largely responsible for the location and growth of cities themselves. The city-forming type of industry has an effect similar to those retail and service functions found within central place cities (see Chapter 6). For example, central place cities interact with people in rural territory. Likewise, city-forming manufacturing plants sell their products to markets at great distances from the city in which the plant is located. Thus the size of any urban place — and its importance — is implicitly assumed to be related to some activity that brings money to the city in question.

According to economic base theory, each city must have one or more city-forming functions. These functions provide the triggering mechanism for urban growth. From these initial functions other employment, activities, population, and of course land uses, develop. A simple example of how growth occurs is demonstrated by a manufacturing plant that sells its products outside its urban area. This plant is thereby a city-forming or *basic activity*, and its workers are called *basic workers*. Let us assume that this manufacturing plant employs 100 workers, who are hired from outside the city. These workers immediately add to the city's population because they are added to the city's employment force. Their wives and children are a further addition to the population of the city. Given an average family size of 3.5 per worker, then some 250 persons are added to the community through the initial employment of 100 workers. Thus some 350 persons (workers and their families) are new to the community (Figure 14.1).

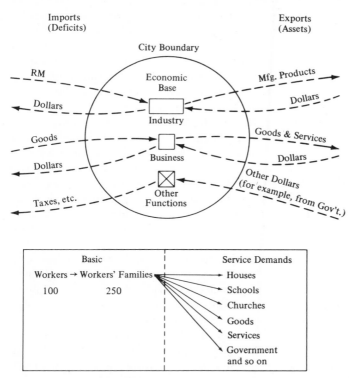

FIGURE 14.1 Urban Economic Base Theory within a Balance of Payments Framework. Within this framework, all imports to the urban community are viewed as deficits because money flows out of the community. Conversely, any activity that brings money into the community from outside is viewed as an asset to the urban economic base. The connection between basic workers and service demands is shown schematically.

The major growth impact of such basic workers, however, is through their family demand for various goods and services within the community. Such basic workers and their families need homes, schools, stores, health and government services, and many other things. Inasmuch as these things must be provided by service workers like building contractors, teachers, merchants, doctors, and civil servants, such service workers and their families are largely supported by the basic workers. If the service workers have families, even more persons will be added to the community through an initial basic worker input of only 100 persons — and the cycle of growth continues. The service workers and their families, in turn, require services similar to those of the basic workers and their families. Thus a second-round effect is set in motion. Of course, with each round the number of additional service workers is reduced. Nonetheless, the process continues through several rounds. Eventually, the catalytic effects are dissipated as fewer services are provided locally.

From the above, another relationship is also evident: the ratio of basic workers to service workers. The higher the basic-service ratio, the higher the growth potential from any given basic worker input. This magnifying feature of basic employment is often called the *multiplier* effect. In small cities, the ratio is often less than one, but in large metropolises it may be almost three — that is, three service workers for each basic worker.

The nature of the multiplier effect is clearly related to the nature of the basic workers. Obviously, the family coefficient is critical. If the basic workers are mostly single, as is commonly the case in mining, lumbering, and military operations, then there will be little demand for housing, schools, and the like. Instead, as in the mythical Wild West town, most of the basic workers' money is spent in saloons, hotels, and in recreational pursuits. And if, in turn, the saloon and hotel keepers have no wives or children, or send their profits out of town on the Wells-Fargo Express, the multiplier effect will be small indeed.

The economic base concept can also be used to provide estimates as to the amount and type of new land that might be added in a city, given a basic activity input. Just as basic employees act as a service employee multiplier, they also act as catalysts for new urban land uses. Given assumptions similar to those in the manufacturing case above, the amount of land generated by such an initial input can be roughly determined if population and employee densities are known. Such information is best based on the densities required for new functions, rather than on average existing densities of residential land or of the number of workers per unit area for commercial land.

Data on marginal land density — the density at which *new* additional workers and their families will occupy the land — is needed. Information like this is always hypothetical, but estimates can be made based on the most recent land-use changes. These figures are commonly called *land absorption coefficients*.

Assume that the land absorption coefficients are 0.034 workers per acre for industrial land, 0.047 persons per acre for commercial land, and 0.059 for residential land.[1] Given the fact that our new plant adds 100 workers, some 3.4 acres of industrial land will be added to the community through the building of the industrial plant on a 3.4-acre site. Given a residential density of 16.9 persons per acre and a family size coefficient of 3.5, then some 20.7 acres will be added in residential land. If the number of required commercial service workers is eighty, then some 3.8 acres of new commercial land will be added. Thus, with the addition of 3.4 acres of industrial land,

[1]These land absorption coefficients are based on the calculations of John H. Niedercorn and Edward F. R. Hearle in "Recent Land Use Trends in Forty-eight Large American Cities," *Land Economics*, February 1964, 105–109.

more than 24.5 acres of urban land will be added in the first round (Figure 14.2).

The argument is increasingly heard that far too much importance has been attached to growth. True, a new basic activity may make a city grow in population, but it may not necessarily make the city a better place in which to live. In fact, some urban-affairs specialists think that many cities are already too large. Certainly, the indiscriminate solicitation of new industry is rarely beneficial. It may cause further pollution and traffic congestion, require the addition of municipal services, and make many functions, such as schools, inadequate — all of which would require the initiation of new spending programs.

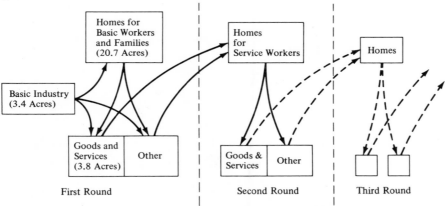

FIGURE 14.2 A Basic Industry and Its Impact on Service Activities. Assuming a basic industry occupying 3.4 acres and employing 100 workers, and using standard land absorption coefficients and certain multiplier assumptions, the amount of land for various uses is shown for three "rounds" of development.

A balance-of-payments approach to the urban economic base also reveals that service activities and imports are as critical as export activities. In fact, it is argued that the service activities are composed of things that make a city distinctive, a good or bad place in which to live.[2] It is reasoned that if a city has good housing, schools, public services, and other amenities that reflect a high-quality urban environment, there is no need to worry about the basic activities. The latter will take care of themselves without any chamber of commerce ballyhoo and land-giveaway programs. Moreover, it is argued that the basic activities may come and go as a city changes its character and responds to new opportunities, but the service activities are the truly permanent and distinctive features.

[2]See Hans Blumenfeld, "The Economic Base of the Metropolis," *Journal of the American Institute of Planners,* 1955, pp. 114–132.

The general pattern of industry

Economic base theory sheds much light on the general relationships among land uses, with particular reference to industry. Nonetheless, very little understanding of the locational pattern of industry has been achieved. Yet in broad form, the pattern is fairly clear. In most American cities, one part of the city is generally dominated by manufacturing and the other by residential land use. The primary locational factor in almost every city is proximity to major transportation routes. Historically, this has meant proximity to water at ports and proximity to railroads. Such a pattern in strikingly evident in Saint Louis (Figure 14.3)

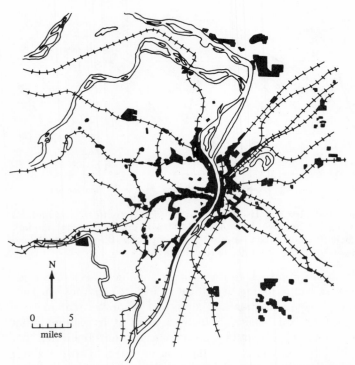

FIGURE 14.3 Industrial Land-Use Pattern in Greater Saint Louis.   Note the affinity of industrial land to railroad routes and to the Mississippi River. Source: W. C. Gilman & Co., *Saint Louis Metropolitan Area Transportation Study*, 1959.

A more careful examination of the pattern, however, indicates considerable variation. In simple terms, three types of patterns are noted: (1) firms occupying small sites fairly close to the center of the city, (2) firms heavily geared to railroad and port facilities, and (3) certain large-scale sites found in rather isolated outlying positions.

The reasons for the general placement of different industrial types within the city can be better appreciated from the vantage point of urban rent theory. In this regard, two types of industries are recognized: (1) *light industry,* and (2) *heavy industry.* This differentiation is related to such factors as intensity of site used, size of site, size of finished product, and the density of employment per unit area. The light industries generally occupy the more accessible positions within the metropolis as compared with heavy industry, because of labor input requirements, needed associations with other similar industries, and other factors. They also, fortunately, can pay much higher per-square-foot rents than can heavy industries like chemicals and steel, which have massive space requirements and a low labor input.

Even so, for light industries there is a play-off between horizontal accessibility and vertical proximity. Traditionally, many light industries occupied upper floors of wholesale and other commercial establishments. Consequently, these have been referred to as "loft" industries. Today, with the development of planned industrial parks in outlying areas, many kinds of light industry are decentralizing.

From the standpoint of transportation, it is noted likewise that two scales of industrial site selection are involved. At the micro scale it appears that industry requires good access to routes within the metropolis. Aside from this, site features such as flat land are often critical. Inasmuch as highways and railroads generally seek out the flat land, a complementary relationship in this regard is easily achieved. At the macro scale, the location of industry appears to be related to transportation routes that offer particular advantages for intercity movement.[3]

The placement of industries with reference to strategic position relative to intercity or intracity transportation requires some further clarification. In the first instance, the location of the firm is determined by exogenous (outside the city) locational forces, whereas in the second instance the location is endogenously determined. It would appear that industries most dependent on rail and port facilities are of the exogenous types. They also commonly require large amounts of space and are usually found in outlying locations or near port facilities. Undoubtedly the location of exogenously oriented industries is much influenced by transportation cost advantages. This is particularly the case with industries that have large or bulky finished products or that require extensive inputs of raw materials. As might be expected, such industries gravitate toward the side of the metropolis facing their largest market, if suitable land is available.

Those industries which primarily sell their wares within a single metropolis are endogenously oriented and are subject to some of the same locational principles as retail business — they attempt to minimize distribution costs

---

[3]For an excellent treatment of industrial location patterns and industrial classifications, see Allan R. Pred, "The Intrametropolitan Location of American Manufacturing," *Annals of the Association of American Geographers,* vol. 54, June 1964, pp. 165–180.

to markets. For manufacturers of many types of small and highly perishable products, the choice location has traditionally been near the central business district. From here, they have the greatest distributional advantage for the entire metropolitan area. Firms that manufacture bread and other bakery products are prime examples. These firms also commonly have wholesale distribution outlets and thus favor locations in or near the traditional wholesaling area of the city. Nonetheless, this locational pattern is being broken by suburbanization and decentralization. For example, a wholesaling or manufacturing firm that distributes food products primarily to supermarkets often finds a location near a circumferential expressway highly advantageous. Other industries that serve primarily a local area might be fixed in their location because of their input source of raw materials. This is particularly the case for firms that receive raw materials by ship. When raw materials like marble, sand and gravel, petroleum, and timber come in by water, the manufacturer often finds it more profitable to locate near these import sources than at other places in the metropolis.

Finally, some industries are closely linked to others in the metropolis. These firms may be using the finished products of another firm as its primary raw material. Thus, industries that use steel products may congregate around steel mills. Chemical industries may cluster about refineries. And various canning and meat-packing plants may seek out locations near slaughter yards.

Residential Land-Use Patterns

Based on urban rent theory, it might appear that residential spatial patterns are relatively easy to understand. Residential land use simply is squeezed outward to the least accessible sites. Thus, it might be expected to be found on the edge of cities and at other less accessible places within the city. That there is general confirmation of this relationship is evidenced by examining the land-use map of any city.

Nonetheless, residential land is also found in some prime positions such as in the inner portions of the city. At first this seems to present some contradiction to the urban rent theory, but in fact it can be partially explained by the varying intensity of space use among various residential structures, ranging from single-family dwellings through high-rise apartments. By building taller structures — that is, increasing the ground floor rents through the vertical compounding of units — some residential uses are able to outbid many other use types. Twenty families on one acre paying $60 a month rent are using the land more intensely than four families paying $200 a month rent, and hence are able to outbid them. The amount of space being used per unit is substitutable for rent per unit area. Given the high priority placed on land space for residential use, the more well-to-do prefer to have larger lots, but not perhaps at the high cost of land in close-in areas.

As expected, multiple-family units dominate the inner zone, double-family units then appear, and single-family residences predominate in the outer zones

(Figure 14.4). This is clearly seen in Saint Louis even though the map shows residential land within the municipal limits only — a territory only one-quarter that of the built-up area. Today the suburban area, while predominantly single-family, low-density residential in nature, is intermixed with a good many multifamily structures. Thus, urban rent theory, which has heretofore been rather effective in giving meaning to population density at any given distance, breaks down as an adequate explanation when residential land is viewed more closely.

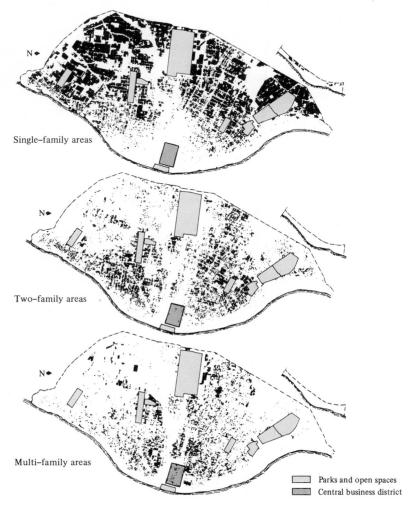

Single–family areas

Two–family areas

Multi–family areas

☐ Parks and open spaces
■ Central business district

FIGURE 14.4 Patterns of Residential Land Use in the City of Saint Louis. Note the general tendency of multifamily housing areas to be located closer to the center than are two-family and single-family housing areas. This "squeezing out" of less intensive residential uses is largely the result of the operation of urban rent theory (see Figure 13.5). Source: Harland Bartholomew, *Land Uses in American Cities*, (C) 1955. By permission of Harvard University Press, Cambridge, Mass.

Nonetheless, in aggregate terms a clear density gradient within cities does exist (Figure 14.5). One interesting facet of this is the manner in which this gradient changes over time. The trend in all American cities is for the gradient (b) to flatten out over time so that a fulcrum point (P) is created. From this fulcrum point toward the center of the city, the population generally declines, but outward from this point the population density increases over time. In the past this decline occurred because the inner zone was invaded by nonresidential uses, which replaced residences. Recently, however, the drop in population here has not been offset by commercial functions. Instead, an actual drop in the intensity of land use in the inner zone of cities has occurred. The rise in population density from the fulcrum point outward occurs primarily as a result of a residential filling-in process. Of course, as raw land is converted from rural to urban uses, densities will rise in the outermost areas and the general built-up area will be extended.

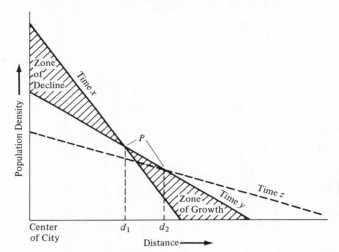

FIGURE 14.5 The Population Density Gradient within Cities over Time. Population density falls off with distance from the center of the city in all cities. In the United States, over time, the inner portions of cities experience a zone of decline, whereas the outer portions experience a zone of growth. At the fulcrum point (P) little density change is experienced between any two time periods. Note also that the edge of the city moves outward over time.

An important implication of the fulcrum principle is that the fulcrum moves outward over time.[4] Moreover, the area near this fulcrum during any given time period remains relatively unchanged. In Figure 14.5 note that at time y the fulcrum point (P) was at distance d_1, but by time z it had

[4]This movement is well documented by Bruce E. Newling in "The Spatial Variation of Urban Population Densities," *Geographical Review*, April 1969, pp. 242–252.

shifted outward to distance d_2. As will be demonstrated in the following discussion, this principle is related to the general stage of stagnancy in population change for any given residential neighborhood (see Figure 14.7, Stage II, which appears later in the chapter).

From the above it is fairly evident that residential land use has a fairly wide range of locational choice. In fact, residential land appears to have more spatial choice than any other type of land use, inasmuch as it is the most widely distributed within the city. For example, commercial land appears to be much affected by strategic points and is limited to highly accessible places in conjunction with proximity to residences. Industrial land is much affected by access to major transportation routes so necessary in the assembly and distribution of materials. Historically, residential land use was highly restrained by proximity to work. However, this proximity is no longer necessary or perhaps even desirable, as long as the worker lives within about one hour's time from his place of employment. Thus most of the metropolis has become one large, generalized housing market. The workplace can no longer be used as an effective way to explain the location of residential land.

The complexity of the residential classification problem increases as one examines the various elements found in residential areas. Residential land may be differentiated as follows, according to such features as structure, occupants, and neighborhoods:

A. By Structure
1. type (brick, frame, one story, and so forth)
2. family accommodation (single, double, multiple)
3. condition (sound, dilapidated, and so forth)
4. proportion of site covered
5. technological up-to-dateness

B. By Occupants
1. family size
2. income
3. age of family members
4. marital status
5. occupation
6. education

C. By Neighborhood
1. low-class (value) residences
2. middle-class (value) residences
3. high-class (value) residences
4. density of population
5. mixed or pure housing types and values
6. quality (parks, schools, and so forth)

Fortunately, there is considerable contamination among all such measures. For example, a high income is highly correlated with a high-priced house and a high-quality neighborhood. This is, in turn, correlated with still other features like family size, type of structure, occupation, and education. Since there is considerable redundancy among the various features, it is necessary to examine only a few in order to reveal the various patterns. The primary basis for residential distinction, as common sense would suggest, stems from the nature of the residential occupants. Two of the most critical variables in this regard are income and ethnic characteristics.

Variations in income patterns

Incomes are more alike within residential neighborhoods than is any other variable. Perhaps one reason for this results from the simple fact that houses within any given neighborhood are all built at about the same price level. Thus, in order to purchase housing in any given neighborhood, the buyers must all have about the same payment potential. Of course, there will be some variation inasmuch as some persons are willing to pay more for housing than others, but with financing as standard as it is, income provides a reasonable explanation. (Incidentally, earnings of the wife are usually not taken into consideration by lending institutions.)

On the other hand, there is some question about which is cause and which effect: homogeneous housing types or a voluntary tendency of people with similar incomes to cluster together. Certainly, the similarity of housing value in any given area is a prime consideration. Nevertheless, there are other good reasons that people with similar incomes might prefer to live in the same area. People with similar incomes are also often similar in age, occupation, and other matters.

The income pattern for Seattle, Washington, is shown in Figure 14.6. Note that again the high-income areas are generally found farthest out from the center of the city. Nonetheless, some qualification should be made. Incomes are highly clustered within areas so that there are pockets of high-income population in certain inlying areas and pockets of extremely low-income population in outlying areas. One spatial pattern is very evident, however. The high-income populations appear to spread out in sectors, particularly along those accessible corridors that offer views of the water. Likewise, hilltops generally have higher-income population than do the valley areas around them. Of course, the latter areas may be adversely affected by their proximity to arterials, which in Seattle generally run along the valleys. Here they cause disaffinities (noise, lack of safety, and congestion) with residential land. Other high-income areas appear to be created in places offering wooded or lake settings. The lot size is another variable, not shown on the map, which varies considerably among income classes; the high-income populations generally have larger lots and hence occupy the land at lower densities for any given location as compared with low-income areas.

It is evident that wealthy persons could, if they desired, occupy close-in sites within a metropolis. Yet in American cities, it is the lower-income populations that occupy the most accessible residential sites. The important paradox to many is how the poorest people in American cities can occupy some of the prime land. Basically, this can occur for two reasons. First, housing stock wears out, and secondhand structures are occupied in a kind of hand-me-down process in which the poor occupy the cast-off housing of the next higher income level. Second, the land is occupied intensively through crowding and high-rise rental structures. In American cities, the wealthy are found primarily in selected outlying locations. By contrast, the wealthy more often occupy the inner zones of non-Western cities, where many of the poor are found on the periphery in squatter shacks. A common explanation for this, aside from historical precedent, is the high friction of distance in non-Western cities. Transportation is too time-consuming for the wealthy in such cities. Consequently, the poor are faced with the burden of daily commuting.

METROPOLITAN SEATTLE
Average Annual Income Distribution

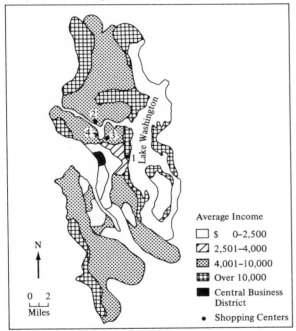

FIGURE 14.6 Average Income Distribution in Seattle. Note the concentration of low-income population near the center of the city and the tendency of high-income population to be sectorized along water-based amenity areas. Source: Based on 1960 *Buying Power Map*, Sanborn Map Co., Seattle, Wash.

While much can be said about the crowded, dilapidated, and slum conditions of the poor in American cities, until recently they have at least been closer to their jobs than have the more affluent. This is changing rapidly, however, and America's poor increasingly find that their jobs have moved to outlying areas of the city. Public transportation is of little value for getting them to outlying areas.

Variations in social and ethnic patterns

Another very noticeable pattern of differentiation among the residential population is according to ethnic background. In Seattle, as in most cities in the United States, the black population, other minority groups, and the very poor occupy areas close to the central business district. These areas were once occupied by some of the more affluent city population. Ethnic concentrations are evident among many groups. The Ballard district of Seattle is predominately Scandinavian; there are Polish districts in Chicago, German districts in Milwaukee, and Jewish and Italian areas in many cities. There would thus appear to be a tendency for people of the same ethnic background to cluster together. How much of this is strictly voluntary and how much a result of general custom or deliberate prior policies of discrimination or balkanization varies from place to place.

Clusters of minority religious groups are also common in many cities. Thus Mormons will often locate in the same area of a large city. Here they have mutual social relations and good access to churches. Occupational clustering is rare but is perhaps more pronounced among university professors than among other professions. Captains of industry and high-echelon business executives often settle in particular districts. These high-income areas, perhaps almost by definition, would be expected to contain similar types of occupations. Finally, there is a tendency of young people, married and single, to congregate in the same vicinity of a city. One suspects here, however, that the stage in the family cycle (no interest in nearby elementary schools) and the need for rental housing (to maintain mobility) are the motivating factors. Inasmuch as such housing is often localized in particular areas, this may be much of the cause.

The trickle-down process and low-income groups

Explanation for income and ethnic variation within cities is also based on historical processes. Traditionally, each higher-income group casts off its housing to the next lower-order group. Thus, a trickle-down process is set in motion whereby definite movement paths occur throughout the city. Under this system the lowest-status income group consistently occupies the oldest, most dilapidated, and least up-to-date housing stock in the city. Generally, this is the housing in the more central locations. Given such a hand-me-down phenomenon, the general placement of the various income and status groups within a city is fairly well predetermined.

Until recently, the most obsolete housing was occupied by the newest immigrant groups. These groups landed in the central portion of cities, became "Americanized," and then began a long series of residential changes in their long, upward climb to the newest housing stock. Thus the occupancy of such inner-zone land by the Negro population, newly arrived from rural areas, was consistent with past patterns. Several factors, however, caused the trickle-down process as a route to upward mobility to become ineffective.

The first major change occurred immediately after World War II, when VA and FHA housing programs made available to young families new, moderately priced housing on the edges of cities. Thus, these people broke out of the long cycle of rentals and the general secondhand housing process as a method of improving their residential lot. Of course, such families still moved to higher-status neighborhoods where many occupied used homes, but the basic cycle of inner-city living had been broken. Even with more potential used housing available, the process did not work for the Negro. Because of housing and employment discrimination, the Negro was unable to achieve upward housing mobility within the city and therefore seemed relegated to occupying slums permanently.

In an attempt to alleviate such a housing stalemate, in the late 1950s urban renewal and redevelopment programs were initiated. Unfortunately, these did not operate to bring Black people into the mainstream of housing changes and to effectuate residential mobility within the metropolis. First, a situation primarily resulted in which the Negro population, which was occupying highly accessible land in the inner city, was merely pushed to nearby neighborhoods, which also became overcrowded. This resulted also, in part, because of the political desire of city administrations to build middle- and high-value apartments on the old slum sites — a move calculated to entice the affluent back to the central city. Although such attempts largely proved futile, they did circumvent any adequate housing program for the Negro. In fairness it should also be pointed out that many high-density public apartments for low-income populations were built. (Low-density housing was ruled out because of the presumed high value of the land.) These, however, were generally unwanted by the low-income population and many became slums of a new type. In fact, most of the low-income population preferred living in inadequate private housing and apartments rather than in the massive, new public housing projects.

During the past few years, housing discrimination has been legally eliminated. Nevertheless, there are few new houses priced for low-income population. Many reasons for this have been given, including high construction costs, high land costs, and, of course, high interest rates; but the truth is that very little profit could be made in low-cost housing by private contractors, in comparison with housing built for the middle- and upper-income groups.

Government effort has been placed on improving the areas now occupied by the low-income population. Local enrichment programs like the Model Cities experiment nonetheless primarily amounted to *situs quo* status for the low-income population. Little attention was given to the question of accessibility to rapidly decentralizing jobs. Instead, emphasis was placed on finding employment in the inner city area, and in some cases even on trying to bring industry to the residential areas, rather than vice versa. Not surprisingly, this approach has not been too successful.

Today, the old trickle-down process has once again been set in motion. The difficulty is that hundreds of acres of formerly middle-income housing has become technologically obsolete in almost every city. Thus, the "middle zone" of the city is faced with a glut of such housing. Should current government programs to provide new single-family housing on the edge of cities for the low-income population succeed, much of the older housing stock will become highly marginal. Because of nonoperation of the hand-me-down housing system for several decades, vast areas of the central city now find themselves with little opportunity for residential survival.

Residential land-use cycles

Any residential area one might choose to examine is probably in a stage of change. In order to assess the nature of the change, close examination of the residential population is required. The two keys to stage of development are the age in which the development first occurred and the location of the settlement within the city. Generally, the closer to the center of the city, the older the development and the more advanced it is in the residential cycle.

In the United States, the cycle for residential change appears to be about fifty years — the general economic life of residential structures. Thus a typical pattern for residential areas built in the 1920s and early 1930s might evidence three stages. (Figure 14.7). Stage I is usually characterized by a physical filling-in process of single-family, owned houses. Such houses built during the 1920s were usually of mixed quality and size within any given neighborhood, but were generally built to fit the technological requirements of that time. Consequently, only the better homes had garages, and these were single garages. The lots were small, averaging about thirty foot fronts, and most houses were of one and a half or two stories. The occupants during the initial settlement stage were young marrieds with school-age children. Consequently, schools were built within walking distance of home and small neighborhood businesses were built close by. Thus, Stage I is characterized by a process of general growth. New functions are added, population grows, and the general future of the neighborhood is one of solidarity and growth. By the end of the first phase, the population for single-family houses had reached its peak. The area is mature.

After an indefinite period of little change, the second stage begins. Density drops as children grow up and leave home (Stage II in Figure 14.7). The families get older and widows occupy some single-family homes. Houses are put into rental status and dilapidation begins to occur among some of them.

It also becomes apparent toward the end of Stage II that the neighborhood is becoming technologically obsolete. Some houses are so dilapidated that they have to be replaced, generally with apartment houses. The rental property further increases, thus emphasizing the growing obsolescence of the neighborhood. The parking problem becomes severe as the public streets become filled with automobiles in the evenings — because suitable parking accommodations are not available at residential sites. Moreover, most of the houses need remodeling and updating, particularly kitchens and bathrooms. By the end of Stage II most of the original families have left the area. Some have died, others have moved to new residential areas, and still others have moved into apartments in other areas. A new group of residents have arrived, and a large percentage of the houses are occupied by renters rather than owners.

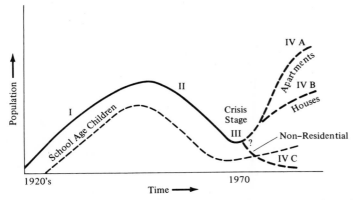

FIGURE 14.7 A Typical Population Cycle of a Residential Neighborhood. In any given neighborhood, over time the population goes through four stages as shown. At Stage III a critical crisis point is reached inasmuch as structures are physically and technologically obsolescent. In most cities, this cycle is about fifty years.

Depending on the location and nature of the original neighborhood, change could then go in several different directions. During Stage III, it might grow in population as single-families homes are torn down or cut up for apartments (IV A). In this case, there would still generally be an oversupply of schools in the area because the new residents have fewer children. On the other hand, the area could continue on a path toward more serious dilapidation and obsolescence. This would be the case if the area proved unattractive for other land uses. In prime areas, the neighborhood might be razed and invaded by commercial uses (IV C). At any rate, it is clear that all residential areas go through some cyclic effects. They have a period of growth, a peak of maximum development, a period of general decline, and the beginnings of a new cycle of development.

American cities today have vast areas of housing, between suburbia and the inner zone, that are well into Stage II. The housing is such that it is not ready for complete clearance, but it is not able to make a viable adjustment to technological change. Thus one of the major problems in cities results from the inherently dynamic nature of their residential land use.

Documentation of the cyclic nature of residential areas has been noted by several specialists in urban affairs.[5] It has been shown that each zone had a period of growth and a period of decline in population density (Figure 14.8). The inner zone *(A)* had growth first, followed by the zones next farther in sequence. However, also note that the more distant zones experience a lower density peak (possibly because of less accessibility potential) and a less steep fall-off in density over time than do inner zones.

Schematic Presentation of Zonal Undulations over Time in a Typical Metropolis

FIGURE 14.8 Relative Density Change over Time for Various Zones within the City.   Each zone contains a period of relative high density followed by a decline. The inner zones of American cities have, of course, peaked first followed by successive zones. Note that there is less density variation within cities now than at any time since the turn of the century. Source: Adapted and modified from Hans Blumenfeld, "The Tidal Wave of Metropolitan Expansion," *Journal of the American Institute of Planners,* 1954.

Residential change on the fringe of cities

Another dynamic feature of residential land use occurs on the edge of cities. Here, land is transformed from rural to urban use. However, the transition does not occur in one fell swoop. The profile of change is fairly complicated. First, there is a series of waves of penetration during which changes in parcel size, ownership, and routes are laid in veneerlike fashion over the original rural pattern. This might be termed a "precession" wave, in that it precedes actual development (Figure 14.9). This wave of preparatory development generally leads, by about fifteen to thirty minutes of driving time, the actual

[5]See Hans Blumenfeld, "The Tidal Wave of Metropolitan Expansion," *Journal of the American Institute of Planners,* Winter 1954, pp. 3–14.

thrust, or tidal wave, of suburban development. As this tidal wave moves over the area, land is assembled, platted, and otherwise prepared on paper for eventual urban use. Although much of the action is visible only at the county courthouses, title offices, and real estate firms, it is nonetheless very real indeed. In fact, the nature of the paper plats and land assembly patterns often have great effect on the future density and settlement patterns of the fringe area.

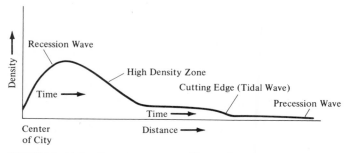

FIGURE 14.9 The Density Profile within American Cities. Density is highest in the inner portions of the city, except for the central business area. Over time, central density declines as it moves outward — the recession wave. The edge of suburban invasion of rural areas is shown by the cutting edge. The precession wave is about fifteen minutes from the cutting edge of the city and is characterized by changes in land ownership, land parcel change, and paper platting; it is a zone characterized by extensive land speculation.

Commercial Land-Use Patterns

A city's pattern of commercial land use is confusing to the casual observer because it is actually composed of a number of business location arrangements. Some commercial uses are aligned along arterials; some are in clusters of varying sizes; and still others are found widely scattered throughout the metropolis (see Figure 14.10). One might thus categorize the first type as highway-oriented, a type in which commercial strip development apparently benefits from automotive traffic; one might categorize the second type as accessibility-oriented, a type in which business is clustered at a hierarchy of strategic sites; and the third pattern might be assumed to reflect low threshold establishments which can be accommodated by neighborhood markets. Therefore, when the general pattern of commercial land use is dissected into various subpatterns, a meaningful distribution can be discerned.

The type of businesses that are found in clusters or nucleations might be considered *intensive* businesses. These are high-rent-paying functions by comparison and are characteristically pedestrian-oriented. Common examples include drug, variety, jewelry, and clothing stores. According to urban rent theory, the intensive establishments can easily outbid the arterial-oriented, or *extensive*, establishments for sites. Hence the intensive functions occupy the most accessible sites. They also often benefit greatly by cluster economies achieved as the result of multiple purpose shopping.

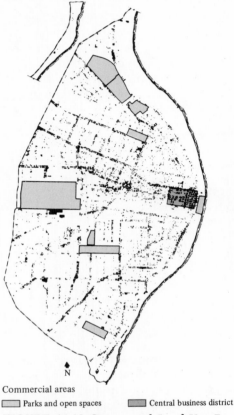

Commercial areas

☐ Parks and open spaces   ▨ Central business district

FIGURE 14.10 Commercial Land-Use Pattern in the City of Saint Louis.   The linear strip development of commercial activities along major streets is most evident. With the development of planned shopping centers, a much more nucleated pattern of business is evident in those areas beyond the central city. Source: Harland Bartholomew, *Land Uses in American Cities*, (C) 1955. By permission of Harvard University Press, Cambridge, Mass.

In contrast, the businesses located along arterials use a large amount of space but pay low rent. Characteristic functions include many drive-in establishments, service stations, automotive sales and repair establishments, supermarkets, and furniture stores. These are usually single-stop functions — shoppers go to only one store and have a definite purchase in mind.

The density of commercial development varies greatly within any given city. As might be expected, it is much more prominent near major employment sources, such as the central business district, than in predominantly residential areas. It is also severely limited in the heavy industrial sector of cities (see Figure 14.10). In the residential sector of the city, commercial development is found in a fairly regular hierarchical pattern, much as might be postulated according to *central place theory*. Especially prominent also is the rise of major regional, planned shopping centers near strategic interchanges of the freeway system. The strip commercial developments are based on automotive traffic and are perhaps related to the commuting work trip.

Central place theory and the business pattern

Much explanation of the distribution of commercial activities can be achieved by applying the principles of central place theory, discussed in Chapter 5, to tertiary activities within cities. Each business requires that a certain threshold or market be met before it can be viable. Thus business activities that require small numbers of customers are the most widespread within the metropolis. These lower-order functions — grocery stores, service stations, drugstores, and other neighborhood-level services like barber shops — are found in centers of almost any size and in many different locations. In fact, the smaller centers will be limited almost exclusively to such low-threshold functions. The next order of functions, those that require a larger number of persons to draw upon, will be found only in centers at the community and regional level. At the highest-level centers, functions that require a large trade area are found. Such activities characteristically include department stores and various clothing establishments.

A point of clarification is the order, however. In fact, the total number of customers of some high-order functions is not necessarily larger than that of a low-order function. The difference relates primarily to the number of persons within any given population who will purchase an item. For example, every family requires groceries, and a high proportion require gasoline — and they require these items frequently. The demand, moreover, is relatively inelastic. Higher-order establishments, on the other hand, commonly find that only a small percentage of the total potential customer market will purchase goods at any one time. Thus it takes many more people in a trade area to supply a viable number of customers for such an establishment than it does for the low-order type, where almost all customers frequently require such goods and services.

Competition among business centers

Many of the smaller and older unplanned business centers are in trouble.

Many businesses in such centers have either moved to planned centers or have become marginal. The villain appears to be the rise of the mighty, planned shopping center. These large centers have affected small business districts, planned and unplanned alike. There appear to be two reasons for this. One is that such centers are simply more attractive and more attuned to the automobile than are the older centers. The second reason concerns the change in mobility within cities, which has had an adverse effect on smaller centers in much the same way that it has placed small towns in competition with metropolises.

The large centers have benefited more from improved transportation than have the small centers. The manner in which this operates is demonstrated below with regard to two business centers — one small and one fairly large and new. Each is in competition with the other for customers in the common territory separating them. Let us assume that the smaller center has five functions, the larger has twenty functions, and that they are thirty blocks apart. Now, by using the standard procedure for computing the breaking point (D) between centers, their respective tributary areas can be estimated (Figure 14.11). If the general accessibility, or friction of distance exponent, is distance squared, than the breaking point between the centers will be ten blocks from the smaller center and twenty blocks from the larger center. (It will be recalled that according to the calculation formula or Reilly's Law, distance from the smaller center (D) equals

$$\frac{d}{1 + \sqrt{\dfrac{P_2}{P_1}}}$$

where d is the distance between centers, P_2 is the size of the larger center, P_1 is the size of the smaller center.)

Now let us assume that accessibility has generally improved between the two centers to the extent that the friction of distance exponent is no longer distance squared, but distance with an exponent of 1 — a reasonable assumption. In this case, the breaking point will have shifted four blocks toward the smaller center so that the trade area boundary (D) is now only six blocks from the smaller center. The result is a drop in customers formerly frequenting the smaller center. In fact, such a drop may result in loss of a function in the smaller center because of inadequate market to support it. If so, then another adjustment would occur and an even further shift toward the smaller center would occur so that the breaking point would now be only 4.8 blocks from the smaller center. Thus an entire series of adjustments results from one change in accessibility. First, the customer-trade-area breaking point (D) is shifted toward the smaller center. Second, the size of the smaller center is made even smaller. Third, other shifts in trade area follow, until some equilibrium is reached. However, quite an opposite effect has occurred with regard to the central business district of cities. In this case, a movement of customers away from this business district has more than canceled out any improvements in transportation.

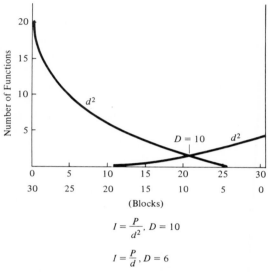

$$I = \frac{P}{d^2}, D = 10$$

$$I = \frac{P}{d}, D = 6$$

FIGURE 14.11 Hypothetical Trade Areas between Two Business Districts. Given one business district with 20 functions and another with 5 functions, the breaking point between the two districts is 10 blocks from the smaller center. With an improvement in transportation such that the friction of distance coefficient is no longer squared but d^1, the breaking point between districts would shift in favor of the larger center by four blocks.

Thus it can be seen that the pattern of business nucleation is constantly in flux. The general effect of improvement in mobility has been an increase in the competitive position of the larger centers, the primary exception being the central business district. In addition, such new innovations as the planned shopping center, with its ability to accommodate the automobile, have rendered the central business district and many of the older, nonplanned centers technologically obsolete.

Competition within business centers

An inverse relationship exists between amount of land used and intensity of urban land use. This relationship is logical if it is assumed that the intensity of use results directly from the bidding process whereby prime land can be occupied only in an intensive manner. In fact, the intensity of retail use decreases with increasing distance from the peak land-value intersection or "100 percent corner" as it is commonly called. Typically, the larger users of space per establishment such as grocery, furniture, drive-in, and automotive establishments are found near the outer edge of the business district. By contrast, functions using relatively little space — barber shops, tobacco shops, jewelry stores, drugstores, and the like — commonly occupy central positions.

There is also variation in rent-paying ability for the same function. The higher the point of accessibility, the higher will be the rent-paying potential. For example, a drugstore located in a large shopping area and thus drawing customers from a wide area may be achieving a more intensive use of its site than a drugstore located in a small neighborhood center and dependent on a more limited number of customers. Therefore, the drugstore in the larger retail center (greater accessibility to a larger market) will be able to pay higher rents than the drugstore in the smaller center. The former will also have to pay higher rents than the latter in order to achieve the same relative position within the center in competition with other functions.

Thus a first clue to the location of any particular business within any given center is a function of the accessibility potential of that center. (This does not apply to planned shopping centers, which will be discussed below.) In small neighborhood centers *(N)*, the highest-level functions will often be a supermarket (Figure 14.12). This function will naturally occupy the prime or 100 percent site. Within community centers *(C)*, functions at a higher level than supermarkets will be found, and these will outbid the supermarkets for prime sites. This will occur even though the supermarket can and will pay more rent in the community center than it would in a neighborhood center. In the regional business districts *(R)*, only the very highest-order functions will be found in the core positions. In summary, the general rent-paying ability of a firm is based on the amount of return that such function can reap at one site versus another; and its placement within a particular center is based on its rent-bidding power relative to other functions within that center.

If it is assumed that a prime reason for differentiation in the location of business types within "unplanned" business centers is rent-paying ability, then it is proper to investigate the reasons for such rent differential in far greater depth. The factors enumerated below affect any retail establishment's ability to pay rent and hence to bid successfully for the most accessible sites: (1) the value of merchandise per unit area, (2) the turnover and markup of merchandise, and (3) the various operational cost peculiarities, such as labor costs, among firms. First, we will see how these operate to affect rents and produce various spatial patterns. Second, we will attempt to determine why there should be variations among establishments with regard to such features as markup — clearly a key item directly affecting profits and, hence ability to pay rents and bid for sites.

The value of merchandise per unit area is a very crude but often effective way of classifying firms on the basis of their potential rent-paying abilities. The method consists simply in estimating the value of the merchandise on site and dividing that value by the square foot of floor area. Establishments with high square-foot merchandise values will generally be found nearer the prime corner than will those with lower values. Nevertheless, there are many exceptions. For example, automobile sales establishments have fairly high values per square foot, whereas variety stores have fairly low values per square foot. Yet, automobile dealers are characteristically found on the periphery of centers and variety stores are found near the 100 percent corner.

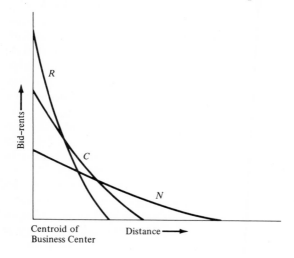

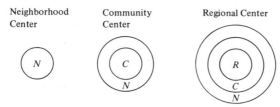

N = Neighborhood Level Functions
C = Community Level Functions
R = Regional Level Functions

FIGURE 14.12 Position of Neighborhood, Community, and Regional Level Functions within Various Center Types.   Regional level functions can bid higher for sites than can community and neighborhood level functions and thereby take prime sites in regional level centers. Wherever a higher level function is absent, as in lower level centers, that function which is highest in the bid-rent hierarchy will occupy the prime sites.

Turnover (or volume) and markup also provide meaningful measures of rent-paying ability. Thus firms with the highest turnovers and markups presumably can pay higher rents, other things being equal, and occupy closer-in locations in contrast to activities with opposite features. Unfortunately, since the same amount of money can be gleaned through substitution of turnover and markup, confusion often occurs. Usually a firm has a high turnover and a low markup or a low turnover and a high markup. For example, dealers in new cars characteristically have low turnover and rather substantial markups — presumably because of salesmen's commissions and the like. By contrast, jewelry stores have fantastically high markups (often 200 or 300 percent over wholesale cost) and low turnover. Grocery stores have low markups but high turnover. Thus, inasmuch as mixing occurs, the locational case is not made clear. Two kinds of firms whose locations do not conform to these measures further demonstrate the problem. Bookshops have moderate merchandise value per square foot, high markups, and low turnover, but rarely occupy prime locations. Music stores likewise have high merchandise value, high markups, and low turnovers, but are invariably in much more obscure and peripheral locations than are bookstores. But why, one might ask, do not firms vary their markups to compensate for turnover and merchandise value per square foot — inasmuch as markup is the only factor not fixed for any location? If this were done, a situation would result in which all stores could compete for sites equally.

The typical response to this question is that the markup over wholesale costs relates to opportunities various sites offer for earnings. In that way, functions fortunate enough to occupy prime locations have somewhat of a spatial monopoly and hence are able to enjoy higher markups without fear of devastating competitive responses from noncentral locations. Thus one might argue that markups reflect the extent of competition as measured by the number of usable sites for that function. (Note that this argument is analogous to that used with regard to rent-paying abilities of different agricultural crops.) Functions with the least choice of suitable sites can charge extremely high markups when they occupy central sites. Nevertheless, there are glaring exceptions to such arguments. Certainly, tradition also might provide a strong explanatory reason inasmuch as some markup rates appear to result primarily from historical precedent. Another explanation for differential markup relates directly to the nature of the item being sold and the advantages derived by proximity to other businesses.

The placement of functions within planned shopping centers is quite different from that in unplanned centers. Given the fact that planned shopping centers are fast becoming the common business medium in most of the newer portions of cities, perhaps it is the "unplanned" districts that are peculiar. Certainly, it is the older districts that are the most anachronistic and most in trouble. Nonetheless, in many respects, the forces that were discussed above with regard to the older centers — and that are most easily seen in such centers — are still somewhat operable in planned shopping centers. It is primarily the nature of shopping center operation that results in a pattern peculiar to this type of business cluster.

On the one hand, the organization of activities within planned shopping centers offers the customer a more advantageous arrangement of goods and services than that found in unplanned centers. First, these centers are commonly free of such nonshopper space use as churches, mortuaries, insurance companies, and similar businesses found within unplanned centers. (While some of these business services are of considerable aid to other businesses in the center, they are of no direct use to the shoppers themselves. Instead, the customer is forced to walk past such establishments in order to assemble the desired items.) Because the placement of functions within planned shopping centers is not based on independent bid rents, many functions are situated more advantageously for the shopper than they commonly are in unplanned centers. As an example, grocery stores are often found in planned centers even though they do not qualify in unplanned centers of equal size.

On the other hand, some aspects of business arrangement in the planned shopping center are less advantageous to the shopper. First a number of functions are commonly excluded from planned shopping centers — functions that are considered very beneficial to shoppers. Often a large department store can dictate terms to the shopping center management and thus force the exclusion of certain otherwise highly competitive stores. In addition, large numbers of extensive businesses normally associated with an unplanned business district are also excluded. Such exclusions commonly include hardware, furniture, lumber and paint stores, some book and most music stores, and all manner of automobile-oriented establishments. One justifiable basis for exclusion relates to the fact that stores in the center carry some of these items — a department store usually carries furniture and books. The usual basis for excluding these stores, however, is the simple fact that they do not contribute many sales to the overall center inasmuch as most of the items they sell are of a single purchase nature rather than part of a multiple-purpose shopping tour.

Another problem for the shopper in many planned shopping centers is the tendency to place a large department store, usually complementary rather than truly competitive, at either end of the shopping mall. (It will be recalled that in unplanned centers, department stores are usually found adjacent, or very near each other.) The result is that people are forced to make the long trek between these stores in order to do comparison shopping. This is a deliberate strategy on the part of shopping center management in order to create as much impulse buying as possible in intermediate stores, a number of which are placed between these major magnets. (In very large centers, the customers have circumvented this somewhat by shopping in only one end of the center, or by driving, rather than walking, to the other end.)

The vertical land-use pattern

Commercial land use is found vertically as well as horizontally within cities. In fact, in the central business districts of American cities, far more square feet of space are found above than at ground level. This is very characteristic of office space. As might be expected, the vertical placement of various business uses does not occur haphazardly but has a distinctive pattern and operates by much the same spatial principles as does economical land use in the horizontal dimension.

Commercial activities place such a high premium on accessibility that rent gradients occur vertically as well as horizontally. Although only the ground floor space has been discussed thus far, it is nonetheless apparent that some measure of vertical height may be substituted for some measure of horizontal distance. Thus a furniture establishment may be found either on the edge of a business district or on the upper floors of a downtown building — in a department store, for example. In this regard, some businesses may have a measure of substitutability between horizontal and vertical proximity to the 100 percent location. Thus at distance X, rents may be the same as at height A; and at distance X_2, comparable to height B. Of course, not all businesses have this substitution capability, since the latter depends on the nature of the business.

The function most capable of such substitution, and most prone to favor vertical to horizontal proximity, are office uses. Typically, these functions, which include lawyers, physicians, real estate and insurance brokers, occupy the upper floors of buildings in which the street level is taken by retail uses. It should also be noted that some of these functions are suitable for both ground level and upper level space; ground floor occupancy, however, occurs only at the periphery of a business district.

Nevertheless, unusually high accessibility indexes are maintained vertically, largely as the result of the efficiency of the elevator versus comparable horizontal movement. In fact, the elevator is far superior to movement made horizontally. This can be demonstrated by imagining a high-speed elevator operating on the horizontal scale (Figure 14.13). Assume that the vertical elevator and the "horizontal elevator" are equal in speed. If so, the vertical elevator would provide access to almost ten times as much space in a given time as the horizontal elevator. (Stop and start time would, of course, diminish this advantage somewhat.) In order to have access to circles of space with 100-foot radii, the horizontal elevator would have to travel 200 feet between stops. But to provide the same access to space vertically, the elevator would have to travel only about 20 feet between stops — that is, the distance between floors.

For any given ground-floor accessibility, there is a fade-off of accessibility upward. The degree of fade-off depends on the accessibility value at ground floor level, the height of the building, and the potential functions that may find such a location suitable. The decrease in rents with height is shown theoretically for three different positions of horizontal accessibility, A, B, and D (Figure 14.14). The ground floor rent is determined by its position in the horizontal accessibility fade-off from the prime site. The rents decrease as one proceeds upward. In fact, the second and third floor show a much steeper fall-off than does any comparable horizontal space extension. Beyond these first few lower floors, however, the drop becomes less.

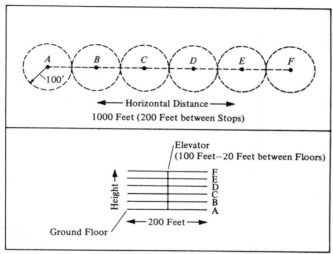

FIGURE 14.13 Comparative Space Efficiencies between Horizontal and Vertical Transportation Systems. Because of the stacking advantages afforded vertical space, the elevator is considerably more efficient than a one-floor horizontal system for reaching small areas. The slower speed of elevators and the high cost of vertical construction largely mitigate this advantage, however, except for intensively used space such as offices.

A special peculiarity of vertical space is the tendency for rents at the very top floors to increase with increasing height (Figure 14.15). This "penthouse" effect evidentally occurs for at least two reasons, one psychological and the other based on the creation of "site" amenities. In the first instance, there appears to be psychic, and hence prestige value, in occupying the top floor or floors of a very high building — a psychic value reminiscent of the native Indonesian hang-up in this regard. Such height also provides certain advantages with regard to view, lack of noise, and, in some areas, diminution of smog.

With regard to retail goods, the effect of height is severe. Most retailing outlets not already operating on the ground floor find anything above the ground floor unacceptable. However, in certain large establishments like downtown department and furniture stores, much use is made of upper floors. Here again, there is a fade-off in intensity of space use analogous to the horizontal scale. The top floor of department stores invariably contains articles that are characteristically single-purchase, or certainly definite-purchase, items, such as furniture, carpeting, and so forth. People will make the trip upward in order to see a particular thing. By contrast, goods usually purchased on the basis of convenience and impulse are placed on the ground floor.

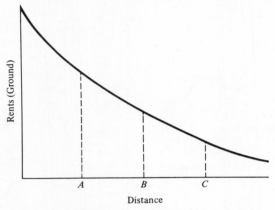

FIGURE 14.14 The Play-off between Ground Floor Rent and Distance from the Prime Rent Site.   Sites at distance *C* bring less rent than those at distance *A* closer to the prime rent site. This is because of the inferior interaction potential of less accessible sites.

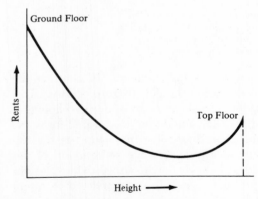

FIGURE 14.15 The Play-off between Ground Floor Rent and Vertical Distance.   The fade-off in rents with height is somewhat similar to that for horizontal distance (see Figure 14.14). However, with increasing height a "penthouse effect" is often achieved whereby the top floors bring higher rents than do those in the center of the building. The reason for this relates to the amenities, such as view, which are created in the upper floors of taller buildings.

Rent-paying ability also differentiates office space use within tall buildings. For example, legal offices are most prominent in the upper stories of office buildings, yet lawyers require considerable interaction with other functions and with clients. By contrast, real estate and insurance offices are characteristically found in the lower floors, even though their need for access to the street is considerably less than that of lawyers. Undoubtedly, rent-paying ability operates here with a double-edged sword. First, some functions, such as lawyers, are high-rent payers yet could more profitably occupy the lower floors. However, perhaps for prestige reasons, they prefer offices higher in the building. The very top floors (penthouse floors) are devoted primarily to legal firms because of their ability to outbid other functions. Real estate offices and insurance offices in downtown office buildings often pay higher rents than they might otherwise have to because, paradoxically, many are squeezed down to lower levels by bidders for space above. Perhaps one result of this is reflected in the increasing tendency for insurance firms to move to ground floor space elsewhere or to separate buildings in outlying locations.

Conclusions

Despite this rather lengthy discussion, only about one-half of the land uses in a typical city was presented. Many other land-use types, particularly the public and semipublic uses, were omitted. An interesting discussion could have been focused on particular activities like hospitals, churches, parks, and cemeteries. Nonetheless, such extended treatment of intraurban patterns would yield little additional knowledge about the nature of urban patterns and the nature of urban location problems. In this regard, it should be recalled that our purpose is not to discuss all possible activities, but only those which provide additional incremental insights and enlightenment about the nature of various locational patterns and problems. The treatment of industrial, residential, and commercial land-use patterns has largely filled this purpose.

The placement of activities within cities is largely affected by competition for accessible sites over time. Thus all types of land use generally seek central locations. Those with the greatest need and greatest rent-paying abilities, however, usually end up with the prime sites. In this regard, commercial functions are the most competitive bidders for space within cities and consequently are found in most of the strategic locations. The possibilities for vertical-scale benefits are often involved in achieving high rents. Farthest removed from the center of the city are commonly single-family residential structures. Thus there is a general fade-off of both land value and population density as one proceeds from the center outward.

Residential land use has become highly independent of accessibility requirements. People can now travel great distances to work, thus making available for residential occupancy a vast area well beyond present-day suburbia.

Moreover, business functions, schools, and other needed services tend to follow the path of residential development, so that residential areas appear to be setting the stage for the future pattern. In this respect, residential areas are becoming less and less dependent on situation, or accessibility features, and more concerned about site features like views, proximity to lakes, and wooded areas. Tremendous importance is also being given to the ability to have large lots. Thus land is being consumed on a per capita basis several times more rapidly than the population is growing in urban areas.

Nonetheless, industrial land is often the triggering element for urban growth. This is particularly the case for those industries which export their products beyond the city. These city-forming industries employ basic workers who indirectly support many other persons and activities within the city. Often these industries select their site within the city based on good access not to areas within the city itself, but to areas outside the city from which they may obtain raw material and ship finished products. Often port locations and railroad proximity, plus flat land, are site requirements that override centrality within the metropolis. In fact, most large land-using primary industries are found on the edge of cities.

There is a strong tendency for like functions to cluster within parts of a typical city. Industry is heavily attracted to other industry inasmuch as one firm's finished products are often another's raw materials. Business, too, is characteristically found in tight clusters because of the benefits one business offers another as the result of comparative shopping by customers. Even residential areas remain quite pure despite the obvious daily interaction with all types of diverse uses.

The fact that various functions within a city are not mixed but largely pure is responsible for the daily ebb and flow of traffic in the city. Foremost among these is the work trip, but shopping, business, social, health, and other trips are also involved.

Finally, there is a pattern of land use in the vertical as well as the horizontal dimension within cities. In fact, there is often a direct substitution between height and distance from the prime center of accessibility for business functions. Thus a stratification of retailing activities occurs as one proceeds upward as well as outward. For example, furniture is often sold on the top floor of a department store or on the edge of the business district in the downtown areas. Likewise, a vertical stratification, based on the ability to pay rent, occurs within office buildings. Lawyers commonly pay high rents and, perhaps for prestige reasons, usually occupy the topmost floors of office buildings. Nonetheless, there are many kinds of lawyers and many different locational choices. Finally, residential land can also effectively compete for central city uses through high-rise structures.

Increasingly, however, most activities are emphasizing the one-story or horizontal dimension rather than the vertical dimension. This is true for industrial, residential, and commercial uses. The horizontal production system (continuous process flow) has become standard through the adoption of assembly line techniques in much of industry. Business uses also increasingly emphasize the one-level approach surrounded by ample parking. Residential land use is perhaps the most land-hungry of all. The rambler concept in home construction alone is responsible for much of the necessity for larger lots. But the major factor necessitating more residential space is the automobile and the attached garage. Two-car garages are now common and three- and four-car garages for the home are increasing.

Perhaps the most important and continually true statement that can be made about the intraurban activity pattern is that it is in rapid and constant flux. Consequently, formerly well-placed functions now find themselves in the backwash locations. Business centers and businesses within them are in severe competition. The older, unplanned centers are often becoming marginal as new, large, planned shopping centers, strategically situated near major freeway interchanges, become more dominant. Even the formerly supreme central business district of many cities is fast becoming technologically obsolescent with respect to shopping. Residential neighborhoods are rarely stable. They are either increasing or decreasing in population. As a general rule, most residential areas in the central city are tending to lose population, primarily because of aging, whereas those in outlying and suburban areas are still tending to grow.

BIBLIOGRAPHY

Blumenfeld, Hans. "The Economic Base of the Metropolis." *Journal of the American Institute of Planners*, November 1955, pp. 114–132.

————. "The Tidal Wave of Metropolitan Expansion." *Journal of the American Institute of Planners*, Winter 1954, pp. 3–14.

Colby, Charles C. "Centrifugal and Centripetal Forces in Urban Geography." In *Readings in Urban Geography*, edited by Harold M. Mayer and Clyde F. Kohn, pp. 287–298. Chicago: University of Chicago Press, 1959.

Donaldson, Scott. *The Suburban Myth*. New York: Columbia University Press, 1969.

Eaton, Leonard K. "The American Suburb: Dream and Nightmare." *Landscape*, Winter 1963-64, pp. 12–16.

Haig, Robert Murray. "Toward an Understanding of the Metropolis: The Assignment of Activities to Areas in Urban Regions." In *Readings in Economic Geography*, edited by Robert H. T. Smith et al., pp. 44–57. Chicago: Rand McNally, 1967.

Lampe, Fred A., and Schaefer, Orval C. Jr. "Land Use Patterns of the City." *The Journal of Geography*, May 1969, pp. 301–306.

Nelson, Howard J. "The Form and Structure of Cities: Urban Growth Patterns." *The Journal of Geography*, April 1969, pp. 198–207.

Nelson, Richard L. *The Selection of Retail Location*. New York: Dodge, 1958.

Pred, Allan R. "The Intrametropolitan Location of American Manufacturing." *Annals of the Association of American Geographers*, June 1964, pp. 164–180.

Reinemann, Martin W. "The Pattern and Distribution of Manufacturing in the Chicago Area." *Economic Geography,* April 1960, pp. 139–144.

Simmons, James. *The Changing Pattern of Retail Location.* Department of Geography Research Paper no. 92. Chicago: University of Chicago Press, 1963.

Smith, P. J. "Calgary: A Study in Urban Pattern." *Economic Geography,* October 1962, pp. 315–329.

Vance, James E. Jr. "Housing the Worker: The Employment Linkage As a Force in Urban Structure." *Economic Geography,* October 1966, pp. 294–325.

part f

Problems of Activity Placements: Micro and Macro Regionalizations

The movement of firms and families out of the central city is now proceeding on such a scale that the problem has become, depending on whether the point of view is urban redevelopment or area development, either how to get them to stay or how to get them to move to more socially desirable locations. On their own, the lagging regions are scarcely able to entice them; and the central cities . . . cannot keep them. This evolution has made the urban problem the most important issue in the United States — next to war and peace.

Lloyd Rodwin, *Nations and Cities: A Comparison of Strategies for Urban Growth* (Boston: Houghton Mifflin, 1970), pp. 219–222.

XV

Some Geographically Based Problems on a Micro Scale – Urban Problems

Unfortunately, application of the concepts and principles discussed above does not always result in making this the best of all possible worlds. This is particularly the case with regard to the way in which land is used within cities. Because space is so scarce and tightly utilized in cities, conflicts among different functions commonly exist. The result is congestion, noise, and other disjunctive features that make cities less desirable places in which to live. Moreover, the city grows unevenly, with some areas growing rapidly and others stagnating or declining. Marginal neighborhoods and business districts, blight, and sprawl are some of the consequences.

However, the most acute problems of cities stem from their very nature — the concentration of many people in a small territory — and have always required ingenuity with regard to providing all manner of "housekeeping" services for the population. Housekeeping functions include, among others, such services as fire and police departments, water supply, health and medical care, and sewerage systems. Housekeeping problems, however, have generally been solved in most American cities — at least technologically speaking. For example, buildings are more fireproof; water systems have been elaborately developed; various public health facilities, such as hospitals and clinics, are legion. Through housing and building codes, many of the severe ills formerly associated with city living have been eliminated.

Nor are environmental problems new. Since the industrial revolution many large cities have been afflicted with severe smoke and smog. In fact, the smog problems in cities like Saint Louis and Pittsburgh were much worse at the turn of the century than they are today. The automobile and the airplane, however, have created a new kind of air pollution. This is particularly critical in cities that are characteristically plagued by air inversions and that have mountains or other barriers on their leeward sides (for example, Los Angeles and Salt Lake City). Cities that are in low-lying river valleys and the like are also much affected if they are the site of obnoxious industries (for example, Lewiston, Idaho, which has a pulp mill).

Equally serious is the problem of land and water pollution. Ground pollution occurs primarily from septic tank development in outlying areas. Much of this has recently been eradicated through the provision of sewers, but many other potentially dangerous areas remain. Water pollution is of a more serious nature. Like air pollution, it often affects other communities near its source. Characteristically, cities dump municipal and industrial wastes in their rivers. Although most of this waste must now be purified to some extent, difficulties with stream ecology are common. Sometimes the water temperature is raised sufficiently to kill certain wildlife in the streams; and, of course, many detergents are almost impossible to remove from industrial and municipal waste.

Territorial Change as an Urban Problem

In many respects the land-use patterns of a city are an ossification of a number of time processes. Thus, a full understanding of land-use problems, and problems related thereto, requires an understanding of the processes that have brought them about and, perhaps even more important, of the forces now operating to change the morphology of the city. Inasmuch as the form of the city is more rigid than the processes that have created or are now acting upon it, tensions and stresses are built up in the spatial pattern. These stresses thus provide insights into reasons for the changing form and land-use characteristics of particular areas within cities.

One of these stresses results from the growing territorial extent and population size of cities. In fact, territorial extent is increasing several times more rapidly than population growth. Thus, the land used per capita within cities has been rapidly increasing. All manner of functions now use greater amounts of land; the spatial result is that cities now occupy far more territory for any given population than they formerly did. Simply put, cities have spread outward very rapidly during the past several decades and such areal spread has resulted in the formation of a number of new urban problems. In some areas, such as the central portions of American cities, problems are created because this territory is declining in growth and importance. In contrast, outlying areas are plagued by too rapid a growth. Such growth or decline is always disruptive and always presents problems. Of the two, growth seems much easier to accommodate than does decline.

Nowhere are conflicts over territorial growth more acute than at the municipal level. As the metropolis has increased in area, it has also increased in its number of municipalities, some of the largest metropolises having a hundred or so separate "cities" and towns within them. Each of these municipalities is primarily concerned with its own welfare, adopting policies and interpreting urban problems from a vantage point that increases its viability as a municipal entity.

As cities have grown outward, the original central city has until recently not desired — or, in some cases has been unable — to annex the new, urbanized territory on its edges. Consequently, much of this territory is still unincorporated and only loosely controlled with regard to land-use placement and the development of needed public facilities and services. On the other hand, many new municipalities have been created to accommodate rapidly growing population on the fringe of cities.

Each of these towns or cities is concerned with its own individual welfare and only indirectly concerned with the metropolis at large. As might be expected, the policies of many of these separate territorial entities are not always in the best interests of the community at large. Some prohibit all but residential uses, even though the residents in that area might benefit greatly by closer provision of business and employment activities.

Nowhere has municipal self-interest been more damaging to the metropolis at large than in the policies of central city governments. Because central cities usually comprise the oldest parts of the metropolis, they are plagued with some of the most difficult problems. Not only are central cities declining, but their problems are further aggravated because many of their structures are fast becoming physically and technologically obsolescent. Some of the newest technologies, such as the freeway, cannot even be effectively accommodated within this older urban framework.

Moreover, such cities have found their tax base shrinking as people and activities have moved outward. To complicate the matter even further, the central city population has become much lower in income as many low-skilled families have migrated to them. The central city is also heavily populated by the elderly and the economically depressed. Consequently, the central city finds itself burdened with increasing demand for public services and decreasing revenues. It is perhaps best described as having a few depreciating assets and a host of compounding liabilities.

Because of this dilemma, caused by spatial growth of the metropolis, central city governments are fighting hard to preserve themselves as viable municipal entities. Central business districts, as a case in point, are promoted by almost any means available. Perhaps this is because central business districts have declined so dramatically in sales and employment in the last few decades. The latest hope on the part of central city government is to develop rapid mass-transit facilities that will, of course, focus on the downtown area. Urban renewal and redevelopment programs, programs pushed through the federal government in part by central city mayors, are another example of a desperate measure to maintain land values.

This attitude is succinctly stated by one eminent political scientist: "Since the positions of power in our society can be expected to fight for survival, it can be expected that the vested interest in downtown should fight as hard for the preservation of our outmoded central city land values as the embattled farmers have to preserve an outgrown pattern of agriculture. When one looks at the vested stake in central city real estate, it is hard to imagine that the fight to achieve public subsidies to resist its obsolescence will be less than that put up by agriculture. Certainly there might seem to be a greater appeal for spending the massive sums that now go into subsidizing an unproductive agriculture on the maintenance of our obsolescent central city plant. The sentimental appeal that persuades us to save the family farm can and has been raised to save downtown. As yet, the appeal goes no further than the appeal for urban renewal, and the subsidization of commuter railways and mass transit. If this does not work, we can expect the ante will be raised rather than the end abandoned. . . . Perhaps one day we will cease to regard Los Angeles as a monstrosity and accept the technological obsolescence of the older city. Our agricultural experience indicates the old will die hard."[1]

The result of the fragmentation of government that exists in the metropolis is inefficient government, in the first instance, and a definite lack of coordination among areas and functions within the metropolis, in the second. Of course, some governments bear more of the burden than do others. In addition to being unfair, this presents the dilemma of finding a way to equalize the burden. It is quite evident that many of our "urban problems" are the result of problems seen from the perspective of a particular municipality. Thus many urban problems are more apparent than real. At the very most, they are problems applicable only to one part of the city.

People-Related Problems versus Thing-Related Problems

The problems discussed above might best be described as thing-related problems. Foremost among them are questions of central city decline, blighted neighborhoods and marginal business districts, decentralization, suburbanization, and sprawl. Yet all these emphasize happenings associated with functions or territories. The really important problems that result from changing spatial arrangements within cities must surely concern the quality of living in an urban environment. These latter kinds of problems are people-oriented rather than thing-oriented.

In this regard, questions of health and general social and economic well-being are of concern. Health problems associated with the physical structure of cities and the concomitant environments thereof include a wide range of phenomena like air and water pollution. Other questions of noise, aesthetics, safety, and the provision of such public facilities as museums and parks are also important features. Many of these people-based problems are the result of the land-use pattern within cities.

From the discussion in foregoing chapters, one might get the fallacious notion that profits are more important than people. Activities seek out the particular location that gives them maximum profitability. When this interferes

---

[1]Norton E. Long, *The Polity* (Chicago: Rand McNally, 1962) p. 163.

with certain human values, however, people should surely be put first. Nowhere has this conflict become more apparent than within metropolitan areas. In seeking out optimum locations for various activities, little attention is usually given to the effect on the quality of the urban environment as a place to live. Consequently, smog, traffic congestion, and various noise and other environmental problems have become the rule rather than the exception.

Part of the problem stems from the system of corporate bookkeeping used within cities. Industrial plants, for example, benefit greatly from the external economies found in cities, but do not reap the penalities for the external diseconomies they help to create. Instead, such external diseconomies as traffic congestion, air pollution, and general hypertension of the population caused by living in large metropolitan areas is passed on to the general population. Yet, these problems do not adversely affect the profits of the firm nor its decision to locate in a particular place.

As will be demonstrated in this chapter, when it becomes a matter of either/or, people and their needs must surely take precedence over the placement of things. Five dicta might be postulated with reference to this issue.

First, people are more important than bricks and stone. Some people would preserve physical artifacts in a metropolis at all costs.

Second, people are more important than land values. It has long been the contention that maximization of land value within a metropolis results in a most efficient system. Nevertheless, when the choice is between providing living space for people and building structures that would yield higher land values, it is fairly clear which of these should be given precedence.

Third, people are more important than land. By this is meant land as a commodity. There are those who would insist that cities be tightly restricted in order to save land on the edge of cities. One might ask, Save land for whom and for what? As will be demonstrated, land on the edge of cities is no longer a scarce item.

Fourth, people are more important than municipal governments and fiscal solvencies. Unfortunately, many of the policies of municipalities are based on maintenance of the tax base and the general financial solidarity of the particular municipality rather than on the needs of the overall urban population in that area or areas beyond. One example of this is the desire on the part of such governments to increase the population, and hence the population density, of the residential areas, although higher densities may not improve the quality of the urban environment. Likewise, through their chamber-of-commerce-type approaches, these governments often solicit industry indiscriminately in an attempt to increase the economic base, and hence the population, of the city. Measures like this have become particularly common in many of the central cities that are experiencing heavy population and business decline.

Fifth, people are more important than cities themselves. There are some who maintain that the city form must be preserved at all costs. Many of them find that the new pattern of urbanization and the new way in which nonrural population occupies territory does not fit their image of a city. These people see a city in its historical and traditional context as a high-density and highly concentrated small area quite distinct from the surrounding countryside. One should not evaluate new patterns in terms of what a city has been, but in terms of the advantages and disadvantages the new modes of land settlement will have for the people who live in the areas.

Urban Problems as Assets and Deficits

Most urban problems should also be understood within the context of assets and deficits. Almost every particular event or land-use arrangement has some advantages and some disadvantages. Inasmuch as it is often difficult to weigh these benefits and costs, the best course to follow often poses a dilemma.

Nowhere is such a dilemma more apparent than in those urban problems that result from the changing spatial structure of the city — urban sprawl and decentralization, central city decline, questions of marginal business districts and area blight, problems of traffic congestion, and many others. Some of these difficulties, of course, are caused by simply trying to use cities that were built for another technological age. Much of the problem in American cities today is the inability of the old framework of the city to adjust to changing social, economic, and technological conditions. It has been said that we build cities too well. If they wore out faster, it would be easier to keep them in tune with the changing conditions. Yet any change creates a general feeling of confusion and chaos on the part of many people. Given the already rapid spatial change in cities, it is little wonder that many urbanites see the city as a seething hotbed of problems.

A more balanced view of the problems of the city, however, reveals that, at least for American cities, things have been getting better rather than worse in terms of overall living conditions. This is not to suggest that everything has been getting better, for no one can deny that in large metropolises such problems as air pollution and other environmental and ecological difficulties arising from urban growth are on the increase. Nonetheless, a number of improvements can surely be listed. These include, first of all, greater choice in the location of homes, factories, businesses, and other activities within the city. In other words, the spatial parameters of choice have been vastly widened during the past several decades. This simply means that people now have greater freedom regarding the types of places in which they can live within metropolitan areas. Of course, many have opted for large lots in amenity-laden areas outside the old city. Such choice has, by definition, benefited some areas and depreciated others.

Nor can anyone deny that major improvements have occurred in the general living standards of the American urban population. These include for most not only more purchasing power and a greater selection of goods and services, but also more leisure time for the pursuit of recreation and pleasure.

There have been major innovations in technology, although some might question whether these changes, which have occurred not only in the United States but in many places around the world, have enhanced the quality of life. Foremost among them have been the rise of the automobile and the freeway, and, of course, the concomitant response in the urban form. Nor should one forget the revolution in communication that has taken place with the spread of television and telephone. Major improvements in building construction, notably prefabrication and the use of the steel girder, have permitted skycrapers to be erected with ease. Improvements in the high-speed elevator, air conditioning, and in various other facilities within buildings have allowed people to live and work in more comfortable surroundings.

There have also been major innovations in the way in which land is utilized. These improvements include the rise of planned shopping centers. Planned industrial parks are another fairly new phenomenon and have been of great assistance to small businesses and small industries. Likewise there have been major changes in merchandising technology such as the standardization of goods, including freezing and processing, that have allowed the consumer to select from a range of items wider than ever before. Nor should one forget the development of credit cards — a boon to many shoppers.

On the positive side also is the simple fact that all kinds of activities are now utilizing more space. Many families now own their own homes and are able to live in larger houses and on larger lots. Despite certain negative connotations, this is definitely an asset and has improved the quality of living in cities for many during the past decade or so.

Finally, at least in newly developing areas and with regard to new structures, the urban environment is generally more aesthetically pleasing now than it was in the past. Note the great amount of nursery stock being sold in new residential areas as contrasted with the past. Indeed, most homes are now landscaped. Attention is given to all manner of underground wiring for power, telephone, and other utilities. The same kind of aesthetic concern is also evident in the attractiveness of both industrial and commercial property. Most industrial firms now spend considerable effort on the appearance of their plants and the areas around them. Businesses have become especially conscious of presenting a pleasing image. Even service stations have now entered into the visual-improvement age. Of course, much remains to be done, but it is not inappropriate at this stage to remind ourselves that all parts of cities are not getting worse.

Problems in Cities

Inasmuch as land-use characteristics vary dramatically within the city, these problems vary in degree of intensity from one part of the city to another. It makes little sense therefore, to generalize about the metropolis as a whole. For a discussion of location-related problems to be relevant, it must apply to a particular region of the city. Almost any statement would be true or false somewhere within a metropolis.

Therefore, in order to understand the nature of our urban problems as these pertain to spatial arrangements, it is necessary to talk about the parts of the city separately. Since all cities have grown outward from a central core such problems are perhaps best discussed from the standpoint of a concentric or zonal approach. In American cities, four zones are evident: (1) an inner zone, which is composed of the central business district and the surrounding high-density residential areas like the Negro ghetto; (2) a "middle zone," which is composed of the outer one-third or so of the central city; (3) a suburban zone; and (4) an outer zone.

Problems in the inner zone of cities

The inner zone of cities primarily includes three types of land uses: (1) the downtown or central business district area, (2) the adjacent wholesale and light manufacturing area, and (3) the high-density and usually low-income residential area nearby. These zones have several important assets. First, they are well situated within the metropolitan area. Indeed, many of the transportation developments like the freeway system have actually improved access to and from these places and other parts of the city.

The fact that this area includes the historical center of the metropolis, with the prestige that it carries, is also a major asset. For many people, the land occupied by the central business district is the sacred cow of American cities. Undoubtedly, historical factors are in part responsible for this attitude. As pointed out in earlier chapters, this concept, though fallacious, is nonetheless important in terms of understanding some people's philosophy and interpretation of such spatial problems.

Another major asset of the central area or inner zone of cities is its sheer mass and high intensity of use. Here are found the highest land values and the greatest population densities in the city — and, according to some people, the greatest opportunities for redevelopment. Unfortunately, the urban renewal and redevelopment programs have not verified this assumption.

If the assets of the inner zone of the city are impressive, the deficits are even more so. As a matter of fact, some people have suggested that the physical layout and structures are so obsolescent that they cannot be saved. Certainly the streets are too narrow, the blocks are too small, and much of this territory has lost its strategic importance as a result of the change in transportation patterns within the metropolis. This decline is reflected in the increasing drop in population, employment, and business activities in the area. Wholesale and distribution warehouses are rapidly moving to outlying areas of the metropolis. Light industry is likewise finding outlying, planned industrial parks more advantageous. Retail establishments have largely decentralized in order to be more accessible to the higher income residential population. More recently, office space has begun to develop in strategic places outside the central city boundaries.

There appear to be about four possible approaches to this spatial problem. The first and most widespread "solution" is to raze, rebuild, and renew the present territory so that it can accommodate future clients and higher uses. Generally the argument has been that in this area the new functions (that is, those replacing the former functions), should be more intensive, whether they be commercial or residential uses. On the other hand, the high density of such low-income population is perhaps one of the main people-problems of the area. By making densities even greater, such problems may actually be compounded. Thus we are left with the recurring dilemma of finding a way to resolve these conflicts between people and things.

Of no small importance is the question of who should pay for such redevelopment. The central cities argue that the federal government and the people who live in the metropolis at large should foot the bill. Yet as far as people in outlying areas are concerned, this money might better be spent in the newly developing part of the city. They argue that it is sometimes more sensible to evacuate a territory than to remodel or rebuild it. Of course, those who say that nothing much should be done for the inner city area advocate and hope for the removal of many of its low-income residents to better housing and more space in outlying areas, where they can improve the quality of their living conditions and also, in many cases, be closer to places of employment.

A further argument along this line is that the inner city is not yet ripe for redevelopment because land prices are artificially pegged at high levels that do not yet reflect the true drop in monopolistic and strategic importance this territory has experienced. This school of thought thus advocates waiting until values drop. Certainly this makes sense from a public investment standpoint inasmuch as the cost of redevelopment after the area has deteriorated considerably more would be much lower than the present cost. (The question remains, however, what about the people who will continue to live in the area during this very dramatic period of declining quality in the urban environment?)

This latter stance is taken also by those who insist that the intensity of use of the city's inner zone be decreased. They suggest that appropriate land uses here would include such things as parks and other municipal functions. This is unreasonable to expect, however, as long as we have a central city government concerned with increasing the tax base of the area. Many of the suggested functions, which would be lower in intensity than those they replace or would be in the public land-use sector, would not add to this tax base.

In order to point out the dilemma with regard to the central business district, various approaches to solutions will be discussed here. The first is the common public policy of augmenting the district. The paradox is that by building up the downtown area, negative features are created. One deficit of this policy is surely the amount of money involved. A second deficit is the haunting fear that the new structures and investment will still not make the area viable. In other words, Will such investment actually pay off? Will the central business district ever return to its former status in the metropolis?

More critically, improving the downtown area, or ensuring its growth, means that restrictions will have to be placed on some of the major improvements occurring elsewhere in metropolitan areas. First there will have to be restriction on mobility. The automobile will have to be discriminated against to a high degree, and rapid transit will have to be pushed. This would place controls on housing location and would decrease the range of spatial choice in business and residential location. It would also, of course, restrict urban growth outward and thereby remove a number of advantages that would otherwise be achieved by more extensive occupancy of the land.

Our new technology can also be used as an argument in favor of augmenting the downtown area and building high-rise apartment houses in the inner part of the city. Such things as improvements in air conditioning and air circulation within buildings, the development of high-speed elevators, and the presumed improvements in rapid mass transit would make this argument seem fairly attractive.

The arguments in favor of doing nothing involve several points. First, many wonder why they should have to subsidize this area or a particular function. They argue that business should pay its own way and remain competitive within the metropolis. Moreover, they argue that adjustments and relocations already occurring are based on solid economic-geographic principles that should not be curbed. Finally, they argue that downtown areas will survive if they have a use and a function. Therefore, why worry about them? If they are viable and if they are truly prime locations within the metropolitan framework, things will take care of themselves.

Surprisingly, a public policy that is deliberately calculated to destroy the central business district and the inner zone of the city would result in a series of benefits to the metropolis at large. First, the central city government would probably go bankrupt. This also, of course, would force the institution of some kind of metropolitan government or, at the least, would make the central city much more cooperative with regard to municipalities in outlying areas. Thus a new governmental structure would undoubtedly replace many of the ill-designed schemes to augment the downtown area, and there would be less worry about local tax bases and more concern about the quality of living and the overall arrangement of land-use patterns within an urban nucleus. Such diminution of the central business district might perhaps also tend to improve the "urban transportation problem," which now means, primarily, getting suburbanites to and from their jobs in the central business district easily and rapidly. If such functions were repositioned within the metropolis, then much of this problem would perhaps be eliminated.

On the other hand, since there is a tendency for people to live at some distance from their place of work, considerable crosstown commuting might be the result. This is certainly the case in Los Angeles. In order to ensure improvement, perhaps places of residence would have to be controlled — with reference to places of work; hardly a very popular notion. The destructive policy toward the central business district would also lead to a dual approach in which the emphasis would be on the most modern technology. Such features as the freeway, the automobile, use of more land, more green space, and perhaps even new towns would then be emphasized. From a human standpoint this might be very desirable. From an ecological standpoint the results would be disastrous.

The inner zone of the city represents a paradox. Rather than being under-developed, as are many areas of the world, this area is overdeveloped. Over-development appears to be a solvable problem until decline begins to set in. Perhaps the real problem is our inability to handle decline. We have many models for growth but practically no way of handling the diminishing importance of places. Nevertheless, the central city and central business district are decreasing in importance, much as are many of our small cities and towns.

The high-density, low-income areas in the inner zone of cities also have almost unsolvable problems. The first problem concerns the general age and dilapidation of many of the residential structures. This results in remodeling costs so high that they often exceed the value of the remodeled structure. Because of such difficulties, much of the housing is rundown and in rental status. In fact, well over half of the housing in high-density areas is rental housing. The result is overcrowding coupled with many other social and economic problems.

To make the matter even worse, major arterials often blanket these high-density areas. Highways were developed primarily to provide outlying areas better access to the central business district. As they converge near the inner zone of the city, however, they become very close together. In many ghetto areas, major arterials are only a few blocks apart. This creates severe land-use conflicts, making the turnover of housing exceedingly high. It also, of course, creates an adverse human environment for the population.

Possible solutions to the problems of the inner zone include: (1) an extensive remodeling and redevelopment program like the various attempts at urban renewal, (2) improvement in the upward housing mobility of the population with the aid of better jobs and nondiscrimination in housing, and (3) encouraging the movement of people out of the area and into better environments.

Problems in the middle zone of cities

In most metropolises the middle zone encompasses the outer third or so of the central city. It is characterized by a mixed land-use pattern and by houses that have reached, or are fast reaching, the limits of their economic and technological lives. As such, these provide some portent for future problems. Because the housing is generally of a mixed quality, many of the poorer homes have become aged and dilapidated. Rental housing is also increasing rapidly. Moreover, much of this housing is owned by very small landlords who are primarily interested in milking the property rather than improving it. In other cases the most dilapidated homes have been torn down and replaced by apartment buildings. This creates conflicts among residential uses and invariably leads to overcrowding in the neighborhood.

The area has also traditionally been interspaced with business uses, which are largely falling into marginal status. Thus residential conflicts also occur near these deteriorating business centers. Finally, the area is interlaced with major arterials, most of which are simply widened residential streets. Heavy traffic is often within ten or twenty feet of the front door of many residents. The environmental problems of noise, air pollution, and general safety have caused many people to move from these houses. In fact, the turnover rate is several times higher for homes along these major arterials than for the better situated homes within the middle zone.

The problems of aging of the population and general technological obsolescence of many structures in this zone were discussed in the previous chapter. Suffice it to say here that the area is oversupplied with business and school uses but undersupplied with regard to many of the other public amenities required by the aging population.

Unlike the inner zone, there is fair potential for maintenance of this middle zone area. Yet, almost no federal programs are aimed at preventing future disaster here. This is doubly unfortunate because of the diversity of the population and structures as well as the possibility for creating a viable urban environment for some time to come. As things now stand, however, the immediate future of this area looks bleak indeed.

Problems in suburbia

Much has been written about the ills of suburbia. The popular studies have primarily focused on certain social problems and on aesthetic concerns about the great homogeneity of residential structures. These, however, are not the major problems concerning land use and spatial arrangement.

Suburbia today cannot be generalized to this extent. In fact, it contains some prime residential areas and many middle-income housing areas as well as some of very low status. Furthermore, suburbia is no longer characterized by a monotonous sea of subdivision. Business has rapidly developed in suburbia, and other employment opportunities are becoming more common. In short, the suburban landscape is rapidly becoming filled in and diversified in function.

Moreover, it has changed dramatically in lot size, types of structures, and other criteria acceptable for residential development since World War

II. The first subdivisions after World War II were primarily two-bedroom houses with carports or detached garages located on front foot lots of about 50-foot widths. Today, the common standard is four-bedroom houses with two-car attached garages on a 70- or 80-front foot lot.

Thus many of the older suburban neighborhoods are almost as technologically obsolescent as homes in the middle zone of cities. In fact, inasmuch as many of the cities' middle-zone homes were large and substantially built, they may actually contain greater potential than the first suburban subdivisions built. Perhaps the saving grace of the older parts of suburbia is that they were all built about the same time with the same kind of structures. Therefore, they should all be right for clearance and redevelopment at about the same time.

The basic problem in suburbia from a land-use standpoint is the general lack of public facilities. Parks are scarce. Schools are constantly inadequate in location and size as the population fills in. Few other urban amenities — street lights, sidewalks, general fire and police protection, and the like — are adequate in the suburbs.

Because of the lower density and the leapfrog development whereby much of the land has become urban by default, the provision of such public services as water, sewerage, and power is more expensive on a per capita basis than it is in a more dense environment. In fact, the expense is so great with regard to sewers, for example, that they are largely absent from many suburban areas. This sprawling, leapfrog development has been lamented by many observers of the suburban scene, who felt that such unused land would unnecessarily increase the territorial extent of cities and cause the residents to purchase more transportation than would otherwise be required.

On the other hand, some astute observers have suggested that these urban-by-default areas have great potential. It was noted that many nonresidential functions were eliminated in the first round of development. It was thought, therefore, that such land would be needed and used for commercial and other functions. This has proven to be partially the case. However, the general trend has been to fill in with new residential structures many of the areas that were passed over in the first round. In fact, the current trend in apartment building has led to rather dense development in some of these places. Unfortunately, the needed parks and other public facilities have generally not been accommodated.

Perhaps the greatest difficulty in suburbia is financial in nature. Because of the low densities and the predominantly residential nature of this territory, coupled with the myriad of small incorporated places, viable sizes have not been reached to provide the necessary services on an efficient basis. Each local municipality often tries to have its own police force and other public services. This leads to tremendous duplication and high costs for its residents. Often, however, school districts, water districts, and the like are not based on municipal boundaries but on more feasible geographical areas. Nevertheless, suburbia is characterized by a vast multitude of different governmental and functional jurisdictions. As might be expected, each of these is trying to improve its own spatial bailiwick. Some are actually improving their importance to the detriment of neighboring communities.

Yet suburbia is best considered as a transition between the older city, characterized by the middle zone, and the future city, characterized by the outer zone. It is, therefore, a compromise between the old city and the future city.

Problems in the outer zone beyond suburbia

Urbanization is also occurring beyond suburbia. In this fringe area, land is being made ready for urban occupancy. Farms are being subdivided, roads are being planned, land is being zoned, and some development is already taking place. Mostly, however, it is an area of seeming disuse. Farms have been abandoned and are now in the hands of large land speculators.

Because of the higher rent-paying ability of urban functions, they can easily invade agricultural lands. This has caused great concern on the part of many observers. Nevertheless, it is difficult to justify the preservation of much local agricultural land. Certainly an industrial plant on such land creates far more jobs than does a farm. Moreover, land for living is surely as important as land for farming, provided there is farmland elsewhere. That there is ample farmland elsewhere appears to be the case. In fact, millions of acres in farms have been abandoned or have become marginal during the past decade or so in the United States, and the highest rate of farm abandonment occurs around large cities. Much of this land is physically inferior, for farming purposes, to land found elsewhere, since much land around cities is agriculturally marginal. Many of these farms were unable to compete with larger-scale farming operations in other areas and would have fallen into disuse even without an urban invasion. There are cases, however, in which irreplaceable agricultural land is being invaded by residential and other uses. The Santa Clara Valley in California is a case in point. Perhaps in areas like this the land should be preserved for agriculture.

In most instances, however, the preservation of agricultural land is of little consideration. After all, it was the city that created the agricultural value of this land by providing an accessible urban market. With improvements in transportation, agriculture has shifted to more distant and more physically advantageous areas. Thus there is plenty of land for settlement around many of our cities. Even along the Eastern Seaboard of the United States, there are vast open spaces between such cities as Washington, Baltimore, Philadelphia, New York and Boston. It is only along the major arterials connecting the cities that any semblance of rural penetration has been made.

Therefore, the outer zone undoubtedly presents a great potential for the utilization of the latest innovations in urban pattern and form. It is a vast area because of its circumferential nature in relation to cities — an area that provides great opportunities for low-density structures. In fact, with guidance and planning, a new and better kind of city could be created here. This city could be coordinated with physical and environmental conditions, thus combining the best aspects of country and city life. Here also perhaps lies an opportunity for the development of new towns and new communities. Unfortunately, almost no real consideration is being given to this vast, new frontier of urban land. As Edward Higbee[2] observed:

> From the standpoint of the greatest good for the greatest number of American citizens at this particular moment in the nation's development, the most important function of the farm on the urban fringe is as a reservoir of space which eventually will be urbanized. Unless a growing community regards the farms on its periphery as the most important raw material out of which its future will be molded and treats them accordingly, there can be no sensible policy for the eventual allocation of their space to urban uses.

It is ironic that most of our attention to cities has been focused on the more obsolete portions. The new urban-land frontier has generally been ignored or treated in sorry fashion. Should current trends continue in this new area, an intermixing of land uses, and the resulting major disaffinities, could occur. Because of the increased spatial choice for all kinds of activities, there is tremendous potential for intermixing of functions. Yet, very little land control is evident here. Should current trends continue, the new urban-land frontier may present far worse urban problems than suburbia initially did. Moreover, the hope of bringing about any semblance of useful compromise between rural and urban occupancy will be gone forever.

Other land-use problems in American cities

Cities are suffering from a multitude of other problems related to land use. Most of them are the result of functions that occupied land properly at some time in the past but face problems at the present — and will face even more in the future. One of the more outstanding problems in American cities, as in many others around the world, is cemeteries. In many of our older cities, cemeteries have been full for many years, yet they remain. They occupy considerable amounts of prime urban land, which is almost impossible to use for a new purpose. (Interstate highways are about the only function that has been able to disrupt the pattern.)

Traditionally, cemeteries were placed on high ground at the city's edge, but today this area is no longer peripheral — it is heavily populated. Yet the cemeteries remain as large pockets of unused urban space, which would other-

[2]Edward Higbee, *The Squeeze: Cities Without Space* (New York: Morrow, 1960), p. 174.

wise offer fine opportunities for the development of needed public services like parks and playgrounds. This space is often ideal, too, as residential property. Unlike most other urban uses, cemetery use is extremely difficult to change — although change is sorely needed.

Churches are another function that in many areas of the city are overbuilt or have outlived their usefulness. Characteristically, large churches are found in the inner zone of the city; yet most of their members have moved to outlying areas where they have built new churches. The old structures remain in marginal status at best. In this case, the tax structure that exempts church property tends to propagate such anachronisms.

Many government properties and installations constitute another case in point. Again, because of their tax-exempt status and their presumed "permanent" nature, they take up vast areas in some cities. This is especially a problem when such installations become surrounded by residential neighborhoods. Many military bases in cities could well be abandoned to make room for a more satisfying use of the land.

On the private side of the ledger, two uses are particularly troublesome. The first of these is golf courses — an extensive and heavy user of urban space. In fact, it is hard to imagine any game that approaches golf in the amount of space it keeps from higher and better uses. Although golf courses take up vast amounts of territory within cities, they are used by very few. In some places, these courses are being removed for housing developments and the like. A better use, however, might well be for open space or parkland. Here is a case where the transition might best be made from the private or semipublic sector to the public sector.

But perhaps the most disruptive and widespread user of land is the service station. Because of the highly competitive nature of oil companies, far more land is occupied by this one activity than can reasonably be justified. In fact, many observers believe that oil companies often buy such land with the ultimate intention of using it for business investment purposes. At any rate, there are service stations in abundance, disrupting the surrounding areas with their flying banners, large revolving signs, and generally noisy operations. One wonders if the urban environment would not be much improved if just this one function were more tightly controlled in respect to the amount of territory allotted to it.

Regional Problems in Other Cities of the World

In many respects, large cities throughout the world reflect some of the same problems of aging and peripheral growth that plague American cities. They also reflect, in some cases even more severely, the disaffinities with regard to certain land uses. An exception to the fringe problem occurs in many European cities, where land use around cities is very tightly zoned and controlled for rural purposes. However, this creates severe crowding in many of these cities and relegates most of the population to apartment living. Moreover, European cities in particular are even more obsolete with regard to their ability to handle the automobile than are American cities. Thus parking and traffic problems are possibly even more severe in them.

Low-income populations have difficulties in all cities of the world. In American cities poor people are forced to occupy the more dilapidated neighborhoods and structures in the metropolis. Nevertheless, they do occupy fairly centrally located property. In contrast, much of the low-income population in other world cities, outside of Europe, live on the edge of the metropolis in shantytowns. Moreover, these squatter settlements are almost totally lacking in any of the utilities of the main city — water, sewerage, fire protection, and in many cases, even streets. Such settlements are built almost overnight on land that belongs to very large landowners or to the government.

Many of the people in these shantytowns, like people centrally located in American cities, are newcomers to the city. They come primarily from the agricultural areas of these underdeveloped countries. Yet jobs are scarce in large cities. Moreover, the jobs are located mostly in the central portion of cities in underdeveloped countries rather than in outlying areas. Thus these people must face a long commuting journey every day in order to work. This is double jeopardy for such populations. Because of the relatively poor transportation, however, the more accessible residential sites are occupied by the higher-income population. There is an analogy with American cities, however, in that here, too, jobs are moving *away* from the low-income population. Over the long run, undoubtedly the low-income population, if they are to improve their accessibility to employment, must move closer to the center of cities in underdeveloped countries and closer to the edge of American cities.

Conclusions

Cities do not occupy some dark and mysterious portion of the earth. Rules of location and problems of territorial growth and decline apply to cities as much as to any larger portion of the earth's surface. Because they contain so many people in such a limited area, however, the location of activities within cities becomes of critical importance. Indeed, if it were not for the great crowding for sites by diverse land uses within cities, including a place for man himself to live, many urban problems would not exist or would be almost identical to those found on a world scale.

It also has been shown that problems vary greatly from one part of the city to another. Thus a first step to geographical understanding and diagnosis is proper regionalization. When areas are delimited on the basis of homogeneous geographical features, better appreciation of the results of locational patterns results. Such regional synthesis provides a solid basis by which the complexity and nature of the locational problems discussed in foregoing chapters can be examined.

Problems of land-use arrangements vary greatly from the inner to the outer zones of cities. In the inner zones, problems related to diminishing importance and decline occur, whereas in the outer zones, the problems result primarily from too rapid and uncontrolled development. Thus, the inner zone is plagued by having the promise of too little, whereas the outer zone is plagued by having the promise of perhaps too much, too soon.

The geographically based problems within cities primarily relate to territorial dynamics as these are augmented by aging of areas and structures over time. These problems cause additional problems pertaining to the quality of the urban environment.

Finally, the city is plagued by multigovernmental jurisdictions in an area that is one economic unit. Such fragmentation of administrative units invariably leads to problems of coordination among areas and functions. It appears that what is described as an "urban problem" may be a problem to only one small segment of the urban population or to only a particular area of the metropolis.

BIBLIOGRAPHY

Abrams, Charles. *The City Is the Frontier*. New York: Harper & Row, 1965.

Applebaum, William, and Cohen, Saul B. "The Dynamics of Store Trading Areas and Market Equilibrium." *Annals of the Association of American Geographers*, March 1961, pp. 73–101.

Berry, Brian J. L. *Commercial Structure and Commercial Blight*. Chicago: University of Chicago Press, 1963.

Gaffney, Mason. "Urban Expansion — Will It Ever Stop?" *The Yearbook of Agriculture–Land*. Washington, D.C.: Department of Agriculture, 1958, pp. 503–522.

Hauser, Philip M., and Schnore, Leo F., eds. *The Study of Urbanization*. New York: Wiley, 1966.

Kinsel, John F. "Planning for People: A Concept of Rural-Urban Regions." *Community Planning Review*, September 1957, pp. 144–150.

McGee, Terrence Gary. *The Southeast Asian City*. New York: Praeger, 1967.

Morrill, R. L. "The Negro Ghetto: Problems and Alternatives." *Geographical Review*, July 1965, pp. 339–361.

Rodwin, Lloyd, ed. *The Future Metropolis*. New York: Braziller, 1961.
    Scientific American. *Cities*. New York: Knopf, 1966.

Ullman, Edward L. "The Nature of Cities, Reconsidered." *Proceedings of the Regional Science Association*, 1962, pp. 7–23.

Webber, Melvin M.; Dyckman, John W.; Foley, Donald L.; Guttenberg, Albert Z; Wheaton William L. C.; and Wurster, Catherine Bauer. *Explorations into Urban Structure*. Philadelphia: University of Pennsylvania Press, 1964.

Wilson, James Q. *The Metropolitan Enigma*. Washington, D.C.: Chamber of Commerce of the United States, 1967.

Wingo, Lowdon, ed. *Cities and Space*. Baltimore: Johns Hopkins Press, 1963.

Wood, Robert. *Metropolis Against Itself*. Washington, D.C.: Committee on Economic Development, March 1959.

XVI

Some Geographically Based Problems on a Macro Scale – Regional Problems

This chapter attempts to provide some insights into the kind of problems that occur in response to the operation of the spatial principles discussed in previous chapters. Thus "problems" as used here will not refer to problems of geographical understanding, but to problems that result from various spatial conditions and patterns. Some problems would result from almost any spatial system devised. The comments below are not meant as an indictment of the present system, but simply as an important adjunct of it.

Certain difficulties were discussed in earlier chapters — for example, questions of resource depletion and trade restrictions. Nonetheless, they were presented in a factual way in order to gain greater appreciation and understanding of the locational process. They were also difficulties that could be remedied within the public policy framework.

In contrast to most of the problems raised earlier, those posed below are not subject to easy solution, or perhaps to any solution at all. The source of these problems is territorial inequality. Yet spatial inequality would occur even on a homogeneous earth. As one locational economist aptly stated: "Even in the absence of any initial differentiation at all, i.e., if natural resources were distributed uniformly over the globe, patterns of specialization and concentration of activities would inevitably appear in response to economic, social, and political principles."[1] To lament the fact that spatial disparities result in almost unsolvable human problems is to engage in a fruitless exercise.

We will first examine, within a broad regional framework, the nature and general causes of areal inequalities on the surface of the earth. It will be shown that the unequal distribution of economic activities results in an interconnected system of problems. The staging mechanism for such problems results from the vastly different economic achievements among and within

[1]Edgar M. Hoover, *The Location of Economic Activity* (New York: McGraw-Hill, 1948), p. 3.

nations. Just as developmental differences within cities result in problems (discussed in Chapter 15), so do differences on a world and national scale cause major concern.

Spatial inequalities result in three general types of problems: (1) problems pertaining to economic characteristics of areas, (2) problems pertaining to people, and (3) problems pertaining to the ecology and environment. The first of these is discussed with regard to questions of regional development strategies and policies. The second is discussed with regard to improving the general standard of living and welfare of people rather than areas. And the third is concerned with environmental difficulties that create problems for both territorial growth and population within the territory. As might be expected, the major problems of areas and peoples are most concentrated in the lagging, or underdeveloped, parts of the world; environmental problems are most pronounced in the highly urbanized and industrialized places. Thus some problems result from areas having too little, and some from areas having perhaps too much.

Synthesis of Regional Inequality — Causes and Characteristics

The reasons for spatial differentiation of particular activities have been previously discussed. In contrast, geographical variation is presented here in terms of areas rather than activities. The general concept of *core*, *central*, and *outlying* areas is most useful in this regard. It is a framework that provides an explanation for regional differences, both present and future, and a synthesis of the foregoing principles applied in an areal context. Moreover, the concept is operable at various territorial scales — at world, national, regional, and even local levels.

Simply put, the concept is based on the idea that for any area there is a prime region for carrying on most economic activities. This *core* area, therefore, has maximum urban and industrial development, a major local market, and good access to all other places. In fact, the core area, because of its importance and dominance, is at the locus of major transportation routes. The core area thus has had first choice in the manufacture and marketing of most products. All other areas are primarily limited to a raw material supply operation whereby they feed the core area with needed commodities.

The classic historical case was the British Empire: A great many areas of the world were supplying Britain with raw materials for her industry, and foodstuffs for her population. In Britain, value was added to these commodities through manufacturing, after which some of the products were returned to other areas at much increased cost. The differential was used by Britain to supply herself with additional means of production, with increased quantities of raw materials and foodstuffs, and, in general, to enhance her economic development. The result was that the core area, Great Britain, got richer faster than the poorer colonial areas.

Somewhat similar spatial arrangements are found at a world scale today. For example, the core area of the world is Western Europe and the northeastern quadrangle of the United States. This region includes — technologically, industrially, and politically — the most advanced nations on earth. Most other areas of the world, with the exception of the Soviet bloc and Japan, supply this core area with raw materials needed to operate its huge urban, industrial, and military complex. In return, the noncore areas receive manufactured goods and technical assistance. Thus, while both areas benefit, the core area appears to be benefiting most. Therefore, the gap in economic development and standard of living between the two areas has been widening. Today, it has grown so appreciable that the core area nations are often referred to as the "have" nations and the other nations of the world as the "have not" countries.

Core area superiority also operates within nations. For example, the core area of the United States is the American manufacturing belt. This area is at the focus of almost all national transportation routes — in fact, it arranges them that way. The core area of the United States includes less than 10 percent of the country's total area, but contains over one-half of the nation's population and much greater proportions of the nation's manufacturing employment. It is the crucible of brainpower and innovation, and the communications, financial, and administrative center of the nation — indeed, of most of the world.

Why this has happened is the subject of much speculation. Perhaps it was due to an early start. Perhaps it was the result of having great quantities of such industrial raw materials as coal and iron ore fortuitously close at hand at the right time. Perhaps it was the result of having great agricultural resources. Perhaps it was based on its early development of international trade. At any rate, the superiority of this area is a fact, and one not easy to change.

One can easily see why other areas might have some difficulty competing with the core area. In the best position to compete, however, are those areas adjacent to it. These *central* areas are often in a fairly good position for developing sizable amounts of economic activity if they have the right resources — resources that the core area lacks. Barring that, the central areas do at least get second choice in the production and distribution of products. Central areas likewise are able to manufacture for a national market if their products are high in value compared with the costs of transportation. Manufacturing plants here are often characterized by having a high weight-loss ratio. Thus these activities are generally the result of central areas having special advantages in natural resources. Central areas also have the possibility of intercepting many flows from distant areas en route to the core.

At least four central areas can be identified within the United States: (1) the South, which can be divided further into an eastern and western portion;

(2) the Western Middle West, which includes much of the Great Plains; (3) the Northwest, or Upper Midwest, which includes portions of Northern Michigan; and (4) the upper portion of New England.

The next tier of regions is called the *outlying* areas. Since these areas are farthest from the core, they get last chance for production geared to national markets. Most of the outlying areas are restricted to the production of (1) raw materials for the industries of core or central areas; (2) foodstuffs for the general population; or (3) resources that cannot be found in comparable quantity and quality closer to the core market.

Thus, in order to compete effectively, outlying areas must have a very superior natural base. This generally consists of utilizing a very specialized resource like timber, minerals, soil, or even sunshine. The Pacific Northwest and California, as outlying areas in the United States, specialize heavily in supplying commodities not readily available closer to the market — for example, timber, agricultural products, certain minerals, and a climate suitable for retirement living and recreation. Australia and New Zealand, which are outlying areas on a world scale, specialize in commodities that cannot be supplied more cheaply, or in sufficient quantities, by countries between them and the European core.

Industrial production in outlying areas is generally geared to local markets. With such limited markets, activities here, in contrast to those found in core and central areas, can profit very little from scale economies. In fact, many outlying areas have a population or market so small that profitable production cannot be undertaken. On the other hand, there are such exceptions as Southern California, whose concentration of population affords a regional market large enough to support the production of many locally consumed items.

On the other hand, outlying areas at considerable distance from the core may have some advantages. Their remoteness may allow them to supply local markets without destructive, core-based competition. Even so, the scale economies achieved by firms located in more central positions often outweigh the advantages that local firms have over them in terms of transportation costs.

In one sense, outlying areas are becoming better off as transportation improves and cuts down on the problems of transferability to the core area. On the other hand, the trend has been to improve methods of transporting raw materials versus finished products so that many of the former are now moving directly to core and central areas rather than being processed in outlying areas.

Considerable distinction should be made among outlying areas. Some of these are only one spatial step removed from central areas. As such, they meet most of the criteria and problems discussed above. Some outlying areas, however, are best described as fringe or corner areas. They are so far removed from the main center of population that they are largely left in the backwash of development.

At this stage some distinction should also be made between outlying areas and stranded areas. Although underdevelopment in outlying areas may occur for a number of reasons, the primary cause is their spatial position relative to other places and materials. Other places having better opportunities for growth thus substitute for the growth that might otherwise occur in outlying areas.

In contrast, the stranded area may occur within either concentrated or outlying areas. Characteristically, it is an area that was formerly in tune with major development in its area but was not able to keep up. This stranded condition may result from a multitude of factors including a change in the transportation network relative to such areas, a depletion of resources, or general inabilities to compete with other places having greater opportunities.

Thus it can be seen why regional disparity is the rule. Vast differences in economic advancement at almost every territorial scale are the result. On a world scale, the advanced and the underdeveloped nations exemplify these differences. Within nations, some regions are fairly well off while others lag or are underdeveloped by comparison. Such regional disparity is found within nations, both rich and poor.

Within the underdeveloped nations of the world, large cities often stand out in contrast to the backward rural areas around them. The disparity here occurs within a very short spatial distance. The growing and rapidly industrializing cities stand in stark contrast to the primitive economy and largely illiterate and unskilled people in the countryside. Such a dual society is especially evident in much of Southeast Asia, where cities like Bombay, Calcutta, Bangkok, Saigon, and Hanoi stand out as pillars of affluence and growth in a sea of rural backwash. (Of course, there are also many poor in such cities so that there is a tremendous regional disparity within them.)

Regional disparity is also the rule in more economically advanced nations. Note the variation in economic activity between the northern and southern parts of Japan, northern and southern Italy, northern and southern Argentina, or indeed, between the North and the South in the United States. (In all but Japan, the northern areas are the more highly industrialized and urbanized.)

A more careful examination of regional disparity, however, reveals that a simple, geographical dichotomy between growing and lagging areas is too crude a formulation. For example, within the United States there are a number of depressed or lagging regions that are geographically separate: (1) an extensive territory in the Appalachians from southern Pennsylvania south to northern Florida; (2) the Ozarks area, including parts of Oklahoma, Arkansas, and Missouri; (3) the Atlantic coastal plain from Carolina to Georgia; (4) the Upper Great Lakes; (5) the "four corners area" in New Mexico, Colorado, Utah, and Arizona; (6) the Mississippi Delta area; and (7) large numbers of isolated areas in the Rocky Mountain West.

The reasons for disparity are multiple. Some places — the Applachians, for example — are suffering as a result of poor farmland and a technology that requires fewer workers in coal production. Other places have found that their resources are no longer competitive with those available elsewhere. Still others find that because of transportation improvements and farming changes elsewhere, they have been left with little competitive potential. As might be expected, many of the farming areas are in difficulty simply because agriculture requires fewer people and fewer areas today than it did formerly. In fact, about one-half the counties in the United States are losing population.

There is also great disparity within states of the United States, as there are within Canadian provinces. Most of the Midwest states show greater prosperity in their northern areas, where the land has been glaciated. Here the land is more level, more agriculturally productive, and consequently more urbanized. In fact, about the only state that does not show startling differences from one part to another is Iowa, yet even its eastern portion is more prosperous than its south-central area.

Problems Related to Regional Disparity

Because areas have vastly different amounts of economic activity and economic potential, the people in such areas are likewise often in comparable economic conditions. If people were distributed in conformance with the economic opportunities of areas, few problems resulting from spatial inequality would exist. To the contrary, at least on a world scale, the areas with the fewest activities and the least hope for economic development also contain the greatest populations. Classic examples in this regard are India, China, and other countries in Southeast Asia. Unfortunately, even in economically backward areas with few people, such limited population often has a low standard of living.

A hasty solution comes to mind: Encourage migration from areas of inferior location to those with superior actual or potential development. This is not much practiced, however, primarily for political reasons. Migration between countries is tightly controlled. Thus most peoples of the world are restricted to their particular nations — whether or not they can earn a livelihood in them. To improve their economic status, their own area must be improved. Even within nations, the facilitation and encouragement of migration is rarely encouraged.

Migration is not the simple solution it appears to be at first glance for yet another reason: Poor people are also found in advanced areas. These people are the less educated and the less skilled — characteristics that apply in abundance to most of the population in underdeveloped areas.

Thus the primary solution consists in efforts to improve the economic potential of lagging and depressed areas. As the concept of core, central, and outlying areas demonstrate, however, this is almost impossible to achieve. In fact, despite major area development programs within and between nations, the gap between the rich and the poor and the have and have-not areas has been widening rather than narrowing.

At the very minimum one might expect that the rich could share their wealth, at least to the extent of keeping people in these areas from starving. Unfortunately, this also does not seem to be the case. In fact, starvation is a fact of life in many of the underdeveloped countries of the world. Their agricultural resources are simply not adequate to support the population properly. It is therefore commonly — albeit superficially — suggested that the problem is overpopulation relative to local food resources.

Yet, as a whole, the world is quite capable of feeding its inhabitants. It has been argued, therefore, that the primary problem is one of equalization of wealth and distribution of foodstuffs. Because of the many political and institutional problems involved, however, this has not developed. Consequently, even in an affluent world, many people are without jobs, without food, and without hope. The fact is that a minority of people in the world have an overabundance of material wealth whereas most others have only a scanty minimum for survival. Moreover, the gap is growing, with those on the lower end of the economic scale becoming more and more discontent.

In this regard, three types of countries are commonly differentiated: (1) the Western countries, (2) the Communist or Soviet-bloc countries, and (3) the Third World countries. The first category commonly includes the industrialized countries of Western Europe, the United States, Canada and such outliers of European colonization as Australia, New Zealand, and South Africa. (Japan, although highly industrialized and urbanized, cannot be considered "Westernized.") The second category, the Soviet-bloc countries, are usually technologically advanced but lack an individual standard of living comparable to that of the West European and North American nations. Finally, the Third World includes the countries of practically all other areas, particularly Asia, Africa, and South America. (Incidentally, the South American nations might be considered still another bloc. They are true outliers of European colonization, but are nonetheless primarily raw-material-oriented in terms of their level of economic development. Internal political problems — and the fact that these countries have been used as a source of raw materials and as a field for investment by the Western countries — have perhaps prevented them from attaining a higher economic level.)

It is the people of the Third World countries who have been most affected by problems of underdevelopment. These countries suffer from a serious imbalance between a rapidly growing population and available resources — an imbalance that grows progressively more serious. Their technology is inferior. Their knowledge and use of their own resources are inadequate. Their transportation remains largely primitive. As might be anticipated, much of the population is plagued by problems of malnutrition, illiteracy, and lack of the skills needed for urban industrial purposes.

Regional Development Dilemmas

Our primary concern with regard to the effects of unequal development of areas should, of course, be the people who are its victims. In practice, however, most of the emphasis, reflected in the programs for change, has been placed on regional improvement rather than on human improvement. This is not an entirely irrational stance inasmuch as people, on a national scale at least, are generally immobile, and are restricted for their livelihood to their own countries. Thus economic improvement of the territory through industrialization appears to be a logical way, although perhaps not the best way, of improving the quality and standard of living for the population.

There are many other ways in which the economic status of the people might be more directly benefited. A better, people-based solution in some places might be improving education and job training, and encouraging and aiding people to move out of areas that have little potential (or that are over-populated in terms of opportunities) and into more advantageous areas. Nonetheless, most government programs are focused on improving employment *within* lagging areas. Very little consideration is given to direct improvement of the people if this involves moving them out of the area.

One reason areas, rather than people, are emphasized is that the various countries of the world and regions within them, are vying with each other to improve the economic status of their territories. Politicians are concerned about serving their constituents in a particular area. If these people migrate out of the area, the politician has presumably gained nothing.

Unfortunately, perhaps because of the governmental systems, more attention is usually given to improvement of places rather than improvement of people. Nowhere is this more evident than at national levels. Every small country wants to improve its economic status. Specifically, most want to develop a major iron and steel industry. Obviously, this is unreasonable for many places in the world, not only because of the lack of a raw material base, but also because of limited local markets. Nevertheless, many nations pursue such a deliberate industrialization policy anyway.

The dilemma is shown by the following example. India could undoubtedly import its motor vehicles much more cheaply than making them. Nevertheless, India has an embargo on foreign-made vehicles, and somewhat similar policies have been developed in Australia. Yet the market in both countries is very limited.

Similar strategies for improving the growth within nations also are much in evidence. The policy has been primarily to bring about more industrialization in the underdeveloped places. One strategy is to develop urban *growth poles* in these outlying areas. For example, noncoastal settlement in Australia was fostered by placing the national capital in Canberra. Brazil has attempted to develop much of its inland area by building its national capital at Brazilia.

To date, the results have been mixed at best. Nevertheless, some development has occurred around the new town of Ciyudad Guyana on the Orinoco River in Venezuela. Where there is a logical economic reason for such a function to occur, success progresses very readily.

In most of these outlying areas, however, it seems much more efficient to transport the resources available there to some other place. Oil from the northern slope of Alaska, for example, is being transported to refineries in the coterminous United States. Refining in Alaska does not seem to be forthcoming. Thus little major or long-term employment is created in many of these outlying places. Similar kinds of events are also evident in the large, mineral-supplying areas of Peru, Venezuela, Chile, and the Middle East.

Ecological and Environmental Problems

If problems pertaining to people and areas are acute, environmental and ecological problems are equally so. Although they exist throughout the world and are usually associated with widespread extraction of resources in outlying areas, they are most acute in the heavily populated core areas because they affect greater numbers of people. Moreover, people themselves bring about many of the problems. Through their cities and industries, people have contaminated many lakes, rivers, and streams in the core areas. In fact, water, air, and land are being polluted to such a degree that serious problems pertaining to man's ultimate survival are at stake.

Environmental and ecological problems are particularly serious in the core areas of the United States. Lake Erie is badly polluted as are rivers like the Hudson, the Ohio, the Illinois, and many others. Air pollution, although primarily associated with large cities, blankets most of the entire core area. Should the present rate of pollution growth continue, the environment for living will continue to deteriorate dramatically.

In other areas of the world, different kinds of environmental problems occur. The classic case was the erosion problem in the South during the heavy period of cotton growing. The dust bowl in Oklahoma is another tribute to man's attempt to exploit the earth at all costs. Great sores on the surface of the earth exist where man has almost wantonly exploited the mineral resources. This is particularly evidenced in Appalachia, in Northern Minnesota, in Bingham, Utah, and in other areas where strip mining is widely practiced. In major oil-producing regions, the area is blanketed with oil wells and other paraphernalia, which create unsightliness and often destroy the area for other use possibilities.

Another example is the destruction of considerable forest areas in the United States. The cut-over area of Northern Michigan and Minnesota is a classic example. Here forests were removed in such a way as to render the area largely unusable for any other purpose. Even the redwood forests of Northern California are quickly falling under the woodsman's ax. Such resources are almost irreplaceable, given the time it takes to grow new redwood trees. But vast areas of forest exploitation occur throughout the West. Although transplanting is now becoming more common, the destruction of the ecological environment is severe. Not only are these areas ruined for recreational and other purposes, but flooding, the destruction of wildlife, and other harmful consequences commonly occur.

Man's role in changing the face of the earth has in many cases been disasterous. Generally, little attention has been given to the future longevity of areas. Instead, they have been exploited on a one-shot basis. Conservation has been much talked about but very little practiced. To say that many areas of the world have become ugly and dilapidated through man's intervention is an understatement. Almost no consideration has been given to the preservation of natural beauty.

The classic endeavor of man has been to change the natural environment. However, his actions have treated the environment more as an enemy than as an integral part of his existence. Thus man has set out, intentionally or unintentionally, to conquer — or at the least, to tame — nature. He now finds, that nature is fighting back. Much of man's natural environment has been ruined and what remains is in dire jeopardy. In fact, many persons suggest that because of man's increasing pollution of his atmosphere, not only by smog but by various other pollutants, man himself may be eradicated some time in the future.

Fortunately, we are entering a new age of consciousness and concern as to how man occupies and utilizes the land. Much more attention is being given to questions concerning proper and wise use of resources. (In fact, a number of prime resources will soon be depleted unless more careful attention is paid to the way in which they are used.) The big consumers, as might be expected, are the core areas of the world. The central and outlying areas are primarily engaged in feeding this massive giant. However, some nations have begun to rebel and to suggest that it is not to their benefit, regardless of price paid and profits gained, to deplete their resource base. Others, however, look upon the sale of their resources — a case in point is Venezuela and its petroleum — as a proper way to get funds to finance other aspects of their regional economy.

Conclusions

It is tempting to draw an analogy between the regional development problems now striking U.S. cities and the regional problems encountered on a world and national scale. On a world and national scale, it appears that rich areas are getting richer whereas those that have little are getting relatively less. Just the reverse, of course, has occurred for various parts of the city, and one wonders whether such events might hold some portent for future world conditions. For example, should world transportation continue to increase and should technological change continue to move in quantumlike jumps, then it is possible that some of the most developed areas of the world might find that they have also reached their peak, much as the inner zone of the metropolises has done, and a decline might occur in the most developed areas. Should such decline begin, then massive problems of adjustment to decline will occur. These problems will be on such a scale that it will make the problems of decline within cities look like child's play.

There is some evidence that growth is slowing down in some of the core areas of the world. The industrial belt of the United States, for example, has not been growing as rapidly as in the past. And it is in the industrial belt that the most serious problems resulting from urbanization and industrialization are occurring. Ecological and environmental problems in this area are but one set of difficulties that seem almost impossible to curb, given more economic development. In fact, some parts of the industrial belt now find themselves declining and assuming certain of the characteristics of stranded areas. With the rapid growth of technology, many of the older industrial plants in the poor areas are becoming obsolete. As this obsolescence continues, not only in plants but in the physical fabrication of the metropolises in which these plants are located, development tends to occur in places other than the core.

Ironically, the very aid now being given to lagging areas may someday upset the spatial balance so that some of these areas will truly reach the "take-off" stage. Should this occur, then the balance of economic growth may well shift to new places. And a new area, with the latest in technology and structures, might make many of the older areas, with their increasing environmental, industrial, and especially urban problems, less desirable places for economic growth.

Certainly, the history of the world suggests that no area for long maintains supremacy over the remainder of the world. Civilization has shifted many times and will surely shift again. Thus in the future new core areas may develop in places presently considered as having little potential. Hope is not completely absent for the more unfortunate people and areas of today. Nonetheless, such spatial change occurs very slowly when balanced against immediate human needs. For the balance of this century at least, the present pattern, and its resultant problems, is the reality mankind must face.

BIBLIOGRAPHY

Berry, Brian J. L. *Strategies, Models, and Economic Theories of Development in Rural Regions.* Agricultural Economic Report no. 127. Washington, D.C.: U.S. Department of Agriculture, 1967.

Estall, R. C. *New England: A Study in Industrial Adjustment.* New York: Praeger, 1966.

Goldman, Marshall, ed. *Controlling Pollution.* Englewood Cliffs, N.J.: Prentice-Hall, 1967.

Landsberg, Hans H.; Fischman, Leonard L.; and Fisher, Joseph L. *Resources in America's Future: Patterns of Requirements and Availabilities, 1960–2000.* Baltimore: Johns Hopkins Press, 1963.

Leighton, Philip A. "Geographical Aspects of Air Pollution." *Geographical Review,* April 1966, pp. 151–174.

Perloff, Harvey S.; Dunn, Edgar S. Jr.; Lampard, Eric E.; and Muth, Richard F. *Regions, Resources, and Economic Growth.* Baltimore: Johns Hopkins Press, 1960.

Phelps Edmund S., ed. *The Goal of Economic Growth.* New York: Norton, 1960.

Thomas, William L., ed. *Man's Role in Changing the Face of the Earth.* Chicago: University of Chicago Press, 1956.

Tunnard, Christopher, and Pushkarev, Boris. *Man-Made America: Chaos or Control?* New Haven: Yale University Press, 1963.

Ullman, Edward L. "Amenities as a Factor in Regional Growth." *Geographical Review,* January 1954, pp. 119–132.

Zelinsky, Wilbur; Kosinski, Leszek A.: and Prothero, R. Mansell. *Geography and a Crowding World: A Symposium on Population Pressures Upon Physical and Social Resources in Developing Lands.* New York: Oxford University Press, 1970.

Index

Abaca, 45
Accessibility, 305–305, 306
  and area differentiation, 61
  and city shape, 262
  and commercial land use, 293–294, 298, 302–304
  and extractive activities, 58, 134–135, 137, 147
  and industry, 281
  and intra-urban land use, 260–263
  and mountain land use, 51
  and residential land use, 282–286
  and transportation routes, 262
  and workplace, 327
Acculturation, and subsistence economies, 118
Activity components, 5 (see also specific types)
Actual range, 103 (see also Breaking Point and Reilly's Law)
Adirondacks, and city pattern, 112
Aesthetics, and city land use, 317
Affinities, and city land use, 265–268
Afforestation, 147
Afghanistan, and primitive economies, 125
Africa, and new nations, 75
  O.A.U, 76
  Trade, 35, 77
Agglomerative economies, 67, 206–207
Agriculture, 35, 155–219
  and cities, 266, 271, 324
  climatic conditions, 58–59
  in primitive economies, 45, 120
  problems in, 62, 183–185, 188, 324, 335–336
  public policies, 313–314
  rent gradients, 161–165
  rent-paying abilities of crops, 157–164
  See also specific crops
Air pollution, 311–312, 339
Alaska, and Indians, 85
  and regional development, 339
Alexandersson, Gunnar, 203, 240
Alfalfa, and crop rotation, 196–197
Alkalinity, of soils, 188, 194
Alliance for Progress, 79
Alliances, 76
Alluvial soils, 52
Aluminum industry, 209
  and scale economies, 66
Amazon Basin, and economies, 123
Amazon River, and use, 52, 53
Amenities, and height, 303
  and industrial location, 70, 210
  in suburbia, 322–323
American manufacturing belt, 32, 260, 341
  city pattern in, 111
  as core area, 333
  infrastructure of, 67
Anadromous fish, 144 (see also Salmon)
Anchovy, 143

Ancillary linkages, 267–268
Annexation, 313
Anthropologists, and primitive societies, 118, 124
Anti-trust legislation, and vertical integration, 64
Apartheid policy, 84
Apartments, and land rents, 264
Appalachians, agriculture in, 169
  cities in, 112
  as lagging area, 335, 339
Apparel industry, and city location, 224
  and labor, 206
  and market, 207
Apples, Washington Delicious, 29, 190
Aquiculture, 143, 166 (see also Fishing)
Arabs, and Israeli conflict, 83
  and Soviet support, 76
Areal integration, 331–332
Areal interdependence, and potato production, 206
Argentina, agriculture in, 32, 171–172
  and economic development, 88
  and urbanization, 251
Arizona, as desert, 51
  and water demands, 54
Arkansas, and rice production, 59
Arterials, and inner zone of the city, 321
  and urban penetration, 324
  See also Freeways
Ash, as tree, 148
Assembly line production, and scale economies, 65
Atlanta, as regional capital, 97, 227, 233
Attorneys, and office location, 268, 306
Australia, agriculture in, 128
  and British Commonwealth of Nations, 77
  industry in, 338
  iron ore, 240
  as outlying area, 334
  population of, 74
  and Tasmanians, 85
  and urbanization, 251
Automobiles, production of, 28, 207
  sales of land use, 271, 295, 299
  and scale economies, 64, 66, 67, 69
Aztec civilization, 83

Back-haul, principle of, 23, 31
  and iron and steel production, 242
Balance of payments, and urban economic base, 277, 279
Ballard, Wash., 288
Ballast, principle of, 31
Baltimore, 31, 324
Banana Republics, 173
Bananas, 29, 35, 157
  as plantation crop, 173
Bangkok, 335

345